Augustus Keppel

The Trial of the Honourable Augustus Keppel

Augustus Keppel

The Trial of the Honourable Augustus Keppel

ISBN/EAN: 9783337320423

Printed in Europe, USA, Canada, Australia, Japan

Cover: Foto ©Lupo / pixelio.de

More available books at **www.hansebooks.com**

THE TRIAL

OF THE HONOURABLE

AUGUSTUS KEPPEL,

ADMIRAL OF THE BLUE SQUADRON,

At a COURT MARTIAL,

Held on Board his Majesty's Ship BRITANNIA, in PORTSMOUTH HARBOUR, on THURSDAY, JANUARY 8, 1779,

BEFORE

Admiral Sir THOMAS PYE, PRESIDENT,

Upon a CHARGE exhibited against him

By Vice Admiral Sir HUGH PALLISER,

FOR

MISCONDUCT and NEGLECT of DUTY.

TO WHICH IS ANNEXED,

Several interesting LETTERS and PAPERS relative to the Subject.

TOGETHER WITH

A GLOSSARY of the TECHNICAL TERMS and SEA PHRASES, used in the Course of the TRIAL.

Faithfully taken down in Court by

THOMAS BLANDEMOR,

For the GENTLEMEN of the NAVY.

PORTSMOUTH:

PRINTED BY MESSRS. J. WILKES, BREADHOWER, AND PEADLE.
SOLD BY S. CROWDER, G. ROBINSON, AND J. BEW, LONDON.

MDCCLXXIX.

A F F I D A V I T.

PORTSMOUTH, *16th Feb.* 1779.

I THOMAS BLANDEMOR, of Fiſh-Houſe, in the pariſh of Titchfield, near Portſmouth, Hants, do hereby make oath and declare, that at the requeſt and under the direction of many Gentlemen of the Navy, and ſeveral other very reſpectable characters, the friends of the Honourable Auguſtus Admiral Keppel, I have, BY PERMISSION of the Court, taken down in Short-hand the minutes of the ſaid Admiral's Trial, hereunto annexed. And I alſo declare upon my oath, that I have, to the beſt of my ability, (after twenty years practice) endeavoured to expreſs every particular VERBATIM, neither adding to, or diminiſhing from, any part of the ſame, knowingly or intentionally to convey a different idea or conſtruction that the genuine ſenſe of the evidence, with a view to criminate or exculpate either party; nor have uſed any device or means whatever, to render this publication partial. In witneſs whereof I have hereunto ſet my name, the day and year firſt above written.

T. Blandemor

Sworn before me, this 16th day of *February*, 1779,

JOSEPH BISSELL, Mayor

ADVERTISEMENT.

WE whose names are hereunto signed, Printers of the following Trial of the Hon. Augustus Admiral Keppel, do hereby declare, that the same is printed literally from the copy taken down in short-hand, and transcribed by Mr. Blandemor, without any alterations, omissions, or additions; and that the original copy, together with Mr. Blandemor's affidavit, remain in our hands for the inspection of any persons who may be desirous of seeing the same.

PORTSMOUTH,
February 23, 1779.

J. Wilkes

J. Breadhower

J. Peadle

A GLOSSARY of SEA TERMS,

NECESSARY FOR

Explaining the Meaning, as generally underſtood, of the TECHNICAL PHRASES made uſe of in this BOOK.

WEAR. To wear, is to bring a ſhip into a different tack, i. e. to turn her head to leeward.

TACK. To tack about, is to go upon another tack, or to bring the ſhip's head another way.

TACKS. Are large ropes, made faſt to the lower corner of the fore and main ſheets; when the larboard tacks are on board, the left-hand corners of the ſheets are pulled forward, and then the left ſide of the ſhip is to the wind; but when the ſtarboard tacks are on board, the right-hand ſide of the ſhip is to the wind.

LINE. A line is the arrangement, or order, in which a fleet of ſhips of war are diſpoſed in to engage an enemy; and that which is beſt calculated is, by drawing up the ſhips in a long file or right line, prolonged from the keel of the hindermoſt to that of the foremoſt, paſſing through the keels of all the others, from the van to the rear; ſo that they are, according to the ſea phraſe, in the wake of each other.

WAKE. A ſhip's wake is the dead water which the ſhip leaves behind; and for one ſhip to come into another's wake, is to come into the ſame track that ſhe ſails in; conſequently, the line for action cannot be formed without the ſhips come into the wakes of each other.

WEATHER LINE. The weather line has this advantage, that it may approach the enemy, and determine the time of action; and if it is more numerous than the lee line, it may ſend

ſend a detachment to cut off part of the enemy's rear; is leſs incommoded by the ſmoke, and may ſend in their fire-ſhips among the enemy's fleet; but then, in rough weather, the leeward ſhips can open their lower ports, and uſe the heavy artillery, when the windward line cannot, leſt the ſhips ſhould take in too much water.

LEE LINE. The lee line is greatly incommoded by ſmoke, but then they can eaſily take away their diſabled ſhips. In ſhort, the advantage or diſadvantage between the windward and the leeward lines, depend much upon the wind and ſmoothings of the ſea, in fine weather the windward line has infinitely the advantage; but in high winds and rough ſeas, the leeward line may be ſaid to have the advantage.

SIGNAL. Signals, are certain little flags or colours hauſed out as a token what to do, or give notice of ſomething; and generally, in engagements, a frigate is appointed to repeat ſuch ſignals of which every ſhip has a book with the different colours painted thereon, and annexed is an explanation of each of the ſignals.

LOG BOOK. The log book is a large demy folio, kept upon the quarter deck, or ſome other convenient part, wherein is ſet down the courſes ſteered, the winds, and all the tranſactions of the day, ſimply as they occur, by the Maſter or Officer of the Watch, from which all the Officers take their Journals: no more than one is ſuffered on board any ſhip, as it is by this alone the conduct of every officer and man on board muſt be determined.

LARGE. To go large, is when a ſhip goes right before the wind: and, to large, is ſaid, when ſhe goes neither before the wind nor upon the wind, but as it were, quartering between both.

STAYS. Are ropes which keep the maſt from falling aft.

STAYS. To ſtay a ſhip, i. e. to bring a ſhip upon the ſtays, is to manage her tackle and ſails ſo that ſhe cannot make any way forward, and BACK STAYS (in a ſhip) are ropes which go on either ſide of the ſhip, and keep the maſt from pitching forward or overboard.

A LIST

A

LIST of WITNESSES,

CALLED upon the TRIAL.

The

The LINE of BATTLE,

Issued the 28th of June, 1778, by Admiral Keppel.

The Monarch to lead with the LARBOARD; and the Ramillies with the STARBOARD TACKS on Board.

Frigts.	SHIPS.	COMMANDERS.	guns.	men.	Divis.
Fox, Capt. Windsor.	Monarch,	Capt. Rowley,	74	600	Vice Admiral of the Red.
	Hector,	Sir J. Hamilton, Bart.	74	600	
	Centaur,	Capt. Cosby,	74	600	
	Exeter	Nott,	64	500	
	Duke,	Brereton,	90	750	
	Queen,	Sir Robert Harland, Capt. Prescot,	90	772	
	Shrewsbury,	Ross,	74	600	
	Cumberland,	Peyton,	74	600	
	Berwick,	Hon. Keith Stewart,	74	600	
	Stirling Castle,	Sir Charles Douglas,	64	500	
Proserpine. Capt. Sutton. Arethusa. C. Marshall.	Courageux,	Rt. H. Lord Mulgrave,	74	600	Admiral of the Blue.
	Thunderer,	Hon. Capt. Walsingham,	74	600	
	Vigilant,	Capt. Kingsmill,	64	500	
	Sandwich,	Edwards,	90	750	
	Valiant,	Hon. Lev. Gower,	74	650	
	Victory,	Hon. Aug. Keppel. Rear Adm. Campbell, Capt. Faulknor,	100	894	
	Foudroyant,	Jervois,	80	650	
	Prince George	Sir J. Lindsay, K. B.	90	750	
	Bienfaisant,	Capt. Macbride,	64	500	
	Vengeance,	Clement,	74	600	
Milford, C. Burnaby.	Worcester,	Capt. Robinson,	64	500	Vice Admiral of the Blue.
	Elizabeth,	Hon. F. Maitland,	74	600	
	Defiance,	Capt. Goodhall,	64	500	
	Robust,	Capt. Hood,	74	600	
	Formidable,	Sir H. Palliser, Bart. Capt. Beazely,	90	772	
	Ocean,	Capt. Laforey,	90	750	
	America,	Rt. H. Lord Longford,	64	500	
	Terrible,	Sir R. Bickerton, Bart.	74	600	
	Egmont,	Capt. Allen,	74	600	
	Ramillies,	Capt. Digby,	74	600	

A LIST

A LIST of the FRENCH SHIPS of the LINE, that failed from BREST in July 1778, according to the beft Intelligence.

Ships.	*Guns.*	*Men.*
Le Bretagne,	116	1600
La Ville de Paris,	94	1200
Le Saint Efprit,	82	1000
La Couronne,	82	1000
*Le Duc de Bourgogne,	82	1000
Le Robufte,	74	800
L'Orient,	74	800
Le Glorieux	74	800
Le Conquerant,	74	800
Le Fendent,	74	800
Le Magnifique,	74	800
Le Partmere,	74	800
L'Intrepide,	74	800
L'Actif,	74	800
Le Zodiaque,	74	800
Le Dauphin Royal,	74	800
Le Artifian	74	800
Le Diadem,	74	800
Le Bien Aime,	64	600
Le Solitaire,	64	600
Le St. Michel,	64	600
*L'Alexandre,	64	600
Le Refleche,	64	600
Le Rolande,	64	600
L'Evellie,	64	600
Le Sphynx,	64	600
Le Vengeur,	64	600
L'Actionaire,	64	600
L'Indien,	64	600
Le Triton,	64	600
L'Amphion,	50	400
Le Feir,	50	400
	2286	24200

N. B. The Duc de Burgogne and Alexandre were not prefent on the 27th of July, the day of the engagement, and therefore their men and guns ought to be deducted out of the above Lift, viz.

	Guns	Men		
Le Duc de Burgogne	82	1000		
L'Alexandre	64	600		
	146	1600	146	1600
			2140	22600

COPY of the WARRANT for holding a Court Martial on ADMIRAL KEPPEL.

By the Commissioners for executing the Office of Lord High Admiral of Great Britain *and* Ireland, *&c.*

WHEREAS Sir Hugh Pallifer did, by his letter to our Secretary, defire we would order a Court Martial for the Trial of the Honourable Auguftus Keppel, for mifconduct and neglect of duty on the 27th and 28th of July, in fundry inftances, contained in his the faid Vice Admiral's Charge. And whereas we have thought fit to order the faid Court Martial to be held on the 7th day of January next, provided the witneffes on the part of the accufer and accufed fhall be ready. We herewith fend you his letter, together with a paper of the charges, and do hereby require you to affemble fuch Court Martial on board one of his Majefty's fhips, either in the harbour or at Spithead; or if the witneffes cannot then be ready, as foon after as they fhall be fo, to enquire into the faid charge againft the faid Admiral, and to try him for his conduct and behaviour therein mentioned.

To Sir Thomas Pye, Knt,
Admiral of the White,
at Portfmouth.

SANDWICH,
J. BULLER,
CHARLES SPENCER,
H. PENTON.

THE
TRIAL
OF THE
Hon. AUGUSTUS Admiral KEPPEL.

FIRST DAY, THURSDAY, January 8.

AT a Court Martial assembled on board his Majesty's ship the Britannia, in Portsmouth Harbour, on Thursday the 8th day of January 1779, and from thence adjourned to the Governor's House, at Portsmouth, before

Admiral Sir THOMAS PYE, President.

ADMIRALS

BUCKLE,	ARBUTHNOT,
MONTAGUE,	RODHAM,

CAPTAINS

MILLBANK,	DUNCAN,
DRAKE,	BOTELER,
PENNY,	CRANSTON,
MOUTRAY,	BENNETT,

W. JACKSON, Esq; Judge Advocate.

Admiral KEPPEL brought on board of the Britannia by the MARSHAL; and Audience admitted.

The Order for the Trial was then read; which named the above Gentlemen *only* to be Members thereof, at which an objection was started by Capt. Faulkner, of the Victory, on account of his not being appointed one of the Members of the Court; in answer to this it was replied, that as a witness on the trial he was ineligible; and the act of Parliament which disqualified him was recited, together with the opinion of Council in support of the rejection of persons so situated, the Captain then withdrew his claim; this being finished, the Court was adjourned to the Governor's house, about half past twelve o'clock, when a letter from Sir Hugh Palliser to Mr. Stephens, Secretary to the Admiralty, praying him to lay before the Lords thereof the following Charge, and to order that a Court Martial should be holden on the Hon. Augustus Admiral Keppel, in consequence thereof.

A CHARGE

A CHARGE *of* Misconduct *and* Neglect of Duty, *against the Honourable* Admiral Keppel, *on the 27th and 28th of* July, 1778, *in divers Instances, as undermentioned:*

I. THAT on the morning of the 27th of *July*, 1778, having a fleet of thirty ships of the line under his command, and being then in the presence of a French fleet of the like number of ships of the line, the said Admiral did not make the necessary preparation for fight, did not put his fleet into a line of battle, or into any order proper either for receiving or attacking an enemy of such force: but on the contrary, although his fleet was already dispersed and in disorder, he, by making the signal for several ships of the Vice Admiral of the Blue Division, to chace to windward, encreased the disorder of that part of his fleet, and the ships were in consequence, more scattered than they had been before; and whilst in this disorder, he advanced to the enemy, and made the signal for battle: That the above conduct was the more unaccountable, as the enemy's fleet was not then in disorder, nor beaten, nor flying, but formed in a regular line of battle on that tack which approached the British fleet, all their motions plainly indicating a design to give battle, and they edged down and attacked it whilst in disorder. By this unofficer-like conduct a general engagement was not brought on, but the other Flag Officers and Captains were left to engage without order or regularity, from which great confusion ensued: Some of his ships were prevented getting into action at all, others were not near enough to the enemy, and some from the confusion fired into others of the King's ships, and did them considerable damage: And the Vice Admiral of the Blue was left alone to engage, singly and unsupported: In these instances the said Admiral Keppel negligently performed the duty imposed on him.

II. That after the Van and Center Divisions of the British Fleet passed the rear of the enemy, the Admiral did not immediately tack and double upon the enemy, with these two divisions, and continue the battle; nor did he collect them together at that time, and keep so near the enemy to renew the battle as soon as it might be proper: On the contrary, he stood away beyond the enemy to a great distance before he wore to stand towards them again, leaving the Vice Admiral of the Blue engaged with the enemy, and exposed to be cut off.

III. That

III. That after the Vice Admiral of the Blue had passed the last of the enemy's ships, and immediately wore, and laid his own ship's head towards the enemy again, being then in their wake, and at a little distance only, and expecting the Admiral to advance with all the ships to renew the fight, the Admiral did not advance for that purpose, but shortened sail, hawled down the signal for battle, nor did he at that time, or at any other time whilst standing towards the enemy call the ships together, in order to renew the attack, as he might have done, particularly the Vice Admiral of the Red and his division, which had received the least damage, had been the longest out of action, were ready and fit to renew it, were then to windward, and could have bore down and fetched any part of the French fleet, if the signal for battle had not been hawled down, or if the said Admiral Keppel had availed himself of the signal appointed by the thirty-first article of the fighting instructions, by which he might have ordered those to lead who are to lead with the starboard tacks on board, by a wind, which signal was applicable to the occasion for renewing the engagement with advantage, after the French fleet had been beaten, their line broken, and in disorder.--- In these instances he did not do the utmost in his power to take, sink, burn or destroy the French fleet that had attacked the British fleet.

IV. That instead of advancing to renew the engagement, as in the preceding articles is alledged, and as he might and ought to have done, the Admiral wore and made sail directly from the enemy, and thus he led the whole British fleet away from them, which gave them the opportunity to rally unmolested, and to form again into a line of battle, and to stand after the British fleet. This was disgraceful to the British flag, for it had the appearance of a flight, and gave the French Admiral a pretence to claim the victory, and to publish to the world that the British fleet ran away, and that he pursued it with the fleet of France, and offered it battle.

V. That in the morning of the twenty-eighth of July, 1778, when it was perceived that only three of the French fleet remained near the British, in the situation the whole had been in the night before, and that the rest were to leeward at a greater distance, not in a line of battle, but in a heap; the Admiral did not cause the fleet to pursue the flying enemy, nor even to chase the three ships

that

that fled after the reſt; but on the contrary, he led the Britiſh fleet another way directly from the enemy.--- By theſe inſtances of miſconduct and neglect, a glorious opportunity was loſt of doing a moſt eſſential ſervice to the ſtate, and the honour of the Britiſh navy was tarniſhed.

H. PALLISER.

So ſoon as the charge was read, Admiral Keppel addreſſed himſelf to the Court, requeſting, "That the log-"books belonging to the ſeveral ſhips which accom-"panied him on this expedition, ſhould be delivered into "Court, and be ordered to lie on the table, for the in-"ſpection of the members, as well as to prevent any un-"fair uſe being made of them, by eraſures or alterations "of any kind."

Sir Hugh Palliſer very ſtrenuouſly objected to this, on the ground that they could be of no value as evidence, until they were ſworn to by the ſeveral maſters, and authenticated in form.

The Court, however, coincided with Admiral Keppel in opinion, that it would be proper to have all the log-books brought into Court, as it would prevent even the idea of an alteration in the favour or to the prejudice of either party.

Orders were then given to the maſters of the different ſhips, whoſe log-books were neceſſary for evidence, to bring them into Court preciſely at ten o'clock to morrow forenoon, then to ſwear to the authenticity of them, and that they had undergone no additions or alterations of any kind whatever, relative to what had paſſed between that time and the twenty-eighth of July following.

The Preſident then made a motion to adjourn, which being unanimouſly agreed to, the Court was in conſequence adjourned to ten o'clock to-morrow morning.

SECOND DAY, FRIDAY the 8th of JANUARY.

THE court met according to adjournment, about ten o'clock, when the Maſters of the ſeveral ſhips that were in the engagement, were ordered to produce their log-books, and to be ſworn ſeparately to the truth of them; and that they had undergone no alterations or additions. The maſters were called in, and ſworn accordingly.

Mr. Moſely, maſter of the Bienfaiſant, ſaid he had no log-book, nor had he kept any during that time.---He ſaid, he had made minutes in his journal, but that was left at Plymouth.

Mr.

Mr. Arnold, maſter of the Robuſte, refuſing to take the oath, was aſked by the Court the reaſon of his refuſal.

A. Becauſe ſeveral alterations and additions have been made.

Sir H. Palliſer. Do you object to the oath on account of any alterations made in your own minutes, or becauſe of any additions to them by others?

A. I object for both reaſons.

Admiral Keppel. Were any of the alterations you ſpeak of made before or after it was publickly known that I was to be tried?

A. They were made both before and after it was known that a Court-Martial was to be held.

Admiral Keppel. Are you poſitive any alterations were made ſince it was determined to hold this court-martial?

A. I believe ſome of them were made only ten or fourteen days ago.

Admiral Keppel. Do you know by whoſe authority the alterations were made?

A. By order of our Captain.

Admiral Keppel. Were thoſe orders verbal or written?

A. Both.

Admiral Keppel. Did you upon the Captain's requiſition refuſe to make any ſuch alterations?

A. No, I could not.

Admiral Keppel. Was any officer or other perſon preſent at the time? A. Yes, I believe the firſt Lieutenant.

Q. Were the written orders in the Captain's own hand writing?

A. No, they were copied by one of the mates.

Q. Were the alterations made by the uſual perſon who keeps the log-book? A. Yes.

Q. Where were they made.

A. In the great cabin of the Robuſte.

Q. Did the Captain ſee the log-book at the time?

A. The Captain ſees the log-book every day.

Q. Did the Captain, after the action, approve of what was put into the log-book relative to that day's work?

A. It was not inſerted in the log-book until it had received the Captain's approbation.

Q. Were the alterations for the 27th and 28th of July inſerted at that time by the Captain's approbation?

A. The Captain frequently thought it neceſſary to add to or interline?

Q. Do you think any alterations were made in conſequence of Admiral Keppel's trial?

A. I believe they were.

 The

The remainder of the masters were next ſworn to their reſpective log-books.

Sir Hugh Palliſer then deſired to have acceſs to all or either of the log-books out of court hours.

The Court took up the conſideration thereof, to be determined to morrow.---The maſters were then ordered to withdraw.

Captain Marſhall, of the Arethuſa frigate, called into Court, and ſworn.

Sir Hugh Palliſer. When was the French fleet firſt diſcovered?

A. On the 24th of July, about half paſt two o'clock.---We did not ſee them, I believe, ſo ſoon as other ſhips.

Q. Were the French fleet during that afternoon, to the eaſtward, and to leeward of the Britiſh fleet; or how otherwiſe ſituated?

A. I cannot ſpeak poſitively to any queſtions previous to the 27th of July; I did not expect to be called to anſwer any queſtions prior to that day; but I will ſpeak to the beſt of my recollection.

Q. How did the enemy appear to be employed; was it in forming their fleet into a line of battle, or in what other way?

A. I was too much employed to look after what they were about.

Admiral Keppel. I apprehend there can nothing be brought againſt me in charge till the 27th or 28th of July. However, I beg leave to be underſtood, that I have no objections to ſuch queſtions being aſked, as will go into the merit of every day's buſineſs; if the accuſer does not go into them, I certainly will myſelf.

Q. In the evening of the 23d, between ſeven and eight o'clock how were the French fleet ſtanding---to, or from the Britiſh fleet?

A. I wiſh I had been better prepared.---We had our larboard tacks aboard, and many ſignals were made and repeated, and the French had their ſtarboard tacks on board---My whole attention was to the flag, and to repeat the ſignals. I cannot ſpeak ſo well as I could wiſh.

Q. At eight o'clock did not the King's fleet bring to on the larboard tack, per ſignal? A. Yes.

Q. Was the wind about weſt at that time? Or how was it?

A. At weſt, by the log-book.---I cannot ſpeak from my own recollection.

Q. From what time or hour was it weſt by your log?

A. From half paſt three to nine o'clock.

By the Court. This is mere log-book evidence. Captain Marſhall

Marſhall ſpeaks only from his log. He anſwers no queſtions from his own knowledge.

Admiral Keppel. I wiſh Captain Marſhall were permitted to withdraw to recollect himſelf, that he may be able to anſwer theſe queſtions with more certainty; for he came prepared to anſwer thoſe only which relate to the 27th and 28th of July.

[Captain Marſhall then withdrew; and in about half an hour came in again.]

Q. Upon the 27th in what ſituation and diſtance was your ſhip from the Victory, at ſix in the morning?

A. Nearly in her ſtation; near the Victory, rather abaft the Admiral's weather beam, about three or four miles.

Q. Was not the Britiſh fleet at that time much extended, ſcattered, and diſperſed?

A. There were ſome ſhips to leeward, of the blue diviſion, and ſome of the red to windward, on the weather quarter.

Q. Was not the fleet ſcattered; ſome ſhips ſeparated more than others, ſome conſiderably more to windward than others, and others to leeward in the morning?

A. In the morning they were ſo.

Q. Do you remember the ſignal being made on board the Victory, on the 27th of July, for ſeveral ſhips to chaſe to windward, eſpecially the blue diviſion?

A. I remember the ſignal; it was not a ſignal I repeated; I have not taken it down. I remember a ſignal being made ſeveral times; I have obſerved before, I did not repeat the ſignal. I ſpeak from memory, without having made a note of it.

Q. There was ſuch a ſignal made then?

A. There was.

Q. Do you know what ſhips the ſignal was made for?

A. I do not; I imagine it was for ſome ſhips of the blue diviſion.

Q. Did you take notice of a number of ſhips making ſail in conſequence of that ſignal.

A. Some ſhips did; the number I cannot recollect.

Q. Did not thoſe ſhips chacing in conſequence of that ſignal become more ſcattered from the Vice Admiral than before?

A. I cannot be a judge of that; I was to windward; thoſe ſhips that ſailed beſt would moſt increaſe their diſtance.

Q. Was not the Britiſh fleet then ſtanding on the larboard tack, till a ſignal was made for the Britiſh fleet to tack altogether? A. They were.

Q. At what hour was such signal made?

A. Half after ten, by my time.

Q. Soon after the British fleet tacked, was not the French fleet discovered to windward, approaching our fleet, on the contrary tack, in a regular line of battle?

A. We did not observe them in a line of battle, nor on a contrary tack, till just before the firing began a-head.

Q. When they had their larboard tacks a-board in the morning prior to firing, what time did you discover them to be in a line of battle?

A. When they laid their heads the other way, as they were standing upon the same tack that we were, they appeared to me to be in a line of battle: I speak before the time of tacking, they laid their heads the other way: we tacked after them just before the firing began.

Q. Did you discover the French fleet in a line of battle before the British fleet began to engage?

A. In the morning, about eleven, they had been in a line of battle, and tacked from it; in the morning they were to windward of us.

Q. What time?

A. I imagine about nine; a little after ten we tacked after them; the first I saw of their being about, was just before the firing began, consequently I cannot know whether they were in a line of battle.

By the Court. The question is, Whether or not he saw the French Fleet before they began to engage, to be in a line of battle?

A. I imagine they were, before they tacked, about nine o'clock, as it appeared to me.

Q. Did Admiral Keppel make signal for the fleet to form into a line of battle, or into a line on any point that day before the engagement began?

A. No, I think not.

Q. Was there time for doing so, from day-light in the morning, till the time the engagement began.

A. Most certainly. Five hours.

Q. Did the King's fleet advance towards that of France, without being in such line or order? A. Yes.

Q. Was there a general signal for the whole fleet to chace at this time?

A. Not that day. But I considered ourselves in chace of them nearly the whole time, except when there was a signal for the line of battle. When the signal to form a line of battle was out, we could not be in chace.

Q. Did the French attack us while we were not in a line, nor in any order upon any point of the compass?

A. They did.

Q. Were

Q. From the manner of engaging was it not impoſſible for our ſhips to engage the enemy ſhip to ſhip?

A. It was impoſſible, ſome of our ſhips were ſo far to leeward.

Q. Did Admiral Keppel make the ſignal for battle, whilſt the fleet were without line of battle, or any other line? A. Yes.

Q. Did the Admiral make the ſignal for battle before the French fleet fired? A. The firing began firſt.

Q. Did the French or Engliſh fire firſt.

A. I know not.

Q. Could you tell what ſail thoſe ſhips were under at the time the ſignal was made for chace?

A. Some of them had their mainſails up, their gibs and ſtay ſails, I think not their top-gallant ſails.

Q. Were not then theſe ſhips a-head of the Admiral on his lee bow at the time the ſignal was made for chace by the Admiral? A. Some of them, I believe, were.

Q. Such of them as were of the blue diviſion in that ſituation, and on the larboard tack, was not that the proper ſtation of that diviſion, to be in readineſs to form the line of battle on that tack, in caſe the ſignal had been made for it, that diviſion being to lead on that tack?

A. The Vice Admiral of the Blue leads on the larboard tack.

Q. Were not ſome of the frigates and fireſhips expoſed to the firing of the enemy again, before they could get out of the way? A. I know not.

Q. Did any of the enemy's ſhot go over your ſhip before you got out of the way?

A. No, not till I was in my ſtation a-breaſt of the Victory to leeward, and after I had brought her up, then, I think, we bore up a little, out of the reach of the ſhot.

Q. When the Arethuſa bore up, were any of the other frigates to windward of the Victory, and a-head of you?

A. There might be; I cannot be poſitive; I endeavoured to keep in my ſtation.

Q. What ſtation did you preſerve with reſpect to the Victory during the time ſhe was going down along the rear of the French line?

A. I endeavoured to keep upon the Victory's beam, out of gun ſhot.

Q. Was you in that Poſition at the time the Victory paſſed the laſt ſhip of the French line?

A. I cannot be poſitive of the exact ſituation; the Victory was in a ſmoke, and we had not ſeen her for ſome time.

Q. When the Victory had paſſed the rear of the French

line,

line, and ceafed firing, did you then fee her, and in what ftation was you then from her?

A. I faw the Victory, but fo long ago, I cannot recollect her exact ftation.

Q. How long, and how far did the Victory continue to ftand at the fame time after paffing the laft of the fleet, before fhe wore?

A. To the beft of my recollection, but a very little while.

Q. What do you mean by a little while?

A. I cannot confirm it, 'tis at fuch a diftance of time.

Q. As to the diftance what will you pleafe to fay?

A. I cannot afcertain the diftance.

Q. At what time did the Victory wear?

A. We repeated the fignals foon after one; as appears by my minutes, taken by the Purfer. He was the perfon appointed.

Q. Do you know by your own knowledge the time the Victory wore, after fhe paffed the line?

A. It muft be foon after one; by the glafs I faw the fignal, and imagine it was foon after one.

Q. Was the fignal for battle aboard of the Victory hauled down before, or after fhe wore?

A. To the beft of my recollection, after fhe wore.

Q. How long time?

A. Not a great while, I think.

Q. Were the minutes taken on board the Arethufa of the fignals made, examined and compared with thofe minutes taken on board the Victory?

A. Thefe minutes I have in my hand were taken by the Purfer, and will be fworn to, and have not been compared with any other minutes except as to time; there has been no alteration.

Q. Do not thofe minutes tell the time the fignal was hauled down?

A. It does; and it was at 26 minutes paft one, P. M.

Q. Did the Victory, at any time, fet her top gallant fails?

A. I do not recollect fhe did.

Q. What was the firft fignal the Admiral made after the Victory wore, and ftood again towards the French fleet?

A. The Union Flag, a blue and red crofs at the mizen peak, and one gun, for the fleet to form a line a cable's length a-head.

Q. What time was that?

A. At forty minutes paft one, and hauled down twenty-three minutes paft three.

Q. What was the next fignal?

A.—At

A. At fifty minutes paſt one, a flag, ſtriped blue and white, at the mizen topmaſt head, the other a pendant at the main topmaſt head, for the Proſerpine to come within hail. Soon after another pendant, yellow, at the fore topmaſt head, for the Arethuſa to come under hail.

Q. What was the next ſignal?

A. I was on board the Victory; the minutes will tell; fifty minutes paſt two a blue pendant at the enſign ſtaff for the fleet to wear.

Q. What was the next?

A. At twenty-four minutes paſt three, a blue flag at the mizen peak, for the ſhips to windward to get into the Admiral's wake.

Q. What was the next?

A. At thirty minutes paſt three a union and blue flag, with a red croſs at the mizen peak.

Q. Was not that up before?

A. We hauled it down for the fleet to form a line a-head, a cable's length aſunder.

Q. At what time was that flag hauled down?

A. At twenty-three minutes after three.

Q. What was the next ſignal?

A. At fifty minutes paſt three, a yellow pendant at the mizen topmaſt head; the Milford's ſignal.

Q. For what purpoſe?

A. No purpoſe; the ſignal was out.

Q. What was the next?

A. A white pendant at the ſtarboard main top ſail yard arm nearly the ſame time for the Duke.

Q. Was the ſignal for battle up at that time?

A. About twenty minutes.

Q. What was the next?

A. A flag ſtriped blue and white, at the main top maſt head, for a particular ſhip to make more ſail.

Q. Do you remember any other pendant out at that time? A. The yellow was out, but I did not haul it down.

Q. What was the next ſignal?

A. At thirty-ſeven minutes paſt four a Spaniſh enſign at the main top maſt head, obſerving the ſhips out of their ſtation.

Q. What was the next?

A. At fifty-ſix minutes paſt four, a red pendant at the mizen top maſt head; the Prince George's ſignal.

Q. What was the next.

A. A blue pendant at the ſtarboard mizen top ſail yard arm, at fifty ſeven minutes paſt four for the Bienfaiſant.

Q. What was the next?

A. There were more ſignals then made, but I have not

not the minutes of more than two ſhips; the Prince George and Bienfaiſant, and ſome other ſhips were out of their ſtation. The Spaniſh flag hung till near dark.

Admiral Keppel. What was the next?

A. At twenty-two minutes paſt five, a yellow pendant at the main top maſt head, the Proſerpine's ſignal.

Q. What was the next?

A. Thirty-two minutes paſt five, a yellow pendant at the ſtarboard main top ſail yard arm, the Fox's ſignal.

Q. What was the next?

A. At thirty-ſix minutes paſt ſix, a red pendant at the larboard main top ſail yard arm, the Fox's ſignal.

Q. What was the next?

A. At thirty-ſix minutes paſt ſix, a red pendant at the larboard main top ſail yard arm. There were other ſignals made between this. The Fox's was at the main top maſt head.

Q. The blue flag was hoiſted, but no account given when it was hauled down?

A. At thirty minutes paſt three.

Q. What was the next?

A. At ten minutes paſt ſix a blue flag hoiſted at the enſign ſtaff, hauled down in three minutes, it was hoiſted by miſtake, and then hoiſted for the ſhips to windward to get into the Admiral's wake.

Q. What was the next?

A. At thirty-ſix minutes paſt ſix, a red pendant at the larboard main top ſail yard arm; that is the third ſignal. The Spaniſh flag ſtill flying.

Q. What was the next?

A. A blue pendant at the ſame time, at the larboard fore yard arm, the Centaur's ſignal. At the ſame time a white pendant, at the larboard mizen topſail yard arm, for the America. At the time theſe ſignals were made, there was either four or five blue pendants flying on board the Victory at different places, but I have only two blue pendants to repeat. I do not know exactly for what ſhips they were, having no minutes of them, but believe them to be the Ramilies, Thunderer, Cumberland, Ocean, Terrible, Bienfaiſant, and Hector, of the blue.

Q. Was there any ſignals made after that time, between thirty-ſix minutes paſt ſix, and dark?

A. I have no minutes of any ſignals after.

Q. After the Arethuſa paſſed the rear of the French fleet, did you look towards the enemy's fleet, and ſee thoſe ſhips of ours which were then engaged. A. I certainly did.

Q. Had

Q. Had you occasion to take any particular notice of the station of the Vice Admiral of the blue at that time?

A. No, I did not. The first I saw of the Vice Admiral of the blue was coming out of action with the other ships.

Q. Was this observation before or after Admiral Keppel had wore? A. Before.

Q. Did you afterwards take notice of the Formidable after coming out of action to wear, and laying her head towards the enemy again?

A. I perceived my station to be to windward, after wearing, made sail and tacked close upon the Formidable's quarter, as I would not go so near to windward of the Vice Admiral, and then formed under the Victory's lee bow, and stood about, while I was in stayes, was hailed by the Victory to come on board her, which I immediately obeyed.

Q. When you first saw the Formidable laying with her head towards the enemy, was that before or after the Admiral made the signal to wear? A. After.

Q. At what distance was the Admiral at that time from the Formidable, when you saw her head towards the enemy?

A. No great distance. The Formidable was upon the Victory's lee bow. I will not say any distance, but we were soon about.

Q. What sail had the Victory, while she was standing from the rear of the French fleet, till she wore?

A. I cannot tell.

Q. What sail had she set, when she was afterwards standing towards the French fleet, after having wore.

A. I positively don't recollect; the main top-sails were unbent.

Q. Did you observe the Formidable, when she wore, lay her head from the enemy towards the Admiral?

A. She must have wore while I was in the boat. I did not see it.

Q. The first time you took notice of her, with her head towards the Admiral, was that before or after you saw the Admiral's main top sails were unbent?

A. I observed the Formidable upon the Admiral's quarter. Indeed the Admiral was upon the leeward tack, and the Vice Admiral was upon the starboard, and I believe the Victory the headmost ship at that time.

Q. Did you continue on board the Victory, till the Victory and Formidable met? A. I was on board the Victory when the Formidable passed to leeward.

Q. When the Victory passed the Formidable to windward,

ward, did not the Victory immediately wear; and pass under the Formidable's stern to leeward of her, and steered a course from the wind. A. Not immediately after.

Q. What did the Admiral do then immediately when he was to leeward?

A. I left the Victory immediately after she wore, the Admiral had discharged me. I left the Victory while she was wearing, and went on board the Arethusa.

President. When the Formidable stood to the Victory, to leeward, was the signal flying for a line of battle a-head on the fore top mast head?

A. To the best of my remembrance.

Admiral Keppel. What was the Vice Admiral of the blue's station upon the leeward tack, when the Admiral's signal was out for a line of battle a-head, on board the Victory.

A. Leaving room for the Foudroyant, Prince George, Bienfailant, Vengeance, Worcester, Elizabeth, Defiance, and Robuste, to form the line.

Admiral Keppel. Was there any one ship a-head of the Victory, in obedience to that signal? A. No, no.

It being four o'clock, the Court adjourned to half past nine tomorrow morning.

THIRD DAY, SATURDAY JANUARY 9th.

AT ten o'clock this morning, the court being assembled, proceeded to give their opinion on the motion made by Sir Hugh Palliser yesterday, "for leave to inspect the "log-books of the several ships which had been received "into court at the request of Admiral Keppel." When Sir Thomas Pye, getting up, declared it the unanimous opinion of the said court, "that Sir Hugh Palliser was "entitled to such an inspection of the log-books after "the rising of the court, if made in the presence of an "officer, who should be sworn to a strict preservation of "their present contents."

The examination of *Captain Marshall* was then resumed.

Sir H. Palliser. As the Formidable was between the Victory and the rear of the enemy's fleet, was not she the nearest ship to the enemy, and the only one between them and the Victory? A. I think she was.

Q. Did you observe three of the enemy's ships standing directly for the Formidable, and at a less distance from her than the Victory was, and with more sail than the Victory, she having unbent her main top-sail, and hauled down the signal for battle?

A. I

A. I was on board the Victory, and cannot think they were at a less distance from the Formidable than the Victory know not what sail they carried; to the best of my recollection, the Victory bent her main top sail about the time she wore from the French fleet. I was on the quarter deck of the Victory, and saw the buntings of the main top sail hauling up, just before I went out of the ship. The signal for battle was hauled down twenty-six minutes past one.

Q. Whilst the Victory was standing towards the enemy, were any of the ships of the Admiral's division in their station in a line a head of him?

A. I believe not. I have already said the Victory after the Formidable wore was the headmost ship.

Q. Did the Admiral make the signal for them to get into their stations, whilst they were standing towards the enemy?

A. The signal for the fleet to form a line a-head a cable's length asunder, by my minutes, and the best of my recollection, was flying at that time.

Q. Was the signal made for observing any particular ships, whose proper stations were a-head of the Admiral, being out of their station at that time?

A. No, I believe not.

Q. Were not the ships of the Vice Admiral of the Blue's division just then come out of action and disabled?

A. I yesterday observed, that the Formidable, and some ships were disabled, but their names I cannot recollect.

Q. Had not the French fleet broken up the line and were then in disorder?

A. I had but a momentary view from the starboard quarter gallery, of the French fleet, and cannot ascertain.

Q. During the time the Admiral was standing towards the French fleet, where was the Vice Admiral of the red and his division?

A. Nearly on the Admiral's lee, or weather beam, or rather before the beam.

Q. At what distance was the Vice Admiral of the red from the Victory, at the time she wore and stood from them?

A. I cannot tell the proper distance at this period.

Q. Were they not considerably to windward of the French?

A. I have observed that I saw the French fleet out of the Admiral's starboard quarter gallery, and that the Vice of the Red's division was rather before the larboard or Weather beam of the Victory.

Q. Where

Q. Where was you when you saw the Vice Admiral to windward, and before the Victory's beam?

A. On the Victory's quarter deck.

Q. Whilst the Admiral was standing towards the French fleet, was any signal made for the ships of the starboard tack in a line of battle, to take the lead at that time? A. No.

Q. Did the Victory wear without standing beyond the Formidable, and first seem to offer to pass again to windward of her?

A. I said yesterday that I left the Victory when she was wearing; I likewise observed, that the Formidable was passing on the starboard side of the Victory.

Q. After you returned on board your own ship, did you follow the Victory, in order to be ready to repeat the Victory's signals?

A. I got into my station as soon as possible.

Q. How did the Admiral steer after he passed to leeward of the Formidable.

A. It appears by my log S. and by E.

Q. Was that upon the wind, or from the wind?

A. From the wind.

Q. How many points?

A. I cannot pretend to say by any means, as we sailed various courses to keep our station.

Q. How was the wind?

A. I have not taken it down till five o'clock, when it was S. W. and by W.

Q. Do you remember what sail the Admiral carried?

A. No, Sir.

Q. When the blue flag at the mizen peak was first hoisted, 24 minutes past three, was the Formidable near to, or a distance from the Victory.

A. I cannot tell, for I cannot recollect.

Q. The Victory having passed to leeward of the Formidable, and the Victory standing upon a wind from that time, could her distance be great at that time from the Victory, if she had laid still?

A. I have not said that the Victory was standing on a wind, if I recollect right.

Q. Whether that space of time would admit of a great distance; whether the Victory was going upon a wind, or going large?

A. It appears by my minutes to be about an hour and half between the making of the two signals; I have not in my log any rate of the ship's going till five o'clock; I cannot ascertain it.

Q. Which

Q. Which two signals do you allude to?

A. The blue pendant at the ensign staff, made 50 min. past two, for the fleet to wear, and the blue flag at the mizen peak, at 24 min. past three, for the ships to windward to get into the Admiral's wake.

Q. As your station was to windward of the Admiral, did you observe any one ship of the Vice Admiral of the Blue's division at that time to windward of the Admiral?

A. Yes, it appeared to me there was.

Q. Can you name any? A. No.

Q. What reason had you for saying any of them were in that situation?

A. I was on the Victory's weather beam, about two or three miles, and there were several ships appeared nearly astern of the Arethusa.

Q. Do you strictly attend to the time I am speaking of, which is 34 minutes after the Admiral wore.

A. I cannot speak to time, not having kept any minutes of the disposition of the fleet.

Q Did you in the Arethusa, get three Miles from the Admiral's weather beam, in 34 Minutes?

A. I should suppose not.

Q. What Distance was the Arethusa from the Victory when you got into the boat?

A. Not a great distance, but the Victory takes a great deal more time in wearing than frigates do in staying.

Q. By the Victory's continuing to stand to the southward, as before, did she not leave the Formidable astern, and somewhat to windward of her wake, she having passed to leeward of her?

A. The Formidable was to windward and astern.

Q. Did not the distance between the Formidable and the Victory continue increasing the whole afternoon?

A. I cannot recollect.

Q. Was not the course that the Admiral did steer directly from the enemy?

A. The enemy appeared to me on the Arethusa's larboard quarter.

Q. Did the Admiral continue the same course till night?

A. I do not know from my own knowledge.

Q. Don't you know from your own knowledge, whether the fleet continued to stand to the southward, in like manner as they steered immediately after the Admiral wore, and stood to the southward?

A. The fleet stood to the southward. My objection to the former question was to the course.

Q. Did they continue to do the same the whole night?

 A. Yes.

A. Yes.

Q. When the Admiral wore, and ſtood to the ſouthward, did the French fleet then begin to form a new line of battle? A. I know not when they began to form.

Q. When did you ſee they were forming in a line of battle? A. ſome time in the afternoon.

Q. Can you recollect whether that was before or after the Admiral had wore? A. After the Admiral had wore.

Q. In forming the line did they point to leeward of the Britiſh fleet? A. Yes, they did.

Q. For that purpoſe did they appear to you to be going large, or from the wind? A. I cannot ſay.

Q. In the afternoon whilſt the ſignal for the line of battle a-head was flying, and ſtanding to the ſouthward, did not the Vice Admiral Sir Robert Harland, with his diviſion, bear down into the Admiral's wake, and at what time?

A. The time I cannot ſpeak to; but Sir Robert Harland did bear down, but I do not exactly know whether into the Admiral's wake.

Q. Was it nearly in his wake?

A. It was to leeward of me, I cannot anſwer poſitively.

Q. Was not the Vice Admiral of the red, then in his ſtation according to the flag then flying, a-head of the Admiral?

A. The Vice Admiral of the red and his diviſion lead with the ſtarboard tack.

Q. Did you obſerve the Vice Admiral of the red afterwards make ſail, and get into his proper ſtation a-head?

A. The Vice Admiral of the red and ſome of his diviſion went down agreeable to the ſignal.

Q. Can you aſcertain the time they made ſail for that purpoſe? A. I cannot.

Q. What diſtance did you obſerve at ſix in the evening the Formidable was left a-ſtern of the Admiral?

A. I cannot ſpeak as to the diſtance.

Q. During that night did you obſerve any ſignals made by the French fleet by ſky rockets? A. No.

Q. Was the French fleet, or any part of it in ſight the next morning?

A. There were three ſtrange ſails, which I imagined to be part of the French.

Q. Was there any more of them obſerved from your ſhip that morning? A. No.

Q. Did any of our ſhips to your knowledge make the ſignal for ſeeing ſtrange ſhips?

A. There were ſome ſignals made.

Q. How

Q. How many?

A. I do not know how many, nor by whom the ſignals were made.

Q. Do you know whether the Admiral's ſhip anſwered them? A. I do not.

Q. Do you know from what quarter of the compaſs the ſignal was made for ſeeing theſe ſhips? A. No, I do not.

Q. Is it noted in your log-book, that ſuch ſignals were made for ſeeing ſtrange ſhips? A. It is not, Sir.

Q. Were not the three ſhips you mentioned, very near to the Britiſh fleet? A. I cannot judge the diſtance.

Q. Did they croud ſail from the Britiſh fleet?

A. Yes, I think they did.

Q. Which way did they go?

A. They ſeemed to me to ſtand away upon our ſtarboard quarter to the S. E..

Q. Did the Britiſh fleet or any part of them purſue thoſe ſhips? A. I know not.

Q. Did the Admiral early in the morning of the 28th wear, and lay his head with the whole fleet to the northward? A. Yes.

Admiral Montague. The three ſhips that you ſaw to leeward in the morning, did you take them to be line of battle ſhips or frigates? A. I cannot ſay what they were.

Q. Can you tell the bearing and diſtance of Uſhant at noon on the 27th according to your ſhip's reckoning?

A. Our bearing and diſtance from Uſhant, at that time, by the log, was N. 86. E. diſtance 28 leagues.

Q. How was the wind in the morning of the 28th?

A. At two o'clock by log the wind was W. and no alteration mentioned in that day's work.

Q. What weather was it then?

A. A freſh wind, thick and cloſe, hazey I think.

Admiral Keppel. On what tack was the French fleet at day light in the morning of the 27th?

A. On their larboard tack.

Q. When did they tack and ſtand on the ſtarboard tack? A. About nine o'clock.

Q. After they were on their ſtarboard tack, did you ever loſe ſight of them for any time? A. No.

Q. When you ſaw them beginning their fire on the headmoſt of the Engliſh fleet, did you obſerve whether the French Admiral was in his own fleet? A. I did not.

Q. Do you know what ſail the Formidable had on the larboard tack when ſhe paſſed the Victory?

A. I cannot deſcribe it.

Q. Was the ſignal for the line of battle a-head ever

hauled down while the Victory was leading to the French fleet on the larboard tack? A. No, Sir.

Q. How many ships of the Vice Admiral of the red were with him at the time he bore down to the Admiral?

A. I do not know.

Q. Do you recollect what ships of the centre division were a-stern of the Victory in their stations?

A. I cannot say what, but there were very few.

Admiral Montague. From the day you first saw the French fleet, to the time you lost sight of them, do you of your own observation or knowledge, know of any act of the commander in chief, Admiral Keppel, behaving or conducting himself unbecoming a flag officer?

A. No, as God is my judge.

CAPTAIN MARSHALL *ordered to withdraw.*

Sir WILLIAM BURNABY, *of the* Milford, *sworn.*

Q. When was the French fleet first perceived?

A. Friday the 24th July, at two in the afternoon, by log.

Q. What was the situation of the French fleet from the British to eastward, and to leeward, or how otherwise situated?

A. They were to the westward of us, nearly a-head, and farther to leeward.

Q. At eight in the evening that night how was the French fleet standing, how did they appear to be employed that afternoon, were they forming their line, or in what other way?

A. They were standing towards us in great disorder. Admiral Keppel made my signal to come within hail of him, and gave me orders to make sail a-head to reconnoitre the French fleet, I made sail directly towards them, the French fleet then standing on towards us, keeping a little from the wind and still in disorder. I stood towards them 'till within a gun-shot and half. The van of their fleet, I judge, was within six or seven miles from the lee bow of the van of Admiral Keppel's fleet. At half past four I tacked from the French fleet, and stood towards the Victory. The French fleet nearly about that time began to form their line a-head, directing their course to leeward of our fleet, very little from the wind.

Q. How did they appear to be employed that afternoon till eight o'clock that night?

A. I observed them under an easy sail from the time I tacked, and to be employed in forming their line, directing their course to leeward of our fleet. It was hazey and late before I joined the Victory a second time, and received orders to go a-head and keep between the French fleet and ours, but cannot say, I observed particularly their motions, (from the thickness of the weather) to the hour of eight. The rear of the French fleet from the time I first speak, were considerably a-head of our fleet.

Q. What was the position of the French fleet with respect to the British fleet at eight o'clock?

A. They were upon the lee bow. Many of them then formed in a line of battle.

Q. Upon what tack? A. The larboard tack.

Q. Did they continue to stretch upon that tack to leeward of our fleet?

A. I did not observe they did after eight o'clock.

Q. Were they then to leeward of the British fleet?

A. Yes, Sir.

Q. How was the wind at that time? A. W. and by S.

Q. Did not the British fleet bring to at eight o'clock on the larboard tack, per signal?

A. Admiral Keppel made signals at half past eight to bring to on the larboard tack.

Q. Did the British fleet lay to all that night?

A. To the best of my recollection they did.

Q. Were not the Milford and another frigate stationed between the two fleets to make signals during the night, to observe the motions of the enemy, and to make signals accordingly.

A. I don't know of any other ship except my own, I cannot tell what orders were given to any other ships?

Q. Was you ordered?

A. The signal being made to bring to, I soon after lost sight of the French fleet, I was stationed a-head betwixt the French fleet and ours, and to acquaint Admiral Keppel if they should be standing towards, or ready to approach us.

Q. Had you occasion to make any signals to the Admiral during that night of the motions of the enemy?

A. No, as I brought to a-head of our fleet along side of the Admiral, it being very late before I reached the van of the fleet.

Q. Did you observe the other signals that were made?

A. No, Sir.

Q. Where was you at noon 23d July, in what latitude?

A. I do not recollect, I have not my log-book.

Q. The French fleet being to leeward of the British fleet, and standing to the southward, and at the same time our fleet was lying to on their larboard tack, with their heads to the north. Are you of opinion that if they were disposed to avoid coming to an engagement they would

 have

have continued to ſtand upon that tack during that night, having the port of Breſt under their lee?

A. I think it poſſible they might.

Q. Do you know that they did not ſtand on all night upon that tack?

A. They did not, becauſe at day break in the morning, it being thick foggy weather, I found myſelf a little to leeward of the French fleet, they being to windward a-head.

Q. What diſtance was you from the Engliſh fleet at that time? A. I cannot recollect.

Q. When did you make ſail afterwards?

A. At half paſt three by ſignal.

Q. In the morning had not the French fleet the weather gage of the Britiſh fleet, who were then between them and Breſt?

A. They were to windward of us, the wind N. W. and by W.

Q. The Britiſh fleet being then to leeward, and the wind at N. W. and by W. were not they betwixt the French fleet and Breſt? A. Yes.

Q. When you brought to at night, the French fleet were rather to leeward you ſaid. In the morning when you made ſail, you ſaid the French fleet was to windward of the Britiſh fleet; do you know from your own knowledge, whether they came there from working to windward, or by a ſhift of the wind?

A. The wind ſhifted to the N.

Q. Did that bring the French fleet to windward or to leeward?

A. I do not know, but have reaſon to believe that the French fleet tacked after dark, and carried a preſſed ſail all that night on the larboard tack, one of the ſhips in the morning appearing to have carried away her fore top maſt.

Q. Were the whole of the French fleet at day light at a conſiderable diſtance from the frigates?

A. I did not ſee it, nor can recollect the circumſtance; they certainly muſt have tacked, or wore, and ſtood the other way, I imagine cloſe upon a wind from the poſition they appeared in.

Q. Had they carried a preſſed ſail all night, would they have been in ſight of you in the morning?

A. 'Tis very poſſible, becauſe they got ſome miles in the wind's eye, and worked directly to windward I judge.

Q. When you did ſee them in the morning, what ſails did they appear to have ſet?

A. I do not recollect the ſails they had ſet, it ſeemed to be ſails ſuitable to the weather.

Q. What

Q. What sort of weather was it? A. Very thick.

Q. Did it blow fresh? A. Yes.

Q. At what time did the French fleet tack in the morning, and come upon the starboard tack?

A. I do not recollect.

Q. Did it not blow very fresh all that night, and in the morning, with a very high sea?

A. I think it blew fresh in the night, but I don't recollect the strength of it.

Q. What sail were you under at day light in the morning, when the fleet made sail?

A. I had two reefs in my top sail.

It being now four o'clock, the Court adjourned, until ten o'clock to-morrow morning.

FOURTH DAY, MONDAY JANUARY 18th.

THE Court being assembled, and the prisoner brought in, the evidence of Sir WILLIAM BURNABY *was re-assumed and continued.*

Q. Whether during that day, it did appear to him, that the French were collecting their ships together, and endeavouring to keep their fleet in a line of battle?

A. I think they were.

Q. During the days of the 25th and 26th of July, was it or not, for the most part, fresh gales and squals, with a heavy N. W. swell.

A. It was fresh gales and squals.

Q. Can you recollect what sea you had that day.

A. I cannot recollect any extreme heavy swell, but such a sea as is usually attendant on such gales of wind and squals.

Q. Did the French fleet during these days keep the weather gage. A. Yes they did.

Q. And did they carry such sail as to preserve their line of battle.

A. I generally observed them in a line of battle.

Q. And did they preserve nearly the same distance from our fleet.

A. I think they rather increased their distance.

Q. At times when the weather moderated, did the French Admiral croud sail away, or occasionally shorten sail for better perfecting his line of battle?

A. At times they seemed to carry a pressed sail, tolerably well preserving their line, at other times they went under an easy sail, seemingly to perfect their line.

 Q. With

Q. With the wind and weather on these days, do you think the ships could have properly fought their lee lower deck guns ?

A. I think it would have been attended with great risque if they had attempted it.

Q. Could ships have fought their weather lower deck guns, or part of them ?

A. I think they might have fought part of them.

Q. Then would it, or would it not, for these reasons, have been disadvantageous to the French fleet to have bore down and attacked the British fleet on these days.

A. I think it would have been disadvantageous to the French.

Q. In the morning of the 27th of July, was the British fleet scattered, extended, and dispersed.

A. They were somewhat dispersed.

Q. Do you remember signals being made on board the Victory, in the morning of the 27th, for several ships of the Vice Admiral of the blue's division, to chace to windward ?

A. To the best of my knowledge, betwixt nine and ten, a signal was made for some ships to chace; but what ships I do not know.

Q. Was that signal to chace to windward ?

A. I do not recollect, the ships seemed to make sail to windward.

President. Do you remember what signal it was ?

A. No, Sir.

Q. Were the ships that did chace, of the Vice Admiral of the blue's division ?

A. I could not discern what they were.

Admiral Montague. When you saw the signal for ships to chace betwixt nine and ten o'clock, did you observe any of the British ships to make more sail than they did before ?

A. I observed several of the ships in the rear of our fleet to make more sail.

Q. Is there any mention of that signal, made in your log ? A. There is not.

Q. What time did the British fleet tack all together by signal to stand towards the French fleet ?

A. I do not recollect.

Q. Is there no notice of that in your log book ?

A. No, Sir.

Q. Did the Admiral make the signal for the British fleet to form into a line of battle a-head, or on any point of the compass, the day before the engagement began ?

A. I do not recollect that he did.

Q. At

Q. At what time did you observe the French fleet to be in a regular line of battle?

A. Tolerably early in the morning.

Q. Did the Admiral make the signal for battle whilst the British fleet was dispersed?

A. The signal for battle was made about half after eleven.

President. Do you recollect who began the engagement? A. The French,

Capt. Millbank. Do you recollect the tolerably early hour in the morning you saw the fleet in a line of battle?

A. About eight o'clock.

Prosecutor. Did you observe some of our frigates and fireships being exposed to the fire of the enemy before they could get out of the way.

A. Both the fire-ships, the Proserpine, and the Milford were in reach of the enemy's fire, before they got out of the way.

President. Do you remember whether the signal was made for battle by the Admiral before the French began to fire. A. It was afterwards.

Q. How long,

A. I suppose the space of seven or eight minutes.

Q. Did the French, by attacking the British fleet whilst in no line, but somewhat dispersed, render it impossible for us to engage ship to ship, or to bring on a general engagement?

A. From their Position, as I have before observed, somewhat dispersed, as far as my little experience in the service will admit me to say, it prevented our ships from a general engagement.

Admiral Montague. If the Admiral had not advanced towards the enemy, although his line of battle was not regularly formed, could he have brought the French to action, had he waited for forming the line?

A. I should think not, if the French had been disposed to get away.

Q. Were the French close hauled, or did they bear down to oppose the British fleet ship to ship, they, the French, being to windward of the British fleet, and had it in their power so to do.

A. I thought they appeared to keep a little from the wind, just about the time of their coming into action.

Admiral Keppel. I beg you would not shake your head at the witness, Sir Hugh.

President. Do you recollect what sail the French were under when they first began the action?

A. I do not recollect.

Q. Had

Q. Had they their fore sails set?

A. I believe they had.

Q. Was their mainsails set? A. I am not certain.

Admiral Montague. You have said they kept their ships a little from the wind, how many points from the wind?

A. I do not know.

Q. Was it to stretch a-head of our fleet, or to keep to windward of them?

A. Their wearing away could not be with an intention to keep the wind.

Q. Had the French fleet lain to, to receive the British fleet, would not the van of our fleet have reached the van of the French fleet, by which a more general action would have been brought on?

A. Yes, to the best of my judgment.

Q. What part of the French fleet did the van of the British fleet fetch, as the wind was?

A. I think it was about the fourth or fifth of their van.

Prosecutor. Whether, upon the whole he does say, that the French fleet edged down, and brought on the engagement?

A. The van of their fleet, by edging down a little, brought their ships sooner into action.

Q. How long and how far did the Victory continue to stand after passing the sternmost of the French fleet, before she wore and stood towards them again?

A. I believe it might be about 25 minutes, but am not very certain.

Q. What distance do you think she was from them when she did wear?

A. I am not able to determine.

Q. Did you observe the signal for battle being hauled down whilst the Admiral was standing towards the enemy, or from them?

A. I think it was a little before the Victory wore, but cannot charge my memory.

Q. Did you observe the Admiral to shorten sail and unbend his maintop sail while standing towards the enemy.

A. I do not remember.

Q. Did you observe him unbend his maintop sail at all.

A. I do not recollect it.

Q. Did the Admiral wear again and stand from the enemy?

A. The Admiral wore and stood upon his starboard tack, being then a-head of the enemy, on the same tack with them.

Q. Did you at that time, from these motions of the Admiral,

Admiral, conclude that he did not intend to re-attack that day? A. No, I cannot ſay that I did.

By the Court. When the Victory wore firſt, did all the ſhips on the ſtarboard tack a-head of her wear?

A. I do not know.

Preſident. Did the Admiral wear by ſignal the firſt time? A. I do not know.

Q. Did the Admiral wear by ſignal the ſecond time of his wearing? A. Yes, I think he did.

Q. How long was the Victory on the larboard tack?

A. I do not juſtly recollect.

Q. Did you ſee any ſhips on the larboard tack with her.

A. I think I did.

Q. Was it the whole fleet, or only part of it.

A. Part of the van.

Admiral Montague. Do you think it would have been prudent in the Commander in Chief to have renewed the action till the ſhips that had been engaged were all put in a proper condition to engage again, eſpecially as night was advancing.

A. I do not think I am a competent judge.

Captain Mowray. I ſhould be glad to know where the Milford was when the action began?

A. I was pretty well up to windward, and aſtern of ſeveral of the line of battle ſhips.

Q. How many? A. About five or ſix.

Q. Was you in your ſtation?

A. I do not know that I was out of my ſtation; there was no line of battle; we were all in chace, and we got in as we could. I had two ſtations, one when there was no line of battle, and another when there was a line of battle.

Q. What diſtance was the Milford from the ſhips that firſt began the action.

A. About a mile, I believe, aſtern, but at this diſtance of time I cannot be certain.

Proſecutor. Did you obſerve the French fleet to break up their line of battle, and to be in confuſion for ſome time?

A. They ſeemed to be in confuſion a little after the action ceaſed.

Q. Was this while the Admiral was ſtanding towards them?

A. I think it was while the Admiral was on the larboard tack, ſtanding towards them.

Q. Had the Vice Admiral of the Red, Sir Robert Harland, before that time, with his diviſion, doubled on the rear of the enemy, and was he to windward of them?

A. I think

A. I think he was on the larboard tack, to windward of them.

Q. Could that division have borne down on the enemy, if the Admiral had advanced with the rest of the fleet, and kept the signal for battle flying?

A. As being to windward, they certainly could have borne down.

Q. Or if the Admiral had made the signal, appointed by the 31st article of the fighting instructions, for ships on the starboard tack, to have taken the lead, could that division, from their situation, have complied with that signal?

Judge Advocate ordered to read the 31st article.

Q. Sir William Burnaby, Do you know that Article.

A. I do know it. To the best of my judgment, Sir Robert Harland's ship, the Queen, could have obeyed a signal for bearing down, but I do not know how many could have followed him.

Prosecutor. If the enemy had been so re-attacked by the Vice Admiral of the red, and his division bearing down, and the Admiral advancing with the rest of the fleet, would it not have prevented the enemy from recovering from the confusion they were in, and from forming a new line of battle?

A. I judge it might have tended to prevent them from forming a line so soon on the starboard tack as they did, provided our ships were then in a condition of renewing the battle: but of that it is impossible for me to be supposed a competent judge.

Q. Did not the French fleet form a new line of battle without being molested? A. I think they did.

Q. After the van and centre divisions had passed the French fleet, did you take notice of the Vice Admiral of the blue, and the ships of his division that remained engaged?

A. The smoke was too thick for my clearly discerning them.

Q. As far as you did take notice of them, did they appear to you to be far separated from each other, or near together?

A. As far as I can recollect, as soon as they came out of action they seemed separated.

Q. Did you observe the Formidable immediately after she came out of the action, to wear, and lay her head towards the French again, and lay so for some time?

A. I cannot say that I saw it.

Q. Did you see her lay with her head towards the enemy soon after she came out of the engagement, though you did not see her when she actually wore? A. At

A. At this distance of time, I cannot say that I recollect that circumstance.

Q. Do you not recollect seeing her soon after she came out of action, when she was the only ship betwixt the rear of the enemy and the Victory? A. I cannot say I do.

Q. Did you at any time observe three of the enemy's ships standing towards the Formidable soon after the Action? A. It does not occur to me that I did.

Q. When the Admiral did wear to stand from the French fleet, did she not then pass under the Formidable's stern?

Court. Did you ever say that the Admiral wore, and stood from the French fleet?

A. I have not said so.

Prosecutor. When the Admiral wore and stood on the starboard tack, being then a-head of the enemy on the same tack with them, whereabout was the Vice Admiral of the blue at that time?

A. Some distance a-stern, and to windward of the Victory.

Q. Did you observe the signal to be made, for ships to windward to bear down?

A. I did not see the signal thrown out.

Q. Did you see it, after it was out?

A. I do not recollect that I did, but I saw the ships bear down.

Q. Is it not in your log-book?

A. No it is not entered.

Q. Did the Admiral with the fleet, continue to stand on the starboard tack till it was night?

A. Yes, I think he did.

Q. Can you not say what sail he carried during that time?

A. I think he had his topsails and foresail, (but I am not very certain), the greater part of the night.

Q. From the time the Admiral wore and stood on the starboard tack, did the French fleet begin to form into a line of battle on the same tack?

A. I think it was about a quarter of an hour the French began to form their line a-head, after Admiral Keppel had made the signal to form the line a-head on the starboard tack.

Q. Do you mean a quarter of an hour after the Admiral was on the starboard tack?

A. The Admiral had made the signal to form the line a-head before he wore, and stood on the starboard tack.

Q. In that afternoon, whilst the Admiral was standing

on

on the ſtarboard tack, did the Vice Admiral of the Red, and his diviſion, bear down into the Admiral's wake, and at what time?

A. At 35 minutes after four that afternoon, Sir Robert Harland, and moſt of his ſhips, were in the wake of Admiral Keppel.

Court. Do you recollect of how many ſhips Sir Robrt Harland's diviſion conſiſted? A. Ten.

Q. What number do you think bore down?

A. I do not recollect.

Q. Where was the Vice Admiral of the Blue and his diviſion, at this time?

A. At ſome diſtance aſtern and to windward.

Q. Was not the proper ſtation of the Vice Admiral of the Red, according to the ſignal for the line of battle then flying, being on the ſtarboard tack, a-head of the Admiral?

A. The ſignal was firſt made to form a line of battle a-head on the larboard tack. I do not recollect any alteration of the ſignal when they were on the larboard tack. About half paſt four Admiral Keppel made my ſignal to come within hail, which I ſoon afterwards did, and received his orders to acquaint Sir Robert Harland that it was his direction that he made all the ſail he could as ſoon as poſſible, and lead the fleet on the ſtarboard tack, and to make the ſignal for his diviſion to come into his wake.

Q. During that afternoon did you obſerve one of the ſhips of the Admiral's own diviſion laying a conſiderable diſtance aſtern of him, in his wake, upon which the van of the French line fired?

A. I do recollect, the Vengeance, Capt. Clements.

Q. What diſtance do you think that ſhip was aſtern of the Victory?

A. As near as I can recollect, about two miles.

Q. Was you at that time under apprehenſions of any danger of her being cut off by the French?

A. I did at the time expreſs my opinion on the Milford's quarter deck, that ſhe would receive the fire of the French fleet as they paſſed under her lee, and thought it very probable ſhe might have been deſtroyed thereby, the Vengeance then laying in a very ſhattered condition, and at that time ſeemed unable to make ſail.

Q. In what ſituation was you, Sir, during the following night of the 27th, reſpecting the Victory?

A. Some diſtance aſtern and to windward, as near my ſtation as I could keep.

Q. Did

Q. Did you observe the French fleet to make any signals that night by sky rockets, or otherwise?

A. I think I saw one light, which I took to come from the French fleet nearly about ten o'clock.

Q. Could you, at that time, see the body of the ships of the French fleet?

A. They were at too great a distance, and so dark that I could not.

Q. Did you perceive them to bear away in the night?

A. I did not.

Q. When you saw that light, how did that light strike you; as a signal from the French, what did you conclude from it? A. I do not recollect forming any conclusion.

Q. Was the French fleet, or any part of it in sight early the next morning?

A. About four o'clock some of the French fleet appeared to leeward.

Q. How many?

A. I do not know the number, but several; three or four I could easily discern.

Q. Were these three or four near the British fleet?

A. I do not recollect the distance they were at.

Q. Did they appear to you to be line of battle ships or frigates? A. I do not recollect which.

Q. Did these three ships croud sail from the British fleet?

A. They seemed to be steering away to the eastward, increasing their distance from the British fleet.

Q. Was the signal at this time made by any of our ships, for seeing a number of strange ships?

A. I did not see it myself.

Q. Did the British fleet, or any part of them, pursue the ships that were in sight? A. I did not observe any did.

Q. Did the Admiral wear early that morning with his fleet to the north?

A. At eight o'clock the fleet wore, and laid their heads to the northward.

Q. What latitude was you in, at noon on 27th?

A. In latitude of Ushant, 35 leagues distant, by my reckoning.

Q. Was your reckoning corrected that day, or corrected from the land since?

A. It was corrected from the day of reckoning.

Q. What was your latitude, at noon on 28th?

A. About 48. 27.

Q. How was the wind the morning of the 28th?

A. At eight o'clock, when we wore, about W. and by N.

Admiral

Admiral Montague. We are come now to the two days, wherein Mr. Keppel is charged with not doing his utmost, to take, ſink, burn, and deſtroy the ſhips of the enemy, and to have diſgraced the Britiſh flag. I muſt therefore aſk you, Whether during the day of the action, to your knowledge, Admiral Keppel negligently performed the duty impoſed on him?

A. 'Tis a queſtion of the greateſt importance, and far above me to determine. This Court are to adjudge of facts by evidence. Admiral Keppel is a brave and gallant officer, and it ill becomes me to give my opinion. I exceedingly reſpect the character of that worthy gentleman. I ſay it from my heart.

Admiral Montague. If the officers that were preſent refuſe to give their opinion, who is the Court to get information from?

N.B. Here the charge againſt Admiral Keppel was read.

Proſecutor. As Sir William Burnaby modeſtly wiſhes to decline giving his opinion, I preſume he is not compellable, as it is a matter of high importance.

Admiral Montague. If every officer has as much modeſty as the evidence, 'tis impoſſible to come at facts, and Admiral Keppel muſt ſtand convicted to all the world that he has neglected his duty, and did not do his utmoſt to take, burn, ſink, and deſtroy the French fleet, but run away from the French. For my part, I ſhall never give it up, but inſiſt on the witneſs giving a direct anſwer.

Sir Hugh Palliſer. I think no witneſs has a right to anſwer queſtions of opinion, and Sir William Burnaby ſhould not be compelled, as the Court have no power to aſk ſuch queſtions.

The Preſident, Sir Thomas Pye, then deſired the Court to withdraw, to deliberate in private on this queſtion, and after being out of Court near an hour, the Members reaſſumed their ſeats, and the Judge Advocate read the reſolution of the Court, which was, "That the Court had a "right to put what queſtions they pleaſed."

Admiral Montague. Sir William, I aſk you, Whether, during the day of action, to your knowledge, Admiral Keppel negligently performed the duty impoſed on him?

Anſwered again, That is a queſtion of the greateſt importance, and is far above me to be able to determine. I have ſaid before, in other caſes, were I to be aſked that, I did not think myſelf a competent judge. It appears to me, that it comes before this Court to judge from facts given in evidence. Admiral Keppel is a very brave and gallant

gallant officer, and it does not become me to presume to give my opinion, which can be of very little weight.

Admiral Montague. Can you say yes, or no.

A. I say as I did before, I think it do not become me to answer, as I am so very young in the service; I exceedingly respect the character of the worthy gentleman in question, and believe him to be a most gallant man. This I say from my heart. No body entertains a higher opinion of that gentleman than I do.

Admiral Keppel. I have some questions to ask Sir William, relative to the frigates and fire-ships.

Q. Had the frigates, or fire-ships, any men killed by the fire of the enemy on the 27th?

A. I had none, nor do I know whether any of the rest had?

Q. Was the Admiral going large, or by the wind, when the signal of the 31st article of the fighting instructions, is alledged to have been proper to have been made?

A. I do not recollect.

Q. Did you recollect the Admiral being upon the larboard tack, with his head towards the enemy? A. Yes.

Q. Inform the Court, whether the Admiral at any one time while he was upon the larboard tack, did lead large?

A. I cannot answer for certain whether he did or not.

Q. Where was you when I laid my head towards the French fleet?

A. I do not know, because I do not recollect the immediate time you did wear. I was somewhat, as far as I recollect, distant a-stern and to leeward.

Q. Did you lead large at that time, or keep to the wind?

A. If I recollect right, I was going on upon a wind upon the starboard tack, or nearly on a wind.

Q. Were the French fleet forming their line near the time the Admiral first made the signal for the line, after wearing and laying his head towards the enemy?

A. To the best of my recollection, the signal was made by Admiral Keppel to form the line upon the larboard tack, before the French fleet formed their line.

Q. Then you do not recollect that they were forming their line, drawing their one two or three ships out of that body of ships you have already described to be in confusion?

A. Soon after that I observed them forming their line upon their starboard tack.

Q. Soon after what time?

A. The time I mentioned they were in confusion.

Q. What was that confusion, was their fleet at that time at all dispersed?

A. No, the greater part of them seemed to be pretty close together.

Q. Whether the English fleet were not dispersed, while the Victory's head was towards the French?

A. I think they were.

Q. Did you, who was then upon the starboard tack, see any one ship in the line, agreeable to the signal then flying, either a-head or astern of the Victory, who was on the larboard tack?

A. I cannot say that I recollect.

Q. How far was Sir Robert Harland's flag, at the time you have described, from you?

A. He was at some distance, but I cannot recollect exactly.

Q. Can you say how far Sir Robert Harland was from the French fleet? A. No, I cannot.

Q. If you do not know the distance that Sir Robert Harland was from the French fleet, what reason had you to say, his leading large might have prevented the French from forming their line again so soon?

A. Although I cannot recollect the immediate distance, yet still had Sir Robert Harland with his division, and Admiral Keppel with his division, bore down provided they were in a proper condition to attack, I think it might have tended to prevent their forming their line so soon on their starboard tack.

Q. How many ships had Sir Robert Harland of his division with him at this time?

A. I cannot recollect.

Q. You have said, you did not know Admiral Keppel had any ships formed in the line of battle a-head, or astern, I ask you positively, whether you knew or saw that there were any ships, except the Victory herself, and the Formidable, in a situation to give any immediate assistance to the Vice Admiral of the red, if the signal had been made for him to bear down?

A. I cannot recollect.

Q. Was there any other ships?

A. I believe there were some, very few.

Q. I ask this positively. This is a matter upon which I am very much concerned. I must have a positive answer. Say either yes, or no, which is in your breast to say?

A. Not that I recollect.

It being now near four o'clock, the Court adjourned to ten to-morrow morning.

FIFTH

FIFTH DAY, FRIDAY the 11th of JANUARY.

THE Court being met about ten o'clock, the evidence of Sir William Burnaby was continued.

Q. Did you ſee the Vice Admiral of the Blue with ſeveral ſhips of his diviſion? A. Yes, I did.

Q. At what time?

A. About half after four o'clock the Admiral deſired me to inform Sir Robert Harland to make what ſail he could to windward, and lead the fleet on the ſtarboard tack, and to make a ſignal for his diviſion to follow him.

Q. Did Sir Robert Harland give directions agreeable to the Admiral's orders?

A. Yes, Sir, without loſs of time.

Q. Was Sir Robert Harland with the diviſion directly in the Admiral's wake, or a little to windward of it at this time.

A. I think they were nearly in his wake, but to windward.

Q. When you ſpoke to the Vice Admiral of the Red, can you inform the Court, how many ſhips there were at that time of his diviſion a head, and a-ſtern of Sir Robert Harland? A. I do not remember.

Q. Did you, in going down to the Vice Admiral of the Red, Sir Robert Harland, ſee the Vice Admiral of the Blue, and ſeveral of his diviſion with him.

A. Not when I was going to the Vice Admiral Sir Robert Harland, being prevented from the View of thoſe ſhips by paſſing under the lee of ſome others of our ſhips.

Q. Did the Vice Admiral of the Red, in making ſail, according to my orders, paſs to leeward of the Vice Admiral of the Blue. A. I believe he did.

Q. Did the Vice Admiral of the Red, in getting into his ſtation a-head, paſs to windward of the Admiral.

A. I believe he did.

Q. Can you tell the time the Vengeance was within two miles aſtern of the Victory, after the Engliſh fleet was ſtanding upon the ſtarboard tack?

A. I believe it might be near five o'clock in the afternoon.

Q. At this time was Sir Robert Harland making ſail in obedience to my orders? A. I think he was.

Q. Was the Milford at this time as near the Victory as ſhe was to the Vengeance?

A. I was nearer the Vengeance than the Victory, I think.

Q. After Sir Robert Harland made ſail at this time, what ſhips were in the Admiral's wake in the line of battle aſtern of him ?

A. I neither recollect the number, nor what ſhips they were.

Q. Do you allow there were any ? A. Yes.

Q. Was there two ? A. Yes, undoubtedly there were.

Q. At this time ?

A. I think ſo, a little before five o'clock.

Q. Then about five o'clock, you ſay, there were ſome ſhips in a line of battle a-ſtern the Victory ; was the Vice Admiral of the blue one of thoſe ſhips ?

A. I have before ſaid, I judged them to be of Admiral Keppel's or Sir Robert Harland's diviſion.

Q. When Sir Robert Harland's ſhips interrupted your ſight of the Vice Admiral of the blue, and his diviſion, where was the Vice Admiral of the red, and his diviſion ?

A. I think he was well a-ſtern, and pretty near to windward.

Q. Was the Vice Admiral of the red, when a-ſtern, and a little to windward, cloſed in the line in the Admiral's rear ?

A. I ſaid before, that he was a little to windward of the wake of Admiral Keppel's ſhips, and cloſed very near ſome of them.

Q. When you hailed the Queen, Sir Robert Harland's ſhip, did you ſee the Vice Admiral of the blue.

A. I cannot ſay I did, my attention being taken up otherwiſe.

Q. At this time was the ſignal for a line of battle flying at the mizen peak ?

A. I cannot recollect now, whether I asked that queſtion.

Admiral Keppel. If the Vice Admiral of the blue had carried his diviſion, into the place where the Vice Admiral of the red had moved from, at this time, would it not have given certain ſecurity to the Vengeance, deſcribed in ſuch danger, from the place where the Vice Admiral of the blue then was ?

A. I ſhould judge ſo, were they in a proper condition to go into action.

Preſident. Did you know at that time, whether they were in a condition to go into action or not ?

A. No, I did not.

Admiral Keppel. From three o'clock in the afternoon of this day, the 27th July, till ſix o'clock, did Sir William Burnaby in any part of this time, obſerve any of the

English

English fleet much to leeward before the beam and on the lee bow of the Victory, when on the starboard tack?

A. I do not recollect that there were.

Q. You said the French fleet was seen on the 24th by log, did the Admiral call you that afternoon within hail?

A. Yes, Sir.

Q. What orders did I give you?

A. To make sail, and keep a-head of our fleet, between us and the French.

Q. Did you discover any motion in the French fleet that night, that enabled you to make a positive signal?

A. No, I did not.

Q. Did I that afternoon pursue the French in a line of battle, by signal by point of the compass, and use endeavours to close in with them?

A. I recollect your carrying a pressed sail on the larboard tack, standing towards the French fleet, the van of our fleet being then in a tolerable line of battle.

Q. The Vice Admiral of the red, with his division, was he a good way a-stern?

A. I do not recollect what distance they were at; but they were not closed with the centre, as the Vice Admiral of the blue's division then was.

Q. Did I pursue the French fleet with a pressed sail, conformable to the worst sailing ships with me, to close and get up with the French, from the 24th in the morning, to the moment I brought them to battle, except those two times that I made the signal for a line of battle, after the 24th in the morning?

N. B. Here the prosecutor gave some interruption. Admiral Keppel then added, I beg the indulgence of the Court, that the accuser may not interrupt me. I am trying for my life; and my honour, that is dearer to me than my life; and therefore I hope I shall have the protection of the Court.

To this the accuser replied, His own honour was as dear to him, and he stood as much upon it.

A. You always carried a pressed sail, and to the best of my judgment, had a great desire to bring the French to battle, and gave every proof of your desire to bring them to it. But I cannot speak to the propriety of it.

Q. Do you remember whether I made a signal for a line of battle a-head on the 24th in the morning, or not?

A. I think I recollect you did.

Q. Do you remember in the afternoon of that day, that I made signal for a line of battle?

A. Yes, I remember you did, about six in the afternoon.

Prosecutor. You have been asked relative to the time when you took notice of the situation of the Vengeance, please to inform the Court, whether it was not after you had spoke to the Queen. A. Before.

Q. Did you make the stretch upon your larboard tack, or did you continue upon the stretch on the starboard tack, the same way as the fleet was standing, after you had spoke with the Queen.

A. I spoke to the Queen when standing upon the larboard tack, and continued so for some time, but cannot recollect how long; then put about, and stood upon the starboard tack, passing along to the windward of several of our ships that were then tolerably well formed in a line of battle.

Q. By standing further from the Admiral than the Queen was, could you have the opportunity of taking notice of the Vengeance's situation; did that enable you to make more observations on the Vengeance?

A. Yes, it did.

Q. Is there not an appointed signal when the Admiral would have any particular ships stay by disabled ships?

Admitted by the Admiral.

Q. Was such signal made at that time?

A. I never saw or knew of any made at that time.

Q. You informed the Court, that you observed the Vice Admiral of the blue well astern, and to windward of the Admiral's wake, did you take notice at that time, of the situation of the Formidable, respecting her sails and rigging.

A. I do not recollect the condition of her; as far as I remember, she appeared disabled in her sails and rigging.

Q. Did she appear to be equally able to carry sail with the Victory, at that time?

A. No, I do not think she was.

Q. Did not the Victory carry her top-sails entire, and foresail at that time, and her courses luffed up?

A. I have said, I believed the Victory, during the greater part of the afternoon, to carry her topsails and foresail, but whether they were whole topsails, I do not know.

President. Did you observe the Vice Admiral of the blue make any signal to the Admiral, of his not being able to keep in company? A. No, I did not.

Prosecutor. Is there any such appointed?

A. I think there is.

Q. Did not the Victory always outsail the Formidable, with equal sail?

A. As-

A. According to the obſervations I made on the rate of their ſailing, I think ſhe did.

Q. As you have informed the Court, that the Formidable was in a diſabled condition, and deſcribed the ſail the Victory did carry, do you ſuppoſe the diſtance between them was occaſioned by the Victory's ſailing from her, or by any neglect on the Part of the Formidable?

A. The little ſail the Formidable carried after the Action, could not poſſibly enable her to keep way with the Victory.

Admiral Keppel. As you obſerved, you were upon the larboard tack, if the Vice Admiral of the blue had had any meſſage to have ſent me, was it in your power to have gone to him in a very little time, to receive his orders?

A. Had ſignal been made by the Vice Admiral of the blue, to ſpeak with me, I could ſoon have joined the Formidable.

Proſecutor. Was the condition of the Formidable very apparent at that time?

A. I have ſaid before ſhe appeared diſabled.

Admiral Keppel. Was her topmaſt, topgallant maſt, lower, or topſail yard, carried away.

Proſecutor. I admit the maſts and yards were all ſtanding.

Sir William Burnaby ordered to withdraw.

CAPT. DIGBY, *of the Ramillies ſworn.*

Proſecutor. Do you remember the Britiſh fleet bringing too, in the evening of the 23d of July, on the larboard tack?

Admiral Keppel. Admitted; at eight o'clock.

Proſecutor. Was the French fleet to leeward at that time, of the Britiſh fleet, ſtanding to the ſouthward, on the ſtarboard tack, in a line of battle, or nearly ſo, as it appeared to you?

A. I recollect very well the Engliſh fleet bringing too, but I cannot ſay exactly at what time. I recollect ſeeing them paſſing to leeward of us, and part of them in a line of battle; whether they were all ſo I cannot tell.

Q. Did you ſay they wore on the ſtarboard tack?

A. Yes.

Q. Was not that their ſituation at the cloſe of the evening?

A. I cannot ſay, but at the cloſe of the evening they were paſſed to leeward of us.

Q. How was the wind?

A. The wind was weſterly, but upon what point I cannot ſay. I have no minutes, but a copy taken by a perſon gone abroad, and therefore cannot ſwear to them. I beg pardon, it was W. and by N. by log.

Q. How did Uſhant bear by your reckoning at noon on the 23d? A. I cannot recollect.

Q. Have you no days work?

A. I have no account of it about me.

Q. When the French fleet was to leeward of the Britiſh, as you have deſcribed, with the ſtarboard tack on board, the wind at W. was not Uſhant then under their lee? A. It was.

Q. Did you ſee any part of the French fleet at any time during that night?

A. It was very dark and blowing, and I ſaw no French ſhips; but I ſaw ſome falſe fires made.

Q. In what ſituation was the French the next morning, from the Britiſh fleet?

A. I think they were to the northward.

Q. At a little, or conſiderable diſtance?

A. They were at a conſiderable diſtance.

Q. Had the French Admiral intended to avoid an engagement, would he not have continued to ſtand on the ſtarboard tack, during that time, towards Breſt?

A. It is matter of opinion.

Admiral Montague. Pleaſe to give your opinion on this trial, as well as ſpeak to facts.

A. I beg not to give my opinion.

Proſecutor. If the French Admiral had continued to ſtand on that tack all the night, with a wind blowing ſtrong, would they not the next morning have been near to the port of Breſt, and at a great diſtance from the Engliſh fleet, which lay the whole night with their heads to the northward?

A. They would have been nearer the port of Breſt, and further from the Engliſh fleet than they were.

Q. But on the contrary, did not the French fleet gain the wind of the Britiſh fleet in the morning, and thereby place it between them and Breſt?

A. They were to windward the next morning, and of courſe we were between them and Breſt.

Q. Do you conſider theſe motions of the French Admiral as marks of his intention to avoid coming to an engagement, or of his intention to do ſo, when there ſhould be a proper opportunity?

A. I did imagine at that time the French fleet intended to attack us.

Q. During the following day, the 24th, did it appear to you that the French were endeavouring to keep their ſhips in line of battle? A. Yes.

Q. You

Q. You have ſaid it blew hard in the night, what kind of weather and ſea was there during the next day?

A. As well as I can recollect, it was more moderate.

Q. Do you recollect that during the 25th and 26th there were freſh gales, and ſqually for the moſt part, or how was the weather on thoſe days?

A. It was very ſqually, and blowing at different times, but I cannot recollect how it was at the exact time. It blew freſh and ſqually part of theſe days.

Q. From your recollection of its blowing freſh and ſqually on part of thoſe days, was it attended with ſuch ſea and ſwell as is uſual upon ſuch freſh gales and ſquals?

A. There was ſome ſwell, but I do not recollect either one day or other particularly.

Q. From your recollection of the wind, weather, and ſea, in your judgment, could ſhips have fought their lee lower deck guns?

A. As well as I can recollect, I could not have fought all mine, moſt part of the time, but I cannot ſay as to the whole time.

Q. If the French had borne down, and attacked the Britiſh fleet, when ſuch ſhips as the Ramillies could not have fought the whole of their lee lower deck guns, would it not have been very advantageous to the French fleet to have attacked under theſe circumſtances?

A. That ſeems matter of opinion, and depended on their ſhips.

Q. Did the French, as it appeared to you, during this day, endeavour to preſerve their fleet in a line of battle, as well as the wind and weather would permit, preſerving their diſtance from our fleet? A. They did.

Q. At times when the weather was more moderate, did it appear to you that the French Admiral crowded ſail in order to get away, or that he made ſail and ſhortened ſail occaſionally, for better perfecting his line of battle?

A. I ſaw many of the ſhips ſhorten ſail and make ſail at different times, but after the firſt day I always imagined they wiſhed to avoid us.

Admiral Montague. When you ſaw the French fleet making ſail and ſhortening ſail in order to form their line, at the time the Proſecutor has asked you, did you ſee the French fleet bring to, in order for the Britiſh fleet to come up to them?

A. I do not recollect ever ſeeing the whole French fleet brought to, at any part of that time.

Q. Did the Britiſh Admiral and fleet endeavour to get

to

to windward towards the French fleet, while they were forming their line to windward?

Admitted by the Admiral.

Q. In the ſhip you commanded that day, was your weather ports up, and could you have fought your weather guns, on the lower deck, had the French brought the Engliſh to action?

A. Frequently I could not.

Q. Were thoſe ports open any part of theſe days?

A. I believe ſome few of them were.

Proſecutor. As you have ſaid that you could fight part of your lower deck guns, could you have fought the weather guns, at the time you could not have fought your lee guns.

A. I have not ſaid ſo. I believe I might have fought more weather guns than lee guns.

Q. As the ſhips or fleet could have fought more of the weather guns than the lee guns, had not the fleet to leeward a great advantage over the other?

A. They that can fight moſt guns, has moſt advantage.

Q. In the morning of the 27th, was the Britiſh fleet much extended, ſcattered, or diſperſed?

A. Much about the ſame as it had been the day before, in the morning, before any ſignal was made.

Q. Inform the Court how they were the day before?

A. As well as I can recollect, not in the ſame order as when there had been a line of battle.

Q. Do you remember a ſignal to be made that morning, on board the Victory, for ſeveral ſhips of the Vice Admiral of the blue's diviſion to chaſe to windward? A. I do.

Q. Did that ſignal cauſe theſe ſhips to be ſeparated from their flag, and that part of the fleet to be more diſperſed than they were before? A. Certainly.

Preſident. Was your's one of thoſe ſhips? A. No.

Q. Do you recollect how many there were?

A. I think four.

Q. At what time did the Britiſh fleet tack altogether by ſignal, to ſtand towards the French fleet?

A. I cannot be exact in point of time, I think between nine and ten o'clock.

Q. Did the Admiral make any ſignal for the Britiſh fleet to form into a line of battle that day before the engagement began? A. None that I ſaw.

Admitted by the Admiral, that he made no ſignal for a line of battle on the 27th, before he cloſed, and paſſed the French fleet.

Proſecutor. Did the Admiral make the ſignal for a line of battle, while the fleet was ſo ſeparated and diſperſed?

Admiral

Admiral Keppel. Has he ever ſaid, that at eleven o'clock the fleet was ſcattered, and diſperſed?

Witneſs. *The witneſs deſired to explain himſelf upon an anſwer given to a former queſtion: viz.* I only meant to ſay, that the fleet was not in ſuch order, as when there had been a line of battle. The different diviſions ſailed ſome a-head, and ſome a-ſtern, in a different form, to be the ſooner ready.

Proſecutor. For what, Sir, for forming a line?

A. I ſuppoſe for forming the line.

Q. Were not ſeveral of the ſhips of each of the diviſions conſiderably to windward, and others conſiderably to leeward of their reſpective flags?

A. I was too far from the red diviſion to judge. With regard to the Vice Admiral of the blue's diviſion, at eleven o'clock, thoſe ſhips whoſe ſignals were made to chace, were conſiderably to windward. As I was to windward myſelf, I could not juſtly judge of the diſtance of thoſe to leeward.

Q. From the deſcription you have given, was not the fleet ſcattered and diſperſed?

A. I do not know what diſperſed means; part of them were ſeparated.

Q. And did not the Admiral make the ſignal for battle, while the fleet was as before deſcribed?

A. I cannot ſay as to the exact time of eleven o'clock, but about that time he made the ſignal?

Preſident. Did he make the ſignal before or after the enemy fired? A. After the enemy fired.

Admiral Montague. I beg leave to aſk Captain Digby relative to the expreſſion, ſcattered and diſperſed. At the time you are ſpeaking of, were the three diviſions of the Britiſh fleet ſailing in the uſual way that fleets ſail, when not in a line of battle?

A. They were in a ſituation to form the line, ſooner than if they were in a common way of ſailing.

Proſecutor. You ſay the whole of the fleet was in a ſituation that they might have formed in a line of battle, ſooner than in a common way of ſailing, if the ſignal for the line of battle had been made, inſtead of ſending out ſhips of the Vice Admiral of the blue's diviſion to chace, which ſeparated that part of the fleet; might not the Britiſh fleet have been formed into a line of battle before the French attacked it?

Admiral Keppel objected to the impropriety of this queſtion, it was therefore waved and put thus:

Q. Might

Q. Might not the English fleet have formed into a line of battle, before the French attacked them?

A. I think there would have been time, if the signal for the line of battle had been made, when the signal for the ships to chace, was.

Q. Did the French by attacking us when we were not in a line of battle, but under the circumstances before described, render it impossible for our Captains to engage ship to ship, or to bring on a general engagement?

A. Certainly.

Q. When you run down along the French fleet, and engaged, did they appear to you to be formed in a line of battle?

A. They did; but part of them were not very regular.

Q. You mean not regular in point of distance, but were they in a line?

A. Part of them were not very regular, the one way or the other.

Q. Did not you say first, neither the one nor the other?

A. The question has been varied a little; I believe they were not in point of time, nor distance.

Q. While you was proceeding along the French line, and engaged, was you at any time interrupted in your fire, by the irregularity of our ships not being in a line, by any other ship falling in your way. A. No, I was not.

Q. Was there any shot fired over you from any of our own ships?

A. I believe not; during the action there was such a report; and I was told so, but don't know by whom.

Q. When you passed the rear of the enemy's fleet, was you a-head or a-stern of the Victory?

A. A-head of the Victory?

Q. How long and how far did the Victory continue to stand, after she had passed the stern of the enemy's line, before she wore to stand towards them again?

A. I was so situated that I could not be a judge of the distance, and I was so much employed, that I did not see her at the time she wore or tacked.

Q. The first time you did observe the Victory had wore, and was on the larboard tack, at what distance then do you think she was from the French fleet?

A. I have said before, that I was so situated, it was impossible for me to be a judge of the distance at all.

Q. Did you take notice of her when she wore again the second time, on the starboard tack?

A. I did see her about that time.

Q. Can you judge of her distance at that time from the French?

A. At

A. At that time the body of the English fleet was between me and the French fleet, and therefore I could not judge of the distance.

Q. Which way was your ship's head at that time?

A. I had wore once before, and was just wearing at that time.

Q. Can you mention how many, if any ships, were laying with their heads to the southward at the time the Admiral was wearing, to lay his head again to the southward?

A. The body of our fleet appeared to me at that time in a cluster; it is therefore impossible.

Q. Did the Victory appear to be in that cluster?

A. She did, though not in the thickest part of it.

Q. Did you observe when the signal for battle was hauled down?

A. I did not.

Q. When did you first observe that it was down?

A. I was so extremely employed, that I did not observe it myself, nor can I recollect when I was first told of it.

Q. Did you observe the Admiral unbend his maintop sail? A. I did not.

Q. Did you take notice of its being unbent at any time?

A. I observed before, that I had not time to look myself, and did not hear of it till afterwards.

Q. You said you took notice of the Admiral about the time he did wear the second time, was that the time when the British fleet was in a cluster, as before described.

A. They appeared to me in a cluster, from my position at that time.

Q. Did you observe the French fleet to break up their line of battle?

A. I was in that position I could not see it, the British fleet being between me and them.

Q. When did you first take notice of them after our firing ceased?

A. Not till they were got to leeward, and extended to the southward?

Q. Did you take notice where the Vice Admiral of the Red and his division was, about the time, the Admiral wore the second time, and stood to the southward?

A. They were to windward of the British fleet, which prevented me from seeing them.

Q. Did you not see them at all?

A. I could not distinguish them.

Q. When the Admiral wore the second time, did you see the Vice Admiral of the blue?

A. I can-

A. I cannot be accurate in point of time, I ſaw the Vice Admiral of the blue not a great while before.

Q. What was her ſituation then with reſpect to the Victory?

A. As they both made a part of the fleet, I could not judge of the diſtance; but the Vice Admiral of the blue appeared to me to leeward of the Victory.

Q. Did ſhe appear, near that time, to be near the Victory?

Admiral Keppel. I have not heard Capt. Digby ſay, he ſaw the Victory wear.

Capt. Digby. I did not ſee her wear.

Admiral Keppel. That's material to me.

Capt Digby. I have mentioned before, I could not tell the diſtance.

Proſecutor. As you have not been able to ſpeak to the time that the Victory continued to ſtand beyond the French fleet, or aſcertain the diſtance, can you eſtimate the diſtance that your own ſhip ſtood from the French fleet, before you wore yourſelf?

A. I cannot; but I know that I was obliged to ſtand a great way beyond the Victory.

Q. Was your ſhip to windward of the Victory, within half an hour after ſhe wore, and laid her head to the ſouthward the ſecond time?

A. I was a great way to leeward.

Q. When did you firſt get to windward of the Victory?

A. Not till late in the evening.

Q. Did you paſs a-head or a-ſtern of the Admiral, when you went to windward? A. I do not recollect.

Q. Cannot you tell what time it was?

A. Somewhere about ſeven o'clock as near as I can recollect.

Q. Can you tell what ſail the Victory had ſet about that time? A. I do not recollect.

Q. Did you tack or wear after you had paſſed to windward, or ſtand the ſame way he did?

A. I ſtood on further to windward, in order to wear, as my foremaſt was ſo much wounded, I was afraid to wear.

Q. After the Victory had wore to ſtand to the ſouthward at the time mentioned, did ſhe appear to keep her wind or ſail large?

A. The fleet appeared to me to be going upon a wind, I did not take particular notice of the Victory.

Q. Did you at any time look at her, and notice what ſails ſhe had ſet, or ſignals flying?

A. I did look at her ſeveral times, but cannot recollect

the

the particular times; I ſaw particularly my own ſignal to get into my ſtation. There were others, but I cannot recollect them.

Q. But as to the ſails ſet, what do you ſay?

A. I cannot ſpeak with any certainty, but think ſhe had her fore-ſail and top-ſails.

Q. Do you recollect any ſtay ſails or gibb?

A. I do not indeed.

Q. Do you recollect what ſail you carried yourſelf at that time?

A. I have mentioned before that I ſtood on to windward of the Victory, as I was afraid of my foremaſt.

Q. Was the Vice Admiral of your diviſion a-ſtern of you, laying his head to the ſouthward?

A. Not after I wore; I wore in order to get into my ſtation, the ſignal was hauled down.

Q. What ſignal do you mean?

A. The ſignal for the line of battle had been hauled down before, and my ſignal likewiſe to get into my ſtation.

Q. Theſe ſignals being hauled down, you then proceeded to take the ſtation with reſpect to the Vice Admiral of blue? A. Not for that reaſon only.

Q. Was your ſtation a-ſtern of the Vice Admiral of the blue then? A. It was.

Q. What was the diſtance of the Vice Admiral of the blue from the Victory about that time?

A. At what time do you mean, Sir.

Q. When you went to take your ſtation a-ſtern of her, I underſtood it was ſomewhat about ſeven o'clock?

A. I cannot ſpeak accurately as to the diſtance, but think it muſt be about a mile.

Q. Was that a-ſtern of the Victory, or ſomewhat to windward of her wake, or how?

A. Both a-ſtern and to windward of the Victory.

Q. Did you obſerve ſignals and lights made by the French fleet? A. I did not myſelf.

Admiral Keppel. I admit the rockets were from the French fleet.

Proſecutor. Did you obſerve the French fleet to bear away during the night? A. No.

Q. What hour was the report made to you of theſe ſignals being made?

A. I think it was about eleven or twelve o'clock.

Q. How many of the French fleet were in ſight the next morning. A. I ſaw but three.

Q. Were

Q. Were these three near the British fleet and to leeward?
A. They were to leeward.
Q. Was not one of them very near the rear of our fleet?
A. I should think not nearer than four or five miles.
Q. Did they appear to you to be line of battle ships or frigates.
A. Line of battle ships.
Q. Was any other part of the French fleet seen from the mast-head of your ship?
A. They were not, that I heard of.
Q. Do you know of any signal being made by any ships of the fleet, for seeing them?
A. I did not know it that day, but there were signals.
Q. Did the fleet, or any part of them, chace these ships?
A. There were signals made for two or three ships, I cannot recollect which, to chace.
Q. Did they chace?
A. I believe some of them made sail.
Q. Were not the signals hauled down before they did make sail?
A. I did not see them all make sail before the signals were hauled down.
Q. What latitude was you in on the 27th at noon?
A. 48° 22″, I believe. The distance from Ushant I cannot exactly recollect; to the best of my memory we reckoned between thirty and forty leagues, we were out in our reckoning too far to the westward.
Q. How was the wind in the morning of the 28th.
A. By log W. N. W.
Q. What kind of weather was it?
A. More moderate than it had been.
Q. Of how many ships of the line was our fleet composed, on the 27th.
A. I believe, thirty.
Q. How many was the French fleet supposed to be?
A. As far as I could judge, there were 29 sail of the line on the day of action.
President. Did you count the number to be twenty-nine?
A. I did, according to their appearance.
Prosecutor. In that number do you know two, that were supposed to be of fifty guns?
A. Upon my word I cannot say, there were forty-one in all; twenty-nine appeared much larger than the rest, and some of them larger than the others.
Admiral Montague. Do you know that there was a fifty-gun ship in the line? A. I do not, Sir.

Q. Do

Q. Do you know of what force the French line of battle was? A. No.

Admiral Montague read the former part of the Charge against the Admiral, "That in the morning of the 27th of July, having a fleet of thirty ſhips, &c. &c. &c. (*ſee the Charge*) *Then asked the witneſs, viz.* Can you acquaint the Court of any inſtance within your own knowledge, during the time the Britiſh and French fleets were in action, that Admiral Keppel neglected to do his utmoſt to burn, ſink, and deſtroy the enemy, having it in his power ſo to do, or negligently performed the duty impoſed on him?

A. I have always had the greateſt eſteem for, and the higheſt opinion of Admiral Keppel, as an officer. I have ſo ſtill, but I have been giving evidence upon facts, and the anſwering that queſtion would be judging upon them; which I have no right to do.

Q. Then I ask one more queſtion. N. B. *Here the next part of the Charge was read*; upon which Admiral Montague obſerved, That in both articles of the charge, the Admiral was accuſed of running away from the French fleet, inſtead of advancing to renew the engagement, as he might and ought to have done. "The "Admiral wore, and made ſail directly from the enemy, "who ſtood after the Britiſh fleet," now let me aſk you on your oath,

Did you, Capt. Digby, that day, run away from the French fleet. For if Admiral Keppel did, Capt. Digby did too, for I ſuppoſe every part of the fleet followed their leader? A. No.

The Court then adjourned, it being near four o'clock, to ten tomorrow morning.

SIXTH DAY, WEDNESDAY, JANUARY 13th:

The Court re-aſſembled about ten o'clock, when Capt. Digby's evidence was continued.

Admiral Montague. Had not the van and centre of the Engliſh fleet been engaged with the French, as they paſſed them? A. Yes, great part of them.

Q. Was the ſhip you commanded engaged? A. Yes.

Q. What was the condition of the ſhip you commanded, after you left off engaging?

A. Our main top ſail was cut to pieces; our running and ſtanding rigging very much cut, ſo that we were not able to wear for ſome time. Our fore maſt wounded in ſeveral places, particularly one that was cut full half

 through.

through. Several other masts and yards were wounded, the main yard and main mast particularly.

Admiral Montague. In the situation you have described your ship to be, was it such as you could renew the attack, if the Admiral had tacked immediately after the enemy?

A. I do not think my ship was in a condition to seek an attack for a great while afterwards.

Q. How long was it after you were engaged, before your ship was in a proper condition to renew the fight, supposing the Admiral had judged it proper so to do?

A. My foremast was so much cut, that I was afraid of its going over the side; but if any ship had come near me, I should have been in a condition to fight before seven o'clock, though it was near that time before I was able to tack; the lee leach of my main sail was so cut, that I could not set it upon the other tack before that time, which was necessary, on account of my being so far to leeward.

Admiral Montague. Was not you to have led the van on that tack, when the Admiral had laid his head to the enemy? A. No, Sir.

Admiral Montague. Did you tack? A. Yes.

Admiral Keppel. I observed that Captain Digby, the day before, said, that though he was not in a condition to seek to renew the attack, yet if an attack had again been made, he considered himself in a situation to support it; there being a great deal of difference between attacking and being attacked.

Sir Hugh Palliser now wished to ask some questions of the evidence; but as he on the day before closed his examination; it was decided by the Court that he could not ask any further questions, till the Admiral had concluded his cross examination.

Admiral Keppel. What force, I mean large ships, did you discover the French fleet to be composed of, on the afternoon of the 23d of July, and how far were they from you, when they permitted you to count them?

A. I could not count them, the weather was so thick it prevented me.

Q. Inform the Court how far the Vice Admiral of the red, and his division, was from you at the latest period in the day?

A. As the fleet had been endeavouring to get into a line of battle, and were nearly so, and as I was not got into my station, I cannot answer in point of distance.

Q. Do you know whether the Vice Admiral of the red was closed in his station in a line of battle?

A. It

A. It was rather thick and hazey, but I think he was; I am not ſure that I ſaw him.

Admiral Keppel. Capt. Digby, would an officer whoſe rank in the ſervice intitled him to a large command, and he had ſuch command, could he with a ſquadron of ſhips of the line of battle under his command in the ſituation the French have been deſcribed to be before him, during the 24th, 25th, 26th, and 27th of July, relative to wind, weather, and ſea, and ſeeing an enemy to leeward of equal force, have heſitated one moment to lead his ſquadron down to battle, on account of ſuch wind and ſea as has been before deſcribed?

A. I believe I ſhould have attacked them.

Admiral Keppel. I ask whether you would have heſitated?

A. I think I ſhould not have heſitated.

Q. Can you inform the Court of the relative ſituation of me and the French fleet, on the 27th of July at day light?

A. As well as I can recollect, we were both on the larboard tack, the French fleet ſix, ſeven, or eight miles to windward of us.

Q. What was the ſituation of the Vice Admiral of the blue, and his diviſion, with reſpect to the Victory at that time?

A. They appeared to me upon the Victory's lee bow, but am not quite ſure.

Q. At what diſtance do you think they were from the Victory?

A. At that time I really cannot recollect with exactneſs.

Q. Can you recollect what ſail they were under?

A. I cannot indeed.

Q. At this time how was Capt. Digby in the Ramillies ſituated, relative to the Vice Admiral of the blue, and to the Victory?

A. I have ſaid that I cannot recollect at that period of time exactly; I remember to have ordered my officers to keep upon the Vice Admiral of the blue's weather beam, and when I did take notice, he had kept ſtill further.

Q. When you did take notice, what hour of the day was it, and where was he then, in reſpect to the Victory?

A. Upon the ſignal being made for the ſhips to chace, in the morning to windward, I ſet my ſtay ſails, and the period that ſtrikes me ſtrongeſt was, after we tacked between eight and nine, I believe I ſaw then a little upon the Victory's weather quarter?

Q. Was there any greater indication at the time the

ſignal was made for ſhips to chace to windward of the French, intending to fight, than there was on the preceding day? A. I do not think there was.

Q. Had the Admiral formed the line that morning, muſt not he have borne down to have joined the ſhips to leeward, or have ſhortened ſail, and called back the Red diviſion, and thereby have increaſed his diſtance from the French fleet.

A. He certainly muſt have borne down, and many of the ſhips to windward alſo, and of courſe increaſed his diſtance.

Q. Can you inform the Court the exact time the French fleet tacked from the larboard tack, to get into the ſtarboard.

A. I cannot but believe about three quarters of an hour before we tacked.

Q. Before the Engliſh fleet were about upon their ſtarboard tack, was there any ſort of change in the wind?

A. It favoured us.

Q. When the weather favoured us a little, did you lay up with the part of the French fleet? A. I did.

Q. On what tack was the French fleet when the engagement began?

A. On the larboard tack.

Q. Do you know how they got upon that tack, and when?

A. It was very thick weather, and I did not obſerve.

Q. Had you loſt ſight of them for any time?

A. We had.

Q. When you diſcovered them again, after loſing ſight of them, were they got then upon the larboard tack?

A. Yes, they were.

Q. Do you recollect how long it was from your diſcovering them again upon their larboard tack, before the firing began?

A. As well as I can recollect, it was upon my officers acquainting me there were guns firing a-head. I was at breakfaſt, I believe, and did not diſcover them upon that tack, till my officers told me there was firing began.

Preſident. What time was that?

A. I mentioned breakfaſt; I believe it was about eleven o'clock.

Admiral Keppel. Were the greateſt part of the ſhips of the Britiſh fleet, when they came into battle, in a ſituation to ſpeedily ſuccour each other?

A. I could be no judge of the Vice Admiral of the Red's

Red's diviſion; in that part that I was in, I was ſupported by the Admiral and his ſeconds; the Admiral came up upon my weather quarter.

Q. Can fleets at any time, being on a different tack, fight ſhip to ſhip, with or without being in a regular line?

A. I think not.

Q. As you have deſcribed yourſelf to have been near the Admiral, and ſupported by him, when you in the Ramaillies, and the Engliſh Admiral, were engaged with the French, was that part of the French fleet in a regular line, as you and the Victory paſſed them ranging along, or in a confuſed ſituation.

A. They were not in a regular line.

Q. Were any of them right to leeward of the others?

A. There were ſome of them a good deal to leeward, whether directly to leeward, I cannot ſay.

Q. Was there to your obſervation more Britiſh or French ſhips engaged. I mean engaged like men; not at a diſtance?

A. My attention was ſo much taken up to my own ſhip, I could only obſerve thoſe juſt about me.

Q. At what hour in the afternoon of the 27th of July, did you firſt ſee the Victory on the ſtarboard tack, ſtanding to the ſouthward, as you have ſaid you did not ſee her wear.

A. I muſt ſay, I had very little idea how time paſſed that afternoon.

Q. Did you ever obſerve the Victory upon the larboard tack at all?

A. I either obſerved her upon the larboard tack, or was told ſo; in conſequence of her being upon the larboard tack, I wore.

Q. Did you ſee her wear from the larboard tack to the ſtarboard tack? A. No, I did not.

Admiral Keppel. Time is the moſt material circumſtance to me; without time, bringing matters before the Court is not giving me the information I want to call for; and Capt. Digby not being accurate in point of time, makes his evidence to be very uncertain. But as he ſaid in a former part of his evidence, when he obſerved the Victory on his ſtarboard tack, with a cluſter of ſhips about her, he did not ſay the Victory was in the midſt of that cluſter; but at that time can he ſay what hour it was?

A. No.

Q. Then you do not know what time it was?

A. Indeed I do not; but it was not long after the Vice Admiral of the blue had done engaging, as I was told.

Q. At what hour was you told ſo?

A. I cannot really anſwer in point of time.

Q. When you was to leeward of the Victory, upon the ſtarboard tack, in any part of the afternoon, from three to ſix, were there any other ſhips of the Britiſh fleet to leeward, near me. A. There were.

Q. Can you ſay how many?

A. There were at one time four, if not five.

Q. Do you recollect the names of thoſe ſhips?

A. I think one was the Robuſte; the Sandwich was another; but I really do not recollect with certainty the others.

Q. Whether, during this time, between three and ſix, he ever noticed the Victory appearing to lead down from the wind towards the van.

A. I was ſo very much employed, as I obſerved before, that I could not be certain, but think ſhe did lead down.

Q. Do you recollect at what part of time, between three and ſix, the ſhips you deſcribed to be near you, one, two, or all of them left you, and which they were.

A. Upon my word I cannot; they left me one after another.

Q. Can you ſay at what hour in the evening of the 27th you ſaw the Victory without the ſignal for the line of battle flying?

A. It was juſt as I was wearing, after I ſtood into the fleet, that my officer came and told me that the ſignals were down, whether I looked myſelf or not, I do not remember.

Q. At what time?

A. I cannot ſay exactly, but I believe, about ſeven or between ſeven and eight; I am not ſure.

Q. Was it near dark?

A. It is impoſſible, at this diſtance of time, to recollect; I wiſh I could. I can ſo far recollect, that I am very ſure it was not a great while before dark, within half an hour or an hour, I cannot ſay which.

Q. How ſoon after you wore at this time, were you aſtern of the Vice Admiral of the blue yourſelf, in that part you deſcribed your ſtation to be.

A. Very ſoon after.

Q. Did you preſerve that ſtation, and keep ſight of the Vice Admiral of the blue's lights all night. A. Nearly.

Q. Was you near the Formidable at day-light?

A. I was.

Q. At what diſtance; how did the Victory bear from the Ramillies at day-light?

A. She

A. She was upon the lee bow. Diſtances ſtrike one differently. As near as I can ſay, I ſuppoſe near two miles from me.

Q. How was the wind the morning of the 28th.

A. At W. N. W.

Q. Did it blow freſh, in ſquals.

A. It was more moderate than the day before; but about eight o'clock it did blow freſh, in ſquals.

Q. Was there a large ſwell?

A. There was a good deal of ſwell.

Q. Was this wind favourable to carry ſhips to the port of Breſt? A. It was.

Q. Was your ſhip in a condition to give chace, as a man of war ſhould chace, without entangling herſelf with a lee ſhore upon an enemy's coaſt? A. She was not.

Q. After I had brought the fleet to, with the ſhips heads to the northward, on the morning of the 28th, do you recollect I made any ſignal.

A. I cannot recollect the ſignal nor time, but I remember there were ſhips made ſignals that they wanted to ſet their rigging up, but I cannot ſay when.

Q. Was your's one of thoſe ſhips?

A. I did make a ſignal, after ſeeing many others had made it.

Court. Pretty early yeſterday, you ſaid, in the courſe of queſtions about the poſition of the French fleet on the 23d, that the enemy did not mean to come to an engagement after the 23d.

A. I believe, I ſaid, after the firſt day.

Q. Be ſo good as to explain it, and give the Court your reaſons why they wiſhed to avoid it after the firſt day. Why did you think they wiſhed to avoid coming to action with the Engliſh fleet, after the firſt or ſecond day.

A. Becauſe they might have come to action, if they had choſe it.

Preſident. If I recollect right, you ſaid in the morning of the engagement on the 27th, there were ſeveral Engliſh ſhips to leeward of the Admiral; had the Admiral formed the line that morning, would it have been in the power of the Engliſh fleet to have brought on the engagement that day. A. I do not think it would.

Proſecutor. If the ſignal had been made for a line of battle, in forming it, would it have been neceſſary for the Admiral to have bore down any further than into the wake of the Vice Admiral of the Red's diviſion; and would not the Vice of the Red in that place have come to action in like manner as they did, excluding only the Duke, that was a long way to leeward.

A. A line of battle always retards, in my opinion; I imagine, had the signal been made, the red division must have shortened sail.

Q. If the French had not intended to bring on the action, would they have tacked the second time, and edged about and attacked our fleet in the situation our fleet was in?

A. I have not said that the French did not mean it at that time; what I mean is, that at day-light they did not seem to mean to bring on the action.

Q. If the French fleet had not intended to come to action, could they not have avoided it that day.

A. They probably might have avoided it sometime, but I was in the rear of the fleet, and cannot possibly say how long.

Q. Was not your ship in the Vice Admiral of the blue's division? A. She was.

Q. You have described your situation in the action to be mixed with the centre division, did you know of any other ships of the Vice Admiral's division being in the same situation, in consequence of the signal for those other ships being made for chasing.

A. I do not know of any others in the same situation, because I don't know any that were a-head of the Admiral.

Q. Since you have described the situation of the fleet to be such, that the ships were situated to support each other; if those ships of the Vice of the blue's division, who chased by signal, or part of them did engage, together with your ship and the centre division, I would ask whether the Vice of the blue, and the rest of the ships he was left with, were in a condition to support each other, equal to the rest of the fleet.

I did not chace; I was a-head of the Admiral and the chacing ships; I believe engaged astern of them; I don't know their situation, but that they were a good way to windward just before I engaged.

Q. You have not said what must be the situation of the rest of the division, and whether they could support each other equal to the rest of the fleet.

A. I have not said where the chacing ships engaged; but if they all were separated from their division, they certainly could not support each other.

Q. You have described the French fleet as not in an exact line of battle, Could you observe one ship in particular being to leeward of their line, and shut out from

it

it by other ſhips cloſing to windward, of which one of our ſhips, ſuppoſed the Courageux, paſſed between her and the reſt of the French line; do you remember any other ſhip of the French ſo far out of their line?

A. There was one ſhip to leeward of us. I cannot judge of the diſtance of the others.

Q. Do you think that the irregularity you have obſerved in their line, was greater than what might have been expected, from their having been engaged with the ſhips that paſſed before them?

A. There was an irregularity in their line, but what it could proceed from I do not know.

Q. After the Admiral, with his own diviſion, and the diviſion of the Vice Admiral of the red, and ſuch ſhips of the blue diviſion as had joined, had paſſed the enemy, did he tack and double upon the enemy, and continue the engagement?

A. The Vice Admiral of the red and his diviſion paſſed to windward of me ſoon after I came out of action, but I believe the action was not renewed upon that tack juſt at the time.

Q. Did the Admiral with his diviſion, and the other ſhips with him do ſo? A. I believe they did not.

Q. Or did the Admiral with the whole of the ſhips, keep ſo near to the enemy as to be ready immediately to renew the engagement, when the Vice Admiral of the blue came out of it, or to ſupport him while he continued engaging with the few ſhips that were with him?

A. I have already deſcribed my ſituation to be ſuch about that time, the Engliſh fleet being between me and the French fleet, that it is impoſſible for me to anſwer how they were ſituated?

Q. Do you know that he did do ſo? A. Do what?

Proſecutor. Keep his fleet at that diſtance, as to be ready at hand to renew the engagement when the Vice Admiral of the blue came out of it, or to ſupport him whilſt engaging, with the few ſhips with him?

A. I have declared I do not.

Admiral Keppel. Do you call this the croſs examination, upon what the evidence has given in anſwer to my queſtions. It is taking up much time, and calling upon me again and again to examine.

Admiral Montague. I am of opinion that we ſhall never get through one evidence before next Chriſtmas. 'Tis unfair to the evidence and leads him to perjury, for he cannot recollect what he has ſaid before, and he may really contradict himſelf.

Proſecutor.

SEVENTH DAY, THURSDAY JANUARY 14th.

THE Court being met, about ten o'clock, the prisoner was brought in, and audience admitted.

CAPT. HOOD, *of the Robuste, sworn.*

Admiral Keppel. Mr. President, It is not only my own opinion, but that of many of my friends, that the alterations already proved to have been made in Capt. Hood's log book by his own direction, is a sufficient and very just ground for my objecting to his evidence being taken; but however I will not avail myself of the advantage that the iniquity of such a proceeding has given me, since it is my wish that every officer who took part in the action, should be permitted to lay before this Court his opinion of the conduct of their Commander in Chief in that affair.

Capt. Hood then addressed the Court, as follows: I must beg the indulgence of the Court to explain the nature, sum, and substance of the alterations in the log book of the Robuste, because I flatter myself that not only this respectable Court, but the public at large, will be well satisfied with the innocence of them; and I trust that they cannot, in any shape, be construed to affect one side or the other. For my own part, I never considered a ship's log book to be material evidence; much less did I ever expect that any words that should be put into my log book would be considered as a charge: God forbid that such a thing should be conceived or adopted! The winds, the courses, the distances in the Robuste's log book, stand unaltered: the corrections in it respect the narrative part only; and when I found that the ship's log book was likely to be produced in Court, perhaps on myself, on that account, not knowing but I might stand here a prisoner, instead of an evidence, I judged it proper to revise and correct it, for the credit of the ship, and for the sake of all her officers; and not in a private, but in a public manner, known to every officer in the ship, and setting forth a fair and faithful representation of the transactions of the 27th of July. I stand here an attacked man, from the 11th of August to the present hour; my character has been wounded; I have seen abuse go forth daily into the world, respecting me: letters have been sent to the first characters in the kingdom, to prejudice me: in one paper I was put under arrest, for disobedience of orders; in others I was said to

be

be broke. Anonymous publications have said, that the rear division was the cause of our not succeeding that day; and had the rear division done their duty as well as the centre and the van, a compleat victory would have been obtained. Since which many other publications of the like kind have been made, which I equally despise; but I was alarmed greatly, when in a public assembly the whole of the rear division was blamed. I therefore thought it necessary to correct my log book, for the honour and safety of the officers of that division. I shall beg leave to call the Master of the Robuste to elucidate and clear up this matter, that when the whole is investigated, I trust I shall not be found to have done any thing to the prejudice of that Honourable Admiral. The Master of the Robuste has acted like an honest man, by having a conscientious regard to truth. I applaud him for it. I beg also to call Lieutenants Pitt and Lumley, who will produce the original log books, and by that the Court will see what alterations have been made; the Court will then be in possession of the whole, and to their judgment I submit my honour. I must beg leave to say one thing more, and that is, if a Captain of the navy has not a right to alter and correct his log book, or if that right is taken away, he is in a most deplorable situation. I think that I am authorized to do it; that I am called upon to do it---the Master is so by his instructions---the Court knows he is to correct his day's work and log book. There is no law against it, and there can be no criminality in it; and I declare, if I have not that power, my honour and reputation is taken from me; and I will never set my foot on board a King's ship again.

When Capt. Hood had concluded the above harangue, he called Lieutenants Pitt and Lumley, who produced their log-books, and being called upon to swear that they were exact copies of the log book of the Robuste, before it had undergone any alterations, they declined taking the oath, saying that they had made some alterations themselves, in the month of October last. They were then dismissed, and Captain Hood's evidence taken, as follows:

Sir H. Palliser. What were the alterations you made in the log book?

A. The first alteration was respecting sending out the ships to chace in the morning; my original log book made the Vice Admiral to send out the ships instead of the Admiral; and that was corrected by saying, "The "Admiral made the signal, instead of the Vice Admiral, "for

" for us and ſeveral other ſhips to chace to windward. The ſecond part ſpeaks more fully of the Admiral's making a ſignal in the afternoon, for the ſhips to bear down.

Q. What ſignal, a general ſignal?

A. I apprehend it was the ſignal for the whole, that is the whole of the ſecond part. The third alteration relates to the ſeeing the three ſhips in the morning of the 28th, which was omitted in the original book, but how it was omitted, I cannot conceive. The log book before the Court ſpeaks of the Robuſte bearing down in the evening, to take her ſtation; and it goes on to ſay, that ſhe continued in her ſtation as well as a diſabled ſhip could do. The Admiral carrying much ſail. The maſter was preſent at the time the alterations were made. I ſhall give the Court all the information I can.

Admiral Montague. At what hour was the ſignal made to bear down into the Admiral's wake, as you was a diſabled ſhip? A. It was night.

Admiral Keppel. I beg the indulgence of the Court to aſk a few queſtions reſpecting the log book. I would aſk you, Where is the firſt entry of the firſt log book of the 27th, and 28th of July, as it ſtood originally?

A. Upon my word, I do not know.

Proſecutor. In what ſituation was the French fleet in the night of the 23d of July, with reſpect to the Engliſh fleet, and upon what tack were they ſtanding?

A. The French were to leeward of the Britiſh fleet at night, ſtanding upon the ſtarboard tack.

Q. How was the Britiſh fleet laying at that time, I mean juſt at duſk?

A. They were laying to on the larboard tack.

Q. How was the wind then?

A. I do not know the time the Admiral made the ſignal, there were many ſignals made that night. I judge the wind was W. N. W. the French upon the ſtarboard tack, and to leeward of the Britiſh fleet.

Q. Had they not the port of Breſt under their lee?

A. They certainly had.

Q. Did the Britiſh fleet continue to lay to all that night?

A. I think they did.

Q. If the French Admiral had intended to have avoided coming to an engagement, would he not have continued to ſtand upon that tack all night towards Breſt?

A. If the French Admiral's orders authorized him to go into port, certainly he had it in his power.

Q. Was

Q. Was or was not the French fleet the next day to windward of the British, and had they not thereby placed us between their fleet and the port of Brest?

A. The French fleet were certainly to windward of the English in the morning, and consequently must have placed the English between the French fleet and the port of Brest.

Q. From these motions of the French Admiral, did you apprehend that he meant to avoid an engagement, or to bring on one, when the wind and weather should be proper for him to do so.

A. From the motions of the French, they indicated to my mind an intention of keeping at sea; of course he did not mean to avoid an action, and from the subsequent matter, I judge he meant to engage the English fleet.

Q. Can you recollect the wind, weather, and sea, during the 24th, 25th, and 26th of July?

A. May I be allowed to look at my log book? *granted.*

Q. During those days, do you think it would not have been disadvantageous to the French, to have attacked the British fleet, considering the wind, weather, and sea, on those days; as in that case they must have fought their lee lower deck guns.

A. The wind and weather, during those days, was squally, sometimes with rain, as far as I recollect, and the sea rather rough. It would have been disadvantageous for any fleet to have engaged on those days, more particularly the French fleet, because they must have fought their lee guns, being to windward, which I think they could not have done to any advantage.

Q. In the morning of the 27th was not the British fleet scattered, I mean several ships of each division being on various bearings and distances from their respective Admirals?

A. I was not on deck till after the signals were made from the Admiral for the Robuste, and, I think, five other ships of the Vice Admiral of the blue's division, to chace to windward, consequently, I cannot speak to the state of the fleet before that period.

Q. Did not the signal cause that part of the fleet to be more dispersed and scattered than before?

A. I think these six ships, the Robuste and five others, chacing to windward, as far as I can recollect, between five and six in the morning till ten, carried, during that space of time, as much sail as it was their duty to do. The signal having been thrown out for them to chace, must of course increase their distance from the centre of

the

the fleet, and thereby may be ſaid to be more ſcattered, and diſperſed.

Q. Did not that ſignal leave the Vice Admiral of the blue with four ſhips only?

A. The Vice Admiral of the blue's diviſion conſiſted of ten ſail; I have given the Court an account of ſix of them having been ordered to chaſe to windward by ſignal, conſequently there could remain but four with the Vice Admiral.

Q. At what time did the Britiſh fleet tack all together by ſignal?

A. I wiſh in the courſe of my evidence this day, not to be confined poſitively to time, it being very much out of my power to do it, as near as I recollect the Admiral made his ſignal for the fleet to tack all together about ten o'clock.

Q. Was there any ſignal for a line of battle made that day, before the engagement began?

A. None, that I ſaw.

Q. At what time did you firſt ſee the French fleet in a line of battle that morning?

A. To the beſt of my recollection they began to form, or were formed, very early in the morning. They were completely formed, I believe, about ten, or between ten and eleven.

Q. Did not the Victory begin to engage the French Admiral in the center of their line?

A. The Robuſte chacing from the fleet, that morning, threw her at too great a diſtance for me to judge preciſely of that event.

Q. Had you an opportunity of ſeeing the Formidable come into action?

A. I ſaw the Formidable go into action, but cannot be exact to ſay at what time.

Q. Did you obſerve that ſeveral ſhips in the van of the French fleet fired at her which ſhe did not make any return to, before ſhe came to a cloſe engagement herſelf?

A. I know the French ſhips fired a great many ſhot at the Robuſte, which ſhe did not return till ſhe came near enough to do execution, and I judge of the Vice Admiral's conduct by my own.

Admiral Montague. Is that an anſwer to the queſtion? we do not deſire your judgment on the matter. Did you ſee the Formidable cloſely engaged with ſome of the French ſhips, a-head of the French Admiral, at the beginning of the engagement?

A. I.

A. I cannot ſpeak poſitively what ſhip the Vice Admiral of the blue engaged.

Sir Hugh Palliſer. Was not the Formidable as long and as cloſely engaged as the Victory?

A. I cannot ſay how long the Victory was engaged; but I ſaw the Vice Admiral of the blue engaged from the time he began his cloſe action till he paſſed the rear of the French fleet.

Q. Was not the Victory, while ſhe was in action, ſupported by the whole of the Admiral's diviſion, and part of the ſhips of the blue diviſion, that had joined him.

A. I take it for granted that the whole of the Admiral's diviſion gave all the ſupport to the flag that they poſſibly could.

Admiral Montague. Speak from your own knowledge; what was in your imagination, I believe, is not an anſwer?

A. 'Tis impoſſible, while in cloſe action, to ſee what other ſhips are engaged.

Q. Was the Formidable ſupported by the whole of her own diviſion, after the ſhips were taken from him by ſignal, to give chace? A. No.

Q. How many ſhips, during the action, were a-ſtern of the Formidable?

A. I believe there were ſix, I cannot ſpeak poſitively. I don't recollect more than ſix ſail.

Q. Was your ſhip one of them? A. Yes.

Q. Can you name any of the others?

A. The Terrible, Elizabeth, Egmont, Worceſter, and America.

Q. Are you certain with reſpect to the Egmont and America?

A. The America was one of the number.

Q. Did the Admiral, with the van and centre diviſions, and with ſuch of the ſhips of the Vice Admiral of the blue's diviſion as had joined him after paſſing the rear of the enemy's line, immediately wear and double upon the enemy, and continue the engagement?

A. I do not know whether the Vice Admiral of the red, or the van, or centre, with ſuch ſhips as had joined, wore or tacked,---I did not ſee it.---I was not got out of the fire of the enemy at that time.

Q. Do you know whether the Admiral kept ſo near the enemy, after he had paſſed them, as to be ready to renew the engagement, when the Vice Admiral of the blue came out of it; or to ſuccour and ſupport him while he remained engaged, with the ſhips that were with him?

A. I do not.

Q. Can you tell at the time when you came out of the engagement, how far diſtant the Admiral was, from the ſhips of the rear of the enemy?

A. I judge the Admiral might be within two miles of the rear of the enemy.

Q. Did you obſerve at that time which way his head was? A. He was ſtanding towards the enemy.

Q. Then before that, had he not been at a greater diſtance?

A. As I could not know how long the Victory ſtood after ſhe paſſed the enemy, I cannot pretend to ſay when ſhe did wear; 'tis impoſſible for me to ſpeak of the diſtance.

Q. When was the ſignal for battle hauled down?

A. The ſignal according to the time in my ſhip, was about two o'clock.

Q. Did you obſerve the Admiral unbend his main top ſail, while ſtanding towards the enemy?

A. I did not ſee the Admiral unbend his main top ſail, but was informed he did.

Q. Did you obſerve the Formidable as ſoon as ſhe had paſſed the rear of the French line, wear, and lay her head towards the enemy? A. I did.

Q. Was not the Victory, and the body of the fleet, ſtanding towards the Formidable and the French fleet?

A. They were.

Q. Did you afterwards obſerve any of the French ſhips, that wore and ſtood with their heads towards the Formidable?

A. I did not ſee the French ſhips wear, at the time the Vice Admiral alludes to.

Q. Did you ſee any of them ſtand towards her? A. Yes.

Q. Did you obſerve her to wear again, and lay her head towards the Victory? A. I did not.

Q. Did you ſee her meet the Victory?

Admiral Montague. I muſt aſk whether the Victory did meet the Formidable, or whether ſhe wore and ſtood towards the Formidable; did you ſee the Victory and Formidable meet each other? A. No; I did not.

Sir Hugh Palliſer. When you ſaw the Admiral two miles diſtant from the French fleet, ſtanding towards the enemy, did the body of the fleet appear to be with him?

A. There appeared a number of ſhips with him, but I did not count them.

Q. Was not that the time you deſcribed the Formidable was laying her head towards the enemy again? how much nearer was ſhe to the enemy than the Victory?

A. The

A. The Formidable, at that time, appeared to be pretty near astern of the rear of the enemy, and within a small distance, as it appeared to me.

Q. Was not at that time the Vice of the red and his division laying to windward of the enemy's rear?

A. At that time the Victory, and the Vice of the red were to windward of the rear of the enemy.

Q. Did you see the Admiral wear again, and stand from the enemy?

A. I saw the signal on board the Victory for the fleet to wear, and they did wear.

Court. At what time?

A. I believe, between two and three o'clock, by the time in the Robuste.

Q. When the Admiral had wore, was the course he then stood from the enemy? A. Yes.

Q. Did you observe the French fleet to break up their line of battle, and become in confusion?

A. The French fleet did break up their line of battle, but at what particular or precise time, I cannot tell.

Q. Was it at or about the time the Admiral wore, and stood from them; or can you say whether it was before or after.

A. To the best of my recollection, it was after.

President. When the Admiral wore and went from the French, did he go close-hauled, or from the wind?

A. I believe the fleet were close hauled.

Court. Were the whole of the red, and the Admiral's division on the larboard tack, when the signal was made to wear?

A. I cannot speak positively to the whole; but the Admiral, to the best of my recollection, was upon the larboard tack.

Q. From the description you have given of the Admiral and the Vice Admiral of the red, being to windward of the enemy, with the body of ships about him, if instead of the Admiral's being about two miles distant from the enemy, he had been as near the enemy as the Formidable was when she wore, and came out of action, would it not have been a favourable opportunity to re-attack the French, when they had broke up their line?

A. I do not recollect that I made use of the word body. [*body* was previously altered to *number.*]

Admiral Montague. Was it when the Vice Admiral wore and stood from the enemy, or when the Formidable wore, as she came out of action, and laid her head towards the enemy; give an account.

 A. If

A. If that number of ſhips I have deſcribed, had been as near to the enemy as the Formidable, and the Admiral had thought that theſe ſhips were in condition to re-attack the enemy, it appeared to me a favourable opportunity for doing it.

Q. Or, if they had advanced, from the ſituation they were in at this time, do not you think that the French fleet might have been attacked and prevented from forming a new line of battle?

A. The ſituation of theſe ſhips being to windward of the enemy, gave them an opportunity of attacking the enemy, provided the ſhips were in condition, of which I could be no judge in my diſtant ſituation, I can only take it from their poſition.

Q. From the firing kept up, and the very diſtinguiſhed good behaviour of all our ſhips, that did get into the engagement, have you any reaſon to ſuppoſe that the French did not ſuffer in proportion to the Engliſh fleet?

A. I have every reaſon in the world to believe, that the ſhips of that diviſion did their duty, to the beſt of their ability. I muſt conclude that the French did ſuffer, from the very briſk fire of all thoſe of the Engliſh fleet that got into action.

Q. Did they ſuffer as much as ours?

A. I judge they did ſuffer in proportion to ours.

Admiral Montague. Did you obſerve the French fleet to have ſuffered ſo much in their maſts, yards, and ſails, as the Engliſh?

A. I do not recollect that any of the Britiſh fleet ſuffered in their lower maſts, I cannot ſay how far they might be diſabled.

Q. Do you think ſhips might be ſo far diſabled, without carrying away their lower maſts, as not to be able to purſue the enemy for ſome time? A. Certainly.

Admiral Montague. You have ſaid that the Robuſte was diſabled after ſhe came out of the action, pleaſe to relate to the Court the ſtate ſhe was in after the engagement, and how many hours, or what time it was before ſhe was in a condition to purſue the enemy, provided the commander in chief had thought proper ſo to do?

A. I deſire to know if I am to relate every particular?

Admiral Montague. I don't mean every brace and bowling; running rigging will come within theſe articles, I mean maſts, yards, and ſails.

A. When I came out of action we had one ſhot through our mainmaſt, one through the centre of our foremaſt, and another oblique; ſhe received alſo two ſhot in her

bowſprit,

bowſprit, one material one in the mizenmaſt; her main topſail yard was ſhot away, part of it hanging down on the quarter deck; her foretop gallant maſt was ſhot in two; ſhe received two ſhot in her mizen yards, I believe, under water and a little above, about eleven, three or four of them under water, one very dangerous; her main topmaſt was ſhot in two or three places, but they were not ſuch as to prevent the ſhip from carrying ſail upon it. 'Tis impoſſible for me to ſay the ſtate and condition of her ſails, they were ſo very much ſhot. Moſt of her braces, bowlings, bows, and running rigging, were ſhot away; many of her ſhrowds, ſome lower, and ſome topmaſt ſhrouds were ſhot away; one of the ſhot, between wind and water, was a forty-ſix pounder; it ſtruck the ſhip about five or ſix feet under water, and took place directly againſt the hollow beam and pudlock rider, which conſequently cauſed the ſhip to make a great deal of water; a very unfortunate one it was. I had given directions to wear my ſhip immediately on the Formidable's wearing, when the carpenter told the Firſt Lieutenant that it was impoſſible to wear. My anſwer was, that it was an evil I would ſubmit to, if needful; and I was obliged to continue on the ſame tack, my purpoſe being to renew the attack with the firſt ſhip I had laid a longſide of. I had forgot to ſay, two of her ſtarboard ports were knocked away.

Admiral Montague. We wiſh only to hear the defects of your ſhip, Captain, and not a relation of your valour and intentions; it is foreign to the queſtion.

Sir H. Palliſer inſiſted that the whole ſhould be put down, to prove what might be done.

Admiral Montague to Sir Hugh. Then let it be put down, as I ſuppoſe it is agreeable to your own generous palate.

Admiral Keppel begged it might be ſo put down, though out of order.

The evidence then went on.---My firſt object was, to repair the damages my ſhip had ſuſtained; there was a great deal of water in the ſhip, and the people extremely alarmed: I ordered the carpenter over the ſide to ſtop the leak.

Preſident. What time was it before you were in a condition to renew the action?

A. Before the leak was ſtopt it might be ſeven o'clock in the evening, or after; it might be eight.

Q. Did you tack your ſhip at that time?

A. I tack'd my ſhip at four o'clock.

 Q. Were

Q. Were your sails and rigging, at that time, in a condition to renew the attack?

A. I should have pursued the attack at that time, if I had been a single ship; but I do not think I was fit to engage in a line of battle.

Admiral Arbuthnot. If the Admiral had thought fit to have renewed the attack, when the French line was broke, could you have obeyed his signal and gone down to the enemy in the condition you was in? A. I could not.

Prosecutor. Did you observe one of the French ships of the line bear away, and go off with a frigate, with her main yard shot away?

This question admitted by the Admiral.

Q. Would the manner of renewing the attack, as you have described in a former question, have required a pursuit, having stated the French fleet to have broke up their line, and beginning to form a new line; with their heads towards the British fleet.

A. It depended very much upon the operation of the enemy's fleet.

Q. Were the enemy's ships permitted to form a new line of battle, without being molested by the English fleet?

A. I don't recollect the time that the enemy began to form their new line again; but in the evening I observed the enemy's fleet drawn up to leeward of us, but not in a well-formed line; part of their rear appeared to me in some confusion.

Admiral Arbuthnot. If you had been one of those ships to windward of the French fleet, could you have obeyed the signal, if the Admiral had made it, and gone down to the attack? A. No, Sir, not at that time.

Q. Did, or did not Admiral Keppel stand away as directly from the enemy as the wind would permit, from the time he passed the last ship of the enemy's line, during the whole afternoon and night of the 27th, except during the interval of the two supposed times of his wearing in the afternoon?

A. I do not admit of two wearings; after the British fleet wore to the southward, with their starboard tacks on board, it continued on the same tack the whole of the afternoon, and during the night. The enemy were on the same tack; we were a-head of the enemy.

Q. At the beginning of the time you have spoken of, when the Admiral wore and stood to the southward, was not this a direct course from the enemy, as near as the wind would permit?

A. The

A. The two fleets were ſtanding on parallel lines, the Engliſh to windward, and the French to leeward.

Q. At the time they were ſtanding upon a parallel line, the Engliſh to windward and the French to leeward, do you think the Admiral of the Britiſh fleet was then flying from the enemy?

A. At that time there was no appearance of a flight.

Q. At any time during that day, or while the French were in ſight, did the Britiſh Admiral ſhew any ſigns of flying from the enemy?

A. The former part of the day was purſuit; the latter part conveyed an idea of flight.

Q. In the deſcription you have given of the two fleets, the French to leeward and the Engliſh to windward, do you think that the French were chacing the Britiſh Admiral, who was ſuppoſed to be running away; and had the French fleet all their ſails ſet?

A. As near as I recollect, the poſition of the two fleets, about eight in the evening, the Engliſh fleet to windward in that parallel ſituation which I have deſcribed, were endeavouring to form a line of battle, and had been endeavouring to form all the afternoon; from three o'clock the ſignal was out to form line of battle. The French fleet being to leeward, appeared to me to be performing the ſame evolutions. At this particular time in the evening, which was the laſt obſervation I made upon the fleet, towards the cloſe of the evening, the van of our fleet ſeemed to be advanced before the van of the enemy, and as near as I can recollect, the Victory ſeemed nearly oppoſed to the van of the French fleet. Fleets in theſe two ſituations cannot be conceived to be either chacing, or running away.

Admiral Roddam. As the enemy had been long in ſight, did you expect to attack, or be attacked.

A. I thought the enemy meant to attack us.

Q. When the Robuſte, and five ſail more were ordered to chace to windward, did you in your judgment as an officer, think that the ſignal was made for thoſe ſhips to cloſe the fleet, or ſcatter them from the fleet?

A. I have already ſaid, that the ſignal being thrown out to chace to windward, muſt have increaſed their diſtance from the centre of the Britiſh fleet.

Q. But I appeal to your judgment; was that ſignal to cloſe the fleet, or ſcatter it?

A. 'Tis impoſſible for me to ſay what the Admiral's intentions were. I can only ſpeak of the ſituation of the Robuſte. I did not aſk the Admiral's reaſons for doing ſo.

Q. Suppose then there had been no signal made by the Admiral, would you have stood on upon that tack till you had lost sight of the Admiral; was there any sail a-head? A. No.

Q. You was to chace to windward, was it to close your own ships or to extend them?

A. Tacking to windward must certainly extend our ships.

Q. When signal was made by the Admiral for your ship and five more to chace to windward, did you then look upon it that you was to make the best of your way to the French fleet?

A. The chacing to windward undoubtedly encreased the distance from the center of the English fleet, and brought us nearer to the French.

The Court now adjourned, being half past three, till to-morrow morning ten o'clock.

EIGHTH DAY, FRIDAY, January 15th.

The Court being met according to adjournment, the Prisoner brought in, and audience admitted, Captain Hood's Evidence was continued.

Q. On the 28th in the morning, when the French fleet was to leeward, not in a line, but in a heap, would it have been prudent, in the situation the British fleet then were, for the Admiral to have pursued them?

A. I did not see the French fleet to leeward, on the morning of the 28th, excepting three sail.

Admiral Montague. Did you see, when the Admiral made signal to chace the three ships in the morning of the 28th, any ships make a signal for setting up their rigging.

A. I saw the flag for some ships to chace to the south-east early in the morning; I do not recollect to have seen at that time any signal being made for setting up rigging.

Q. How long after this was the signal made?

A. I cannot say what time.

Q. Did you make that signal?

A. I did Sir, but not till after the Admiral had made the signal for setting up rigging; to the best of my recollection the whole fleet made the signal.

Prosecutor. Do you know any good reason why those three ships were not chaced?

A. I cannot pretend to give reasons for the Admiral; he is to judge whether the ships are or are not to chace.

Q. Was the signal made for setting up rigging by any

of

of the ships, before the Admiral laid his head to the northward?

A. I cannot speak with respect to other ships, I can only say that I did not make the signal for setting up rigging till the ships heads were laid to the northward, to the best of my recollection, I have not taken any minute of it.

Q. Whilst your ship was engaged, was any other ships so near to you as to be a support to each other?

A. I did not see any ship a-head of me, or any astern of me, in passing along the French line, nearer than a mile; to the best of my judgment, there were none.

Q. As you have related the damages your ship sustained in the action, was it, or was it not occasioned by the ships being scattered, separated, and dispersed, so as not to support each other?

A. I have given my answer to the distance of the Robuste from the ships astern, which is all that I can say upon the subject.

Q. Whether by the Admiral's shortening sail, while standing towards the enemy, hauling down the signal for battle, wearing and standing to the southward with the French fleet then astern, did you, or did you not then conclude, that the Admiral had determined not to re-attack that evening?

A. I have already said, that I did not see the Admiral shorten sail when the signal for battle was hauled down, I cannot pretend to judge of the Admiral's determination.

Q. Have you since been of that opinion, from the various motions of the Admiral at that time, and from the Admiral's own account published by authority?

Admiral Keppel. I beg pardon, that letter of mine ought to be commented upon by itself.

President. I do not think he ought to judge of it afterwards, Capt. Hood is to give an account of things as they appeared to him at the action, not two or three months afterwards. Did you know the letter you saw in print, to be the just copy of Admiral Keppel's letter, but whether this is a proper question is to be determined by the court.

The Court withdrew to settle the propriety of this question, and resolved that this question is not a proper one to be asked.

Prosecutor: The Court having decided, I shall beg leave to call Capt. Hood, and to put that question to him, after I have proved the Admiral's letter.

Admiral Keppel. When you propose that question, the Court will judge whether it is improper; whenever that letter

letter is ſhewn to the Court I ſhall admit it, and after that object to that queſtion being asked of any witneſs.

Proſecutor. I beg leave to obſerve that I ſhall then take the ſenſe of the court, whether I might not then put the queſtion. Did not the Vice Admiral of the red and his diviſion, bear down into the ſtation of the Vice Admiral of the blue that afternoon?

A. I was too much engaged with the buſineſs of my own ſhip to obſerve that operation.

Q. I aſk you, as an old officer, who has ſeen a great deal of ſervice, whether you ever knew, whilſt the ſignal for line of battle a-head was flying, the commander of ſhips to order the van or rear diviſion to take the place of the other, without being ſatisfied that one of thoſe diviſions was diſabled from taking his proper ſtation?

A. During the courſe of my ſervice, I do not remember to have ſeen that done.

Q. Was not the Vice of the blue, with his ſhip, and thoſe then with him, the laſt that came out of the engagement, and diſabled?

A. They were the laſt that came out of the engagement, and were diſabled; I cannot ſpeak poſitively as to all of them.

Q. Is there not a ſignal appointed, when the commander in chief wants the commander in the 2d or 3d poſt, with their diviſions, to make more ſail?

A. Before I give my anſwer, may I be permitted to look at my fighting inſtructions. *Admitted*. Yes, there is one.

Q. Is there not a ſignal for all flag ſhips to come into the Admiral's wake?

A. Yes, 'tis the 11th article of the fighting inſtructions.

Q. Was your ſhip to windward of the Victory, within half an hour after the Victory wore and ſtood to the ſouthward?

A. She was at that time to leeward of the Victory.

Q. Did you obſerve any ſignals made in the night of the 27th by the French fleet?

A. In the early part of the night I ſaw ſome ſignals, ſome rockets, or ſomething of that kind.

Q. Did you obſerve them to bear away in the night?

A. I did not.

Q. Do you know if any ſignal was made on the morning of the 28th, of ſeeing the French fleet?

A. I do not know of any ſignal being made, but I heard there was.

Q. At what diſtance were thoſe three ſhips that you have mentioned, from the Britiſh fleet?

A. I

A. I cannot pretend to aſcertain the diſtance with exactneſs; they appeared to me, if my eyes did not deceive me, to be about four or five miles from the Robuſte.

Q. Where about was the Robuſte at that time with reſpect to the Formidable and Victory?

A. She was to windward of both.

Q. Were thoſe ſhips nearer to any other of the Britiſh ſhips, than they were to the Robuſte? A. They were.

Q. Did they appear to be line of battle ſhips or frigates?

A. They appeared to me to be line of battle ſhips.

Q. Did the Admiral lay the fleet, early in the morning of the 28th, with their heads to the northward?

A. The Admiral did lay the ſhips, in the morning, with their heads to the northward, but I do not know the preciſe time.

Q. Which way did thoſe three French line of battle ſhips ſtand?

A. They made ſail to the eaſtward, going large, or rather before the wind.

Q. In what latitude was the Robuſte, on the 27th at noon?

A. In lat. 48° 16″ as it was delivered to me, by the maſter of the Robuſte.

Q. What was the bearing and diſtance of Uſhant at that time?

A. North 81, eaſt 45 leagues, but I believe the ſhip was nearer the land, than ſhe appeared by our reckoning.

Q. What are your reaſons for ſuppoſing ſhe was nearer to land, than ſhe appeared by her reckoning at that time?

A. The reaſon ariſes from the ſailing of the ſhips from that day till we had made the land.

Court. What land? A. We made Scilly firſt.

Q. Had you any reaſons at that time? A. No.

Q. Suppoſing yourſelf was at that time forty-five leagues from Uſhant, do you apprehend there would have been any immediate danger, if the fleet had purſued thoſe three French ſhips, as well as as the reſt of the French fleet, ſaid to be in ſight?

Court. He has not ſaid ſo.

Evidence. I muſt beg leave to obſerve to the Court, that on the 28th at noon, the Robuſte was but thirty-eight leagues from Uſhant, I only ſtate the time that there may be no miſtake in the day; there did not appear to me to be any immediate danger.

Q. How was the wind and weather on the 28th?

A. The wind was weſterly, and the weather moderate, I think.

A. Being

Q. Being the middle of ſummer, ſhort nights, and moderate weather, do you apprehend there was any imminent danger, if the fleet had chaced till they had ſeen thoſe three ſhips, and the reſt of the French fleet into port?

A. I do not think that there was any imminent danger, but the Admiral muſt be the beſt judge.

Capt. Duncan. Was your ſhip, on the morning of the 28th, in a condition to have chaced as a man of war ſhould do, when a ſignal is made her to chace?

A. The Robuſte in the morning of the 28th was not in a perfect condition to chace.

Admiral Montague. Do you think ſuppoſing the Britiſh fleet to ſail equally well with the French fleet, there was a probability of the Admiral's coming up with them before night, provided they continued to fly from him?

A. I think not.

Q. Suppoſing the Britiſh Admiral had chaced the French fleet, and ſeen them go into port, and ſuppoſing himſelf to be within four leagues of the French coaſt, and a gale of wind had come on, would not the Britiſh fleet have been in great danger in the condition it was in, making the enemy's coaſt a lee ſhore?

A. I certainly think the diſabled part of the Britiſh fleet would have been in danger.

Q. Had the French fleet after the action of the 27th when to leeward, continued to lay to till day-light the next morning, do you not think that Admiral Keppel would have borne down and engaged them, provided the ſhips were in a proper condition to to do?

A. Yes, he certainly would.

Capt. Cranſton. On the morning of the 27th, when the Robuſte's ſignal was made to chace to windward, what was her ſituation with reſpect to the Victory and Formidable?

A. I have already given in evidence, that I was not on the deck till after the Robuſte had chaced by ſignal, or words to that effect. I therefore cannot ſtate the ſituation of the Robuſte before that ſignal was made, but from the information of the officer.

Q. Can you recollect whether ſhe was to leeward of the Victory?

A. She was not much to leeward of the Victory when I came upon deck, and ſhe was to windward of the Formidable, it may be a mile and a half, or two miles, and by report of the officer, was within three cable's length of the Formidable.

Capt. Duncan. By your having chaced to windward, did you

you not get ſooner into action than you would have done, had you not chaced ? A. I believe not.

Q. Had you been in a line of battle on the ſtarboard tack, and of conſequence in the Victory's wake, would you not have paſſed the enemy at a much greater diſtance than you did? A. I cannot anſwer that queſtion.

Q. Was the enemy's ſhore a lee ſhore, as the wind was on the 28th in the morning?

A. The wind was at W. N. W. on that morning.

Q. Was that a lee ſhore or not?

A. It blew upon the port of Breſt, I believe right into Breſt.

Admiral Keppel. May I be permitted to ask the witneſs ſome queſtions, relating to the alterations made in the log-book? (*granted*)

Q. Where are the entries of the Robuſte's log-book of the 27th, and 28th of July, as they ſtood originally?

A. I really do not know.

Q. Did you ſee any rough minutes of theſe two day's tranſactions, before they were entered in the log-book; and were they approved by you?

A. I certainly did ſee them, in a rough paper, and not knowing at that time, but that they were correct, they were inſerted in the log-book?

Q. Were they inſerted by your approbation?

A. I directed them to be entered in the log-book.

Q. When was it that the alterations and additions were made?

A. I do not remember the day; but the maſter having been already before the Court, I ſubmit the day to his recollection.

Q. As you cannot be preciſe as to the day, can you ſay, whether you then had heard of Admiral Keppel's intended Court Martial?

A. When I took into conſideration, the alterations and corrections of the Robuſte's log-book, I had not heard of any intentions of trying Admiral Keppel.

Q. When you ordered theſe alterations and corrections to be inſerted, had you not then heard of Admiral Keppel's intended Court Martial?

A. I had not, but it was rumoured here.

Q. Explain what you mean by a rumour of a Court Martial, which you had not heard of.

A. What I mean by a rumour, is a great many people were talked of to be tried, in common converſation.

Q. When the alterations were actually made in your preſence,

presence, had you not then heard of Admiral Keppel's intended trial, or not?

A. I have already said, that I had not heard of Admiral Keppel's intended trial.

Admiral Keppel. Captain Hood has referred to what the Master said relating to those alterations; may I beg to have the Clerk's minutes on that article read. *This was accordingly done, and the minutes related,* "That to the best "of his (the Master's) knowledge, the alterations were "made in the log-book after it was known that Admiral "Keppel was to be tried by a Court Martial."

Q. "By whom were these alterations made?

A. "By the Captain, dictated by him, and copied by "the mate.

Q. "Were they written or verbal?

A. "They were written.

Q. "Was any officer present?

A. "Yes, the first lieutenant.

Q. "Where were the alterations and additions made, "and in whose presence?

A. "In the presence of the Captain and first lieutenant "in the Captain's apartments.

Q. "Did the Captain see them before they were in-"serted? A. "Yes.

Q. "Did you ask the Captain whether he approved "of the minutes after the action?

A. "The Captain saw and approved them."

Captain Hood. To prove to the Court how very incorrect the master is, with respect to the day, I shall beg leave to observe, that on the 4th of December, I applied for public leave of absence to the Admiralty; it arrived here by the 7th, and the Admiral gave me notice of it: Business of Court-martials detained me here till the 16th; from the 16th of December to the 3d of January I was in London: Now I only mention this to shew the incorrectness of peoples memory, as to time. I can produce the Admiralty letters and precedents, and prove my return to this port was on the 3d of January; so that this makes a space of twenty days, directly contrary to what the master has asserted; not with an ill intention, I believe, but for want of recollection. In regard to the log, I will state an extraordinary charge in regard to the log book of the Robuste. The master said I looked at the log book every day; I may perhaps have paid more attention to the log than many others. On the 9th of September or October I sent for the master.---*Here he was interrupted by the Court, who said* "We have nothing to do with this at Court-martials."

President.

President. I believe it was known at that time that the Admiral was to be tried, tho' not officially: Can you recollect the precise time they were made?

A. I do not pretend to ſay the day.

Admiral Keppel. Am I to underſtand, upon the oath you have taken, that you had not heard of my intended trial, when you directed theſe alterations to be inſerted?

A. I believe I have anſwered that queſtion already.

Admiral Keppel. I do not underſtand you have: I beg you will anſwer it ſtreight and direct?

A. I heard it as common converſation, but no further.

Q. Had you not heard when the alterations and additions were inſerted, thar Sir Hugh Palliſer had charged me with ſome offence.

A. I never heard of any charge, I don't know what the offences were, they were not come out to my knowledge.

Q. Had you not then heard, that Sir Hugh Palliſer had exhibited a charge againſt me, tho' you did not then know the particulars of it?

A. I have already acknowledged that I had heard of the intended Court martial, therefore if there was to be a Court martial, conſequently there muſt be ſome charge.

Q. Had you ever converſed or correſponded with Sir Hugh Palliſer, directly or indirectly, before you had made the alterations in the log book, on the ſubject of Admiral Keppel's trial?

A. I never converſed with Sir Hugh Palliſer upon that ſubject.

Q. Nor correſponded?

A. Letters certainly paſſed betwixt us, but not relative to this charge.

Q. Have you not converſed with him on the log book.

A. Never.

Q. Do you mean to ſay, that neither your correſpondence, or converſation with Sir Hugh Palliſer, have ever been on the ſubject of the trial, or alterations of the log book?

A. Never a word about the log book, and I believe Sir Hugh Palliſer never heard a ſyllable about the log book, till after the trial came on.

Q. Am I to underſtand you, that there was nothing ſaid with regard to the trial neither?

A. At what time?

Q. Before the alterations were inſerted in the log book.

A. Nothing about the trial in the ſmalleſt degree.

Q. What then led you to diſcover, in four months after

ter the action, any error in the ſtate of the tranſactions of thoſe two days, which you did not obſerve at the time?

A. I was led to the diſcovery of the truth for the ſake of myſelf.

Q. Now we muſt come to the alterations which you admitted to be made, in order to fully aſcertain them: I muſt aſk you this plain queſtion, Did your original log book ſtate, that the Admiral was making much ſail on the evening of the 27th?

A. I do not recollect that it did.

Q. Do you recollect it did not?

A. I yeſterday declared that it did not; I don't unſay what I have ſaid before, ſo that is impoſſible.

Q. What hour does that inſertion ſpecify in the log book?

A. It relates to part of the night, not to any part of the day.

Q. What hour is it put to?

A. I believe it is put, as far as I can recollect, to part of the firſt watch, and part of the middle watch; but I believe no hour is put down, tis only a narration and running on, but as I am called upon to declare, I will do it to the beſt of my judgment.

Admiral Keppel. Mr. Preſident, as that alteration in Capt. Hood's log book tends to affect my life, I ſhall aſk him no more queſtions.

Sir H. Palliſer. Give me leave to offer a few words to the Court, in conſequence of what Admiral Keppel has juſt ſaid. *Court.* Agreed to.

Sir H. Palliſer. The croſs examination of Admiral Keppel, tending to attack the credit and character of Capt. Hood, I think it proper to give notice, that in the further progreſs of this trial, I ſhall examine the Maſter of the Robuſte, and other witneſſes, to reſiſt ſo cruel an attack on the character of a gentleman of his ſervices and merit, and confute the invidious attempt that has been made to -----*Here the Court interfered, and declared they could not ſit and hear it called a cruel and invidious attack.*

Admiral Montague. I muſt beg leave to ſay, that the Priſoner has a right to aſk ſuch queſtions, where his life is at ſtake; I do not underſtand that the character of Captain Hood is impeached by it; I am ſure if I did, I ſhould put a ſtop to it; this is not the form of a Court martial, tho' it may be the form of Weſtminſter hall.

Admiral Keppel. He, Captain Hood, has acknowledged, that the Admiral's making more ſail, is added and put into the log book; I have therefore ſaid, that I will

not

not ask him any more questions, because he has committed an act that affects my life, and therefore I reject his further evidence. Admiral Keppel then, *with a most feeling sensibility, the tear starting from his eye, exclaimed, that his astonishment could not be expressed, when he first heard that his conduct on the 27th and 28th days of last July was accused, he knew of no one that could prove the charges laid against him, and was so unprepared that he had almost determined to set up a paper to the public, intreating all those that could, to come and clear his innocence, and from that moment prepared what evidence he could attain; and he hoped that his honour would come out unsullied.*

Admiral Montague. Upon the whole of the transactions of the 27th and 28th of July, relative to the British fleet, did it appear to you, as an old and experienced officer, that Admiral Keppel by his conduct on either of those days TARNISHED the honour of the British flag.

A. Before I can give an answer to that question, I must beg to know, whether any part of the evidence that I have given, is to be taken.

President. Your depositions are taken down, and stand part of the evidence.

Admiral Montague. Tho' the prisoner does not chuse to ask any more questions of the evidence, the Court is not to be barred asking questions of any evidence, in order to get at facts.

A. I have long had the honour of knowing the honourable Admiral, and I still respect him, notwithstanding my evidence will not be further required. His character is above my praises. I have given my evidence as far as it has gone, with honour and integrity, the Court must therefore judge and decide upon that question.

Admiral Montague. I do not think that an answer to my question; it is a part of the charge against the Admiral, and I should think that every Captain, commanding the British ships on those two days, can acquaint the Court, whether by the misconduct or negligence of Admiral Keppel, the honour of the British navy was tarnished.

A. The Court must judge of it from my evidence, I cannot be a judge.

Admiral Montague. Did you see any?

A. I have given my evidence.

Q. Your evidence, if I understand right, is to answer all such questions as shall be asked you, to the best of your knowledge, to speak the truth, the whole truth, and nothing but the truth, so help you God.

A. I have done ſo.

Preſident. Take the anſwer.

Here he was ordered to withdraw.

AARON GRAHAM, *late Purſer of the Arethuſa, now of the Valiant*, ſworn.

Q. Are thoſe minutes you have in your hand, the original minutes you made on the 27th of July?

A. They are not the original ones, they are a copy of them.

Q. Where are they, then?

A. The original ones were kept in a book, which was made for the quarter deck in particular, and copied into the log book every night, by the mate or maſter, and was kept there continually, for three weeks after the 27th of July; when they were miſſing. I took a copy of them the morning after the 27th; the Mate took a copy of them the evening of the 27th.

Q. How do you know that he did?

A. He ſhewed them to me at the ſame time, and told me they were a copy of them, in order to inſert them in the log book, as he had done every day previous to the 27th.

Q. Did you compare your minutes and the Mate's together? A. I do not recollect I have.

Q. Have you ever compared them with the original?

A. I compared them at the time I made the copy, and examined them myſelf.

Proſecutor. Do you know if they were entered into the log book by the Mate, the evening of the ſame day?

A. I believe they were not.

Q. Do you know what is become of that original minute book that was taken off? A. I do not.

Q. You ſay, that about three weeks after, it was miſſing; has it ever been ſeen ſince that time?

A. Never by me.

Q. Do you know of any one elſe having ſeen it ſince that time? A. I do not.

Q. During thoſe three weeks, where was it kept?

A. Upon the quarter-deck in the binnacle.

Q. Are the minutes you are going to produce, an exact copy of what was entered originally in that old minute book, and nothing more or leſs?

A. They are an exact copy, and nothing more, but there is leſs; I am not particular as to the time when the pendants were hoiſted.

Q. Then you ſay it is not a compleat copy of the whole, ſomething being omitted? A. The

A. The queſtion was asked me before, there is leſs not more, I am not particular as to the time the pendants were hoiſted, as I took the copy more for my own ſatisfaction, than for public inſpection.

Q. If you omitted any part of it, what was your reaſon for omitting that part?

A. As I wiſhed to know the particular ſignals that were made, I took an exact account of the general ones, not only of their being made, but of the time in which they were made: But as for the pendants, I only put them down in regular order as they were made.

Q. Do you mean in the original one, or in the preſent one?

A. The following copy in my hand, I ſhall give in, as they ſtand in the original, though the time is not expreſſed in this.

Q. In the original book, were thoſe ſignal pendants entered regular and in order, with the time againſt them?

A. They were.

Q. Let me know your reaſons for omitting the time againſt their particular ſignals, in your copy?

A. As I obſerved before, it was more for my own information than for public inſpection. I thought if I could be particular as to general ſignals, the time of particular ſhip's ſignals being made, was of no conſequence.

Q. Is the time omitted againſt every ſhip's ſignal, or only particular ones? A. Againſt every ſhip's ſignal.

Q. Is it the firſt copy?

A. No, but the original one I can produce; I received Sir Hugh Palliſer's ſumnions not above five minutes before I came into court, and therefore have not got it with me.

Q. Why did you take a copy of it?

A. Becauſe it was not quite ſo fair.

Q. When did you take the copy?

A. About eight or ten days ſince.

Q. Is it an exact copy of the firſt copy? A. It is.

Q. Were the times omitted in that book?

A. They were.

Q. What was the firſt ſignal on the 27th?

A. The ſignal for tacking, union at the fore and mizen top-maſt head.

Q. At what hour?

A. Thirty minutes paſt ten. When I ſay it was made, I mean, it was repeated on board the Arethuſa.

Q. What was the next?

A. Red flag at the fore-top-maſt head, a ſignal to engage.

Q. Does

Q. Does the time of the ſignals being hauled down, ſtand in the minutes againſt the ſignals that were firſt made, or are they not placed againſt the ſignals, but apart?

A. They ſtand upon the minutes as they are entered in this minute book.

Q. When was that ſignal hauled down?

A. Twenty-ſix minutes after one.

Q. After the ſignal was made for battle, what was the next ſignal?

A. Blue pendant at the enſign ſtaff.

Q. At what time was that?

A. Two minutes after one.

Q. What ſignal was that? A. The ſignal for wearing.

Q. What was the next?

A. Blue and white ſtriped flag at the mizen top-maſt head, a ſignal to ſpeak to a particular ſhip to come within hail, fifty minutes paſt one.

Q. What was the next?

A. Yellow pendant at the main top-maſt head, the Proſerpine's ſignal.

Q. The next?

A. The union, with a blue flag and red croſs at the mizen peak.

Q. At what time?

A. Forty minutes after one.

N. B. *The union flag, with a blue pendant under it, was prior to this.*

Q. When was it that the union and blue flag, with a red croſs under it was hauled down?

A. Twenty-three minutes paſt three.

Q. When was it again hoiſted?

A. At thirty minutes paſt three.

Q. When was it again hauled down?

A. On board the Victory, I do not know; on board the Arethuſa at day-light the next morning.

Q. What was the next ſignal to the union and blue flag, after its being firſt hoiſted?

A. A blue pendant at the enſign ſtaff.

Q. What time? A. Thirty minutes paſt two.

Q. What was the next?

A. Yellow pendant at maintopmaſt head?

Q. At what hour?

A. I have not the time expreſſed againſt the pendants.

Q. What was the next ſignal in order?

A. Blue flag at mizen peak.

Q. What ſignal was that?

A. A ſig-

A. A ſignal for ſhips to windward to bear down into the Admiral's wake.

Q. At what time?

A. Twenty-four minutes paſt three?

Q. When was that hauled down?

A. Thirty minutes paſt three.

Q. When was that hoiſted again?

A. At thirteen minutes paſt ſix.

Q. When was it hauled down?

A. At day dawn the next morning.

Q. What was the next ſignal in order, after twenty-four minutes paſt three?

A. A union and blue, with a red croſs at the mizen peak, for ſhips to form a line of battle, a cable's length aſunder a-head.

Q. What was the next ſignal in order, after twenty-four minutes paſt three?

A. Yellow pendant at the main topmaſt head.

Q. Have you any time to that?

A. I have no time to any of the pendants.

Q. What ſhip was that for? A. The Proſerpine.

Q. What was the next ſignal?

A. Blue and white ſtriped flag at the main topmaſt head, thirty-three minutes after four, for a particular ſhip to make more ſail. It was hauled down within a minute.

Q. Were there any ſhip's pendants out at that time?

A. I believe not.

Q. Does it appear in your minutes, that the Duke's ſignal was made with that flag?

A. I have ſeveral pendants out at the time the Spaniſh flag was flying at the maintopmaſt head, but none while the blue and white ſtriped flag was flying at the main topmaſt head.

Q. Can you recollect what ſhips the pendants were for?

A. I think not.

Q. What time was the Spaniſh flag hoiſted?

A. Thirty-ſeven minutes paſt four.

Q. What was the firſt pendant let fly after that?

A. A red pendant at the mizen topmaſt head.

Q. Was it immediately upon the Spaniſh flag's being hoiſted?

A. I do not recollect they were flying together.

Q. What was the next pendant?

A. Blue, at the ſtarboard mizen topſail yard arm.

Q. Do your minutes mark the ſhips thoſe pendants were for? A. They do not.

Q. In the original minute-book, was not the time, as well as the names, set down?

A. There was a column for it, but I believe the significations were not inserted.

Q. As you cannot name ships or time, go on then and name the pendants in the order they were made---What was the next?

A. Yellow pendant at the starboard main topsail yard arm. These are all the pendants I have down.

Q. Are the three that you have mentioned all that were in the original minute-book?

A. There were two signals intervened between them and a number of other pendants that were let fly, when the Spanish flag was at the main topmast head.

Q. Were the other pendants, and the ships names they belonged to, particularly ascertained in the original minute book?

A. Yes; but whether the significations of them were, as I have already observed, I do not recollect.

Q. Do you mean to say, the pendants and names were inserted, without the names of the particular ships?

A. Yes, I do.

Q. You said you had omitted the time in your last copy; but that you had entered the order in which they were made, I should be glad to know your reason, why you have omitted both the pendants and ships names, that were made with that signal by the Spanish flag.

A. I have not omitted the pendants, I said before that the two signals intervened between the three last pendants I mentioned, and the several others that were thrown out whilst the Spanish flag was flying at the main topmast head.

President. Now tell us what were those two flags that intervened?

A. A blue flag, which was hoisted by mistake, at the ensign staff. It remained there three minutes, and then was hoisted at the mizen peak. I do not mean to say that this mistake happened on board the Victory.

Q. At what time was that mistake made;

A. It was hoisted by mistake at the ensign staff, ten minutes after six, and at the mizen peak thirteen minutes after six.

Q. Can you name the number of pendants you said were thrown out? A. I can.

Q. Name them?

A. Red pendant at the larboard main top sail yard arm, blue pendant at the same place, blue pendant at the larboard

fore

fore yard arm, white pendant at the larboard mizen top ſail yard arm, white pendant at the fore top maſt head, blue pendant at the ſtarboard main top ſail yard arm, red pendant at the ſame place, blue pendant at the main top maſt head. Theſe are all the ſignals I have.

Q. Did you make any diſtinction of time between the pendants? A. None at all.

Admiral Keppel. I ſhould wiſh to know whether the Vice Admiral has done with this evidence?

Proſecutor. No.

It being now four o'clock, the Court adjourned, until ten o'clock to-morrow morning. Mr. Graham ordered to attend.

Ninth Day, SATURDAY the 16th of January.

The Court being re-aſſembled, about ten o'clock, the evidence of Mr. Graham was concluded.

Sir Hugh Palliſer. Have you brought with you the firſt copy? A. I have.

Q. When was it taken?

A. In the morning of the 27th July.

Q. Is there any alteration made in this book in your hand, from the day it was wrote, to the preſent?

A. There is ſome little difference, and therefore, I have not given my evidence as they ſtand upon that book, but as they ſtand upon this; becauſe therein I had put down the ſignal hauled down at forty-ſix minutes paſt one, inſtead of twenty-ſix minutes. One miſtake I have made; I put down a pendant not hoiſted, but recollected ſince where it was, and have given evidence accordingly.

Q. Is there any other difference between theſe two books?

A. No, in every other particular that is a fair copy of this.

Q. Who was the mate that took the original copy in the log book you mentioned yeſterday? A. Mr. Chewſey.

Ordered, *That Mr. Chewſey be ſummoned to attend, and bring the ſhip's log-book.*

Mr. Graham ordered to withdraw.

Capt. Allen, *of the Egmont, ſworn.*

Proſecutor. When did you firſt ſee the French fleet?

A. Upon my word I cannot juſtly tell: the log book is left at Plymouth, and I muſt refer you to that, Sir.

Q. Upon the day when you did ſee them, do you remember what time of the day it was?

A. About two or three o'clock; I will not be poſitive.

Q. During that afternoon and evening, did they appear to be employed in forming a line of battle? A. No.

Q. How were they situated, with respect to the British fleet, then?

A. I do not recollect, it is a long time ago, and I have not charged my memory with any thing of that sort, I assure you?

Q. Do you remember the situation of them the following morning? A. No, I do not.

Q. Do you remember when you first saw them on the morning of the 27th? A. I do.

Q. At What time, Sir? A. At five o'clock.

Q. When did you first discover them to be in a line of battle? A. Not at all.

Q. On which tack were they when you first saw them?

A. On the larboard tack?

Q. About what time was that?

A. Between five and six o'clock.

Q. Did they not appear to you at any time to be in a line of battle? A. No.

Q. In the morning of the 27th, how was our fleet situated, with respect to each other?

A. I cannot positively answer that question, I don't know; the position of the Egmont being far to leeward.

Q. Do you remember the Admiral making a signal, for some ships of the Vice Admiral of the blue's division, to chace to windward? A. I do.

Q. What time? A. Near six o'clock.

Q. For how many ships of that division?

A. I do not know. The Egmont was one of them.

Q. Can you name any of the others?

A. The Terrible. I do not recollect the others.

Q. Were there several pendants?

A. I do not recollect any more than two pendants.

Q. Did you see a number of ships make chace, in consequence of that signal?

A. There might be three or four of the blue.

Q. Did those ships, three or four, whatever their number were, by chacing, separate and scatter that part of the fleet more than they were before?

A. They made a greater distance, no doubt, but they were not scattered.

Q. Did they all preserve an equal distance from each other while they were chacing? A. No, they did not.

Q. When did the French fleet tack from the larboard tack, to come to the starboard?

A. I cannot ascertain the time.

President.

President. When that ſignal was thrown out, to chace to windward, what reaſon did you form within yourſelf at that time, as the cauſe of that ſignal being thrown out?

A. To get to windward, and cloſe with the Admiral.

Q. When the French fleet tacked, did they tack together, or ſucceſſively in each other's way.

A. It is out of my power to tell.

Q. At what time did the Britiſh fleet tack all together by ſignal?

A. The ſignal was made to tack at ten, but I had tacked before that time. They did not tack all together.

Q. At what time was the ſignal made for battle?

A. I ſaw it a quarter after eleven.

Q. What part of the French line did you begin to engage with?

A. I engaged the third ſhip; but they were not in a line.

Q. Were you at that time accompanied with any other ſhips of your diviſion, ſo near as to ſupport each other?

A. I was ſo attentive to my own ſhip, that I do not recollect any other than the Formidable, about a mile from me.

Q. Was that a mile a-head or a-ſtern of you?

A. A-ſtern of me.

Q. How near was the ſhip next a-head to you?

A. I do not recollect any other ſhip being near me as we came up, (there being ſo much ſmoke) except French men of war.

Q. In that part of the engagement, did you receive any conſiderable damage from the enemy?

A. I cannot ſay that I recollect what damage we received; we did not conſider damage, we were ſo attentive in firing at the enemy.

Q. Do you not think, that the damages you received in that part of the engagement, were greater than they probably would have been, if you had fought in a body with the reſt of the ſhips of the blue diviſion? A. No.

Q. If you had engaged in a body, would they not have ſhared in the fire from the enemy, that was wholly levelled at you, when you was alone?

A. That is as the enemy pleaſed; they may have fired at me alone, or they might not have fired at me at all.

Q. From the place where you began to engage, did you proceed till you joined ſome other part of the Britiſh fleet, and was that the Vice Admiral of the blue's diviſion, or the Admiral's diviſion?

A. I proceeded and joined the Admiral's diviſion.

A. In

Q. In doing that, did you not paſs a-head of the Admiral of your own diviſion? A. No.

Q. Did you paſs a-ſtern of him?

A. We did not paſs a-ſtern of him.

Q. In what ſituation was the Vice Admiral of the blue from you, when you joined the Admiral's diviſion?

A. He was a-ſtern, upon the lee-quarter.

Q. Was he in that ſituation from you, when you firſt began to engage? A. No.

Q. How then?

A. Upon the lee beam, about three miles and half, or four perhaps, to the beſt of my recollection.

Q. When you joined the Admiral's own diviſion, did you continue to engage there? A. I did.

Q. Did the confuſion of that part of the fleet you was in, occaſion ſome of our own ſhips to fire into your ſhip?

A. I ſaw no confuſion at all?

Q. Was you fired into by any of our ſhips? A. I was.

Q. By what ſhips? A. The Thunderer.

Q. What damage did you receive by her ſhot?

A. The ſheet anchor was broke, two cutter boats were ſhot through, ſome ſhot in the ſhip's ſide, but no man killed or wounded.

Q. Was not your main maſt wounded, by a ſhot on the larboard ſide? A. Not that I recollect.

Q. Was it not underſtood at the time, that a man was killed upon the quarter deck, by the Thunderer's fire?

A. No, it was proved that he was killed by the three deck French ſhip that lay along ſide.

Q. Did any other of our ſhips fire over or into you that day? A. No.

Q. Whilſt the Thunderer and you lay in that poſition, did not the enemy's ſhot go over both, or hit both?

A. I cannot ſay that they went through us, and into us.

Q. Were they within diſtance for the ſhot to reach you both? A. Yes, within piſtol ſhot.

Q. Was you at that time a-head or a-ſtern of the Victory? A. A-ſtern of the Victory.

Q. Did you proceed on in that ſituation from her, till you paſſed the rear of the French fleet? A. I did.

Q. How far do you think the Britiſh fleet was extended, from van to rear, at the beginning of the engagement?

A. I do not know.

Q. Was not the Victory, whilſt ſhe was in action, ſupported by the whole of the Admiral's own diviſion, and part or the Vice Admiral of the blue's?

A. I

A. I cannot tell that there were many ſhips engaged.

Q. Can you tell by what ſhips the Formidable was ſupported during her engagement?

A. I cannot particularize, but there were three ſhips a-ſtern of the Egmont, among which ſhips was the Vice Admiral of the blue?

Q. After the Admiral, with the ſhips of his diviſion, and the others with him, had paſſed the rear of the enemy, did he wear and ſtand towards them? A. He did.

Q. At what diſtance from the ſternmoſt of the enemy's ſhips, did he wear?

A. I cannot aſcertain the diſtance, it was not far.

Q. How long was it after he paſſed the rearmoſt ſhips?

A. That I do not know neither.

Q. Did you continue to ſtand beyond them longer than the Admiral did, or did you wear at the ſame time?

A. I continued on the ſtarboard tack, till ſix o'clock in the afternoon, having four feet water in my hold, which obliged me to continue ſo.

Q. From the very briſk fire kept up by our ſhips that were engaged, do you think that the French ſhips were not damaged, at leaſt as much as ours?

A. I can anſwer for no ſhip's firing but my own, neither what damage the French may have received.

Q. Have you any reaſon to think the French were damaged in proportion to what our's was?

A. I cannot ſay, I have reaſon to ſuppoſe they muſt have been damaged, no doubt.

Q. After you ceaſed firing, did you take notice of the Vice Admiral of the blue of your own diviſion?

A. Not till ſix o'clock in the evening.

Q. Did you ſee the Victory when ſhe wore?

A. I have already ſaid, I did ſee the Victory wear.

Q. Did you ſee the Vice Admiral of the blue at that time? A. No.

Q. When was the ſignal for battle hauled down?

A. I cannot immediately ſay.

Q. Can you ſay whether it was before or after the Admiral wore? A. I cannot.

Q. Did you obſerve the Admiral unbend his main top ſail? *Admitted by Admiral Keppel, whilſt ſtanding towards the enemy, and bent again in half an hour.* A. Yes.

Q. Where was the Vice Admiral of the red and his diviſion, at the time the Victory was ſtanding towards the enemy?

A. I was ſo attentive to repairing my own damages that I cannot immediately ſay.

Q. Did

Q. Did you fee the Victory wear the fecond time?

A. I have faid before, I did not.

Q. When did you firft fee her with her head towards the fouthward? A. Between four and five o'clock.

Q. Was there a number of fhips about her at that time? A. There was.

Q. Did you take notice when the French broke up their line?

A. I did not perceive them in any line, as I have faid before.

Q. Did you perceive them to be in a crowd, different to what they had been during the action?

A. I did not fee them in a crowd at any time before or after the action, nor at any time.

Q. Did you obferve them when they began to form a line of battle, with their heads to the fouthward?

A. I did not.

Q. Was the Vice Admiral of the blue, and part of his divifion, the fhips that came laft out of the engagement?

A. I cannot tell. Mr. Keppel admits they were.

Q. When the Victory wore the fecond time, did fhe ftand to the fouthward?

A. I did not fee the Victory wear the fecond time, after fhe had wore fhe was ftanding to the fouthward; between four and five o'clock.

Q. Was the French fleet then a-ftern?

A. They were not.

Q. Where were they?

A. They appeared to me, the greateft part of them, a-breaft of the Admiral, to leeward.

Q. At what time are you fpeaking of?

A. About fix, I believe, in the evening.

Q. Did you obferve what fail the Victory had that afternoon?

A. I was in fuch a pofition as not to be able to judge.

Q. Did you fee the blue flag, at the mizen peak, hoifted on board the Victory that afternoon? A. I did.

Q. At what time, Sir?

A. About five o'clock, I think.

Q. Was your fhip then to windward or to leeward of the Victory? A. A-head, and to leeward withal.

Q. At the time you mentioned to have feen the French fleet, about fix o'clock, were they forming in line of battle?

A. They appeared to me to be forming.

Q. Did the Vice Admiral of the red bear down into the Admiral's wake that afternoon?

A. I did

A. I did not ſee him bear down, but he was, or appeared to me to be a-head of the Admiral.

Q. Before that happened, did you take notice of his being a-ſtern of the Admiral in his wake? A. I did not.

Q. At what time that evening did you get to windward of the Victory?

A. I tacked at ſix o'clock, and was to windward of the Admiral a little before ſeven.

Q. Did you obſerve that evening, a number of ſhips pendants out to bear down, and yours amongſt them, on board the Victory, and on board the Formidable?

A. I did.

Q. Where was your ſhip at that time, with reſpect to the Formidable? A. To windward.

Q. At what time was that? A. Near ſeven o'clock.

Q. Did you obſerve the Fox come to the Formidable?

A. I did not.

Q. After you had made ſail in conſequence of that ſignal, and your pendant being hauled in, did you again bring to?

A. I did, for we had much water in the hold at that time, and were going too faſt for the people that were over board to ſtop the leak.

Q. Did you obſerve any ſignals made in the night by the French fleet, or were you informed of it at the time?

A. I ſaw ſome rockets hove, which I apprehended were from ſome of the French ſhips.

Q. Did you percieve them from that time to go away?

A. No, I did not.

Q. Were they, or part of them in ſight the next morning from your ſhip?

A. I ſaw three ſail betwixt three and four o'clock in the morning of the 28th.

Q. Was you informed that there were any more ſeen from the maſt head of your ſhip that morning, ſuppoſed to be the French fleet?

A. I neither was informed, or did ſee any more than the three ſail.

Q. What did you judge theſe three ſail to be, line of battle ſhips or frigates?

A. I judged two to be line of battle ſhips, and one frigate; but in that I might be miſtaken.

Q. How far do you think theſe ſhips were from the British fleet? A. They might be ſix miles.

Q. Do you ſpeak of them all, as being at equal diſtance, or the furthermoſt of them?

A. The neareſt of them.

Q. Do

Q. Do you mean at day-light when you firſt ſaw them?

A. I mean at day-light, when I firſt ſaw them.

Q. Whereabout was the Egmont at that time, from the neareſt of the Britiſh fleet?

A. About four miles a-ſtern of the Vice Admiral of the blue.

Q. Were not thoſe three French ſhips nearer to other parts of the Britiſh fleet, than they were to the Egmont?

A. I think they were.

Q. When you was four miles aſtern of the Formidable, was you to leeward or to windward of the wake of the Admiral, and of the reſt of the ſhips?

A. It appeared to me, the Egmont was to windward.

Q. Were thoſe three ſhips to leeward of the Britiſh fleet? A. Yes.

Q. Did the Admiral lay the fleet with their heads to the northward the next morning, I mean the 28th?

A. Yes.

Q. What latitude was your ſhip in at noon on the 28th, by reckoning?

A. That the log book and journals will ſatisfy.

Q. Did the Maſter give you his day's work?

A. He did, but I have it not with me. The Maſter and Lieutenant being detained at Plymouth, they ſent me neither journal nor log.

Q. Then you do not remember what it was?

A. No, I do not.

Q. Do you remember by the Maſter's reckoning, what diſtance you was from Uſhant that day?

A. No, by the ſame reaſon.

Q. What ſort of weather was it that morning?

A. As near as I can recollect, it was hazy.

Q. I mean as to the wind? A. It blew freſh.

Admiral Keppel. At the time the ſignal was made for the Egmont to chace to windward, and the other ſhips of the Vice Admiral of the blue's diviſion on the 27th, can you remember what ſail the Vice Admiral of the blue was under?

A. She carried her top-ſails and fore-ſail; but the Egmont being a-head, I cannot recollect ſeeing whether ſhe had her main-ſail and her main-top ſtay-ſail, or not.

Q. As an Officer of experience, when a ſignal is made for your ſhip, or a ſhip to chace to windward, does it direct you to ſtand upon the ſame tack five hours, from the tack you ſet off from, or to tack and ply to windward in the wind's eye?

A. No, Sir, it does not, but to tack and ply to windward.

Q. You

Q. You ſaid you did tack before the general ſignal was made; if the other ſhips had tacked as you did, I would aſk whether they would not have got to action as ſoon as you did, and given you ſupport and ſuccour; and whether their ſtanding ſo much longer, was not the reaſon, why they were ſo extended and ſcattered; if that was not the reaſon of it, was it the fault of the ſignal to chace to windward?

A. There is no doubt but if the ſhips had tacked as I did, they might have been in action as ſoon as the Egmont; it was not the fault of the ſignal to chace to windward.

Q. If then they had got into action as ſoon, or nearly as ſoon, and had bore down and cloſed with the center diviſion, as the Egmont did, whether that would not have given ſtrength to the center diviſion, and ſtrength to the diviſion aſtern of her?

A. Undoubtedly it muſt.

Q. I think you ſaid, while you was in action, you ſaw the Vice Admiral of the blue, and two ſhips of his diviſion a-ſtern of the Egmont; the ſituation that the Egmont was then engaged in, did not that give ſuccour and ſtrength to the Vice Admiral of the blue? A. It did.

Q. Some ſtreſs has been laid upon the Thunderer's firing through, or over, or hitting the Egmont; I would aſk, if in a number of ſhips following one another, do you imagine that it is uncommon for ſuch an accident to happen in ſome part or other of the fleet ſo engaged, and ſo obſcured from one another by ſmoke?

A. It often happens in great fleets unavoidably.

Q. You have ſaid you ſtood upon the ſtarboard tack till ſix o'clock, in repairing damages; and have alſo deſcribed ſeeing the Victory upon the ſtarboard tack, betwixt four and five o'clock; then I am going to ask, whether you obſerved at that time the Victory leading two or three points from the wind, down upon the ſhips to leeward?

A. I did obſerve it, and judged it was to ſuccour the crippled ſhips then laying to, and repairing their damages, a head and to leeward of the Britiſh fleet.

Q. I would ask, whether the Victory's ſtanding two or three points from the wind was wearing the enemy's fleet, or going from it?

A. It was wearing the enemy's fleet; but they appeared to me to edge away alſo.

Q. Do you know, between four and five o'clock, what other of the Engliſh ſhips were down to leeward, upon the lee bow of the Victory, somewhere about the Egmont, in the same condition as herself?

A. There were four sail to leeward, besides the Egmont.

Q. When you joined the Vice Admiral of the blue, about seven o'clock, did you then see the signal on board the Victory for a line of battle a-head, and the blue flag under it? A. I did.

Q. Had you ever seen it before, in the course of the afternoon? A. I had.

Q. When you was to windward, at seven o'clock, of the Vice Admiral of the blue, did you observe him with the same signal out as the Victory had?

A. I only saw the signal for bearing down into the Vice Admiral's wake, with my signal.

Q. Whether in the condition your ship was in after the action, and on the 28th in the morning, it was such as to permit you to chace like a man of war, without danger of being entangled with a lee shore upon an enemy's coast, in imminent danger to your ship?

A. She was not in a condition to chace, much less to be entangled with a lee shore, on an enemy's coast.

Admiral Montague. You will please to acquaint the court with the defects of the Egmont, after the action of the 27th, as to masts, yards, sails, rigging and hull?

A. I must beg leave to refer the Court to the defects given in to the Commander in Chief, the morning after the action. One of the assistant builders is here, I have summoned him to bring them.

Court. They are too many and too long to trouble the Court with. Name some of the worst of them.

A. I will. We received six shot between the lower part of the whale on the starboard side, and five streaks below it; the head of the main mast had two or three shot thro' it; the head of the mizen mast shot totally away; the crotchet and mizen top sail yard, the main yard, and the starboard yard arm, shot through; one shot through the slings of the main yard, one shot through the larboard, and most of the larboard yard arms shattered; the head of the fore top mast was shot away; the fore yard shot through in two places; the fore main top sail yard shot through; the foremast had one shot through the centre; the head of the foremast much shattered.

Admiral Montague. I am very well satisfied with the account you have given, if you will leave off there.

A. Whenever you please to order me.

Admiral Montague. Then, Sir, how long was it after, that you was in a condition to renew the attack, if the Admiral

Admiral had judged proper to have done ſo; how many hours?

A. Three hours and a half.

Q. Then, Sir, was it not more proper and prudent in the Admiral to lay to and repair his diſabled ſhips, before he renewed a ſecond attack? A. Aſſuredly.

Q. Then, Sir, upon the whole, did it appear to you, as an old experienced officer, That Admiral Keppel, by his conduct either on the 27th or 28th of July, tarniſhed the honour of the Britiſh navy?

A. No; and I ſhould not take upon me to ſay ſo much, if I had not been forty years at ſea, and thirty-three years an officer, that I look upon it the Admiral did behave with great honour, inſtead of tarniſhing, the Britiſh flag.

Capt. Allen, ordered to withdraw; and it being near four o'clock, the Court adjourned till Monday ten o'clock.

TENTH DAY, MONDAY the 18th of JANUARY.

Court met according to adjournment; but Rear Admiral Rodham, one of the members, being taken ill, the Court adjourned till to-morrow morning ten o'clock.

ELEVENTH DAY, TUESDAY, JANUARY 19th:

Rear Admiral Rodham having recovered from his indiſpoſition ſo as to be able to attend in his place, the Court was opened a little after ten o'clock, when

MR. CHEWSEY, *Maſter's Mate of the Arethuſa, was called in, and ſworn.*

Sir H. Palliſer. Have you got the ſhip's log-book?

A. Yes.

Q. Is that the original log book? A. It is.

Q. Have you ever made any arrangements or alterations? A. I never made any.

Q. Have any been made?

A. I do not know that there have.

Q. Did you enter the two days work of the 27th, and 28th of July, in it?

A. I did, they are the ſame I entered.

Q. At what time did you make your entries?

A. Generally in the evening.

Q. Was there a minute book of ſignals kept?

A. There was.

Q. Did you take a copy of this minute book on theſe days? A. I did.

Q. Did you enter the ſignals in that minute book, into the log-book? A. I did not.

Q. Did you uſually enter the ſignals from the minute book into the log-book? A. I did.

Q. Did you enter other days, and not theſe two days?

A. I did, as it will appear by the book.

Q. What was the reaſon of your not entering theſe two days, as it was uſual to enter all other days?

A. The reaſon was, that there was not room in the book, and it took up ſo much time, and we were all in a hurry and confuſion.

Q. Was there not room on the following leaves; were not all the next leaves blank at that time?

A. Yes, Sir, there was room; but Capt. Marſhall had intended to keep a minute book, and the Maſter told me it was not material.

Q. Then you underſtand you was in a manner forbid doing of it, as not neceſſary, becauſe the Captain meant to keep a ſeparate account?

A. No, Sir, I did not underſtand that; I was not forbid.

Q. Where is the original minute book?

Judge Advocate. Here it is; the Preſident received it yeſterday, and on the evidence being asked if he knew any thing of it, he acknowledged it to be his own hand writing.

A. That was loſt that was taken by the pencil; and the paper I have taken ſince was copied from it.

Q. In whoſe care was that book before it was loſt?

A. It remained in the binnacle drawer, on the quarter deck, the day after the engagement.

Q. How long was it after that time, that the book was loſt?

A. I believe it was eight or ten days, I cannot be certain.

Q. Where is the firſt copy you took from it, of thoſe two days work; I mean the copy that you took in the evening yourſelf? A. This is the firſt copy that I took.

Q. Have you had that in your cuſtody ever ſince?

A. No, Sir.

Q. What did you do with it?

A. When the book was loſt, Capt. Marſhall applied to me, and I delivered it to him.

Q. Have you examined it, to ſee whether it is preciſely the ſame, or to ſee whether there is any alterations?

A. I think it is the ſame; I have a copy that was taken afterwards.

Q. Have

Q. Have you ever made any alterations or additions to it since the day it was first made, of the first entry?

A. I have not, Sir.

N. B. *The signals were then read in Court by the Evidence, but as they agreed exactly with Capt. Marshall's, they are here omitted [See them particularly stated in Capt. Marshall's examination before the Court,* p. 10, &c.]

Ordered to withdraw.

CAPT. ROBINSON, *of the Worcester, called and sworn; and permitted by the Court to make use of some minutes in his own hand writing, which he had made every day.*

Prosecutor. When was the French fleet first seen?

A. On Thursday, 23d July.

Q. About what time?

A. I believe it was about one o'clock, but cannot be certain as to the exactness of the time.

Q. During that afternoon, and in the evening, did they appear to be forming the line of battle?

A. There was an appearance of it, but I cannot be certain.

Q. On what tack was the French fleet then with us that evening?

A. I believe on the starboard tack, standing to the southward.

Q. Was it towards or from the British fleet?

A. Towards them rather.

Q. Was they at that time to leeward of the British fleet?

A. They were to leeward.

Q. At what time in the evening?

A. About eight o'clock, near sun-set.

Q. How was the wind then?

A. About W. N. W.

Q. As you have described the French fleet to leeward of the British, with the wind westerly, standing to the southward, were the French then between the British fleet and the port of Brest? A. Most certainly.

Q. Where was the French fleet the next morning?

A. In the N. W.

Q. Was the British fleet then between the French and the port of Brest? A. Certainly.

Q. What do you apprehend was the cause of the French getting to the N. W. and placing the British fleet between them and Brest?

A. I apprehend it was caused when the wind shifted, and by the fleet laying to.

Q. Do you apprehend, that the French carried sail in the night for that purpose? A. I do not know.

 Q. When

Q. When they were in the N. W. the next morning, had they not the weather gage of the British fleet?

A. They had.

Q. At what time did you first see the French fleet in the morning of the 27th?

A. I did not see them myself till five o'clock.

Q. Did they appear to you to be in a line of battle, at any time in the morning of the 27th?

A. They did, a straggling line, but not a close one.

Q. At what time do you speak of?

A. About five o'clock in the morning.

Q. At that early period in the morning, did their line appear to be more perfected, or more closed?

A. I did not observe them immediately after, for I was engaged in making sail.

Q. In the morning of the 27th was not the British fleet scattered and dispersed?

A. They were not in a line of battle, but in the usual state of sailing.

Q. What was the occasion of your making sail in the morning?

A. The Worcester's signal was out in the morning to chace, with several other ships, to windward.

Q. What did you judge, at that time, the Admiral meant by making that signal?

A. Why Sir, my judgment was, that as every effort had been made to bring the French to battle, after the 23d, the intention of the Admiral's signal for ships to chace to windward, was to bring the French fleet to action.

Q. How many ship's signals of the Vice Admiral of the blue's division were made at that time?

A. I believe about that time there were six, but am not perfectly clear as to the number.

Q. Did that signal leave the Vice Admiral of the blue with more than four ships of his division? A. No, Sir.

Q. Did not these signals cause that part of the fleet to be more separated and dispersed than they were before?

A. It certainly tended to enlarge their distance between the center and the chacing ships.

Q. Did it not also separate them from their own flag?

A. Certainly it did.

Q. Did the British fleet tack all together by signal, to stand on towards the French fleet on the 27th, and at what hour?

A. At ten o'clock or very near, the Admiral made the general signal to tack altogether, and the chacing ships complied with that signal as soon after as could be done.

Q. Before

Q. Before the ſignal was made for chace, was the Vice Admiral of the blue, and his diviſion, a-head of the Admiral, and ſomething under his lee bow, or how were they ſituated? I mean at five o'clock, before the ſignal was made for chace?

A. The Vice Admiral and his diviſion were a-head of the Commander in Chief, but a little on his lee beam.

Q. Were not the ſhips that chaced in different ſituations, ſome a-head, ſome a-ſtern, ſome to windward, and ſome to leeward, at the time the ſignal was made for them to chace?

A. I cannot ſay, I can only anſwer for the ſituation of the Worceſter, becauſe I had the honour of commanding her.

Q. When ſhips chace from different ſituations as before ſuppoſed, and differ in their rate of ſailing, can they all become in the proper ſtation at one and the ſame time for attacking? A. No.

Q. Was it not the Admiral's practice to make the ſignal for ſhips chacing, to tack alſo, when he judged that they ought to do ſo? A. Generally ſo.

Q. Did he make any ſuch ſignal that morning to the chacing ſhips? A. Not that we could obſerve.

Q. Were not four of the ſhips that were ſent out to chace, the whole of the Vice Admiral of the blue's diviſion, with their ſtation in the line of battle, between the Vice Admiral and the Admiral's own diviſion?

A. I have not given the names of any ſhips that chaced to windward.

Q. Was not the Worceſter one, the Elizabeth, and the Defiance?

A. I believe they may; the Robuſte was one.

Admiral Montague. Did the Robuſte chace?

A. Yes, Sir.

Proſecutor. Did not that leave a wide ſpace, by taking theſe ſhips away, between the Formidable and the Admiral's own diviſion?

A. It certainly extended the diſtance to what it was before.

Court. As you were in chace at that time, could you ſee the diſtance the Vice Admiral was from the Admiral?

A. It is impoſſible for me to aſcertain the diſtance with certainty.

Q. If thoſe four ſhips had been permitted to take their ſtations, inſtead of chacing, would not the two diviſions of the fleet have been more connected, the centre and the

Vice Admiral of the blue, than they were after those ſhips were ſent to chace, and were ſeparated?

A. Undoubtedly they would.

Q. Do you think that ſhips proceeding along an enemy's line ſingly, are expoſed to more or leſs damage from the enemy, than if a number of ſhips proceeded cloſely connected, ſo as to ſupport each other?

A. Undoubtedly more, ſuppoſing the enemy's line to be compact and cloſe.

Q. Did not the chacing ſhips, ſo far as you know, come into action ſeparately, and at conſiderable diſtances from each other?

A. The four ſhips that chaced together, came into action ſeparately, and at ſome conſiderable diſtance from one another.

Q. Were any ſhips ſo near to you as to be of ſupport to each other?

A. I don't know what time you allude to; I was two hours in action, and conſequently nearer ſometimes to our ſhips than at others.

Q. Did part of the chacing ſhips go a-head, and join the center diviſion?

A. I really do not know that.

Q. If the ſix ſhips had not been taken from the Vice Admiral of the blue's diviſion, and ſent out to chace, might not the Vice Admiral of the blue, with his whole diviſion, have gone into action in a connected body, and have ſupported each other?

A. Yes, I ſhould think ſo.

Court. Do you think, that if the Admiral had made the ſignal for forming a regular line, and chacing in that regular line, he could have brought the French fleet ſo ſoon to action? A. No, by no means.

Proſecutor. Was it the van diviſion of the Britiſh fleet, or the chacing ſhips in the rear diviſion, that firſt began the engagement?

A. About eleven o'clock in the morning, I obſerved the van diviſion of the Britiſh fleet engaging with the enemy.

Q. Captain Robinſon ſaid, that at different times of the engagement, you was at different diſtances from other ſhips; now I would aſk, if at any time during the action, theſe ſhips were at ſuch diſtances, as to be able to ſupport each other, and at what diſtances they were at different times from him; how far were the headmoſt and ſternmoſt ſhips from you?

A. I do

A. I do not think any of the four chacing ſhips, that I could ſee, could ſupport each other within my view.

Admiral Keppel. I beg Capt. Robinſon's own words may be taken down; he ſaid four, the Vice Admiral ſays ſix; whatever Capt. Robinſon chuſes to have ſet down, I hope the Court will admit of.

Proſecutor. Were there not ſix ſhips chaced?

A. Four I was ſure of, and I believe there were two more at a greater diſtance, the Defiance and Egmont.

Q. Do you think the damages you received in the engagement, were probably greater than they would have been, if you had engaged in a body with the reſt of your own diviſion?

A. That depends greatly on the circumſtances, the enemy's ſituation, and the number of ſhips engaged.

Court. Was the enemy's line a cloſe one during the engagement?

A. No, Sir, far from it; they were much ſcattered.

Proſecutor. How far do you think the Britiſh fleet was extended, from van to rear, at the beginning of the engagement?

A. I look upon it to be very difficult to aſcertain diſtances between ſhip and ſhip at ſea; but I thought myſelf, who was in the rear of the Britiſh fleet, full three leagues from the van, who were in action.

Court. You ſaid the French fleet was much ſcattered, then their line was extended?

A. I do not know, I was too much engaged, as the Worceſter was the ſternmoſt ſhip from the van.

Q. In what part of the French fleet did you begin the action?

A. I received the fire of two ſhips of the French van, at ten minutes after twelve at noon, for I had a very good obſervation before I began the action.

Q. What part of the French line was it that you received the fire of?

A. Two of the headmoſt ſhips of the French van, about ten minutes after twelve o'clock; I did not return the fire to thoſe ſhips, as I thought they were at too great a diſtance.

Q. With what part of them did you firſt come into action?

A. With the third ſhip of the French van, which was cloſe to me.

Q. Did any of the enemy's ſhips a-head of you bear down, as appeared to you, with an intention to cut you off?

 A. Several

A. Several of them did bear down, but I do not know their motives: I apprehended it was to engage me close, which they did.

Q. Did any of them bear down astern of you, to rake you after you had passed?

A. As I observed before, several ships bore down to engage me, but one particularly bore down right before the wind, came within pistol shot under her top-sails, then her helm, let fall her fore sail, stood on the Worcester's stern, and raked her fore and aft.

Q. Was any of our ships near you at that time, and at what distance was the nearest?

A. I do not know what ships were near me at that time, but believe the Formidable could not be a mile from me.

Q. Did you observe the Formidable when she went into action?

A. In the intervals, when the fire and smoke was clear of me, I observed the Formidable; but I don't know when she went into action.

Q. In the course of the engagement, what ships remained astern of the Formidable?

A. As the engagement continued some time, (I was full two hours engaged) I do not know what time you mean.

Q. From the first time she was in action?

A. I did not come into action till twelve o'clock, and it was past two before I fired the last broadside.

Q. From the time you saw her last, can you recollect the distance?

A. In the course of the engagement I remained astern of the Formidable.

Q. From the time you first saw her, and the distances and situations they were in with respect to each other, were they at wide distances or close?

Court. This is three questions.

Prosecutor. In the course of the engagement, what ships remained astern of the Formidable?

A. There were four sail.

Q. What were their distances and situations with respect to each other, were they close, or at wide distances?

A. At wide distances, or at least I did not observe any of them close, I was so much engaged with my own ship.

Q. Did you observe the Formidable with her mizen top-sail aback, to let those ships close her, the whole time she was engaged, or any part of it, that you looked at her?

A. I did

A. I did not see the mizen top-sail of the Formidable aback, but I observed, as we came up, that the Worcester came up with the Formidable faster, in the latter part of the action, than she did before in different parts of the action; sometimes I could not see at all for smoke.

Q. At what time did you pass the sternmost ship of the enemy?

A. About five minutes after two o'clock in the afternoon.

Q. When the Admiral with the van and center divisions and the ships with him, had passed the rear of the enemy, did they immediately wear, or tack and double upon the enemy, in order to renew the action?

A. I did not see them either wear or tack; I saw the red division making sail to windward, and standing, upon the northward towards the enemy, and they were to windward of us.

President. Do you judge that the action would have been brought on that day, if the Admiral had waited for the fleet to have been more closely connected?

A. No, I don't think they would; I believe the French used their utmost efforts, in the morning, to avoid coming to action, and they tried to get away; they had avoided it every day since the 23d, and had not the wind shifted, they would have availed themselves of it, and not come to action at all.

Court. You said the French fleet was a mile ahead of you, and four ships were astern of the Formidable. Was you the sternmost ship of the British fleet?

A. There is two hours of time difference in that question: when there was four ships astern of the Formidable, it was early in the action; in the latter part of it, a little before two, or half past one, I was not more than a mile from the Formidable.

Prosecutor. Did the Admiral, with the ships that had passed the rear of the French fleet, with him, keep so near to the enemy, after they had passed, as to be in immediate readiness to renew the engagement, when the Vice Admiral of the blue came out of it, or to countenance and support him at the time he continued engaged, with the few ships that were with him?

A. I did not see the Commander in Chief immediately; they had done action before we had, a considerable time.

Q. The first time after you ceased firing yourself, when you did see the Admiral and the ships with him, were they

they then in a ſituation to be ready immediately to renew the engagement?

A. No, I did not; I obſerved when the Worceſter came out of action, that the ſignal for battle was hauled down; how long I cannot tell; and that the Vice Admiral Sir Robert Harland, together with his diviſion, or part of them who were to windward, had ſhortened ſail, and I think had brought to with his main top-ſail to the maſt, as appeared to me, but am not poſitive.

Court. When the French ſhips raked you, what tack was the French fleet upon?

A. I obſerved before, that the ſhip bore down right before the wind, and gave me her broadſide; then he put his helm a ſtarboard, and laid his head to the north, edged away, and raked me fore and aft.

Proſecutor. At the time you mentioned, when you firſt took notice of the Admiral after he came out of the action, and that you obſerved the ſignal for battle was hauled down; how far, according to the beſt of your recollection and judgment, was the Admiral then from the Worceſter?

A. I cannot be clear of the diſtance; as ſoon as I got out of action, I brought too as ſoon as I could get my fore-ſail up.

Q. After you came out of action, did you obſerve the Formidable's motions? A. I did.

A. Did you obſerve her wear, and lay her head towards the enemy, immediately after ſhe came out of the action?

A. The firſt time I obſerved her, I thought ſhe was laying too, but ſoon after that, I obſerved her wear ſhip and lay her head towards the northward, towards the French fleet.

Q. What diſtance do you judge, ſhe was then from the ſternmoſt of the enemy? A. I cannot tell.

Q. While ſhe was wearing, did you obſerve that the ſternmoſt of the French ſhips fired her ſtern chace at her?

A. No, I did not.

Q. If the Admiral, with the body of the fleet, had tacked or wore within the ſame diſtance from the rear of the enemy's fleet, as the Formidable did; might not the French have been immediately re-attacked with that part of the fleet, and Sir Robert Harland's diviſion, that you had deſcribed to windward?

A. As to Sir Robert Harland's diviſion, or part of it that were to windward, had he had ſufficient ſhips, I think he might have done it, but I cannot ſay that of the commander in chief, becauſe I could not ſee him ſo plain.

Court.

Court. You are directed to speak to that part of the question which supposes, that if the Admiral had wore as near to the rear of the French, as the Formidable had wore?

A. The Formidable wore in a line with the French fleet, or part of them; consequently if the Commander in Chief had been in the same situation with the Formidable, and his ships in a proper condition for action, he might have brought the French to action again. 'Tis matter of opinion, I cannot be clear.

Prosecutor. From the very brisk fire that was kept up from our ships that day, have you any reason to suppose that the French were not damaged in proportion with the English?

A. If I might judge of the French by myself, I make no doubt but they received damage. One I saw bear away before the wind, with a frigate to attend her, she must have received considerable damage.

Admiral Montague. As you passed from the van of the French fleet to the rear, when you came out of action, did it appear to you that the French fleet had received as much damage in their masts, yards, and sails, as the English fleet had?

A. As I could form no judgment at that time of the damage sustained by the whole English fleet, I can form no judgment on the comparison between the damages of the English and French fleets in general; but I observed that the French fleet had sustained considerable damage as they passed me, most of them having been in action before.

Q. Except the ship that bore away with her main yard gone, and the frigate that attended her, did you see any other of the French line that had lost their masts and yards, as you passed by?

A. I do not recollect that I did.

Prosecutor. Was there any appearance of any other ship, either English or French, being totally disabled by the loss of any mast?

A. I cannot recollect any, either in one or the other.

Q. When the Formidable wore, and laid her head towards the enemy, did you do so in the Worcester?

A. I did, that was my ship.

Q. Whilst the Formidable and your ship were laying with their heads towards the enemy, did you observe any of the French ships make sail towards them?

A. Yes, several.

Q. Was that the reason of your wearing again, and standing towards the body of the fleet? A. It was.

Q. Was

Q. Did the Formidable do the ſame, about the ſame time?

A. There was very little difference of time between the Formidable and the Worceſter's wearing to the ſouthward, towards our fleet?

Q. After you had wore, and ſtood towards the Admiral, did he appear to you to be alone, or a great body of the fleet about him?

A. There was ſeveral ſhips that paſſed me, before the Admiral came up; I think ſo, I cannot be poſitive.

Court. Was the Worceſter in a condition to renew the action, after ſhe wore the firſt time?

A. No, by no means.

Court. Pleaſe to give an account of the Worceſter's defects, as to maſts, yards, ſails, and rigging?

A. Our main top maſt was ſhot more than two thirds through, about ſix feet above the cap; ſeveral ſhot thro' and thro' the fore-maſt and bowſprit, one in particular in the bowſprit, juſt within the gameling, with a forty-two pounder, the mizen yard ſhot in ſeveral places, a great many ſhot through her ſide and ſtern frame, moſt of the ſtanding and running rigging ſhot away, and all the ſails, eſpecially the main top-ſail, cut to pieces; all the ſtays and back ſtays, in ſhort the whole of her ſtanding and running rigging, the greateſt part of it at leaſt, cut to pieces, together with the braces and bowlings, and I believe there are two or three double headed ſhot in her fore maſt.

Here the Court thought it a ſufficient explanation.

Admiral Montague. Then in the condition you have repreſented the Worceſter to be after the action, ſuppoſing the Admiral had wore, could you have been in a condition to have aſſiſted him, in caſe he had thought proper to re-attack the enemy?

A. Not immediately, by no means.

Q. How long do you think it was before you were in a condition to do it?

A. We were upwards of three hours and a half before we edged down into the line of battle, in our ſtation; we could not get her ready before.

Q. Did you obſerve when the Admiral wore again to ſtand to the ſouthward?

A. I cannot be particular as to the time; about four, I believe, I obſerved him with the ſignal for the line of battle, ſtanding to the ſouthward.

Q. Did you obſerve the Victory and the Formidable meet? A. No, I did not.

Q. When

Q. When the Formidable and Worcester wore the second time, and laid their heads to the enemy, did you observe those French ships you have mentioned to be making sail towards them, then edge away, and begin to form a new line of battle, steering somewhat to leeward of the British fleet?

A. Yes, I saw them undoubtedly edge away, and I thought they were forming a line again to the leeward of the British fleet.

Q. When the Worcester had wore, was the body of the French fleet nearly a-stern of her, or in what position from the Worcester, after you had wore and laid her head to the southward?

A. As near as I can recollect, the body of the French fleet was a-stern of the Worcester, to leeward withal, and forming into a line of battle with their heads to the southward, with their starboard tacks on board.

Prosecutor. You said your ship was not in a condition to renew the attack; I would ask you, in case you had come along side of a French ship, that might have been supposed to have received as much damage in the engagement as yourself, was your loss of men so great, or the number of your guns disabled so many, that you could not have engaged such ship?

A. If she had been complaisant enough to lay a-long side of me, I would have engaged her as long as I had had a barrel of powder on board----I had no guns dismounted.

Q. During that afternoon was you in the Admiral's wake, or nearly so?

A. I was a-stern of the Admiral, and to leeward withal, and got into my station in the line about six o'clock in the evening, or rather before.

Q. What situation was you in on the morning of the 28th at day light, with respect to the Victory?

A. I got into my station I believe in the Vice Admiral of the blue's division, at day light, and a-head, and to windward withal.

Q. Did you see any of the French ships that morning?

A. I saw three large ships, that I took to be French.

Q. Where-about were they?

A. On the lee beam, rather abaft the beam.

Q. At what distance do you reckon them separately?

A. One of them I took to be a large ship, was not more than a mile and half from the Worcester, according to the best of my judgment, and the other two were about three or four miles.

Q. Were any of them, as they appeared to you, nearer

to

to any other parts of the English fleet, than to the Worcester?

A. I believe there were two ships a-stern and to leeward of the Worcester, who were nearer to them than I was.

Q. Were these three ships chaced by the British fleet, or any part of them?

A. I did not see them chaced.

Q. Do you know if the rest of the French fleet were seen that morning, from the Worcester?

A. There were no other ships seen at that time.

Q. Was the signal made for seeing them, by any other ships in the fleet?

A. I did not observe any signal made, but I observed on board the Victory two or three ships signals made, which I apprehended then were for ships to chace, but did not see the chacing flag.

Q. Was you informed by your officers, of any signal being made, of seeing the French fleet to the south east.

A. Of none but the three ships that we saw to the westward; I did not see the body of the French fleet.

Q. Did these three ships crowd sail from us, and which way did they stand in the morning early?

A. At dawn of day I saw them plain; they had much more sail set than we had; they kept the same course so soon as it became clear day, and made all the sail they possibly could from us.

Q. Which way?

A. I cannot be certain as to the point of the compass; but it was to the southward, south east, or south east and by east.

Q. In case the British fleet had chaced those three ships, and suppose the French fleet to be in the direction that they steered, was there not a probability of our undamaged ships coming up with their disabled ships, and in that case might we not have taken them, or if the rest of the fleet had stayed to defend them, might not another engagement have been brought on?

A. With respect to the chacing, there is no doubt of it, the ships that were not damaged might have chaced the ships in sight. As I saw nothing of the body of the French fleet, I can be no judge of their situation, or what they would have done, as it depended wholly on the distance we was then from Ushant or Brest, the port the three ships seemed to be steering for?

Admiral Montague. You say the body of the French fleet were not seen from the mast head of the Worcester; then if Admiral Keppel had ordered the undamaged ships

to

to chace those three ſhips that were running away with all the ſail they could ſet, do you think that the undamaged ſhips might not have been led into the mouth of the enemy, before our damaged ſhips could have come up to their aſſiſtance?

A. That depended wholly upon the diſtance between the body of the fleet and the enemy, and likewiſe whether our chacing ſhips went better than the ſhips chaced?

Court. When did you firſt loſe ſight of the French fleet, in the night of the 27th?

A. I ſaw them very plain, betwixt eight and nine o'clock, at the diſtance of two miles to leeward of the fleet, as near as we could judge, and about ten o'clock at night, or ſoon after, the Maſter and fourth Lieutenant who were upon deck came and informed me that they ſaw ſeveral rockets fired from the French fleet, after which we ſaw their lights no more.

Q. On the 28th at day break, how was the wind, when you diſcovered theſe three ſhips?

A. W. N. W. ſometimes N. W. freſh gales and hazy weather.

Q. Was the ſhip Worceſter under your command, then in a condition to go down upon an enemy's lee ſhore, having a port perhaps to leeward, and begin a general engagement?

A. The Worceſter was in a condition to engage any ſhip at that time, but not in a condition to chace, or to go upon a lee ſhore by any means.

Proſecutor. In caſe the fleet had chaced nearly before the wind, could or could not the Worceſter have carried all her ſails, to have kept company with them?

A. As the Worceſter's main maſt was not injured much, I apprehend before the wind I could have carried all her ſails, having got my main top-maſt fiſhed and ſecured the night before.

Q. What latitude was the Worceſter in at noon on the 27th?

A. In lat. 48° 32" by obſervation, Uſhant eaſt forty leagues diſtant, by the Maſter's account.

Q. What was it at noon on the 28th?

A. In 48° 26" by obſervation, Uſhant N. 80 degrees eaſt 28 leagues.

Q. In ſummer time, ſuppoſing a chace of thirty leagues, was the chance moſt probable of having fair weather, or gales of wind?

A. The wind and weather at that time was extraordinary. We had freſh wind and hazy weather for ſome days. It blew freſh for ſeveral days before. *Admiral*

Admiral Montague. During the courſe of your ſervice, have you not frequently known in ſummer time, very ſevere and hard gales of wind?

A. Undoubtedly, Sir, during a ſervice of forty years; but at the ſame time I think we are not to expect ſuch bad weather in the month of July.

Preſident. How was the weather two or three days after?

A. The next day ſqually, with rain; the next day moderate breezes, but cloudy and likely to rain; the 31ſt moderate and cloudy weather, with rain at times. Wind weſt.

Proſecutor. Being the middle of ſummer, and ſhort nights, do you apprehend it would have been attended with any immediate or imminent danger, if our fleet had purſued the three ſhips, at leaſt ſo far as till they had ſeen them into port, or made the land of Uſhant?

A. This I apprehend depends upon the certainty of the diſtance, as we in a fleet are frequently out in our reckoning.

Q. Independent of reckoning, my queſtion is, till we had ſeen the fleet into port, or made the land of Uſhant?

A. If I had been a ſingle ſhip, and in chace of an enemy, I certainly would have ſtood in till I made the land, or judged myſelf near it. As to a fleet, it depended entirely upon the ſituation of that fleet. If the fleet had been in good order and condition, I ſhould not have heſitated about it.

Q. Are you acquainted with that part of the French coaſt about Uſhant?

A. I am not ſo well acquainted as to run a riſque, without the Maſter on board, who is better acquainted than myſelf with the coaſt?

Q. Is Uſhant at the bottom of a bay, or is it the extremity of the coaſt?

A. Uſhant I apprehend is upon an iſland, detached from the main.

Q. In the morning of the 28th, did the Admiral lay the fleet with their heads to the northward? A. He did.

Q. Before the fleet were laid to the northward, did you obſerve any ſignals made for ſhips to ſet up rigging?

A. No, I did not, if I had, I ſhould have made the ſignal too.

Admiral Montague. Upon the whole then, Sir, did it appear to you, as an old experienced officer, that Admiral Keppel, by his conduct either the 27th or 28th of July, tarniſhed the honour of the Britiſh flag?

A. No,

A. No, I have had the honour of knowing the honourable Admiral for many years; I have always looked upon him as an exceeding good officer, and inwardly a good man, and believe him to be so still, having no reason to think him the contrary.

Adjourned till to-morrow morning ten o'clock.

TWELFTH DAY, WEDNESDAY, JANUARY, 20th.

The Court being met according to adjournment, the evidence of Capt. Robinson was re-assumed.

Admiral Keppel. When you saw the French fleet in the afternoon of the 23d, inform the Court of what force it consisted?

A. I really cannot tell their force, I counted upwards of forty-four sail, large and small.

Q. How was the Vice Admiral of the red division situated at that time, relative to the rest of the British fleet?

A. I do not know, I did not take particular notice.

Q. Do you think the French any time on the 23d, could discover what force the British fleet consisted of?

A. Upon my word, I cannot say.

Q. You was much nearer to the French fleet than the red division was? A. I believe we were.

Q. Did the Admiral pursue the French fleet in the afternoon of the 23d, in a line of battle, carrying a deal of sail? A. He did.

Q. On the 27th July in the morning, how far was the Vice Admiral of the blue, and his division, from the Victory, when the signal was made to chace to leeward?

A. I was not on deck when the signal was made, but came soon after five o'clock, at which time the Victory was a-stern, and to leeward withal, and I apprehend to the best of my judgment, could not be less than two miles a-stern, and to windward.

Q Under what sail was the Vice Admiral of the blue, and the ships in his division, at the time you came upon deck?

A. I cannot say what sail the Vice Admiral was under, but the Worcester was under close reefed top sails, fore sail, main top stay sail, I think, and fore top stay sail.

Q. Do you understand, when the signal is made to chace to windward, that it obliges you to stand upon one tack, till the Admiral makes his signal for you to tack?

A. I always understood when a ship's signal is made to chace to windward, that he was obliged to continue and make sail in compliance with the signal, till he got to such a diſtance as that he could ſee the Admiral's ſignal to call him in again, or tack when the Admiral thought proper.

Q. Could you not have tacked upon that ſignal, without the Admiral's making the ſignal for you to tack?

A. Yes undoubtedly.

Q. Was you authorized?

A. Not in that caſe, when we chace, I apprehend I am not.

Q. Are there not quarter ſignals for ſhips to chace upon, when the Admiral would have them to chace upon a quarter, between any two points whatever; ſuppoſe the N. and W.? A. Certainly there are.

Preſident. When ſignal is made to chace to windward, do you or do you not think, that you are authorized to take advantage of the wind, by tacking without ſignal?

A. Yes, when I have an object in view.

Admiral Montague. Suppoſe you have not an object in view, but if ſignal is made by the Admiral to chace to windward, do not you look upon it as your duty to get ſo far to windward in the wind's eye, as you can? A. I do.

Admiral Keppel. Would you not have tacked before you did, without waiting for the ſignal, if you had expected the fleet to cloſe with the enemy ſo ſoon?

A. Certainly I ſhould have tacked, when I found the object of our chacing anſwered, and that was to endeavour to bring the French fleet to action, as I apprehended.

Q. When you ſaw the Engliſh fleet engaging, did you keep your wind, or could you by leading with a very rapful ſail, have cloſed in with thoſe ſhips ſooner than you did?

A. If I had kept my wind, I could have weathered more than half the whole French fleet, the wind having ſhifted two or three points to the weſtward, but I was obliged to keep away, in order to join my diviſion as ſoon as I could; in the mean time the French fleet edged away, and I was afraid they would have cut me off from my diviſion.

Q. Could you imagine it poſſible for the Admiral to make a ſignal, that ſhould put you in that ſituation?

A. Not intentionally, I am clear.

Q. At the time there were four ſhips, as you deſcribed yeſterday, a-ſtern of the Formidable, what ſhip was the neareſt of theſe four to the Worceſter?

A. I believe it was the Robuſte. I think ſo.

Q. Was it at this time that you ſuppoſed yourſelf about a mile from the Formidable? A. No, by no means.

Q. Were there any ſhips between you and the Formidable, at the time you came out of action?

A. There were not. Q. Can

Q. Can you inform the Court, what became of the four ſhips that you mentioned a-ſtern of the Formidable, during the action?

A. Every one of the ſhips a-head of the Worceſter were engaging the enemy, conſequently ſtood on, and I believe went to leeward of the Formidable, to the beſt of my knowledge, when the ſmoke would admit of my taking notice of any of the ſhips a-head of me, which was ſeldom.

Q. Was the Formidable's mizen top ſail a-back, at any of thoſe times when thoſe ſhips paſſed, as you believe?

A. I never ſaw the Formidable's mizen top ſail a-back.

Q. Did thoſe ſhips paſs to leeward and a-head of the Formidable; when in action, in conſequence of the Admiral's ſignal at five o'clock, to chace to windward?

A. Had the ſignal not been made to chace to windward, it is poſſible thoſe ſhips would have been in a different ſituation to what they were in at that time.

Q. That does not anſwer my queſtion. My queſtion is, whether they ran to leeward, and a-head of the Formidable, in conſequence of my ſignal being made at five o'clock, to chace to windward?

A. I do not know their reaſons, it is impoſſible for me to know, for they engaged the enemy before the Worceſter, being a-head of me on that tack.

Q. Do you mean they were never ſo cloſe as to give ſuccour to the Vice Admiral of the blue, and to one another?

A. I don't know, during the action, that we were ever nearer than half a mile of one another, and ſometimes more, when the ſmoke would permit us to ſee one another.

Q. Does *ſometimes* mean the beginning of the action, or what time; ſince *ſometimes* takes in various periods?

A. I cannot be particular as to the time, but it was between five minutes after twelve o'clock at noon, and five minutes after two in the afternoon, the time I was engaged.

Q. Does he mean to ſay, that at no time between five minutes paſt twelve, and five minutes paſt two, the ſhips were not cloſed together, ſo as to ſupport each other, nearer than half a mile?

A. I do not recollect their being cloſer during that time.

Q. Do you recollect that they were not?

A. I really cannot judge of the whole.

Admiral Keppel. I apprehend, as I ſtand to examine Capt. Robinſon, I may aſk him queſtions that he has anſwered before; and I now remind him, that he takes in a large time of two hours; I muſt by all means pin him to time directly.

Prosecutor. I desire the indulgence of the Court, to order what Capt. Robinson has said, to be read to him.

Agreed. It was accordingly read.

Admiral Keppel. As you have said that three ships passed a-head of the Formidable, and to leeward during the action, how do you reconcile that, with their never being nearer than half a mile?

A. I did not say that they passed a-head of the Formidable; they passed a-head of the Worcester, from the situation they were in, astern of the Formidable.

Court. The Court informed the evidence that he said the Formidable.

Admiral Keppel. If they were a-stern of the Formidable when in action, and got out of the action before her, must they not have passed her during the action?

A. I do not know.

Q. You have stated the ship to be much exposed, and that you began to engage with the second or third ship of the enemy's van, till you got to the rear; how many men had you killed or wounded?

A. I had only three men killed, and five wounded, but some of the men died of their wounds in two days after.

Q. Was the Victory standing towards the enemy, on the larboard tack, when you first saw her after you came out of the action?

A. I think she was.

Q. Can you inform the Court the positive time you first wore, after you came out of action and laid your head towards the enemy?

A. I cannot say the positive time.

Q. Can you say any time near the positive time?

A. I believe it was near twelve, but cannot be positive.

Q. How long did you stand upon the larboard tack, after you had wore towards the enemy; and when standing you wore back to the Admiral, was it by signal?

A. The moment I wore, I brought to; I did not make sail; I was not in a situation to make sail.

Q. When you wore, standing back to the Admiral, was it by signal? A. No, I did not see the Admiral.

Q. After you wore back to the Admiral, how near did the Admiral pass to the Worcester.

A. I really do not recollect how near; but no great distance? Q. Did you pass her?

A. I believe the Admiral passed the Worcester.

Q. Do you mean after the Worcester wore the second time? A. Yes.

Q. Was the Admiral then upon the larboard tack.

A. I believe he was.

Q. Did

Q. Did you see the signal flying on board the Admiral at that time, for a line of battle a-head ?

A. No, I did not see the signal for a line of battle at that time ; I saw it about four o'clock.

Q. Had you no officer appointed to observe the Admiral's signals ?

A. I had, but he was wounded early in the action.

Q. When you passed the Admiral, or the Admiral passed you, do you recollect where the Formidable was at this time ?

A. To the best of my knowledge she was to windward of the Worcester.

Q. How near ?

A. I cannot ascertain the distance ; but not far ; a very little way, I think.

Q. Do you say positively, that when you wore the second time, after the action, to stand towards the Admiral, several ships passed you a-head of the Victory, on the larboard tack ?

A. I am positive that some ships did ; what they were I don't know ; and that one of the ships, to the best of my remembrance hailed the Worcester, and told her to get out of the way, for that the Admiral was coming up.

Q. Was the Worcester and that ship to the southward of the Victory at the time she hailed her ?

A. I do not recollect.

Q. I would remind you the southward is astern of the Victory, when the Victory was upon the larboard tack ?

A. I do not recollect.

Q. Do you know of any other ship ?

A. I was so much engaged putting my ship to rights at that time, that I really did not observe.

Q. What time did you first observe the French fleet forming their line on the starboard tack and standing towards the British Fleet, on the 27th, after the action ?

A. I observed some of the French ships standing with their heads to the southward, between two and three o'clock. I cannot positively say the exact time.

Q. Was it before you wore towards the British Admiral ?

A. Yes, sir.

Q. When you say you got into your station in the Admiral's wake, at six o'clock in the evening, on the 27th, do you then mean you was in the wake of the Vice Admiral of your own division, or of the Commander in chief ?

A. I mean, that I was in my station in the Vice Admiral of the blue's division, as near as I could get, between the Vengeance and the Elizabeth. The Vice Admiral of the Blue was then to windward of us, and the Commander in Chief a-head, and to windward withal.

Q. Do you mean that the Commander in Chief was upon the weather-bow of the Worcester?

A. He was certainly to windward, but how many points I do not know; a-head and to windward withal, as near as we could obferve on board.

Q. When the Admiral laid his head to the northward, on the 28th, did he bring to on the larboard tack?

A. I believe, on the 28th in the morning, when the Admiral made the fignal to wear, they laid their heads to the northward, and brought to. I think fo, to the beft of my recollection.

Q. Did he not ftand before the wind at all after wearing?

A. I do not recollect with certainty that he did; he might.---I recollect myfelf, he did make the fignal for the line, and ftood on a little while.

Q. After the fleet was laid to on the larboard tack, was your fhip one of thofe that made the fignal to fet up her rigging?

A. I made none at all; nor did I fee a fignal. I wanted it.

Q. There was one queftion that I am afraid I did not fpeak diftinctly, relative to Capt. Robinfon's paffing the Victory; as you faid, that while he was paffing, feveral fhips paffed him after the action, and gave this reafon for it, that he was hailed by a fhip that told him to get out of the way, for the Admiral was coming up; what does he mean by faying, that he don't recollect, whether the fhip that hailed him was a head or a-ftern of the Admiral?

A. Upon recollection, I think that he muft be a-head, upon the larboard tack, or elfe he would not have told me to get out of the way; but I cannot be pofitive.

Q. Do you not recollect, whether the fhip that hailed you was upon the larboard, or ftarboard tack?

A. As I have obferved before, I cannot be pofitive.

Q. Do you recollect whether it was a two-decked or a three-decked fhip that hailed you? A. I really do not.

Admiral Montague. Do you remember what anfwer you made to the fhip that hailed you?

A. Perfectly well, Sir, my anfwer was, that they faw my fituation, and it was out of my power to get out of their way, but would as foon as ever I could.

Q. When you was hailed, did not you naturally look to fee where the Admiral was?

A. I did not fee the Admiral, but they told me, the Admiral was aftern coming up.

Prefident. What happened in confequence of that anfwer; did the fhip that hailed you, pafs by you to windward, or leeward, or bring to?

A. To the beft of my recollection, fhe paffed on.

Q. Did

Q. Did the Admiral paſs you, ahead, to windward or to leeward?

A. I do not recollect, being ſo much engaged to get my ſhip in order for action.

Captain Robinſon was ordered to withdraw, and JOSEPH SEWELL, *Maſter of the Worceſter, called and ſworn.*

Proſecutor. Do you remember ſeeing three ſhips of the enemy, on the 28th of July, at day-light? A. Yes.

Q. At what diſtance do you reckon they were from the Britiſh fleet?

A. The ſternmoſt ſhip of the three, was from the Worceſter, a ſhort mile and a half, as I judged.

Q. Was ſhe nearer to any other part of the fleet, than to the Worceſter?

A. There was a ſhip a little aſtern of the Worceſter, rather upon the larboard quarter, which appeared to me to be a little nearer than we were.

Q. Do you remember when the Worceſter came out of the action, at what diſtance the Admiral, and the body of the fleet, then was beyond the rear of the enemy?

A. As near as I can judge, they were to the ſouthward of the Worceſter about two or three miles, their heads towards the enemy, with their larboard tacks on board: I remember ſeeing the Vice Admiral of the red, and ſome ſhips with him, to windward of the Admiral, and a-head withal.

Q. Were they alſo upon the larboard tack?

A. The ſhips I ſaw were upon the larboard tack.

Admiral Keppel. The witneſs has ſaid, that when they diſcovered the ſhips to leeward, in the morning, upon their lee quarter, there was another ſhip nearer than the Worceſter, and he deſcribes himſelf to be within a mile and a half of theſe ſhips? did the Worceſter, or the ſhips near her, lay their heads to theſe ſhips ſo very near, or hoiſt any ſignal to the Admiral, informing him that they were enemies?

A. The Worceſter did not.

Q. You don't know whether the other ſhips did?

A. No, my attention was otherwiſe engaged.

Q. What time did the Worceſter come out of action on the 27th. A. About two o'clock.

Preſident. Had your ſhip's ſignal been thrown out to chace at that time, was you in a condition to chace at the time you ſaw the ſhips about a mile and a half from you?

A. No, we were not.

Q. When you came out of action about two, did you ſee the Victory then? A. I did not.

Q. How ſoon did you ſee her afterwards?
A. About three o'clock.
Q. Was ſhe then upon the larboard tack?
A. She was bearing down, and had the ſignal flying for a line of battle.
Q. Did you at that time ſee any ſhips formed in a line of battle, ahead or aſtern of her?
A. No, I did not, there was a great many ſhips around her.
Q. Do you mean a-head of the Victory?
A. There were ſome a-head and ſome on each ſide of her.
Q. Can you name any? A. No, I cannot.
Q. Do you mean the Vice Admiral of the red, amongſt this number, and the ſhips of his diviſion?
A. They were to windward of them; I cannot recollect whether any of thoſe ſhips bore down with him at that time.
Q. Then you cannot name any individual ſhip?
A. Not one of them.
Q. Can you ſay whether theſe ſhips ſo around the Admiral, or ahead of the Admiral, were with their larboard or ſtarboard tacks on board?
A. They were going down before the wind, the Admiral having the ſignal for the line of battle flying at the ſame time.
Q. Are you quite exact as to the time?
A. It was between three and four in the afternoon.
Q. Did the Worceſter wear, and lay her head towards the enemy, after ſhe came out of the action? A. She did.
Q. How long did ſhe continue on that tack before ſhe wore again? A. About half an hour.
Q. How near did ſhe paſs the Victory, ſtanding upon the larboard tack after wearing again, and ſtanding to the ſouthward? A. About a mile.
Q. Do you recollect what time it was?
A. About three o'clock I think.
Q. Do you recollect any ſhip hailing you at this time of paſſing the Victory?
A. I recollect to the beſt of my knowledge, there was a ſhip that hailed us, and deſired us to endeavour to make more ſail to get out of the way of her, as the Admiral was then aſtern of him, and other ſhips on each ſide of him.
Q. Was that ſhip then upon the larboard or ſtarboard tack?
A. Neither one, nor the other, ſhe was coming down upon us right before the wind.
Q. Do you recollect the name of that ſhip? A. I cannot.
Q. Was ſhe a two or three decker? A. A three

A. A three deck ſhip.

Q. You have ſaid the Admiral was coming down before the wind, am I to underſtand ſhe was ſailing before the wind, or in a ſtate of wearing?

A. She was going before the wind in a ſtate of wearing, to haul up with the ſtarboard tacks to form the line.

Q. Did you ſee the ſignal flying for wearing at that time?

Preſident. Did you ſee the ſignal for the line at that time?

A. I did.

Q. I would ask whether that is the time that you meant the ſhips were a-head of the Victory?

A. No, afterwards.

Court. When you came out of the action, what diſtance was you from the Formidable?

A. About a quarter of a mile.

Q. Did you make your ſignal for ſetting up your rigging, in the morning of the 28th.

A. We did; we hoiſted the pendant at the enſign ſtaff, and ſeveral other ſhips did the ſame.

Evidence ordered to withdraw.

GEORGE DUNN, *ſecond Lieutenant of the Worceſter, called and ſworn.*

Court. *Ordered the Judge Advocate to put the ſame queſtions to him, as had been put to the Maſter by the Proſecutor and Priſoner, which being put in order, his anſwers coroborated the Maſter's.*

Proſecutor. When you ſaw the Vice Admiral of the red, as you mentioned, upon your weather beam; was he making ſail, or laying to?

A. To the beſt of my remembrance he was laying to.

Ordered to withdraw.

Proſecutor. *Deſired the approbation of the court, for the Judge Advocate to read the Admiral's letter to the Admiralty, of 30th of July, which was read as follows:*

SIR, *Victory at Sea, July 30th*, 1778.

" My letters of the 23d and 24th inſtant, by the Peggy and Union cutters, acquainted you for their Lordſhips information, that I was in purſuit, with the King's fleet under my command, of a numerous fleet of French ſhips of war.

" From that time to the 27th, the winds conſtantly in the S. W. and N. W. quarters, ſometimes blowing ſtrong, and the French fleet always to windward going large; I made uſe of every method to cloſe in with them that was poſſible, keeping the King's ſhips at the ſame time collected, as much as the nature of a purſuit would

admit

admit of, and which became neceſſary from the cautious manner the French proceeded in, and the diſinclination that appeared in them to allow of my bringing the King's ſhips cloſe to a regular engagement: This left but little other chance of getting in with them, than by ſeizing the opportunity that offered, the morning of the 27th, by the wind's admitting of the van of the King's fleet under my command leading up with, and cloſing with their center and rear.

" The French fleet began firing upon the headmoſt of Vice Admiral Sir Robert Harland's diviſion, and the ſhips with him, as they led up; which cannonade the leading ſhips and the Vice Admiral ſoon returned, as did every ſhip as they could cloſe up: The chace had occaſioned their being extended, nevertheleſs they were all ſoon in battle.

" The fleets, being upon different tacks, paſſed each other very cloſe: The object of the French ſeemed to be the diſabling the King's ſhips in their maſts and ſails, in which they ſo far ſucceeded, as to prevent many of the ſhips of my fleet being able to follow me when I wore to ſtand after the French fleet; this obliged me to wear again, to join thoſe ſhips, and thereby allowed of the French forming their fleet again, and ranging it in a line to the leeward of the King's fleet towards the cloſe of the day; which I did not diſcourage, but allowed of their doing it without firing upon them, thinking they meant handſomely to try their force with us the next morning; but they had been ſo beaten in the day, that they took the advantage of the night to go off.

" The wind and weather being ſuch, that they could reach their own ſhores before there was any chance of the King's ſhips getting up with them, in the ſtate the ſhips were in, in their maſts, yards, and ſails, left me no choice of what was adviſeable and proper to do.

" The ſpirited conduct of Vice Admiral Sir Robert Harland, Vice Admiral Sir Hugh Palliſer, with the Captains of the fleet, ſupported by their officers and men, deſerve much commendation.

" A liſt of the killed and wounded is herewith incloſed.

" I ſend Captain Faulkner, Captain of the Victory, with this account to their Lordſhips, and am, Sir,

" Your moſt obedient, and humble Servant,

A. KEPPEL.

Philip Stephens, Eſq.
Secretary of the Admiralty.

Liſt

List of men killed and wounded, in the action with the French fleet, the 27th of July, 1778

Ships Names.	Killed.	Wounded.	Ships Names.	Killed.	Wounded.
Monarch	2	9	Vengeance	4	18
Exeter	4	6	Worcester	3	5
Queen	1	2	Elizabeth	0	7
Shrewsbury	3	6	Defiance	8	17
Berwick	10	11	Robuste	5	17
Stirling Castle	2	11	Formidable	16	17
Courageux	6	13	Ocean	2	18
Thunderer	2	5	America	1	17
Vigilant	2	3	Terrible	9	21
Victory	11	24	Egmont	12	19
Foudroyant	5	18	Ramillies	12	16
Prince George	5	15	Total	133	373

Officers wounded.

Lieut. Nicholas Clifford, 2d of the Formidable.
Lieut. William Samwell, 3d of the Shrewsbury.
Lieut. John M'Donald, of the marines--Prince George.
Surgeon of the Elizabeth.

A. KEPPEL.

Prosecutor. I desire that the Admiral's journals of the 27th and 28th of July be read, from the beginning of the action, till the losing sight of the French fleet.

The Court then ordered them to be read from the ship's books, as follows:

July 27, 1778.

AT Ten A. M. made the signal and tacked; a large body of the French fleet appeared in great confusion.

At half past eleven, the ships a-head began to engage, the French ships having fired at the van of our fleet first. Ditto, made the signal for our fleet to engage; we were now on contrary tacks with the French, they striving to fetch as far to windward as they could, firing as they passed our ships; several of them fired at the Victory; but seeing we could fetch the Bretagne, we passed two of their ships; and reserved for the French Admiral's ship.

At three quarters past eleven, got along side of the Bretagne, and at noon engaged La Ville de Paris.

At one, P. M. engaging the six sail that were a-stern of the French Admiral.

At half past one made the signal, and wore our ship greatly damaged in rigging and sails.

At two made the signal for the line of battle a-head, at one

one cable's length diſtance, and brought to, to repair the rigging.

At half paſt two, one of the French ſhips who had loſt her main-yard and mizen top-maſt ran away to leeward, and a frigate to attend her.

At three quarters paſt two the French wore and formed the line with their heads towards us.

At ſeven minutes paſt three, made the ſignal for the ſhips to windward to bear down into our wake, that they might ſee it more diſtinctly, we hauled down the ſignal for the line of battle.

At fifty minutes paſt three, finding the ſignal for bear-down into our wake was not ſeen, we hauled down that, and made the ſignal for the line again, we now ſteered S. S. E. to join our ſhips to leeward and form the line of battle.

At half paſt four repeated the ſignal for the ſhips to bear down into our wake.

At five made the ſignal for the ſhips to get into their ſtations in the line, and ſent the Milford to deſire Sir Robert Harland to make ſail with his diviſion and form the line in the van, which he did.

The French line formed with twenty-eight ſail, and two ſhips of fifty or ſixty guns. Employed in ſplicing the rigging, which is very much damaged, having loſt ſeven main ſhrowds and the major part of the top-maſts and running rigging, with all the top-ſails, courſes and ſtay-ſails very much damaged. At ſeven made each particular ſhip's ſignal of the Vice Admiral of the blue's diviſion, except the Formidable, who has not got her fore-top-ſails bent, to come into their ſtations for the line. The French line coming up, they have thrown the ſhips that received the leaſt damage, into their van. The French Admiral has fourteen ſail of the line a-head, and thirteen a-ſtern of him, with two fifty or fifty-four gun ſhips, four frigates, one ſchooner and three brigs.

At eight o'clock, three of the French ſhips nearly abreaſt of us to the leeward, we ſtanding on under double reefed top-ſails and fore-ſails to give Sir Hugh Palliſer and his diviſion more time to get into the line, preparing to renew the engagement at day-light.

At eleven minutes paſt eleven, one of the headmoſt ſhips of the French fired two rockets, and ſoon after one falſe fire, and at twelve loſt ſight of their lights.

At four o'clock in the morning of the 28th, wore ſhip, and made the Prince George and Bienfaiſant ſignal to chace three ſail in the S. E. quarter, which were all we could ſee, and them we took to be French. At

At nine called them in. The fleet all employed in ſplicing the rigging, and our carpenters employed in fiſhing the main and mizen maſts that were ſhot through.

Captain Beazely, *of the Formidable, was then called and ſworn.*

Proſecutor. Do you remember ſeeing the French fleet, in the morning of the 27th? A. Yes.

Q. Did they appear to you, at any time, to be in a line of battle? A. They did.

Q. Do you remember the ſituation of the Vice Admiral of the blue, and his diviſion, that morning, with reſpect to the Admiral, whether they were a-head of him, upon his lee bow, or how otherwiſe?

A. The Vice Admiral of the blue was upon the Admiral's lee bow, and a-head withal.

Q. Do you remember a ſignal being made for ſix ſhips, or how many, of the Vice Admiral of the blue's diviſion, to chace?

A. To the beſt of my recollection, ſix ſhips of the blue diviſion.

Q. Did that ſignal cauſe thoſe ſhips to be diſperſed and ſcattered from their Admiral, and from each other?

A. It cauſed thoſe ſhips to be extended from their Admiral; but whether they were ſcattered more, I cannot recollect.

Q. In the morning, when the Vice Admiral and his diviſion were ſituated as you have deſcribed, were they not in a proper ſituation and diſtance for readily taking their ſtation in a line of battle, if the ſignal had been made?

A. They appeared ſo to me, if the ſignal for forming a line of battle had been made upon the larboard tack.

Q. If all the ſhips of that diviſion had been ſuffered to remain with their Admiral, might they not have gone into action with him in a joint body, ſo as to ſupport each other? A. Yes.

Q. Did the chacing ſhips, ſo far as you know, come into action ſeparately, and at great diſtances from each other?

A. They appeared ſo to me, as they were aſtern.

Q. Did part of them by chacing, go a-head of the Formidable, and join the center diviſion?

A. Yes, two of them.

Q. Did the taking away of theſe ſhips from the Vice Admiral, leave him to go into action equally ſupported as the other flag officers? A. No.

Q. Was

Q. Was any of the ſhips of the Vice Admiral of the blue's diviſion within gun-ſhot of the Formidable ?

A. When ſhe began the action, except the Ocean, then to leeward of us, the neareſt ſhip that I recollect, was more than half a mile from us.

Q. During the action, were not four of our ſhips at a diſtance aſtern, not together, but ſeparated from each other ?

A. They appeared ſo before the action began, but afterwards I cannot anſwer to it.

Q. During the time the Formidable was engaged, and paſſing along the French line, were any ſhips ſo near her as to afford a ſupport to each other, except at one time a ſhip ſhot up under her ſtern ſo cloſe in the thick ſmoke, that to avoid being on board her, was obliged to run to leeward, which rendered our fire uſeleſs ?

A. After the Formidable had opened her firing, I obſerved no ſhip whatever, except one of the Vice Admiral of the blue's diviſion, coming under her lee.

Q. What ſhip was that ſuppoſed to be ?

A. I cannot ſpeak to that.

Q. With what part of the French line did the Formidable begin a cloſe action.

A. One ſhip a-head of the French Admiral, in the center of their fleet.

Q. Did ſhe not receive the fire of ſeveral ſhips of the French van, which ſhe did not return, 'till ſhe began a cloſe action herſelf ? A. Yes.

Q. Do you think the damages the Formidable received, were not much greater than they probably would have been, if ſhe had gone in a body with the reſt of the Vice Admiral of the blue's diviſion ?

A. Moſt undoubtedly.

Q. As you paſſed along the French line, did they appear to be more irregular than might reaſonably be expected, after having been engaged with the van and center diviſions, before we came the length of them ?

A. No.

Q. The four ſhips you ſpoke of aſtern being at a diſtance, did not the Formidable back her mizen topſail, in order to proceed ſlow along the enemy's line, and let thoſe ſhips cloſe ?

A. The mizen topſail was backed to prevent her from ſhooting a-head, in the way of the Ocean's fire, and was alſo for the ſhips to cloſe us aſtern.

Q. Did not the Formidable begin the engagement within muſket ſhot? A. Yes.

Q. Did

Q. Did ſhe paſs within the ſame diſtance along every ſhip of the French line, to the rear-moſt ſhip?

A. Nearer to ſome of them, and at a greater diſtance from others.

Q. I think you have ſaid, that ſome of the Vice Admiral of the blue's diviſion joined the center diviſion, then was not the Admiral ſupported with the whole of his own diviſion, and with that part of the Vice Admiral of the blue's diviſion?

A. I have ſaid before, that the Vice Admiral of the blue's diviſion had paſſed, but what number the Admiral was ſupported by, I cannot ſay.

Q. In paſſing along the enemy's line, did it, or did it not appear to you, that ſeveral of them were much damaged, they not keeping up ſo briſk a fire as many of the reſt.

A. I did not perceive any particular damage that any of their ſhips had received, but that the center Admiral, and two other ſhips, returned us very little fire.

Q. Did you obſerve one of them diſabled, and run down to leeward out of the line, attended by a frigate, after we had paſſed them?

A. One ſhip with her main yard down, quitted the line, attended by a frigate.

Q. How long upon the whole do you reckon the Formidable was engaged?

A. I cannot ſpeak exactly as to the time, to the beſt of my recollection, an hour and forty minutes.

Q. When the Admiral, with the van and center diviſions, had paſſed the rear of the French fleet, did he immediately wear and double upon the enemy, and continue the engagement?

A. 'Tis impoſſible for me to ſay when the Admiral did wear.

Q. When the Formidable came the length of the rear of the enemy, was the Admiral and the reſt of the fleet ſo near to the rear of the enemy, as immediately to renew the engagement, or to have ſuccoured the Vice Admiral of the blue, in caſe the rear of the enemy had bore down to cut him off? A. No.

Q. When the Formidable ceaſed firing, do you not remember that you and myſelf took notice that the Admiral, with the body of the fleet about him, were ſtanding towards us, and that I therefore ordered the ſhip immediately to be wore?

A. I recollect, that after the Formidable had paſſed the enemy's rear, the Vice Admiral of the blue directed the

the ſhip to be immediately wore; I then obſerved the Victory, with ſeveral ſhips about her, ſtanding towards the enemy.

Q. At what diſtance do you reckon the Admiral, and thoſe ſhips that were with him, were at that time from the Formidable? A. Two miles.

Q. When the Formidable wore, as you before mentioned, were we then directly in the ſtream of the enemy's line, or in the wake of the ſternmoſt ſhips?

A. In the wake of the ſternmoſt ſhip of the enemy.

Q. About what diſtance from them?

A. Random ſhot.

Q. Was that the time you ſpeak of, when you reckoned the Victory was two miles diſtant from the Formidable?

A. At the time ſhe was wearing.

Q. Whilſt the Formidable was wearing, did not the ſternmoſt of the enemy's ſhips fire her ſtern-chace at her, and edge away and bring ſome of her after guns to bear on her?

A. I recollect, after the helm was a-weather, one or two ſhot was fired at her.

Preſident. Were they near enough to hit her?

A. Yes, the ſhot paſſed clear under her quarter.

Proſecutor. Whilſt the Formidable lay with her head to the enemy, were not the officers and men ordered to return to their quarters, in expectation of going again into action, when the Admiral ſhould come up with the fleet?

A. Yes, immediately after the ſhip was wore.

Q. After laying that way a little while, did you obſerve three of the enemy's ſhips making ſail directly towards the Formidable?

A. Yes, pointed immediately to her.

Q. At this time was not the Formidable nearer to theſe French ſhips, than the Victory was to her?

A. The Formidable was nearer to the Victory, than the enemy's three ſhips.

Q. When the Formidable wore again, did theſe French ſhips edge away, and begin to form into a line of battle a-head, pointing to leeward of the Engliſh fleet?

A. Yes.

Q. Did you ſee the Vice Admiral of the red, and his diviſion, at the time the Formidable was laying with her head towards the enemy, and whereabouts were they?

A. I ſaw them to windward.

Q. If the Victory, and the other ſhips with the Admiral, had wore as near to the rear of the enemy as the Formidable

midable did, after coming out of the engagement, the Vice Admiral of the red having doubled upon the rear of the enemy, might not the engagement have been immediately renewed, when the Vice Admiral of the blue came out of the engagement, and by that means prevented the enemy from forming a new line?

Admiral Montague. If the Admiral with his division, immediately after he came out of the action, had wore as near as the Formidable did wear, the Vice Admiral of the blue and his division being then in action, would it not have endangered the ships falling aboard each other, one upon one tack, and the other upon the other?

A. I apprehend not.

Prosecutor. Suppose, Sir, the Admiral with the ships that were with him, had continued to advance towards the enemy, with the signal for battle flying, at the same time the Vice Admiral of the red had bore down upon the enemy, do you not conceive, that the French, in that case, might have been attacked, and prevented forming a new line, which they were doing with their heads towards the British fleet?

A. If the Vice Admiral of the red, and his division, had bore down, I conceive it would have prevented the French from forming their line so immediately as they did.

Prosecutor. You have not attended to that part of the question that supposes, "If the Admiral had advanced with the rest of the ships at the same time."

A. If the Admiral had advanced with the ships, it would have very much assisted in obstructing the forming their line.

Court. Do you know the state of the Admiral's ships that were about him? A. No, Sir.

Q. Do you know the state of the Vice Admiral of the red's division?

A. I know the state of no ship, but that I commanded in battle?

Q. What condition was the Formidable in when she came out of action?

A. All her sails, that were set, were cut to pieces, the gibs and all the stay sails.

Q. In general, was she much damaged?

A. Very much.

Q. Was she fit immediately to go again into action?

A. She was, but not to pursue an enemy.

It being now four o'clock, the Court adjourned, until ten o'clock to-morrow morning.

THIRTEENTH DAY, THURSDAY, JANUARY 21st.

The Court being met at ten o'clock, and the Prisoner brought in, Capt. Beazely's evidence was continued.

Prosecutor. Capt. Beazely, if the Admiral, at that time, did not think fit to re-attack in a line of battle, might he not have immediately formed one, by making the signal for the Vice Admiral of the red, with his division, who was then to windward, to take the lead on that tack, in place of the Vice Admiral of the blue, who was then just come out of action?

A. I saw nothing to the contrary.

Q. Did the enemy, from their motions, shew a disposition towards renewing the engagement?

A. Not till after they began forming their line to leeward, as I saw.

Q. Did the British fleet appear to avoid renewing the action? A. Yes.

Q. After the Formidable wore a second time, did the Victory and Formidable meet?

A. They passed each other.

Q. When the Victory and Formidable had passed each other, did the Victory stand on, or did she wear under the Formidable's stern?

A. She wore a-stern of the Formidable.

Q. Did she first run to leeward, and afterwards haul her wind?

A. She appeared to me to go from the wind.

Q. Did this leave the Formidable a-stern, and to windward withal, of her wake? A. Yes.

Q. When the Victory had wore, and run a little to leeward, as you have described, did she afterwards haul her wind to the southward?

A. She appeared to do so, to me.

Q. Were not the French fleet a-stern? A. Yes.

Q. Did not the Victory continue to stand the same way the rest of that afternoon? A. Yes.

Q. And the following night?

A. Till day-light the next morning.

Q. Do you recollect what sail the Victory carried during the afternoon?

A. I do not recollect that particular.

Q. Did not the Victory always out-sail the Formidable with the same sail? A. Yes.

Q. After the Victory was standing to the southward, did

did the French stand the same way, pointing somewhat to leeward of the British fleet? A. Yes.

Q. Did the Vice Admiral of the red, and his division, bear down into the Admiral's wake that afternoon?

A. Yes.

Q. Was that his own, or the Vice Admiral of the blue's station upon that tack?

A. In a line of battle, on the starboard tack, it was the Vice Admiral of the blue's station.

Q. Do you know whether that was done in consequence of the signal flying, or by particular orders from the Commander in Chief? A. I do not.

Q. Did you observe him afterwards make sail a-head of the Admiral, into his own station? A. Yes.

Q. From the various motions of the Admiral during that afternoon, did you conclude that he had no intention to renew the engagement till the next morning?

A. It appeared so to me; and I expressed these sentiments to the Vice Admiral at the time.

President. When was that?

A. In the afternoon, after the signal for battle was hauled down, when he pointed to the southward.

Q. Can you say any hour?

A. The time betwixt the signal for battle being hauled down, and the fleet's pointing to the southward, at the time it was dark, when he sent for me from the forecastle, the ship was in so much confusion that I could not attend to any particular hour.

President. Do you know of any conversation that passed between the Captain of the Fox and the Vice Admiral?

A. I never heard the Fox hail the Formidable.

Q. Did you see the Fox come under the Vice Admiral's stern?

A. I did not see the Fox till I heard her ship's company cheer the Formidable.

Q. Was not you informed what brought the Fox there? A. Not at that time.

Q. At what time afterwards? A. After dark.

Q. How far do you reckon the Formidable might be from the Victory, half an hour after the Victory passed to leeward of her?

A. Not more than half a mile.

Q. After the Admiral stood to the southward as before mentioned, did the Formidable first haul out of the way of other ships, to take their station betwixt her and the Victory? A. Yes.

Q. How many ſhips, in the line of battle, were ſtationed betwixt the Victory and the Formidable?

A. The Formidable was the ninth ſhip from the Admiral, in the line of battle.

Admiral Montague. Then there were eight betwixt, were there? A. Yes, Sir.

Proſecutor. After the Formidable had ſo got out of the way of other ſhips, did ſhe not ſtand after the Admiral with all the ſails ſhe could ſet, and trimmed as well as the condition of her ſails and rigging would permit of?

A. Yes.

Q. Did not the Formidable ſteer all the afternoon after the Admiral, keeping him a little open on her lee bow?

A. Yes.

Q. Was not that a proper courſe for getting into her ſtation in the line of battle, if ſhe could have come up with the Admiral.

A. Yes, I judged it ſo at the time.

Q. So ſoon as the Admiral wore, and ſtood to the ſouthward, were not the officers, and all hands on board the Formidable, ſet to work to get the rigging knotted and ſpliced, and to repair damages? A. Yes.

Q. Do you recollect the diſtribution that was made of the officers for that purpoſe? A. Yes.

Q. Do you remember the Fox coming to the Formidable? A. I have already anſwered.

Q. At what diſtance do you recollect the Formidable was from the Victory, when the Fox came down to her?

A. One mile or better, in the Victory's wake, and three miles a-ſtern withal.

Q. About what time was that, do you reckon, Sir?

A. Near ſun-ſet.

Q. Was you in a ſituation to hear the meſſage delivered by the Captain of the Fox? A. No.

Q. Was not the ſignal for the line of battle a-head kept flying on board the Formidable, till dark night?

A. Yes.

Q. Was the ſignal for the ſhips to windward to bear down, with many ſhips pendants of the Vice Admiral of the blue's diviſion, let fly on board the Formidable, before or after the Fox ſpoke with her?

A. Before the Fox cheered the Formidable; I did not hear the Fox ſpeak to her.

Q. Were not theſe ſignals made in repetition of their being out on board the Victory? A. Yes.

Q. Had not two of theſe ſhips pendants been hauled down? because the ſhips had anſwered them before the Fox

A. I do

A. I do not recollect that circumstance.

Q. Did the Fox's men cheer the Formidable first, or did the Formidable's men cheer the Fox first?

A. The Fox first cheered the Formidable; and the expression I made use of to the officers and men on the forecastle was; "That's hearty my lads, return the cheer."

Q. Please to give the court some account of the most material damages of your masts, yards, sails, and rigging, and I desire you would first speak of what relates to the fore-mast?

A. The fore-mast was very much wounded, and rotten, the fore top-mast wounded, the fore yard, and the bowsprit; the gib, and fore topmast stay-sail, cut to pieces and carried over board by a cannon shot; the fore-topsail cut to pieces, the foresail very much damaged, the fore stay and spring stay shot away; all the fore-shrouds on the starboard side, except one, shot away, and only three remaining on the larboard side; all the fore-topmast shrouds and backstays, except one on the larboard side; all the top-gallant shrouds and stays; all the braces, bowlings, and running ropes, leading in or about the foremast, very few excepted; fore tacks and sheets shot away on both sides.

Sir Hugh Palliser. Is not this a more full and exact state of the damages, than what could be collected the day after the action, when an account was delivered to the Commander in Chief? A. Yes.

Admiral Montague. Notwithstanding the description you have given of the damages of the foremast, fore topmast, bowsprit, and rigging of the Formidable, did not the Formidable wear twice, before any of the rigging belonging to her bowsprit or foremast was repaired? A. Yes.

Q. And before the signal to come down into the Admiral's wake was made?

A. Yes, we wore twice. I did not observe the signal for coming down into the Admiral's wake, 'till I was sent for from the forecastle, and we had then just wore, with temporary ropes.

Prosecutor. Do you not conceive that any ship, with all her masts standing, whilst she has any canvas abroad, and moderate weather, will wear by putting the helm a-weather, although her masts and rigging may be in such condition that she cannot carry sail upon a wind, to keep company with other ships?

A. Yes, we had that instance in the Formidable.

Q. As you mentioned that there was only one fore-shroud remaining to windward, and two or three to lee-

 ward,

ward, I would ask whether several of those shrouds were not cut in two places? A. Yes.

Admiral Arbuthnot. You have just mentioned that you made tackle falls about your yards; then is it not your opinion, that you could have braced these yards up short, to have stood upon a wind with them?

A. We did brace them to follow the Admiral.

Q. Because the last question was, Whether the ship could not wear without these ropes, and your ship was an example of it?

A. I have said previous to that, we made use of temporary ropes.

Q. Mention the damages of the mainmast rigging?

A. The main top mast was very much wounded, the main yard, and main top sail yard wounded; the main spring stay shot away; seven or eight shrouds on the starboard side, and five on the larboard; the main top stay and spring stay; our main top mast shrouds and all the back stays; the mizen mast and top gallant stay shot away; four channel plates, and three chain plates shot away.

Court. You need not go any further, if the Vice Admiral is satisfied, the Court is.

President. After you passed the French fleet, did they bring to, or make sail?

A. They broke up their line, and appeared to me to be under sail, not laying to.

Q. Was the Formidable then in a condition to follow them to renew the engagement, if the Admiral had thought proper to have done it?

A. She was in a condition to renew the action, but not to carry sail after an enemy.

Admiral Montague. The Vice Admiral asked you if there was not some difference between the defects that you produced in Court, and those you delivered in to the Commander in Chief the day after the action; I should be glad to know, how long after the action the defects you have now delivered, were taken?

A. Immediately on our arrival at Plymouth.

Prosecutor. Were not the officers and men employed on board the Formidable the whole afternoon, and all the following night, in repairing her damages? A. Yes.

Q. Did not the Formidable get into her station by day light the next morning?

A. She got into the line, but I cannot answer whether she was in her proper station in the line, or not.

Q. Did not the drums beat to arms at two o'clock in the morning? A. Yes. Q. All

Q. All hands at quarters, and in all respects ready for action before day light, expecting immediately to engage? A. Yes.

Q. During the afternoon of the 27th, notwithstanding the damages you have mentioned the Formidable received, could she not have bore down upon an enemy, and have engaged, having only had two guns dismounted, although she was not able during the afternoon to reach her station in the line of battle, with the sail the Admiral carried?

A. Yes; such was the Vice Admiral's declaration to me some time in the afternoon; I cannot recollect the particular time.

Q. In the morning of the 28th, do you remember seeing three French ships to leeward?

A. I remember seeing three strange sails.

Q. Did you suppose them to be three French men of war?

A. I did imagine them to be the remaining part of the French fleet.

Q. Did you take them to be line of battle ships?

A. I did.

Q. At what distance do you judge the nearest of them was from the British fleet?

A. Not more than a mile from the Formidable.

Q. What number of men on board the Formidable, were hurt by an explosion of powder?

A. Reported to me twenty-seven.

Q. Were any of them killed out right upon the spot, by that explosion?

A. The officer who commanded that deck, where the explosion happened, informed me, that no man was killed by the explosion.

Q. What number of killed and wounded did you report to me, that was sent to the Commander in Chief, after the engagement, the 29th?

A. To the best of my recollection, fourteen men were killed, one of which was the Boatswain, two since died of their wounds, and forty-nine wounded, one of which was the second Lieutenant.

Q. Have you made a comparison of the killed and wounded in the respective divisions of the fleets, from the account that was published by authority from Admiral Keppel?

A. I did at the time when it was just published.

Q. What was the amount of the number killed in the Vice Admiral of the Red's division together?

A. I do not immediately recollect the number killed.

Q. Do you recollect whether it was more or less than the number in the Vice Admiral of the Blue's division only?

A. To the best that I can recollect, nearly the same.

Q. And as to the wounded, how does the comparison stand? A. Nearly the same.

Q. Were these three strange ships you speak of chaced by any of the British fleet? A. None, as I observed.

Q. Do you know of any signals being made, of seeing more strange ships to leeward?

A. I do not recollect that circumstance.

Q. If the British fleet had pursued these three ships, and supposing the French fleet to have been in the same direction as they steered, was there not a probability of some of our undamaged ships coming up with the disabled ships of the French fleet, and have taken them, if the French fleet abandoned them, or if they had staid by them, another engagement might have been brought on?

A. That being matter of opinion, I would wish to decline to answer.

Q. Do you remember what kind of weather it was that morning? A. Moderate weather.

Q. How many knots do you suppose a ship might run with all her sails?

A. Between seven and nine knots.

Q. Can you judge what time the French fleet made sail? A. I cannot.

Q. Do you know of any signal made in the night, by the French fleet to make sail? A. Not to my knowledge.

Q. What was your distance from Ushant on the 28th at noon?

A. N. 81. E. lat. 48° 11" distance forty-five leagues by reckoning, but afterwards in making land we judged we were nearer to it by thirteen leagues, as near as I can recollect.

Q. Being the middle of summer, short nights and moderate weather, do you apprehend it would have been attended with any immediate and imminent danger, if the British fleet had pursued that of France, for the chance of coming up with some of them, at least so far as till we had seen them into port, or made the land?

A. There appeared to me to be no imminent danger.

Q. If you had had an engagement with a single ship, at that distance you have stated from Ushant, and had beat her to occasion her to run away, do you not think that

you

you ought to purſue her till you ſaw her into port, or to have made the land, all your own maſts being ſtanding?

A. In a ſingle ſhip I ſhould not have heſitated one moment.

Proſecutor. I have done with Captain Beazely.

Admiral Montague. In the courſe of your examination you have ſaid, the chaſing ſhips appeared to come into action ſeparately, and at different diſtances: Do you know the cauſe that they did ſo; and could they not have got into their ſtations in the line of battle, after they gave off fighting?

Captain Beazely. Before I anſwer this queſtion, I deſire the evidence I have already given may be read.

Admiral Keppel. I object to this, upon the evidence's croſs examination, becauſe I ſhall be obliged to examine this evidence very cloſely.

Evidence. In all Court Martials that I have been concerned in, it has been always the cuſtom for the evidence, on his croſs examination, to refer back to the queſtions and anſwers, which have been allowed to be read to him, on which account I beg that indulgence of the Court, as I conceive I have a right to it, on the trial of a flag officer.

The Court withdrew, and came to the following reſolution:

" *That the witneſs, upon his croſs examination by the Court and priſoner, ought not to be allowed to have recourſe to the queſtions and anſwers put to, and given by him, on his firſt examination by the Proſecutor.*"

Proſecutor. As by this reſolution of the Court, Capt. Beazely has been deprived of that indulgence which other witneſſes have had, I beg that the Court will have that attention to him, as not to ſuffer him to receive any extraordinary treatment.

The Court withdrew to conſider the propriety of taking down the Proſecutor's addreſs: Reſolved, " *that the words made uſe of by the Proſecutor, ſeem to convey an idea, that this Court acts upon intereſted and partial motives; they ſhall not therefore be admitted as part of the minutes of the Court, nor ſhall be inſerted in the evidence.*"

Admiral Montague's queſtion was then repeated, viz.

Q. In the courſe of your examination, you have ſaid, that the chacing ſhips came into action ſeparately, and at different times; do you know the cauſe that they did ſo, and could they not get into their ſtations in the line of battle, after they had fought?

A. The reaſon appeared to me to be occaſioned by their chacing to windward per ſignal.

Admiral Montague. The latter part of the queſtion is

not

not anſwered; " And could they not get into their ſtation in the line of battle, after they came out of action?

A. That I cannot be a judge of.

Q. You have ſaid, that two of them went ahead of the Vice Admiral of the blue, and joined the center; did they do it by any ſignal from the Commander in Chief?

A. Not that I know of.

Q. Did the Vice Admiral of the blue make their ſignal to come into their ſtations, when he ſaw them go ahead and join the center? A. No.

Q. Then if he had made their ſignal to come into their ſtations, and they had obeyed it, don't you think he would have been better ſupported?

A. I do think ſo.

Q. You have ſaid, that the neareſt ſhip you can recollect in the Vice Admiral of the blue's diviſion, to leeward of the Formidable, meaning the Ocean, and that the four ſhips aſtern of the Formidable before the action began, were at a diſtance from each other, and half a mile aſunder, and that the damage the Formidable received, was greater than if ſhe had fought in the body of the Vice Admiral of the blue's diviſion; do you not think, if the Vice Admiral of the blue had made the ſignal for the four ſhips aſtern to cloſe the line, and come nearer to each other, and nearer to him, agreeable to the 7th Article of Admiral Keppel's fighting inſtructions, they would not have ſupported him, and taken off a great deal of the fire from the enemy?

A. In the firſt place, I do not recollect what the ſignal of the 7th Article is.

Admiral Montague. I will tell you; 'tis a pendant at the crotchet yard arm, if aſtern; if ahead, at the end of the gib boom.

A. It appeared to me, that if the ſhips alluded to aſtern, had had ſignals made to them to have cloſed the Vice Admiral, they could not have done it more expeditiouſly than they did, as they appeared to me to have all neceſſary ſails ſet to cloſe in the action.

Q. I mean while they were engaging?

A. After the Formidable had began the action, I can anſwer to nothing relative to thoſe ſhips aſtern, except to one that paſſed under our lee, when we were going down the French line.

Q. Was the van of the Vice Admiral of the blue's diviſion ahead of him, and near, to ſupport you in the time of action?

A. I don't apprehend your queſtion, the fleet was not in a line.

Q. Were

Q. Were any of that division that should have been a-head of him, a-head of him in whatever situation they were, on the weather bow, lee bow, or right a-head?

A. I can only answer for two ships that passed the Formidable before the action, but which those ships were, I cannot tell.

Q. What ships did you follow in the action?

A. I do not recollect them.

Q. How far was the nearest ship ahead of the Formidable, just before you came into action?

A. A good half mile.

Q. You do not know whether she was one of your division? A. I do not.

Q. Did you on the 27th of July see any act in Admiral Keppel, that indicated a flight from the enemy, or see the French fleet pursue, and offer him battle?

A. The British fleet stood upon their starboard tacks, forming their line; the enemy forming astern on the same tack; whether that had the appearance of flight, or not, I beg leave to submit to the better judgment of the court.

Q. Admiral Keppel is charged with negligently performing the duty imposed on him; inform the Court if you know of any instance on the 27th of July, in which he was guilty of such negligence, or did not perform the duty imposed on him?

A. I do not allow myself a competent judge of the conduct of an Admiral in such a high department as the honourable Admiral. I stand here as an evidence, not as a judge.

Q. You are not asked as a judge, 'tis a fair and honest question.

A. I wish to decline giving an answer to it: I don't think it would be right in me, who am so young an officer, to answer that.

Q. I must ask it, because it is a part of the charge.--- Then, Sir, did Admiral Keppel, as far as came within your observation, by his conduct, either the 27th or 28th of July, tarnish the honour of the British flag?

A. I must beg leave not to answer that question, for the reasons offered in answer to the previous questions.

Admiral Rodham. You have said that the French fleet seemed, in your opinion, to have an intention to renew the action; what do you mean by that?

A. The French were forming a line to leeward of the British fleet.

Q. When they were forming a line upon the starboard tack, if they had inclined to renew the action, could not they have formed within pistol shot of the British fleet?

A. They

A. They could have formed within pistol shot.

Q. You say you expressed your opinion, that you judged the Commander in Chief did not intend to renew the action, that afternoon, with the enemy, after hauling down the signal for battle; what are your reasons for so judging?

A. Standing from them, and making so much sail, that we could not keep or preserve our distance.

Q. Did you, from the Formidable, ever make any signal, that you could not follow the Admiral?. A. No.

Q. If you had made such signal, do not you think the Commander in Chief would have shortened sail?

A. It appeared to me, that the state of the Formidable was so apparent, that there was no occasion to make such a signal.

Q. Is it the Commander in Chief's business to look out to other ships, or they to look to him?

A. 'Tis the duty of officers to look out for their signals.

Q. Was not the signal on board the Commander in Chief for a line of battle, when the Victory was standing towards the enemy?

A. I never saw it or heard of it.

Q. Why did not the Formidable fire at the French ship, which you said was near you on the 28th, in the morning, which would have shewn the Admiral that they were within a mile of you.

A. I beg to refer this question to the Vice Admiral.

Q. Did you receive any orders to do it.

Capt. Duncan. Was the Formidable, at any time of the day of the 27th, in such condition as not to be manageable? A. No, Sir.

Admiral Keppel. Capt. Bazeley has upon some questions refused giving his opinion, on other questions, he has freely given it, that does not correspond; but, I will ask him now, in order to confirm the opinion he has given, that the Admiral did not intend to renew the battle that afternoon, from the sail he carried; what sail did he carry, as he stood to the southward on the afternoon of the 27th of July?

A. I cannot recollect the particular canvas that she had set, my reasons for so saying was, the Victory getting so far from the Formidable.

Q. Were her top-gallant sails set?

A. I do not recollect they were.

Q. Was her main-tack on board?

A. I did not see her main-sail set.

Q. Were

Q. Were all the reeves out of her top sails?

A. That I cannot anſwer.

Q. Was her gib or ſtay-ſail ſet?

A. From the ſituation the Formidable was in, a ſtern of the Victory, 'tis impoſſible for me to ſay, whether the gib or what ſtay-ſails were ſet.

Q. Pray then inform the Court, how you know the Victory carried much ſail?

A. What I meant to ſay by much ſail being ſet, was in compariſon of the diſabled ſtate the Formidable was in, and what I have related to the Court reſpecting her ſituation; the Victory being at that time, to the beſt of my recollection, under her top-ſails and fore-ſail.

Q. Now I underſtand, you ſay ſhe was under her top-ſails and fore-ſails; did not that ſail ſuffer the French leading ſhip to range up a-breaſt, under her top-ſails, going parallel to the Victory?

A. To the beſt of my recollection, the van of the enemy's fleet appeared to me to be a-breaſt of the Victory about dark.

Q. Now anſwer the other part, under what ſail they led up a-breaſt of the Victory?

A. It appeared to me that the firſt, ſecond, and third ſhips had only their topſails ſet.

Q. At what time do you mean to ſtate, that the Vice Admiral of the red ſhould have fallen down, to have formed in the line on the larboard tack?

A. I do not pretend to judge; but the time the Vice Admiral alluded to in his queſtion, appeared to me to be very applicable for the Britiſh fleet to form in that poſition, as the 31ſt Article in the fighting inſtructions directs.

Q. Do you underſtand the whole of the 31ſt Article alluded to?

A. I think I do; I may be miſtaken; but I think I comprehend it.

Q. Were any part of the Britiſh fleet leading with a large wind. A. None that I ſaw.

Q. I beg the Article may be read.---*It was read accordingly.*

Admiral Keppel. Now do you take upon you to ſay, that the Vice Admiral of the red was not called down by meſſage? A. I do not know.

Q. Do you know how many ſhips the Vice Admiral of the red had with him at this time?

A. To the beſt of my recollection, including himſelf, there were nine.

Q. That

Q. That was the whole of his division, one only excepted, was it not?

A. I can answer to nine, but not to ten.

Q. Then you are sure of nine?

A. To the best of my recollection; but to be positive, I cannot.

Q. Was the Vice Admiral of the red, at this time, or the Admiral of the fleet, nearest to you?

A. I should beg leave to know what time.

Q. The time when you saw the Vice Admiral of the red with nine sail, and made the 31st article applicable to the motions of the fleet, in your opinion?

A. If you want to draw me into opinion, I will answer it possitively; immediately as the Formidable passed the enemy's rear, it struck me in that position.-- My honour is at stake.

Admiral Keppel. I stand for my life, as well as for my honour.

Here Admiral Montague called the evidence to order.

A. As to the nearness of the Vice Admiral of the red, and the ships with him, appeared to me, to be a mile aweather of the Formidable, and the Victory at that time, at two miles distance, when we passed the enemy's rear.

Q. Was it at this time that you thought the Formidable in danger of being cut off by the enemy's rear.

A. No, Sir, not after we passed them.

Q. When was it then?

A. Before we opened our fire, there appeared to me to be great probability that the French Admiral would have made that attempt.

Q. Do you know the condition of the center, and those ships of the Vice Admiral of the red's division, that came out of action, before the Vice Admiral of the blue came out of action?

A. I know the state of no other ship, but the ship I commanded in the day of battle.

Q. Then do you feel yourself justified, as an officer, in swearing that the action might have been renewed with advantage, if the Admiral had wore and stood to the rear of the enemy as the Formidable did, and doubled on the enemy with the rest of the ships; at the same time that you confess yourself ignorant of the condition of every ship in the fleet but your own?

I. I have said, if the Vice Admiral of the Red and his division had bore down, and if the Admiral had advanced with his division to have renewed the engagement, it would have obstructed the enemy from forming a line so immediately.

Admiral

Admiral Keppel. That does not anſwer my queſtion.

A. That's the anſwer I would wiſh to make to it.

Q. Do you take upon you now, uninformed of the ſtate of any ſhip but your own, to ſay, that the Admiral had a ſufficient number of ſhips with him, formed in a line on the larboard tack, and near enough on a line to ſupport him, ſo as to have prevented the French fleet forming on the ſtarboard tack ?

A. I do not recollect the Admiral's being on the larboard tack in a line, with ſhips with him.

Q. When the Formidable paſſed the Victory, while the Admiral was advancing towards the enemy on the larboard tack, after the action, were there any ſhips a-head of the Victory on the ſame tack with her ?

A. I do not recollect ſhip or ſhips.

Q. At what time did you ſee the Vice Admiral of the Red, formed in the rear of the Engliſh fleet in the afternoon of the 27th, while on the ſtarboard tack ?

A. The time I cannot ſpeak to.

Q. Speak within half an hour. A. I cannot.

Q. Not within half an hour ?

A. Only two particular circumſtances, that I can recollect that afternoon, of ſomething very particular happened in the ſhip.

Q. Then you do not recollect the time that the Vice Admiral of the Red quitted the ſtation in the rear, for forming a line a-head ? A. I do not.

Q. You ſaw the Vice Admiral of the Red in the Admiral's rear, did not you ? A. Yes.

Q. Can you inform the Court, what was the ſituation of the French fleet, at the time you did ſee the Vice Admiral of the Red in the Victory's wake ?

A. To the beſt of my recollection, forming their line to leeward and a-ſtern.

Q. What was the ſituation of the Vice Admiral of the blue, at this time ?

A. Do you mean with reſpect to the Victory ?

Q. Yes, and with reſpect to the Vice Admiral of the Red ?

A. To the beſt of my recollection, the Vice Admiral of the Red was formed rather before the lee beam of the Formidable, and a-ſtern of the Victory.

Q. What courſe upon the wind ſhould the Formidable have ſteered, to have come into the Admiral's wake in her ſtation ?

A. That muſt depend upon particular circumſtances, how

how far the Formidable may be a weather of the Admiral's wake, and at what rate ſhe failed.

Q. You have placed the Vice Admiral of the Red, a little before his lee beam, now I may ſuppoſe the Victory at that time, with the wind we had, went two knots and three fathom; what then would have been the courſe neceſſary to have ſteered, to have bore up into her wake, from the ſituation ſhe was in?

A. half a point, or betwixt that and a point, would have increaſed her diſtance, by falling a-ſtern.

Q. Would you not have gone faſter by ſteering a little away from the wind?

A. Not faſter than we did.

Q. Did you ever ſet the Victory by compaſs?

A. I never did that afternoon.

Q. Were there any minutes kept on board the Formidable of the ſignals, or of the bearings of the Admiral, or any thing about him?

A. There were minutes taken of ſignals, very incorrect ones, but nothing about bearings, which I am ready to explain.

Q. Who took them?

A. Two Midſhipmen that were appointed for that buſineſs, their names Geer, and Hoggard.

Q. Do you know where theſe minutes are?

A. No, I never ſaw them after the battle.

Q. How do you know they are incorrect?

A. From the Maſter's report to me, who wrote the log from them, and he obſerved it to me immediately after he ſaw them.

It being four o'clock, the Court adjourned till Monday ten o'clock.

FOURTEENTH DAY, FRIDAY JANUARY 22d.

At ten o'clock this day, the members being aſſembled, and the Court formed, Captain Bazely's evidence was continued.

Admiral Keppel. By whoſe nomination were the Midſhipmen appointed to take the ſignals?

A. By the Vice Admiral's.

Q. Do you mean in time of battle, or in general?

A. In time of battle, by the aſſiſtance of another, one that the Vice Admiral appointed as his Aid-de-camp, a Mr. Montague.

Q. Have not the Midſhipmen, appointed to obſerve and take ſignals, the beſt opportunity of obſerving them correctly.

A. That

A. That I cannot anſwer.

Q. Did they acknowledge at any time, and when, that their ſignals were erroneous?

A. They never did to me, nor I to them.

Q. Was it the Maſter that took upon him to enter the ſignals in the log book, different from the minutes of thoſe appointed to obſerve them?

A. I do not know that the log book differed from the minutes taken by the Midſhipmen, but I obſerved there was very little mention of ſignals in the log book.

Q. Can you repeat, to the Court, the difference?

A. I cannot immediately; they were not taken carefully, but there are no eraſements.

Q. Can you take upon you to ſay, that the minutes and the log book differ or agree as to ſignals?

A. I cannot ſay.

Q. Do you know where theſe minutes are?

A. Since leaving the Court yeſterday, I have enquired of the maſter and different officers of the Formidable, if they knew any thing of the minutes of the ſignals taken before the day of battle, and after the arrival of the ſhip at Plymouth, and I am informed that a Mr. Perry, late Midſhipman of the Formidable, now Lieutenant of the Triumph, at Chatham, had taken theſe minutes with him, out of the ſhip, which I never knew or heard of till this morning.

Q. Were you told when they were delivered to Mr. Perry?

A. Yes; when Mr. Perry was appointed to obſerve the ſignals, in the room of Mr. Geer and Mr. Hoggard, who were appointed to do their duty as Mates of the ſhip.

Q. Are thoſe gentlemen who took the minutes, here?

A. Yes, and I believe the Vice Admiral intends to call thoſe gentlemen; the minutes if they are in being are ſent for.

Q. In the morning of the 27th, how far was the Vice Admiral of the blue to leeward of the Victory, when the ſignal was made for ſhips to chace?

A. About half a mile upon the Victory's lee bow, and a mile a-head withal, to the beſt of my judgment.

Q. Do you recollect what ſail the Formidable was under?

A. I beg leave to aſk what hour in the morning.

Q. I mean at day-light in the morning.

A. Cloſe reefed top-ſails, fore and main top-maſt ſtay-ſails, and fore courſes.

Q. At the time the ſignal was made for the ſhips to chace to windward ?

A. Upon ſignal being made for the ſhips to chace to windward, the main-ſail was ſet, and two reefs let out of the top-ſail.

Q. You have ſaid that the Vice Admiral of the blue, and his diviſion, were in their proper ſituation and diſtance, to have readily taken their ſtation in the line of battle on the larboard tack, had ſignal been made for that purpoſe ; I would aſk you, whether the Formidable, and the reſt of the diviſion, could have got a-head of the Victory without their making aboard, or the Victory bearing down to leeward to them.

A. I apprehend the Formidable could not go right a-head of the Victory, without making aboard for the line to have been compleatly formed, in her ſituation, without the Admiral had edged away for that purpoſe.

Q. Was not the Vice Admiral of the red, and his diviſion, conſiderably to windward of the Victory ?

A. To the beſt of my recollection, upon the weather quarter, and a-ſtern withal of the Victory, three miles diſtant from the Formidable.

Q. Muſt they not have bore down likewiſe, as far to leeward as the Vice Admiral of the blue, and thereby increaſed the diſtance of the whole fleet from the enemy ?

A. Yes.

Q. When ſignal was made for the whole fleet to tack together, at ten o'clock that morning, did the Formidable tack immediately when the Admiral tacked ?

A. I think ſhe did.

Q. You are not ſure ?

A. I think ſhe did, Sir, to the beſt that I can charge my memory.

Q. At what hour did the Formidable back her mizen top-ſail, when drawing to the enemy ?

A. I cannot anſwer particularly to time.

Q. You ſay the mizen top-ſail was backed, to prevent getting into the Ocean's line of fire ; how long did it continue a-back ?

A. Till ſhe had paſſed the French line.

Q. Were the ſhips a-head and a-ſtern of the Formidable, when the mizen top-ſail was backed, joined to the center, ſo as for ſome of them to be obliged to go to leeward, out of the line, on account of the ſhips coming up a-ſtern, preſſing upon them ?

A. To the ſhips a-head I cannot ſpeak, only to one

ſhip

ſhip that paſſed under the Formidable's lee, whilſt ſhe was engaged, or at leaſt running down the French line.

Q. Do you know the ſhip that bore away under the lee of the Formidable? A. I do not.

Q. Do you know what ſhip was next a-head of the Formidable during the action? A. No.

Q. Did not you back your mizen top-ſail for the Ocean?

A. Yes, ſhe was not a-head of us, ſhe was upon the lee bows; as well as for the ſhips a-ſtern to cloſe.

Q. How many of the French ſhips did you paſs a-ſtern of the French Admiral, after you began to engage, I mean the Admiral with the flag at the main top-maſt head, in the 100 gun ſhip?

A. I did not count the ſhips at all whilſt we were running down the French line.

Q. May I aſk where you was yourſelf at that time, when going down the French line?

A. On the fore part of the quarter deck, on the ſtarboard ſide, moſt of the whole time of action, looking at the enemy as we paſſed along the line

Q. How many three decked ſhips had the French?

A. There appeared to me two.

Q. Were they tolerably near together?

A. That I cannot anſwer.

Q. Can you inform the Court, how many French Admirals were tolerably cloſe together? A. I cannot.

Q. Was the irregularity of the French line, the cauſe of the irregularity of the diſtance at which you have ſaid the Formidable engaged different ſhips, as ſhe paſſed along the line; or did the Formidable bear away?

A. The Formidable did, at the time of action, bear up to one of the enemy's ſhips, to avoid being aboard of her, whoſe gib boom nearly touched the main top-ſail weather leach of the Formidable, and I thought we could not avoid being on board.

Q. Did that ſhip ſo near, give a warm fire into the Formidable?

A. No, ſhe appeared to be ſilenced before we reached her.

Q. Then was not the Formidable, and the ſhips a-ſtern, ſupported and ſuccoured by thoſe ſhips that had engaged the French line before ſhe came that length?

A. They certainly received leſs of the enemy's fire, in conſequence of the centre diviſion, and Vice Admiral of the Red, paſſing along the French line before us.

 Q. As

Q. As you have said the Formidable wore after passing the rear of the French ships on seeing the Admiral advancing towards the enemy on the larboard tack, that the officers and men on board the Formidable were ordered to quarters, expecting to renew the battle when the Admiral came up; I desire to know whether the Formidable did not wear again, and pass a-stern of the Admiral without signal, whilst her head was towards the enemy?

A. Yes.

Q. When you passed the Victory, was the signal for the line of battle then flying? A. I believe it was.

Q. When the Vice Admiral of the Red, and his division, made sail in order to get into his station, after being in the rear of the Admiral, upon the starboard tack, did he not pass between the Formidable and the centre division? A. I do not recollect.

Q. You think you saw the signal for the line of battle on board the Victory as you passed her, can you say it was ever hauled down?

A. I cannot charge my memory.

Q. Do not you know when the signal for a line of battle was hoisted on board the Formidable? A. I do not.

Q. Are you positive it was flying at five o'clock on board the Formidable, in the afternoon?

A. I think it was, but I cannot speak positively as to that.

Q. How do you know the time the Fox came to the Formidable, having before said you never observed time?

A. I judge it to be near about sun-set.

Q. What was the confusion you spoke of on board the Formidable?

A. Nothing more than what is natural to happen to a ship coming immediately out of battle.

Q. At what time do you mean the confusion was?

A. The confusion continued the whole afternoon, to get the ship into a situation to obey the Admiral's signals.

Q. When you beat to arms at two o'clock in the morning of the 28th, was it upon the approach of any ship to leeward of you? A. No.

Q. Where was the Formidable at two o'clock in the morning with respect to the Admiral?

A. A-stern and to windward withal.

Q. Did you see the Admiral's lights during the night?

A. Yes, most of the night, at different times that I looked for them.

Q. Were the distinguishing lights of the Formidable burning at that time? A. No, they were not.

Q. Were

Q. Were there any ſhips between the Formidable and the French ſhips that you ſaw in the morning of the 28th?

A. I ſaw none of the Britiſh ſhips between them.

Admiral Keppel. I have nothing more to ask Captain Beazely.

Preſident. I think you ſaid, when the Fox cheered the Formidable firſt, you was upon the fore-caſtle; can you take upon you to ſay, that there was no cheer from the people upon the poop, or quarter deck, at the time the Captain of the Fox delivered the meſſage to the Vice Admiral? A. None that I heard or knew of.

Q. Can you refer to the queſtion asked by the Vice Admiral, reſpecting your engaging with a ſingle ſhip. If you had had an engagement with a ſingle ſhip at that diſtance from Uſhant; I ask whether, if the Formidable had been that ſhip, and in the condition you have reported her to be, to the Court, when ſhe ran away, would you have ventured to purſue her upon a lee ſhore?

A. That would depend upon the diſtance I was from land. In the ſituation the Formidable was in on the morning of the 28th, I would not have heſitated one moment to purſue her, at leaſt till I had made the land, provided the weather had been clear. Nor ſhould I have thought my conduct juſtifiable if I had not.

Q. I mean in the condition the Formidable was on the 27th, at the time you came out of action, when, if the French ſhip had run away, would you have purſued that ſhip?

A. Knowing myſelf upon a lee ſhore, it muſt depend chiefly what courſe I was going on: what I call a lee ſhore, is in ſight of land. If I had been upon a lee ſhore, I would not have done it; but I would on the morning of the 28th.

Admiral Montague. From the ſtrange account Captain Beazely has given us of the minutes taken on board a flag ſhip, it has naturally led me to the Formidable's log book to examine that day's work, and to ſee whether there are any remarks of the ſignals made that day. I ſind three leaves cut out, from the 25th to the 28th of July incluſive; can you inform the Court, how theſe leaves came to be cut out of this book?

A. I do not know, ſo help me God.

Ordered to withdraw.

Sir Richard Bickerton, *Captain of the Terrible, ſworn.*

Proſecutor. At what hour did you firſt ſee the French fleet, on the 27th in the morning? A. At five o'clock.

 Q. Did

Q. Did they appear to you any time that forenoon, to be in a line of battle?

A. They did, but they were not in that regular line that I saw them in afterwards, when I came to range along the French fleet.

Q. At what time had they that appearance to you, Sir?

A. Soon after they tacked.

President. What occasioned your tacking?

A. Agreeable to signal to chace to windward.

Prosecutor. Do you remember signal being made, for some ships of the Vice Admiral of the Blue's division, to chace to windward that morning? A. I do.

Q. Do you remember the time?

A. About six o'clock, for some of them.

Q. For how many ships of the Vice Admiral of the Blue's division, were these signals?

A. I think there were four; but I am not certain.

Q. Do you remember whether there was not more than four that chaced, when these signals were thrown out?

A. I did not chace then.

Q. Was your signal among those that were thrown out?

A. Not at first.

Q. Do you know the names of those four ships?

A. Two of them I do, the Egmont and Robuste.

Prosecutor. Sir Richard speaks of his signal being made after the four; can he recollect whether there was a sixth signal made with the Terrible's?

A. I believe it was the Worcester's.

Q. Did this signal for those ships chacing, cause that part of the fleet to be dispersed and separated from their flag, and from each other?

A. It certainly occasioned them to separate.

Q. In the morning of the 27th, was the Vice Admiral of the Blue, with his division, a-head of the Admiral, some of them somewhat upon his lee bow, and others of them somewhat to windward, or how situated otherwise?

A. I think the Vice Admiral of the Blue was to leeward of the Victory, and a little before his lee beam, the Terrible upon the Vice Admiral's lee bow.

President. Was the signals being thrown out for six ships to chace to windward, a means of their coming to action sooner, or prevented their coming to action sooner than they otherwise would?

A. It was a means of their fetching further to windward, and engaging most of the enemy.

Q. Was there any signal made for the whole division to chace? A. I did not see it.

Q. When

Q. When ſhips chace from different ſituations, and who differ in their rates of ſailing, can they all come into a ſtation at one and the ſame time, proper for tacking?

A. I ſhould think not.

Q. Was it not the Admiral's practice to make the ſignal for ſhips chacing, to tack when he judged they ought to do ſo?

A. I do not remember he often made that a rule.

Q. Did the Admiral make ſuch ſignals that morning for particular ſhips? A. I did not ſee them.

Preſident. I ſuppoſe you tacked according to your own judgment?

A. I certainly tacked according to my own judgment.

Proſecutor. Do you mean to ſay, that you tacked by the general ſignal, for the whole fleet to tack together?

A. We tacked a little before.

Q. If theſe ſix ſhips had not been taken from the Vice Admiral, might not the whole of that diviſion have gone into action together, with their Admiral, in a connected body to ſupport each other, at the time the Vice Admiral himſelf did?

A. We certainly ſhould have been more connected, if we had not chaced.

Preſident. Was you cloſe upon a wind, when you attacked the enemy?

A. Cloſe upon a wind the firſt ſhip, but afterwards we were obliged to keep away.

Q. When ſignal was thrown out to chace, was you to leeward or to windward of the Vice Admiral of the blue?

A. I think I obſerved before, that we were upon his larboard bow.

Proſecutor. Do you think that ſhips, while proceeding along an enemy's line, ſcattered and ſeparated from each other, are expoſed to more or leſs damage from the enemy, than if a number of ſhips proceeded together properly connected, ſo as to ſupport each other?

A. I think the more ſhips are together, the leſs damage each muſt receive.

Q. Did not the chacing ſhips, ſo far as you know, come into action ſeparately, and without any others near enough to ſupport them?

A. There were three ſhips aſtern of us, that appeared to be pretty near together.

Q. Does Sir Richard remember when the Terrible, in the thick ſmoke from the Terrible and Formidable, ran cloſe under the Formidable's ſtern?

A. I remember the Formidable coming acroſs me, when I was eng aging the ſhip ahead of the Bretagne.

 Q. Till

Q. Till the time I am ſpeaking of, was there any other of our ſhips ſo near the Terrible, as to afford ſupport to each other? A. I believe not.

Q. Do you know whether part of the chacing ſhips paſſed ahead of the blue diviſion, and joined the center diviſion? A. I do not.

Q. At the time you ſpeak of, when you was near the Formidable, did you ſhoot ahead of her, or remain aſtern?

A. I remained aſtern for ſome time, but was afterwards obliged to bear up, to prevent being on board the Formidable.

Admiral Montague. Was the Formidable's mizen topſail aback at this time?

A. I do not remember that it was at that time, but I ſaw it aback.

Q. Did you ſee it aback before you ſhot ahead of her, or to leeward, for fear of being aboard her?

A. I really do not know. It was in the heat of the action, and I did not take notice.

Court. Were there any other ſhips nearly aſtern of you at that time?

A. I did not obſerve them; there was one to leeward of us.

Proſecutor. Proceeding along the French line, did not the ſhips go large from the wind?

A. They went from the wind.

Q. When you ſhot to leeward of the Formidable, as you mentioned, how many ſhips of the Vice Admiral of the blue diviſion then remained aſtern of him?

A. I knew of none but the three chacing ſhips.

Q. Were they cloſe up with him?

A. I did not take notice.

Q. After running to leeward to avoid being on board the Formidable, did you ſhoot ahead of her?

A. Yes, upon her larboard bow.

Q. Did you ſee any other ſhips then near her?

A. The America was very near her.

Q. Did you and the America go on ahead?

A. I know nothing of the America, the ſmoke was ſo thick. I went on myſelf, but did not go far ahead.

Q. When you paſſed ahead of the Formidable, and ſpeak of ſeeing the America, was ſhe then upon her lee, or weather bow?

A. Upon the lee bow I think.

Q. You ſaid the French fleet was not in ſo regular a line when you proceeded down their line, as they were before; if, when you proceeded along the enemy's line, it was not perfected,

perfected, was it otherwise than might be expected, after having been engaged with a number of ships that had passed before you?

A. I really don't know.

Q. How far do you think the British fleet was extended from van to rear, at the beginning of the engagement, after the ships had chaced?

A. The Vice Admiral of the red appeared to be very well together. The chacing ships might be about seven or eight miles distant from the Admiral.

Q. In what part of the French line did you begin first to engage? A. The third ship.

Q. By your description of the van and center divisions being pretty well connected together, were not the Admiral's of those two divisions well supported, with the whole force of their respective divisions?

A. At the great distance I was from them, I should think they were.

Q. By your description of the separation of the ships of the Vice Admiral of the blue's division, did he go into action equally supported with the other flag officers?

A. I believe not.

Q. Or was he so during the whole, or any part of the time he was in action?

A. It is out of my power to answer that.

Q. When you had passed the rear of the enemy's fleet, did you observe where the Admiral and the center division was, and where the Vice Admiral of the red and his division was?

A. They were ahead of the Terrible.

Q. Which way were they standing?

A. Towards the enemy.

Q. At what distance do you judge them?

A. I cannot say.

Q. As you cannot speak to the distance, I would ask whether the Admiral, and the ships with him that had passed the rear of the French fleet, were so near to the enemy as to be ready immediately to renew the fight, when the Vice Admiral of the blue came out of it, or to countenance and support him whilst he continued engaged, and the few ships with him, after the Admiral had passed the whole?

A. My ship was just come out of action, and greatly disabled. I was anxious then to get her repaired to renew the attack, and therefore took little notice of any thing else.

Q. From the very brisk fire kept up by our ships that

got

got into the engagement, do you not think that the French ships must have suffered in proportion with ours?

A. Some of them appeared to be greatly disabled, and others did not.

Q. Inform the Court of some of the most material defects of your ship, respecting her masts, yards, sails, and rigging.

A. The fore yard was shot half through, fifteen or sixteen feet from the larboard yard-arm; the main mast had two shot in it, about ten feet below the hounds; one about seven feet above the quarter deck; the main topmast was shot through, about eleven feet below the hounds; the mizen mast received a large shot, about ten feet above the poop; the mizen yard, about twelve or fourteen feet from the parallel, much wounded; the rigging was very much damaged, the main topsail and foresail were cut to pieces, and the other sails very much damaged.

Admiral Montague. You just now said, that the French were some of them disabled; were the English ships that had been engaged, in a condition to renew the attack, at the time the Vice Admiral of the blue speaks of, which was immediately after he came out of action?

A. From what appears to me, I don't think they were.

Q. Was your own ship in a condition?

A. She was not.

President. Suppose you had been engaged along-side of a ship on the same tack, not passing each other upon a contrary tack, was not your ship in a condition to have continued the action with any ship that might have been along-side, in that situation, till it had been more decisive?

A. Yes.

Q. Or was you in such condition as to have been obliged to quit the ship you might have been engaged with?

A. No, I certainly should not have quitted the ship, while I had steerage way, or had the least command of the ship.

President. You have described the Vice Admiral of the blue to be to leeward of the Admiral, on the morning of the 27th; if the Admiral had then bore down into the Vice Admiral's wake, to form the line, as the wind then was, do you think the enemy would probably have been brought to action on that day?

A. The answer to that question must depend entirely upon the enemy; but I believe, if the Admiral had bore down, that we should not have brought them into action, as they always avoided coming to action.

Admiral

Admiral Montague. Did not you come into action as soon, although you chaced, as you would have done provided the Admiral had made the signal for a line of battle, and you had not chaced?

A. I believe sooner.

Prosecutor. Do you remember what part of the French fleet the Formidable began action with; was it a-head of the French Admiral, or a-stern?

A. I never saw the Formidable in action till she began with the Bretagne; she might have formed with the ship a-head of the Bretagne, but reserved her fire for the Bretagne.

Q. Where did the Victory begin action?

A. I really cannot tell.

Q. Then if the Formidable began the action with the ship next ahead of the French Admiral, suppose the Victory had been in a line with her ahead of her, might they not have begun the action successively in the same place?

A. If the Victory had been in a line ahead, there is no doubt but she would have engaged where the Formidable did.

Admiral Montague. In the situation you was in, could you be a judge at the distance you was from the centre and van, whether they were properly supported or not, and how they engaged, or with what ships?

A. It was impossible.

Prosecutor. You omitted, that if the Victory had been in a line with the Formidable, she might have fetched up with that part of the French fleet, where the Formidable did fetch. If the Victory did not begin close action as far ahead of the French Admiral as the Formidable did, would she not have been in a more advantageous situation for attacking the enemy, if she had been in a line with the Formidable?

A. I observed before, if the Victory had been where the Formidable was, she would have engaged where the Formidable did.

Q. I shall ground a question upon one or two that was asked yesterday; I ask you, as an old officer, and one who knows the service well, Whether you understand that a flag officer of a division, has a right to call ships in from chacing, after the Commander in Chief has sent them out to chace by signal, without the Commander in Chief first makes signal to call them in?

A. I have not seen that done without the Commander in Chief's signal.

Q. I ask your opinion, whether from the discipline of the

the ſervice, ſuch flag officer commanding a diviſion only, has a right to do ſo? A. I do not know.

Admiral Montague. I beg leave to aſk you one queſtion, as an old officer; in the ſituation the French fleet were then in, and the wind came ſo far favourable as to admit the Britiſh fleet to bring them to action, do you, altho' your ſignal had been made to chace, and no object in view but the French fleet, do you not think, as an officer, it was your duty to return to the Britiſh fleet, and get into your ſtation as ſoon as poſſible?

A. I do think it was my duty, and I did ſo. When I firſt ſaw the Admiral make the ſignal for the chace, I mentioned to my officers that the intention of that ſignal was to bring the enemy to action at all events, and as ſoon as I ſaw the wind become more favourable, I tacked.

Proſecutor. Do you mean to ſay by this, that you thought it your duty to go into action as ſoon as poſſible, in preference to any thing elſe, under that ſignal, and that you did ſo?

A. I have obſerved before, I thought it my duty to go into action.

Q. Do you think that the Vice Admiral of the Blue was authorized to call chacing ſhips in, on the 27th, on pretence of taking their ſtations in the line, the Commander in Chief having made no ſignal for the line?

A. I cannot ſay.

Q. After you had paſſed the rear of the enemy's line, did you take notice of the Formidable? A. No.

Q. When you firſt ſaw her afterwards, was it while ſhe remained engaged, or after ſhe came out of the action?

A. I took notice of the Formidable when we bore up to get clear of her, I was got upon her lee bow, I did not till then take any notice of her.

Q. Do you remember when you firſt took notice of her, after you came out of action, ſhe being the flag of the diviſion you belonged to?

A. About three o'clock in the afternoon, I think, I cannot be certain.

Q. You have ſaid you took notice of the Admiral as ſoon as you came out of action, but was not able to mention the diſtance he was at; do you remember at that time when you ſaw the Admiral, whether the ſignal for battle, was hauled down or flying? A. I do not.

Q. Where was the Vice Admiral of the Blue, when you firſt ſaw him, about three o'clock, and where was he with reſpect to the reſt of the fleet?

A. I

A. I really cannot tell.

Q. At what time do you recollect feeing him, when you can give account of his fituation ?

A. After I wore, I think I went to windward of the Vice Admiral of the Blue, and got into my ftation.

Q. I think you faid the Admiral, when you firft faw him, was ftanding towards the enemy ; did you fee him wear again to ftand to the fouthward ? A. I did not.

Q. Did you continue upon the ftarboard tack ?

A. Yes.

Q. Whilft you continued upon the ftarboard tack, did you pafs the Admiral ? A. Yes, I did.

Q. Did you pafs to windward or to leeward of him ?

A. To leeward of him, I think. I believe I cheered him.

Q. Where was the Vice Admiral of the Red, when all firing ceafed with his divifion ?

A. I believe that the Vice Admiral of the Red was a little to windward of the Admiral on his bow, but I am not certain.

Q. Did you obferve when the French broke up their line of battle, and began to ftand to the fouthward ?

A. I did not.

Q. When did you firft obferve that any of them were ftanding to the fouthward ? A. A little before I wore.

Q. Was it the Vice Admiral of the Blue, and part of his divifion, that laft came out of the engagement, or what other fhips, if it was not them ?

A. They were the laft, and were the Terrible, America, Elizabeth, and Worcefter. I cannot fpeak to any others.

Q. Whilft you was ftanding with your head to the fouthward, were the French fleet aftern of you ?

A. We lay to, and did not ftand to the fouthward, and I think the French fleet were aftern of us, but am not certain whether we were laying to or falling off.

Q. Did the Admiral with the fleet ftand to the fouthward all the reft of the afternoon, till night ?

A. They had their heads to the fouthward.

Q. Did the Vice Admiral of the Red with his divifion, bear down into the Admiral's wake that afternoon ?

A. I did not obferve it.

Q. Did not you fee them in the Admiral's wake any part of that afternoon, aftern of the Admiral ?

A. No, I do not recollect it upon my word.

Q. Did you ever know, in the courfe of your fervice, that whilft the fignal for a line of battle ahead was flying, the Commander in Chief to order the van or the rear divifion to take the place of the other in the line, without he he was satisfied that one of these divisions was disabled from taking his proper station? A. I have not.

Q. Which division, according to the line of battle, was to lead on the starboard tack?

A. The Vice Admiral of the red.

Q. Do you remember the signal being made, for ships to windward to bear down, with a number of particular ship's pendants flying? A. I do.

Q. Was the Terrible one of them? A. Yes.

Q. Do you remember the first time I had the favour of seeing you, after your expressing a little concern, that it should be thought necessary to make you a signal, and that I replied to you, that I only repeated the signal from the Admiral? A. I believe I do.

Q. Did you at the same time inform me, that when you got down amongst the ships, you was not able to keep your station exactly, your rigging and sails not being compleatly refitted, and that other ships called to you to keep out of their way, or something to that purpose.

A. I believe I do.

Q. About what time was it that you bore down, in consequence of the signal we have been speaking of?

A. A little before seven, I think.

Q. Whereabout was the van, the leading ships of the French, that were forming a line to leeward at that time?

A. Before the beam, I think so.

Q. What sail had the Victory set, any time that afternoon, when you looked at her?

A. I do not recollect.

Q. Do you know of any signals being made by the French fleet, that night, and at what time?

A. There were some false fires about eleven o'clock that night, I think.

Q. Was it perceived, at that time, that they bore away?

A. I did not observe them, because I kept my men to quarters all night, and had lights on the lower gun deck.

Q. Were they pretty near to you during the night, before the signals were made?

A. We judged them at dusk, to be about four miles distant.

Q. What part of the French fleet were in sight the next morning? A. Three sail.

Q. Were they line of battle ships or frigates?

A. I took one of them to be a line of battle ship, the other frigates.

Q. How far do you reckon the nearest of them was from the Terrible? A. From

A. From four to five miles diſtant.

Q. In what poſition were they from the Terrible, a-fore or a-baft the beam?

A. On the larboard quarter.

Q. At what time was it when you firſt ſaw them?

A. Soon after dawn.

Q. Which way did they ſtand?

A. To the ſouthward.

Q. Did they croud ſail away, or bear away more afterwards, or how?

A. They did bear away as ſoon as they diſcovered us.

Q. Were theſe ſhips purſued by the Britiſh fleet?

A. They were not, as I ſaw; there were ſignals out for ſome ſhips to chace, which were ſoon called in again.

Q. Was any other part of the French fleet ſeen that morning, as you know of?

A. I did not ſee any.

Q. Do you know of the ſignal being made by any ſhip for ſeeing them? A. I do not.

Q. Suppoſe, Sir, the Britiſh fleet had chaced theſe three ſhips, and ſuppoſing the reſt of the French fleet to be to leeward, was there not a probability of our undamaged ſhips coming up either with theſe three ſhips, or the diſabled ſhips of their fleet, if the reſt of the fleet left them; or if they had ſtaid by them, might not another engagement have been brought on?

A. I think not.

Q. What ſort of weather was it in the morning of the 28th, as to wind and ſea?

A. I think it was rather hazy, not much wind; I believe a popling ſea.

Q. If our undamaged ſhips, had chaced thoſe three ſhips, what is the reaſon of your ſuppoſing there was no chance of coming up with them?

A. There appeared to me very few of our ſhips fit for chacing.

Q. Do you ſuppoſe there were none?

A. There might be ſome to be ſure.

Q. You have ſuppoſed two of theſe ſhips were frigates, had we not four frigates with us? A. We had.

Q. Some of them upon copper bottoms, clean frigates?

A. Yes.

Q. It being the middle of ſummer, ſhort nights, and you have ſaid not much wind, a popling ſea; do you think it would have been attended with any immediate and imminent danger, if the Britiſh fleet had purſued, at leaſt ſo far as till we had ſeen the French fleet into port, no ſhip in our fleet having loſt her maſt? A. I think

A. I think carrying a fleet, disabled as that was, upon a lee shore, must be attended with great danger.

Q. How was the wind? A. W. N. W.

Q. With the wind at W. N. W. and in moderate weather, if the fleet had gone so far as to come in sight of Ushant, supposing three or four leagues, would that have been running a fleet into imminent danger upon a lee shore? A. No, because the channel was open.

Q. What distance was you from Ushant on the 27th and 28th July?

A. It bore E. N. E. thirty-seven leagues on 27th; on the 28th E. and by N. thirty-four leagues.

Q. Is that a corrected back reckoning, or the current reckoning at the time?

A. The master's reckoning at that time.

Admiral Arbuthnot. You observed the French ships were steering to the southward, the medium of the two days is about E. and by N. from Ushant, do you think, for a ship to have steered that course down, there would have been a probability of seeing the French fleet on the 28th?

A. I should not have steered that course, I should have steered E. S. E. We might have seen them, but I think it would have been at a very great distance.

Admiral Montague. Supposing the French fleet had not run away in the night, but had continued to lay to, to leeward, as they were the night before, jogging on, on a parallel line with the English fleet, do you not think Admiral Keppel would have attacked them in the morning, although he did not pursue them, or think it proper to chace the three sail seen in the morning?

A. I do most certainly think he would.

Q. You are an old officer, you have been more than once in action; you served under a very brave man, Admiral Boscawen; the Admiral now here to be tried, and is trying, is charged with negligently performing the duty imposed on him, I beg you will acquaint the Court, if you know of any instance on the 27th of July, in which he was guilty of such negligence, or did not perform the duty imposed on him?

A. Ever since I have had the honour to know and serve under Admiral Keppel, I have had the greatest esteem for him, and the highest opinion of him as an officer, and I have so still; but as I have been giving in my evidence upon facts, I think my answering that question would be judging of them, which I have no right to do.

Q. Then I am to suppose that you know no act of the Admiral, wherein he neglected, or did not perform his duty? A. I do not.

Admiral

Admiral Keppel. It gives me pain to detain the Court beyond the usual hours of adjournment; but the three leaves containing the narrative of the 26th, 27th, and 28th of July, being taken from the Formidable's log book, and supplied by others, carries with it so extraordinary an appearance, that I trust the Court will not think me unreasonable, in begging that the master may be called in to explain it.

In a case like this, where there is such just ground to expect unfair dealing, it is necessary to prevent any intermediate steps being taken with the master.

Prosecutor. I beg leave to remind the Court, that it is not conformable to rule, to call in one evidence while another is under examination, which would occasion disorder; and this is the more unnecessary, as I intend to call the master myself in the course of the trial, to examine into the affair of the log-book.

ORDERED, *by the Court, That the master may attend to-morrow morning at ten o'clock.*

The Court then adjourned till to-morrow morning ten o'clock.

FIFTEENTH DAY, SATURDAY, JANUARY 23d.

The Court being assembled at ten o'clock this morning, the evidence of Sir Richard Bickerton was continued.

Admiral Keppel. On what tack was the French fleet, when they appeared to you to be in a line of battle, at ten o'clock on the 27th of July? A. The larboard.

Q. Did you lose sight of them at any time afterwards? A. No.

Q. Did the Formidable fetch in a head of the Terrible with the French fleet? A. She did.

Q. How many ships of the rear of the French had the Formidable to pass, when you was compelled to bear up and go to leeward of her?

A. I think there were three of them together.

Q. Did the ships of the Vice Admiral's division you have mentioned before astern of the Vice Admiral of the Blue, come out of action nearly the same time with the Terrible? A. I cannot say.

Q. Can you inform the Court at what time the Terrible did come out of action?

A. At half past one, or rather sooner.

Admiral Keppel. I will not trouble Sir Richard any more.

Ordered to withdraw.

Prosecutor. Mr. President. The cutting the leaves out

 of

of the Formidable's log book, is a fact which I was totally ignorant of, till it was observed yesterday by a member of the Court; nor could any person be more astonished at it than myself. It is my anxious wish to have this matter fully investigated, and for that purpose I have desired the master of the Formidable, and the mate who made the entries in the log book, to attend this morning; and that in giving their evidence on this point, they may be put to the severest test; I desire they may be examined by the Court and Admiral Keppel, without any previous question from me.

Mr. FORFAR, *Master of the Formidable, sworn as follows:*

"*You shall swear that the book you have delivered into Court, now upon the table, is your ship's book, containing the transactions from day to day, without any alteration or addition made, so far as relates to the 27th and 28th of July.*"

Admiral Keppel. My reason for requesting the Court, yesterday, that the Master of the Formidable might be instantly examined concerning the state of his log book, was, to prevent any immediate communication betwixt him and others upon this subject, I must therefore ask the Master; who was the first person that told you, the Court had discovered any extraordinary appearance in the log book?

A. I heard it in a shop, yesterday about noon, the woman in the shop was telling another person that there had been some leaves torn out of the Formidable's log book, which was the first I ever heard of it.

Q. Have you had any conversation with any body, and with whom, before the Court rose yesterday?

A. There were several, I do not exactly know their names, that asked me relative to the book.

Court. At what time was it those people asked you those questions?

A. As soon as I heard of the log book's being in question, I came into the witness's room about one o'clock on purpose to have been examined if I had been called.

Q. Can you name no body that spoke to you when you went into the witnesses room?

A. I shall, Sir. I met, as I was coming along, Mr. Bayley, master of the Foudroyant, who told me I should be wanted, I said very well, I am going to the court, for I had heard of the leaves being cut out.

Admiral Keppel. Did any body else besides the master of the Foudroyant speak to you?

A. I don't recollect any body, till I came into the examining room.

President.

President. Was there any body ſpoke to you in the examining room?

A. I think Capt. Walſingham did; he ſaid, he ſuppoſed I was there on account of the log book? I ſaid yes.

Q. To whoſe houſe did you go after the court broke up?

A. I went to the houſe next door to the Vice Admiral's, where we generally reſort, and ſleep there.

Q. Do you live there?

A. No, I do not ſleep there; I have ſometimes, but did not laſt night.

Admiral Keppel. Had you any diſcourſe about the log-book after the Court broke up yeſterday? A. Yes.

Q. With whom? A. Capt. Beazely.

Q. Does he live at that houſe you went to when the Court was up? A. Yes, Sir, he ſleeps there.

Q. How long did you remain at Capt. Beazely's houſe before you went to Sir Hugh Palliſer's?

A. I cannot juſtly ſay how long, perhaps half an hour.

Q. How long did you ſtay at Sir Hugh Palliſer's?

A. I cannot exactly tell you; it might be an hour, or an hour and an half.

Q. Who was preſent?

A. Almoſt all the officers that were on ſhore, Capt. Beazely, Mr. Dickenſon, firſt Lieutenant, Mr. Waller, ſecond Lieutenant, Mr. Hills, third Lieutenant, Mr. Moor, Lieutenant of Marines, and Mr. Hoſe another, Mr. Thomas, and Mr. Hartwell, and two lawyers.

Q. Were there any queſtions put to you about the log book? A. Yes.

Q. When was the preſent account of the tranſactions of the 25th, 26th, and 27th of July entered in the Formidable's log book; the 27th, when?

A. It was not entered in that book for a day or two; I believe it was put in the 30th, to the beſt of my recollection.

Q. What was the meaning of that delay?

A. I took it off from the log board upon a ſheet of paper to ſhew it to the Admiral, and Captain, before I put it into the book.

Q. Was it approved of?

A. What I took off, was approved of.

Q. Without alteration or amendment?

A. Some things were added to it by recollecting what was omitted.

Q. Do you recollect what they were?

A. I do not recollect exactly what they were; they were with reſpect to ſignals and time, I believe.

M 2 Q. Were

Q. Were there any minutes of ſignals taken by any body, that this log book was copied from?

A. There were, before we came to action, to the time we came out of action.

Q. Were there no minutes taken after that time till dark, during the day?

A. None that I ſaw, except by recollection.

Q. Is there more than one log-book?

A. Yes, ſir, I have another here.

Q. Is it the ſame as that on the table?

A. Except the three ſhips whoſe ſignals I have made to chace in the morning of the 28th, interlined in the one I have with me, and put in ſince, otherwiſe it is exact. That is the reaſon I gave my oath to the book on the table, but I could not to the one now with me.

Q. When was that interlination made?

A. About the time, or before, I cannot ſay which, that we came to an anchor at Spithead, it may be a day before that.

Q. 'Tis not in the log-book upon the table?

A. I believe it is not.

Q. Do you know who cut theſe leaves or entries out of the log-book, of the 25th, 26th, and 27th?

A. One of the mates, Mr. Winckworth.

Court. What was the occaſion of thoſe leaves being cut out?

A. Mr. Winckworth had ſpilt ſome ink upon one I ſaw torn out.

Q. When was that torn out?

A. To the beſt of my knowledge it was the 25th or 26th, the day before the action, or the next to it.

Q. Do you know when the reſt of the leaves were cut or torn out?

A. I did not ſee the reſt torn out, he had done it before I came down. To the beſt of my remembrance when I came down, he told me he had ruled one of the leaves for two days work, and it would not contain it, to put it all in one; I believe it was this, the 26th. The other he had omitted putting in the minutes of the ſignals, taken by the midſhipmen; he had not put them down againſt the hour, and that was the reaſon of his tearing that leaf out. The third, as I before obſerved, he ſpilt the ink upon.

Admiral Keppel. Does he mean relative to the minute ſignals of the 27th and 28th?

A. No, only the 27th; there was nothing wrote upon the 28th.

Q. Did the mate ſhew you thoſe minutes?

A. I gave

A. I gave him the book, and he had wrote the log off upon the leaf before I came down, to the best of my knowledge.

Q. Did you see the minutes he wrote it from? A. Yes.

Q. Did those leaves so wrote agree with the minutes?

A. The entries in the book upon the table do agree with the minutes.

Q. Do you know what became of those leaves that were cut out?

A. I do not know indeed, they were thrown away, I believe.

Q. Do you know where the original minutes now are, from whence the signal minutes were entered in the log-book? A. No.

Q. As the day's work of the 27th and 28th were not entered 'till the 30th, how could they make an entry of them before you went down on the 26th?

A. He took them off the board before I came down.

Q. Did the board continue marked from the 26th to the 30th?

A. No, I took them off upon a piece of paper, when he spoiled this.

Q. Did you ever go to the masters of any ships in the fleet under my command, to ask to see their log-books?

A. No.

Q. Did you not ask Mr. Reade, master of the Queen, to let you see his log-book, and compare it?

A. I went on board the Queen once, and he was then writing his log, in his place, and I looked at it. I do not remember that I mentioned my book at all. It was much the same as my own, I said.

Q. Had you the Formidable's log-book with you when you was on board the Queen?

A. No, never.

Q. Did you compare the entries from the sheet that was blotted, to see that it was fairly transcribed?

A. I do not recollect that I took any notice of the sheet.

Q. Was the log-book now under your arm made since the cutting out the leaves from that on the table, or before; was it copied from the original entry, before the leaves were cut out?

A. I know the 27th and 28th were.

Q. Do you mean to say that they were not copied till the 30th?

A. Yes, I think it was a day or two after the action, the 27th and 28th were; but I cannot say any thing about these two?

Q. Admiral Montague. After the action was over, 'did you see the minutes kept by the midshipmen on the poop, stationed for that purpose, from the morning of the 27th, 'till the action was over, I do not care whether in, after, or before the action?

A. I saw what he had made before ten o'clock, but I saw none afterwards.

Q. Had you these minutes in your possession?

A. Yes, I had them after the action, the midshipman gave me the book.

Q. Did you shew these minutes to the Captain, to know if he approved them?

A. Not till I had inserted them in the paper I took the log on.

Q. Did you not tell the Captain, that the minutes taken on the poop were erroneous?

A. No, I told him they were not all put down, for the midshipmen had taken no notes from the time the action commenced.

Q. How do you know they were not all put down?

A. By seeing the book, and recollecting what was done.

Q. Did you order the minutes to be entered on the log board, or did you make any alteration in them, they being erroneous?

A. They never were entered on the log-board in general.

Q. Is it not usual, for the mate of the watch at sea, to mark the board every hour, and to put against it the remarks and transactions that has happened during that hour?

A. It is customary; but I apprehend in a fleet, the signals are so numerous, that the board would not hold it; we had two mates that had never been in a man of war before as mates, and they were not so expert as I could have wished, so that the mate took it from the midshipman's minute book.

Q. Then the mate entered the midshipman's minutes upon the log-book, for there is but one remark of the transactions of that day upon the book, the signal for the line, and the signal for bearing down? A. Yes.

Q. How comes it these minutes do not appear with the midshipman's book, upon this day's work?

A. The only minutes he has that day were taken, I believe, in the afternoon of the 26th, which was the 27th, of the ship's chacing; I do not recollect any more being taken.

Q. From what book did you take your day's work, in order to work your reckoning?

A. From

A. From the board generally.

Q. Did you take them every four hours off the board, or did you take them off at mid-day?

A. I generally worked my day's work in the morning about eight o'clock, for fear I ſhould be aſked any queſtion about the bearing of the land, by my Admiral or Captain.

Q. You have ſaid, that two of the maſter's mates had never been in the King's ſervice before as mates, and therefore you was fearful they were not ſo expert in marking the log-board, or writing it down in the log-book, as thoſe mates are that have been long in the ſervice; did thoſe two mates, or any of the mates on board of you, conſult with you, before they entered upon the log-board the tranſactions of the day?

A. Sometimes they did.

Q. Did you give any orders, or point out any thing that was wrong on that board, to either of thoſe mates, during the 27th and 28th of July?

A. I do not recollect I did, particularly on either of thoſe two days.

Admiral Keppel. You ſaid that you ſaw thoſe minutes; do you take upon you to ſwear, poſitively, that there were no minutes made of the ſignals from the time the action ceaſed, 'till dark?

A. I ſaw none kept by the midſhipmen, that I can recollect.

Q. As the midſhipmen were appointed to obſerve ſignals, and enter them in a book, why were thoſe entries diſcontinued on ſo important a day as the 27th?

A. I can give no other reaſon, than that they were employed in refitting the ſhip, as they were the only two midſhipmen that we could depend upon.

Admiral Keppel. Mr. Preſident, I ſhall aſk no more queſtions concerning minutes, but I cannot help expreſſing my ſurpriſe, that the midſhipmen ſhould only take down the ſignal for chace, which the proſecutor dwells ſo much upon, and omit all the others by which they were called together again, during the reſt of the day. I have only one more obſervation to make on the accuſer's addreſs to the Court; his offer was intended to carry the appearance of candour, when he requeſted the maſter may be expoſed to the ſtricteſt examination by the Court and me, without any previous queſtion by himſelf; whereas it now turns out juſt as I expected yeſterday, when the Vice Admiral reſiſted my application to call the maſter immediately, that he has been previouſly examined by Sir Hugh Palliſer and his friends.

Court.

Court. Did you enter this signal, that the midshipman omitted, by recollection?

A. Yes, Sir, by recollection.

Prosecutor. Mr. President. The postponing the examination of the master yesterday, was the act and proposition of the Court, before I said any thing. As to my speaking to the master since that time, about cutting out the leaves, it was natural that I should make enquiry into a fact I was ignorant of, and so much surprised at yesterday. And I shall continue to give the Court the utmost information on that point, and for that purpose I have sent expresses to find the succeeding midshipmen, that were appointed as signal midshipmen, to the one that was signal midshipman before. He is supposed to be somewhere in a tender in Wales, or he may be on board the ship he belongs to. I have sent expresses each way, that if he has by him the signal minute book, it might be produced.

Admiral Keppel. I beg to refer to the Court, whether the Prosecutor did not desire that he might not be interrupted in his evidence, when I begged the master might be called yesterday, though past the usual hour of adjournment, before the Court interposed at all.

President. You are right, Sir.

Admiral Montague. Before I put my question, I beg leave to know of the Court, whether I may be permitted to read this day's work in the Formidable's log book, to the Court. *Permitted*.

Q. You have said, you did not dictate to the mates what should be put in the log book, either the 27th, or 28th of July; I desire to know if this account now in the log book, be the mate's own remarks, or yours. I will read them to you.

"The 27th moderate and clear, at ten minutes past one "firing ceased. We saw without a mizen yard and mizen "mast, one of their ships, that seemed to be otherways "much damaged, and who, as soon as the firing ceased, "bore away, and run to the southward, accompanied by "a frigate.---After we passed the last ship, we wore and "laid our heads towards them, as did the Admiral, and "Vice Admiral Sir Robert Harland. Soon after the "French wore, and laid their heads to the southward. "We did the same, and repeated the signal for the line of "battle ahead a cable's length asunder. Our sails and "rigging being very much damaged, we hauled to wind- "ward to *knot and splice*. Sails most of them rendered "unservicetable. At six o'clock P. M. signal made for "us to bear down into the Admiral's wake.---At dusk

" the French formed in a line to leeward, extended parallel to us. The French Admiral, and those nearest to him in the centre in the action, appeared to be almost in the rear, being the ships that had suffered most. Fresh gales and squally, with rain most part of the night, and exceeding dark. At three A. M. having *knotted* and *spliced* most part of the rigging, and shifted some of the sails, bore down into our station in the line, expecting to engage at day-light; but to our great surprise, at day light we found the whole French fleet had stole away under cover of a dark night, except three sail which remained in sight, and immediately crowded all the sail they could to the southward. It is uncertain whether these ships had or not observed the motions of the rest of the fleet in the night, or whether they were left to leeward, and by shewing lights, to make us believe they remained in a line to leeward, as at dusk, and thereby deceive us, to cover their retreat. Thus after the two fleets had been in sight of each other four days, during which time we used every means we could to bring them to battle, and thereby crippled some of our ships breasts by carrying sail, the French keeping to windward of us. In the action we lost our fore top mast stay sail jibb, and top gallant mast stay sail jibb, top-gallant mast stay sail, and main top gallant mast stay sail. In clearing ship lost two cutters, which by lowering down filled, and obliged us to cut them away. Several were employed in *knotting* and *splicing* the rigging, and shifting the sails."

Q. Were these their remarks of this day's transactions, or your dictating to them?

A. I took the log off the board myself, upon a piece of paper; I put down what signals I could recollect myself, and by asking the signal midshipman. I shewed it to the Captain, he desired me to shew it to the Admiral, the Admiral approved of some, and disapproved of others, with the remarks I had made myself, and gave me a piece of paper with respect to some remarks that he had made, so that *between the two*, I made the log up for that day, of what I thought were facts.

Admiral Keppel. So this log is as approved by the Vice Admiral.

Prosecutor. I admit it, the master has stated the facts.

Q. Do you know, or have you reason to believe, that Captain Beazely or myself had ever any knowledge of the leaves in the book being cut out, before yesterday, when it appeared to the Court?

A. No,

A. No, I do not believe either had?

Capt. Duncan. When did you leave the witneſs's room yeſterday?

A. When the Court broke up, I ſaw a number going out.

Q. Was you directed to leave it or not? A. No.

Q. Do you recollect what time you was on board the Queen?

A. Some time before ſhe ſailed for Plymouth, the week before I went on board to get a paſſage for myſelf.

Q. Can you recollect the day, or about the day?

A. No. It was the week previous to the time Lord Shuldham ſailed.

Ordered to withdraw.

GROSVENOR WINKWORTH, *maſter's mate of the Formidable, called and ſworn, and ordered to withdraw, without any queſtions being put to him.*

CAPT. KENYEAR, *late firſt lieutenant of the Formidable, now Capt. of the Salamander, called and ſworn.*

Proſecutor. Can you remember the time after the Formidable had ceaſed firing, and came out of the action, and had laid her head towards the enemy again, the officers and men being ordered to return to their quarters, in expectation of renewing the engagement when Admiral Keppel ſhould come up? A. Yes, Sir.

Q. When did you firſt take notice where Admiral Keppel was?

A. Not till we wore the ſecond time.

Q. At what diſtance do you reckon he was then from you? A. Between a mile and a half and two mile.

Capt. Duncan. Where was you quartered on the day of battle? A. On the main deck.

Q. Do you remember the Victory and Formidable meeting after that?

A. I remember the Victory's paſſing to windward, and under the Formidable's ſtern.

Q. Did the Victory ſtand to the ſouthward after ſhe had wore? A. Yes.

Q. Do you remember the ſignal for the line of battle being then flying, for a line of battle ahead a cable's length aſunder, on board the Victory and Formidable?

A. I do on board the Victory, but am not certain with reſpect to its flying on board the Formidable.

Q. Do you remember the Formidable firſt hauling ſomewhat to windward out of the way of other ſhips, to

take

take their ſtations between us and the Admiral, and afterwards to ſtand after the Admiral with all the ſail ſhe could ſet, and trimmed as well as her condition would admit? A. I do.

Q. Did not the Victory increaſe her diſtance from the Formidable during the whole afternoon? A. Yes.

Q. Did not the Formidable ſteer the whole afternoon, keeping the Admiral a little open under the lee?

A. Yes, Sir.

Q. Was that a proper courſe for fetching into her ſtation, in a line of battle, if the Admiral had not ſailed faſter than us?

A. I think it was.

Q. As the Admiral ſailed faſter than the Formidable all the afternoon, whilſt ſhe continued ſo to do, was it poſſible for the Formidable to get into her ſtation in the line, agreeable to the ſignal then flying?

A. I do not think in was poſſible.

Q. Then whatever ſignals might be made, or whatever meſſage might be ſent, I repeat it again, was it poſſible for the Formidable to have complied with them, to have got into her ſtation in the line of battle that afternoon, unleſs the Admiral had waited for her?

A. I think not, Sir.

Q. Do you remember the ſignal being made in the evening, for ſhips to windward to bear down, with ſeveral ſhips pendants let fly about that time?

A. I obſerved the general ſignal, and the pendants for ſeveral ſhips of the Vice Admiral's diviſion, to bear down at the ſame time; but I cannot ſay whether they were all let fly together, or not.

Q. Were theſe ſhips pendants repeated on board the Formidable, before or after the Fox frigate came to ſpeak with her?

A. To the beſt of my recollection, the ſignals were made before the Fox hailed the Formidable.

Q. Do you remember the Fox cheering; or whether the Fox cheered the Formidable firſt, or whether the Formidable cheered her firſt?

A. I am pretty clear the Fox cheered the Formidable firſt.

Q. Where was you ſtationed at that time, in carrying on the buſineſs of repairing the rigging?

A. On the poop, and was then there.

Q. Did the people on the poop of the Formidable cheer the Fox firſt? A. No.

Q. At

Q. At what diſtance, do you reckon, the Formidable was from the Victory at dusk that evening?

A. I believe the Formidable was about one mile to windward of the Victory's wake, and about two miles from her.

Q. About what time, to the beſt of your recollection, was it when the Fox ſpoke to the Formidable?

A. I believe it was after ſeven.

Court. What was the meſſage the Captain delivered, as you was upon the poop?

A. I did not hear it diſtinctly.

Q. Can you tell what you did hear?

A. I underſtood from the people, that the purport of the meſſage delivered by Capt. Windſor, was for the Vice Admiral's diviſion, to bear down into the Admiral's wake.

Q. Did you hear any anſwer to that?

A. No, Sir.

Proſecutor. Do you remember whether any of thoſe ſhips ſignals, that had been hung out, had been hauled in, becauſe they had been obſerved before the Fox came to us?

A. Two ſhips to windward of the Formidable, which I believe were the Egmont and America, bore up when the ſignal was made, and upon theſe pendants being hauled in, brought to again to windward of the Formidable.

Q. You have repeated the Formidable, as not being able to keep way with the Admiral, or with ſhips carrying ſail upon a wind; don't you apprehend, if the fleet had bore down upon an enemy to renew the attack, notwithſtanding ſhe was not able to carry ſail upon a wind, that ſhe could have gone down into action, though ſhe was not able to carry ſail upon a wind?

A. Yes, but ſhe could not have maintained her ſtation in the line, at a cable's length aſunder.

Q. Did the Admiral, in the afternoon, bring to, to let the ſhips come up with him, that you know of?

A. Not that I obſerved, but I was employed the whole afternoon, after we came out of the action, in repairing damages done to the rigging and ſails.

Q. Were not the officers and men employed all that afternoon and night, in refitting the rigging and ſhifting the ſails? A. Yes.

Q. Was every thing done that could poſſibly be done, for the beſt diſpatch, in getting the ſhip in a condition to get up with the Admiral?

A. I believe there was nothing neglected by the officers or men.

Q. Did

Q. Did not the drum beat to arms at two o'clock in the morning of the 28th?

A. The drum did beat to arms nearly about that time.

Q. Were not all hands at quarters, and the ſhip in her ſtation, a-ſtern of the Admiral, at the proper diſtance, as well as could be eſtimated, in the night, before day-light in the morning, ready immediately to engage?

A. All hands were at quarters, and the Formidable was in the line a-ſtern of the Admiral, but I cannot ſay whether ſhe was exactly in her ſtation, or how many ſhips were a-ſtern of her; and we were expecting to begin firing when it was diſcovered there were only three ſtrange ſail in ſight.

Q. At day-light, when you ſaw thoſe three ſhips, how near do you reckon the neareſt of them were?

A. I did not ſee them till the guns were ſecured, and then they had bore away, and I believe the neareſt at that time was ſomething more than a mile from the Formidable.

Capt. Botteler. As you was upon the poop of the Formidable, I ſhould be glad to know if the log was hove from three o'clock in the afternoon of the 27th, till four o'clock in the morning of the 28th?

A. I did not ſee the log hove at any one time betwixt the dates you have mentioned, being ſo much engaged about the rigging.

Admiral Keppel. Captain Kenyear; you ſaid that the Formidable, after having wore, and laid her head towards the enemy, wore back towards the Victory, whilſt the Victory was with her head towards the enemy; did the Formidable wear towards the Victory by ſignal?

A. I have already ſaid, that I did not ſee the Victory until the Formidable had wore the ſecond time, conſequently cannot know whether the ſignal for wearing was out or not.

Q. When you firſt ſaw the Victory, how were the Victory and Formidable ſituated in reſpect to each other?

A. The Victory was upon the Formidable's ſtarboard bow, and was ſtanding towards her, I believe in a direct line on the oppoſite point of the compaſs.

Q. Did you then obſerve the ſignal for a line of battle ahead, on board the Victory, exactly at that time?

A. No, Sir.

Q. Did you when you paſſed her?

A. No, not till ſhe went under the Formidable's ſtern.

Q. What ſail had the Formidable ſet when ſhe paſſed the Victory? A. I do not recollect. Q. What

Q. What fail had fhe fet when fhe laid her head towards the enemy, before fhe wore to the Victory?

A. I do not know this, I was at my quarters upon the main deck.

Q. What fail did the Victory go under in the afternoon on the 27th, when fhe ftood to the fouthward, the whole afternoon, or any part of it when you faw her?

A. I took very little notice of her during the afternoon, being employed, as I obferved before, in repairing the damages.

Q. How did you take notice that fhe increafed her diftance from the Formidable?

A. I obferved that the Victory was further from the Formidable in the evening, than about three o'clock, when we were aftern and ftood to the fouthward.

Q. Was fhe further from the Formidable at four o'clock? A. I took no account of time.

Q. Did you ever fet the Victory by compafs that afternoon? A. No.

Q. Did the Formidable unbend any of her fails that afternoon, in order to wear others?

A. I believe the fore and mizen top fails were fhifted about eight o'clock.

Q. Do you remember when the fore topfail was unbent? A. No, Sir, not exactly.

Q. Do you remember within an hour or two?

A. No, Sir, but I believe our fore and mizen topfail were fet about half paft eight.

Q. Do you know whether they were both unbent at the fame time? A. I do not know.

Q. Then you don't know whether the fore top fail was unbent? A. No, I do not.

Q. You fay it was bent and fet about half after eight?

A. No, I faid I believed fo.

Q. Was there any fore top fail to the yard at half paft feven o'clock? A. I cannot tell.

Q. Was there any at half paft fix? A. I cannot tell.

Q. Was there any at half paft five? A. I cannot tell.

Q. Was there any at half paft four?

A. I do not know from my own obfervation?

Q. Do you know when you firft faw the fignal for fhips to bear into the Admiral's wake?

A. I believe it was about feven o'clock?

Q. Did you not fee it fooner?

A. I did not fee it till the time the pendants were let fly. I cannot fpeak with certainty as to time.

Q. How long was you employed on the poop?

A. I was

A. I was ordered on the poop, I believe about three o'clock, and was there and about the aft part of the ship most part of the afternoon.

Q. The log was never hove during the whole time you was upon the poop?

A. I have said, I did not see the log hove.

Q. There was no want of seamen in the Formidable to expedite the business, as a well manned ship could expedite?

A. The Formidable was manned as other ships are in general, seamen, landsmen, and ordinary seamen.

Q. Then she was but indifferently manned?

A. There was nothing remarkable either the one way or the other.

Q. Were they sober and orderly, all that afternoon, or was there any drunkenness?

A. I believe they were sober and orderly in general, there might perhaps be one or two a little in liquor.

Q. You said it was seven o'clock when the Fox came to the Formidable, are you sure it was seven o'clock upon recollection?

A. I have not spoke to time with any certainty.

Q. Do you think it was after six?

A. I believe it was later.

Capt. Duncan. What sail did you wear the Formidable down under?

A. The fore sail and top sail I believe only, as the jib and fore top mast stay sail were cut away in the action.

Q. Were the top sails crippled?

A. I cannot recollect, as most of the running rigging was cut away.

Court. You said sometime ago, that on the morning of the 28th, one of the three strange ships that were seen then, were within or about one mile from the Formidable, did you fire at her, or make any signals to the Admiral of these ships being in sight, or make any preparation for chacing them?

A. I believe I said the nearest of these ships was above a mile from the Formidable; we did not fire at her, neither did we make any signal to the Admiral to my knowledge.

Q. Do you recollect at what hour it was quite dark that night?

A. I believe the sun sets a quarter before eight o'clock in the lat. of 48, 27th of July.

Q. What time was it quite dark then?

A. I cannot tell.

Capt. Kenyear was then ordered to withdraw, and the Court adjourned till Monday morning ten o'clock.

Six-

Sixteenth Day, MONDAY, January 26th.

At ten o'clock this morning the Court being met, the prisoner was brought in, and audience admitted.

Capt. Goodhall, *of the Defiance, called and sworn.*

Prosecutor. When you began the engagement, wereany of our ſhips then near you, ſo as to be of ſupport to each other?

A. I ſaw no ſhips engaging the enemy, but the ſhip that was ahead of us, which I took to be the Prince George; not when I firſt began the engagement, I drew up to her ſoon after I began the engagement.

Q. When you drew up to the Prince George, had you then joined the centre diviſion?

A. Yes, I apprehend ſhe belonged to the center diviſion.

Q. Your ſhip was properly one of the Vice Admiral of the blue's diviſion, was it not? A. Yes.

Q. During the engagement, did any of our ſhips fire over you, or fire over any Engliſh ſhips? A. No.

Q. When you paſſed the rear of the enemy, where was you with reſpect to the Victory?

A. The Victory was on the Defiance's lee bow.

Q. At what diſtance did the Victory ſtand, after ſhe paſſed the rear of the enemy, before ſhe wore?

A. She might be about half a mile, or ſomething more, upon the Defiance's lee bow, and wore I apprehend ſoon after.

Q. What diſtance do you reckon the Defiance was from the rear of the enemy, at that time?

A. Three or four cable's length.

Q. What time are you ſpeaking of?

A. The time I obſerved after the Victory had paſſed the Defiance. The rear of the enemy had paſſed the Defiance.

Q. Speak to the time when the Victory wore, and laid her head towards the enemy again, what diſtance do you judge the Victory was from the rear of the enemy?

A. At the time the Victory wore, ſhe might be a mile, or a mile and half from their rear.

Q. Do you know when the ſignal for battle was hauled down?

A. I believe about two o'clock.

Q. Was that before or after the Victory wore?

A. After

A. After.

Q. Did you see any of the ships at that time dismasted?

A. None.

Q. Did you see the Admiral wear the second time?

A. Yes.

Q. Where was the Vice Admiral of the Red, and his division, at that time?

A. They were to windward of the rest of the fleet.

Q. Had they wore and stood to the northward, before the Victory and centre division?

A. I think so.

Q. Then were they more advanced towards the enemy, than the centre division, at the time the Admiral wore the second time? A. They appeared to me to be so.

Q. When did you first take notice of the Vice Admiral of the blue, after you ceased firing?

A. At the time he was near the Victory.

Q. Did you never look towards the ships that remained engaged, after you came out of the engagement?

A. No, not to retain any idea about them.

Q. Then you did not see the Vice Admiral of the Blue, till she was near the Victory?

A. Not till she was near the Victory, I think I saw her edge down towards the Victory.

Q. Did you know of any reason, why the Admiral, and the rest of the fleet, might not have wore much nearer the enemy, than a mile and half, or mile distant, after they passed them? A. I do not.

Q. If they had done so, do you know any reason why the engagement might not have been continued, or immediately renewed, as soon as the Vice Admiral of the Blue came out of the engagement with the ships with him; the Vice Admiral of the Red being at that time to windward of the Admiral?

A. The situation of several of the ships, and the disabled state that others appeared to be in, was the reason, I think, why the Admiral could not have collected a considerable body of ships so easily.

Q. Do you know of the disabled state of any other ship but your own?

A. There were several appeared to be so in their sails and rigging.

Q. From the very brisk fire that our ships kept up during the engagement, had not you reason to suppose that the enemy suffered in proportion to the British fleet?

A. The enemy did not appear to have suffered so much in their sails or rigging, as the English, I am persuaded

they

they muſt have ſuffered much more in the hulls and loſs of men.

Q. You ſaid the ſhips were ſcattered and ſeparated much on coming out of the engagement; would that have been the caſe, if the fleet had been formed in a line of battle, in which caſe a Captain cannot quit his ſtation, according to his fighting inſtructions?

A. They were ſeparated from each other, but not ſcattered or divided, ſo as not to be able to be collected in a certain time; they certainly would have been more collected had they engaged in a regular line of battle, parallel to each other.

Preſident. Do you think the engagement would have been brought on that day, had you been in a line of battle; I mean in the poſition they were then in, if the Admiral had made a ſignal to form a line of battle in the morning?

A. No, the Admiral had always offered the enemy battle, it was in their breaſts to have bore down. I do not think if he had formed a line of battle that morning, he could poſſibly have attacked the enemy.

Q. Did not the French fleet edge down and make the attack?

A. They partly edged down, and were partly met by the Engliſh fleet.

Q. Did they edge down before the engagement began?

A. I cannot poſitively anſwer that, but I think their van did edge down.

Proſecutor. Did it appear to you, by the enemy's ſtanding towards the Engliſh fleet, and forming a new line of battle in the evening, that they ſhewed a diſpoſition to renew the engagement by that motion?

A. It indicated a diſpoſition to receive an attack, for they had it in their power, by making more ſail, to have made one.

Q. You have ſaid after you came out of the engagement, that ſeveral ſhips appeared, to you, to have ſuffered in their ſails and rigging, how many of them did you obſerve in that ſtate at that time, without regard to any thing that you have heard ſince?

A. To the beſt of my recollection, there were ten or twelve, I ſaw them with my own eyes.

Q. Do you think they were not in a condition to have attacked an enemy, who you ſaid ſhewed a diſpoſition to receive them?

A. Towards the cloſe of the day, I believe they were.

Q. Was your ſhip in ſuch condition, that you were not fit

fit to continue in action, if you had had an opportunity of laying along side of a ship, after you came out of action?

A. We were ready for action in thirty, or forty minutes after.

Q. Did you see the Vice Admiral of the red and his division, bear down into the Admiral's wake that afternoon?

A. I saw the Vice Admiral of the red bear away, but in a position to go a-head of the center division, to the best of my judgment, pass under the lee of the Vice Admiral of the blue, and to windward of the Commander in Chief.

Q. Do you know whether the Vice Admiral of the red, was ordered to take the station of the Vice Admiral of the blue, a-stern of the Admiral? A. No.

Q. Were not the ships of the Vice Admiral of the blue, the last that came out of the engagement?

A. I believe so.

Q. Were not the ships you speak of, that you saw disabled in their sails and rigging, chiefly of that division?

A. There appeared to me to be some of that division, and I imagine some belonging to the others; I could not imagine the whole of the blue division were in that state.

Q. Can you speak with certainty, that part of them were of the other divisions?

A. I cannot, but I presume so; some of them were a-head of me at that time, and upon my lee bow, at a considerable distance.

Court. How many of the Vice Admiral of the blue's division did you see disabled?

A. I did not, at that particular time, make any observations of what division the ships belonged to.

Prosecutor. Did you observe what sail the Victory carried that afternoon, after she stood to the southward?

A. I think, soon after she stood to the southward, she had her fore-sail and top sails, and soon after her top-sails only; but I cannot be certain as to every particular sail, or change of sail.

Q. What part of the enemy's fleet were in sight the next morning?

A. Three sail of ships were about a mile and an half from the Defiance, and taken for French men of war, but the body of the French fleet were not seen from the Defiance.

Q. Did you take these three ships to be line of battle ships or frigates?

A. The nearest I took to be a line of battle ship, the others were smaller.

Q. Were they chaced by the British fleet?

A. I believe they were.

Q. How long, and by what ships?

A. For a short time only, by what ships I do not recollect.

Q. Did they set all their sails?

A. That I cannot speak to.

Q. Was there any signal made for leaving off chace?

A. I do not recollect.

Q. I think you said they were about a mile and an half or two miles from the Defiance; did they appear to be nearer to any other part of the English fleet?

A. They must have been somewhat nearer to the ships that were a-stern in the line.

Q. Amongst those ships you mentioned to have seen, when you came out of the engagement, in a disabled state, as to their masts and rigging, were any of them of the red division?

A. I cannot recollect that any of them were of the red division.

Q. Besides these ten or twelve ships that appeared to have been disabled in their masts and rigging, immediately after coming out of action; was there not eighteen or twenty that did not appear to be so?

A. The ships that had suffered in their sails and rigging, drew my attention, but I suppose there might be so many.

Q. Were the frigates disabled?

A. I do not remember having seen them from the time I engaged, or during the whole afternoon.

Admiral Montague. You have heard the charge read against Admiral Keppel; by the first articles of which, he is charged with negligently performing the duty imposed on him; by the third, in not doing the utmost in his power to take, burn, sink, and destroy the French fleet, by the fourth, with running away from the French, and that the French offered him battle, and published to the world that the British fleet avoided it; by the fifth, that by his misconduct and negligence, the honour of the British navy was tarnished. Now, acquaint the Court if you know of any act of Admiral Keppel, either on the 27th or 28th of July, wherein he was guilty of the charges alledged against him, in the different articles of the charge: and you will remember, I do not ask your opinion, but from your own knowledge?

A. No

A. No man can have more esteem or respect for Admiral Keppel than I have. I think him highly valuable as an officer and gentleman, but as this is a question that tends to my passing judgment, who am only a witness, I must beg leave to decline answering it. It appears to me to be rendering my evidence nugatory, and I think it an assumption on the court, whose judgment upon my evidence rests in them alone, and not in mine.

Admiral Montague. Sir; I have not asked for your judgment, I am one of the people here who are to judge, acquit or condemn. A charge is sent to us, which charge we are ordered to try by. In order to come at facts, evidences are examined, and I have heard every thing that has been said by the evidences. I am to judge of that afterwards, how far it will acquit or condemn. But in order to prove the charge, I ask a fair and honest question, both for my country and the prisoner. For my country, if he has done that which has disgraced it, I desire the court may know it; for the prisoner, if he has not done it, that they may also know it; I therefore ask you, from your own knowledge, as Commander of one of the King's ships, whether you saw any act of Admiral Keppel, in which he falls guilty of the different articles of this charge?

A. As a witness, I have further objections to answer a question, which is giving judgment on a charge, from the possible situation that I, or some men I love in the service, may be placed in by a malignant prosecution; and the evidence that can be called to support the charge, drawn from the source of discontent, and therefore as this consequence may be fatal to my own honour, my own character, and perhaps my own life, or perhaps of those I love, I wish to decline answering that question.

Admiral Keppel. Where was the Defiance on the morning of the 27th?

A. On the lee quarter of the Formidable.

Q. Did you see the signal for any ships to chace to windward?

A. I was not upon deck when that signal was made.

Q. Did the officers inform you of it?

A. Afterwards I was informed of it.

Q. Do you recollect what sail you was under at that time?

A. Foresail and double reefed topsails.

Q. Did you make more sail upon the signal being made for ships to chace?

A. No, we did not.

Q. You ſaid you came to action aſtern of the Prince George; were not ſeveral ſhips engaged ahead of the Prince George?

A. The enemy had fired twelve or fiſteen minutes upon the Defiance, before ſhe returned any fire. Soon after we came to cloſe action, and when the ſmoke cleared away, we perceived the Prince George in action, and drew cloſe to her.

Q. At this time was the Sandwich, or any other of the center diviſion, drawn nearer up aſtern of the Defiance?

A. There was no ſhip aſtern of the Defiance, as I obſerved, though I judge there was at ſome diſtance.

Q. You ſaid you received the fire of ſeveral French ſhips ſome time before you returned the fire; with what ſhip ahead or aſtern of the French Admiral, did you begin with, or was it with the French Admiral you began action?

A. The ſecond ſhip ahead.

Q. How many French Ships was there aſtern of the French Admiral, the 100 gun ſhip?

A. I really don't recollect, nor could I count them, the ſmoke and fire was ſo heavy.

Q. Were there ſix or ſeven aſtern of him?

A. I ſhould be apt to think there were.

Q. Was there eight or nine?

A. There might be ſo many.

Q. Did you ſee the French flag ſhips together?

A. I think there were two very near together.

Q. Was the French Admiral in the center of his fleet?

A. I think he was not.

Q. Did you ſee the ſignal for a line of battle a-head, flying on board the Victory, whilſt ſhe was advancing towards the enemy on the larboard tack, after the action was over?

A. I did.

Q. Did you ſee any, or many ſhips formed in a line ahead or aſtern of her, while ſhe continued to ſtand on the larboard tack?

A. To the beſt of my judgment there were not many.

Q. Do you know there were any?

A. I think there were ſome.

Q. Can you name them?

A. The Foudroyant was one, if I miſtake not, the Prince George might be a-head of her, but am not certain.

Q. When you had repaired your own damages, ſo as to be able to get into the line yourſelf, was it whilſt the Victory

Victory was ſtanding upon the larboard tack, with the ſignal for a line of battle flying?

A. We had then wore, and were ſtanding on after Sir Robert Harland's diviſion.

Q. Did you ſtand a-head of the Victory whilſt ſhe was upon the larboard tack, with the ſignal out for a line of battle, I mean, was your rigging repaired time enough to do it?

A. We had wore with our rigging ſtill in a diſabled ſtate, except what contributed to wearing; we were much to windward of her, and I apprehend ſhe was upon our lee-beam or lee-quarter.

Q. Were your damages ſo repaired that you were able to take your ſtation a-head of the Victory, which was your ſtation in a line of battle?

A. Had the ſignal for the line been out at the time the Defiance wore, ſhe could have done it; but ſhe had ſtood on to Sir Robert Harland's diviſion, and had got ſo far a-head as to bring the Victory upon the lee-beam before the ſignal was ſeen, and ſoon after, to the beſt of my judgment, the Admiral ſtood with his head to the ſouthward.

Q. At what time in the afternoon did you rejoin the diviſion of the Vice Admiral of the Blue, after you came out of action.

A. I edged down to the Vice Admiral of the Blue, when the Red diviſion bore away, and ſtretched a-head to get a-head of the center.

Q. How was the Vice Admiral of the Blue ſituated with reſpect to the Victory, when the Vice Admiral of the Red paſſed betwixt her and the Formidable, in order to go a-head?

A. At the time I joined the Vice Admiral of the Blue, the Victory had her head to the ſouthward, and was not at any great diſtance when the Red diviſion began to paſs between the center and the rear.

Preſident. Do you know any part of the day of the 27th and 28th of July, that the Britiſh fleet ran away from the French fleet, or had any appearance that could be ſo conſtrued?

A. No.

Q. Do you know any part of the day of the 27th and 28th of July, that the French fleet ran away from the Engliſh, or ſhewed any appearance that could be ſo conſtrued?

A. On the 28th of July the French fleet avoided it, and fled before the Engliſh fleet.

Admiral Montague. The evidence you have given to this court to day, to me has given more satisfaction than any that has appeared before us; but upon the question that I asked you, you seemed to make a doubt whether you had a right to give an answer, or whether this court was to enquire of you of the charge; I only beg the warrant to Sir Thomas Pye, may be read, so far as relates to the trial of Admiral Keppel. This court is strictly to adhere to the charge, and the accuser and the evidence that has been produced before him, is mere matter of opinion in general.

The Warrant was read accordingly; after which CAPTAIN GOODHALL *was ordered to withdraw.*

LIEUT. WALLER, *of the Formidable, sworn.*

Q. At what distance do you judge the Victory, and the body of the fleet was, beyond the rear of the enemy's fleet, at the time the Formidable passed the last of the French ships, and ceased firing?

A. I do not recollect to have seen the Victory, at the time of passing the rear of the enemy.

Q. Did the Formidable, immediately after passing the rear of the enemy, wear, and lay her head towards the enemy again? A. Yes.

Q. What time do you recollect it was, when you first took notice of the Admiral and the rest of the fleet?

A. I don't recollect seeing the Admiral until we wore the second time, as to the time of the day I cannot speak of it.

Q. What distance do you think he might be then?

A. To the best of my recollection the Admiral was then a mile and a half, or more.

Q. Whilst the Formidable lay with her head towards the enemy, were not the officers and men ordered to their quarters, in expectation of renewing the engagement, when the Admiral with the fleet should come up?

A. Yes, we were ordered to our quarters; I suppose it was expected we should engage.

President. Where was you quartered?

A. On the lower gun deck.

Q. When the Formidable wore the second time to stand towards the Victory, was not the signal for battle then hauled down, or was it flying? A. I do not recollect.

Q. While the Victory and Formidable were standing towards each other, was not the Victory on directly towards the Formidable?

A. We were standing parallel of each other, nearly on the opposite points of the compass.

Court,

Court. Do you think ſhe was ſo far to windward?

A. Very little way to windward.

Proſecutor. Did you ſee the ſignal for a line of battle on board the Victory, before the Formidable came cloſe to the Victory?

A. I do not recollect to have ſeen the ſignal, till the Victory came very near the Formidable, and was wearing under our ſtern?

Q. Whilſt the Formidable was ſtanding towards the Victory, did you ſee any one ſhip betwixt them, that appeared to have taken her ſtation in a line ahead of the Admiral?

A. I do not recollect to have ſeen any.

Q. When the Victory and Formidable met, did the Victory wear under the Formidable's ſtern, run to leeward, and then haul her wind to the ſouthward? A. Yes.

Q. Did not that leave the Formidable aſtern, and to windward withal?

A. We were cloſe to windward, and as the Victory went ahead of us, we muſt be a-ſtern of her.

Q. After the Formidable had got out of the way of other ſhips, did ſhe ſtand after the Admiral with all the ſails ſhe could ſet, and trim as well as the condition of her rigging would admit? A. Yes.

Q. Was ſhe at that time in a manageable condition, to keep her ſtation in a line of battle betwixt two ſhips a cable's length aſunder, if ſhe could have got into that ſtation? A. I don't think ſhe was.

Q. Did not the Victory increaſe her diſtance from the Formidable during that afternoon? A. Yes.

Q. Did the Formidable ſteer that afternoon, keeping the Admiral a little under her lee?

A. To the beſt of my recollection ſhe did.

Q. Was that a proper courſe for fetching into her ſtation, as the Admiral was under ſail, not laying to?

A. I think it was.

Q. Was every thing done on board the Formidable that was poſſible, to repair her with the utmoſt diſpatch?

A. To the beſt of my judgment every thing was.

Q. As you have ſtated that every thing was done that poſſibly could be, and with the utmoſt diſpatch, that ſhe ſtood a proper courſe for fetching into her ſtation---that the Admiral continued to increaſe his diſtance---that he did not bring to, to let the ſhips get into their ſtation. I ſhall now ground the queſtion upon theſe conſiderations, That whatever ſignals were made, whatever meſſages were ſent, and at whatever time ſuch ſignals might be made,

made, or ſuch meſſages ſent, was it poſſible for the Formidable to have got into her ſtation in the line, unleſs the Admiral had waited for him ?

A. I have before obſerved, I believe, that we did every thing we could to get into our ſtation, and that the Admiral gained upon us ; of courſe we could not get into our ſtation without the Admiral waited for us.

Preſident. If the Admiral had wore down, and waited for you, ſhould you have been able to renew the attack ?

A. I cannot be a competent judge, in a queſtion of ſo much importance.

Proſecutor. Do you know if the Admiral did bring to any part of that afternoon, for ſhips to get into their ſtations ?

A. I do not know that the Admiral did bring to.

Q. Did you happen to obſerve at any time what ſail the Victory was under, during that afternoon ?

A. I do not recollect that I do.

Q. From the ſtate you know of the rigging about the fore maſt, was it ſafe to carry ſail upon that maſt upon a wind, till ſtays were got up and the rigging repaired ?

A. I think not ?

Q. Was it not in danger without any ſail upon a wind, till ſome of the rigging was repaired ?

A. That was the general opinion on board the Formidable.

Admiral Montague. From the time the Formidable hauled out of action, and laid her head towards the enemy, how long was it before you went upon the fore-caſtle, to ſee the ſtate of the rigging, being quartered upon the lower deck ?

A. I do not recollect that I was upon the forecaſtle.

Q. Then you don't anſwer the queſtion from your own knowledge, but from hear-ſay ?

A. I believe I have ſaid ſo.

Q. Do you remember the ſignal being made in the evening, for ſhips to windward to bear down, and ſeveral ſhips pendants let fly ?

A. I remember ſeveral pendants flying, for what ſhips or for what purpoſe, I cannot pretend to ſay.

Q. Were theſe ſignals repeated on board the Formidable, before or after the Fox came to ſpeak to her ?

A. I believe before.

Q. Do you remember whether the Fox's people, or the Formidable's people cheered firſt ?

A. I perfectly remember the Fox cheered firſt.

Q. Where

Q. Where was you stationed for carrying on the repairs, and for refitting the rigging?

A. I was stationed at the main rigging.

Q. Did you happen to be in the way, to hear the message delivered by the Captain of the Fox?

A. I remember to have heard something pass, but I do not recollect what it was.

Q. Notwithstanding the damages you mentioned the Formidable had received, although she was not able during the afternoon to reach her station in the line of battle, as the Admiral did not stay for her, do not you think she was capable of going down before the wind, and engaging the enemy, if the Admiral and the rest of the fleet had done so?

A. We were certainly capable of going to leeward and engaging, if we had been a long side of a ship at a proper distance.

Admiral Arbuthnot. But do you mean that you had been in a condition, if the Admiral had made the signal to keep your station in a line of battle?

A. We were capable of going to leeward; I have before observed we were not capable of keeping our station.

Admiral Montague. To be sure you were capable of going to leeward, unless there had been an anchor out astern.

Admiral Keppel. Did you, when the Formidable was upon the larboard tack, standing towards the French, see the repeating frigate at all?

A. I did not attend to the repeating frigate.

Q. Did you at any time in the afternoon set the Victory by compass? A. No.

Q. Did you at any time in the afternoon observe the signal for a line of battle, and the blue flag at the mizen peak on board the Victory, after the Victory wore with her head to the southward?

A. I do not recollect to have attended to any signals on board the Victory, after she was on the starboard tack.

Q. Then I am to understand, that your atention was to the employment you was stationed to, *knotting* and *splicing* the rigging?

A. That engaged the greatest part of my attention.

Q. Was you assisted by the men properly, and like good seamen, all that time? A. I think I was.

Q. Had they any wine, or grog given them, to cheer them up that afternoon?

A. Not to my knowledge.

Q. What

Q. What time was the fore topſail unbent, on board the Formidable?

A. I cannot charge my memory with the time.

Q. Do you know within half an hour, an hour, or two hours?

A. I cannot pretend to ſay what time.

Ordered to withdraw.

LIEUT. HILLS, *of the Formidable, ſworn.*

Proſecutor. Do you recollect the firſt time you took notice of the Victory, and the body of the fleet, after the Formidable came out of the engagement?

A. I ſaw her ſoon after the Formidable wore, and laid her head towards the enemy.

Q. At what diſtance was ſhe then from the rear of the enemy, at the time the Formidable had paſſed the rear of the French fleet? A. I ſuppoſe her to be near two miles.

Q. Did not the Formidable immediately wear, and lay her head to the enemy, after ſhe had paſſed the ſternmoſt of the enemy's ſhips? A. Soon after ſhe did.

Q. When you firſt ſaw the Victory, and the body of the fleet, were they ſtanding towards the enemy, or towards us, as we were juſt by them?

A. I juſt recollect they were, the Victory was ſtanding towards the Formidable.

Q. Were not the officers and men ordered to their quarters, in expectation of renewing the engagement when the Admiral, and the reſt of the fleet ſhould come up? A. They were ordered to their quarters.

Q. When the Formidable wore again to ſtand towards the Victory, was not the ſignal for battle hauled down?

A. I did not ſee it flying.

Court. Did you wear by ſignal or not?

A. I do not know.

Q. Did you ſee any ſignal for wearing? A. I did not.

Q. Whilſt the Formidable was ſtanding towards the Victory, was not the Victory's head directly towards the Formidable?

A. To the beſt of my remembrance it was.

Q. Can you remember when the firſt ſignal for a line of battle on board the Victory, was ſeen on board the Formidable? A. I cannot tell.

Q. Was you in a ſituation when your head was towards the Victory, that the ſignal for a line of battle might have been flying (without your ſeeing it) on board the Victory?

A. It is very poſſible.

Q. Where was you quartered?

A. On

A. On the lower deck, in the time of action; at the time that fhe wore, on the forecaftle.

Profecutor. While we were ftanding towards the Victory, can you remember whether you faw the repeating frigate, or not?

A. I did not fee her as I remember.

Q. Suppofe fhe was nearer to the Victory, and fteering the fame courfe as the Victory, might not a fignal on board her be equally as imperceptible to the Formidable as it was on board the Victory? A. I think fo.

Q. Did you obferve as we ftood towards the Victory, whether any fhips had taken their ftations ahead of us in a line, or whether there were any fhips between us and her? A. I did not obferve any.

Q. When the Victory and Formidable met, did the Victory wear under the Formidable's ftern, run to leeward, and then haul her wind to the fouthward?

A. I think fhe did.

Q. Did not that leave the Formidable aftern, and to windward withal?

A. Yes undoubtedly.

Q. After the Formidable got out of the way of other fhips, did fhe not ftand after the Admiral with all the fails fhe could fet, trimmed as well as the condition of her fails would admit? A. It appeared fo to me.

Q. Notwithftanding, did not the Victory increafe her diftance during that afternoon?

A. The Victory did increafe her diftance from us that afternoon.

Q. Did not the Formidable fteer all the afternoon, keeping the Admiral a little open upon her lee bow?

A. I was not on deck all the afternoon, when I faw her fhe did.

Q. Was that a proper courfe for fetching into her ftation in the line of battle, as the Admiral was under fail?

A. I fhould think fo.

Q. Was not every thing done for refitting the fhip with the utmoft expedition? A. I think fo.

Q. Where was you ftationed for carrying on the works of refitting? A. On the forecaftle.

Q. Who elfe of the officers were there at the fame time?

A. Capt. Beazely and the mafter fometimes.

Q. Had you not almoft all the ftanding rigging about the foremaft to new rigg, as well as all the running rigging to knot and fplice, and a new fore-ftay and fpring ftay to get up? A. We had.

Q. Was not the boatfwain killed in the action?

A. Yes.

A. Yes.

Q. Was not the loss of him very severely felt, in getting the ship refitted in her rigging and sails?

A. Very much so.

Q. Were you not deprived of the assistance of three of the Lieutenants for that purpose, two of them being sick, and one wounded?

A. Two of them were sick and unable to do duty, and one was wounded.

Q. Did you take notice of what sail the Victory was under, at any time that afternoon?

A. I did not observe it.

Q. Do you remember at what time the fore top-sail was unbent?

A I do not exactly remember the time.

Q. At what time was the new one set?

A. At eight o'clock.

Q. Was that as soon as it was safe to set upon the mast, being upon a wind? A. I judge so.

Q. During the time you was employed in refitting the rigging, did you observe any tardiness amongst the people, or any disorders or confusion, that prevented them carrying it on, was not all dispatched with propriety?

A. I saw none, and I believe there was every dispatch possible.

Q. Was not some wine given them, to encourage and refresh them, or was that before the work was done, and the new sail set, or at what time was it?

A. The sails were set, and half a pint of wine given to each man; I judge it to be, between nine and ten o'clock at night.

Q. Did that occasion any interruption or retardment to the duty of the ship, or was it of use and encouragement to the men?

A. I think it encouraged them very much, and was by no means the cause of any retardment.

Q. Do you remember signal being made in the evening for ships to windward to bear down, several ship's pendants being let fly for that purpose?

A. I remember several ship's pendants let fly on board the Formidable, and under, was a signal for them to bear down.

Q. Were these ships pendants let fly on board the Formidable, before or after the Fox frigate came to speak with her?

A. Before the Fox came down.

Q. Do you remember whether the Fox's people or the [Formi]dable's people cheered first? A. I re-

A. I remember the Fox's people cheered firſt, from an expreſſion of Capt. Beazely's at that time, which was "That's hearty my lads, return the cheer."

Q. During the afternoon of the 27th, notwithſtanding the damages you mentioned the Formidable received, might ſhe not have bore down and engaged an enemy to leeward, if the Admiral and the reſt of the fleet had done ſo, although ſhe was not able, during the afternoon, to take her ſtation in the line, upon a wind, except the Admiral had waited for her?

A. I believe ſhe might have bore down, and engaged an enemy, though not able to follow the Admiral upon a wind in the line, and keep in company.

Court. You have ſaid your fore top ſail was not ſet till eight o'clock?

A. It was ſet while I was off the forecaſtle. I ſuppoſed by that, it was not ſet before that time.

Q. Was your ſhip in a condition to go down, and ſeek an engagement, without her fore top ſail?

A. She might have gone down to an enemy.

Q. Where was you, when you heard the two cheers exchanged on board the two ſhips?

A. On the forecaſtle.

Q. Did you hear what converſation paſſed between the two ſhips? A. No, I did not.

Admiral Keppel. You have obſerved, that the Victory was upon the Formidable's lee bow, did you ever ſet her by compaſs? A. I did not.

Q. In your obſervation of her, did you obſerve any ſignals ſhe had flying from half after three to the period of the afternoon, till dark?

A. I did not ſee any ſignal on board the Victory.

Q. You ſaid, when you caſt your eye upon her, you ſaw her upon the lee bow?

A. I ſaw her upon the lee bow ſeveral times.

Q. And at no one of theſe times ſet her by the compaſs?

A. I did not ſet her by the compaſs at all.

Q. But as a ſeaman, you can ſay what that lee bow is, whether one, two, three, or four points. I am ſ[illegible] I could anſwer to it?

A. I beg to know at what time.

Q. What time did the Victory and Formidable paſs one another?

A. I do not recollect the time of the day.

Q. Then I would aſk you, at one hour before the Fox ſpoke to you?

A. If

A. If I can judge of time, ſhe was about a point or a point and an half upon the lee bow.

Q. Was the Formidable cloſe upon a wind at that time?

A. It appeared ſo to me, or nearly.

Q. Then, at the lateſt period of the day, half an hour after ſeven, how did the Victory bear then from the Formidable?

A. I had ſaid, I did not know the hour of the day, but late in the evening, ſhe was upon the lee bow about one point.

Q. In regard to her cheering, you ſaid the Fox cheered firſt. How many cheers did the Fox give her?

A. I cannot charge my memory with that, I think one.

Q. Was there no other cheer given, at any ſeparate time, to the Fox?

A. I do not remember any.

Ordered to withdraw.

Sir JOHN ROSS, *called and ſworn.*

Proſecutor. Do you remember the firſt time you ſaw the French Fleet, in the morning of the 27th of July?

A. At four o'clock in the morning, I ſaw the French fleet ſtanding to the N. W.

Q. How long did they continue upon that tack?

A. They began to wear about eight in the morning.

Q. Did the van or the rear wear firſt? A. The van.

Q. Did they wear ſucceſſively in each other's wake?

A. They did.

Q. How long did they continue to ſtand upon that tack, after they had all wore?

A. At half paſt nine, I loſt ſight of them, being ſqually and thick to the ſouth-weſt.

Q. After they had wore ſucceſſively, as you deſcribed, in each other's wake, did they appear to you, to be in a line of battle?

A. They did appear to be in a line of battle, after they had all wore, ſtanding to the ſouthward.

Q. What diſtance might they be from you and the van diviſion, when they wore at eight o'clock in the morning?

A. I cannot anſwer that exactly, but at four o'clock in the morning, they were eight or nine miles to windward of me.

Q. When did they change their tack again?

A. At ten o'clock when it cleared up, I ſaw ſeveral before

fore the wind, the whole fleet immediately hauled their wind to the N. W.

Q. Then they wore a-head upon the larboard tack to come to the N. W? A. Certainly.

Q. After their heads were to the N. W. did they appear to you to be in a line?

A. More irregular than I had seen them for several preceding days.

Q. I think you was in one of the first ships that was fired upon by the French; when the French began the attack, did they edge down upon that part of the fleet where you was, and begin to fire upon you?

A. I cannot say I recollect whether they bore away or not; I was so attentive in conducting my own ship, that I cannot answer this question.

Q. You recollected that the first motion you observed of them, was wearing successively in each other's wake, and that they appeared to be formed in a line; that they wore again a second time, and attacked the British fleet; do you consider these motions?

A. They certainly fired first upon us; they fired two shot without colours being hoisted.

Q. Do you consider their wearing twice, when they might have tacked, to be an indication of avoiding coming to action, or of their intending to come to action?

A. In answer to that, when I lost sight of them in a squall, I told my officers, that if the squall continued much longer, we should see them to leeward of us, judging from their former conduct; that they intended to push for Brest; when I saw them then, there were six of them before the wind; at one time, I gave orders to bear away two points, but I had no sooner ordered it, than they then hauled their wind to the N. W.

Q. As they hauled their wind to the N. W. if you had kept your ship in the situation you were in, would you not have been able to have fetched their van?

A. I never bore away, the orders were given, but it was impossible to execute them.

Q. Was your ship considerably to windward of the rest of the division, at the time you were speaking of?

A. I was a-head, but whether to windward I cannot say. I was the headmost ship.

Q. Did you chace by signal that morning?

A. I did so, at a quarter after five o'clock, my signal was made to chace to windward, we being the weathermost ship of the fleet at that time.

Q. When the French got upon the larboard tack, and fired upon you, did they seem at that time to keep their wind?

A. They seemed to be close hauled, as Frenchmen generally go a point from the wind.

Q. Did they seem so after they had passed you, and whilst the French and British fleets were passing each other; or did they appear to edge away?

A. Do you mean while I was engaged myself: I was so much employed in the business of my own ship, and on account of the action, that I could not observe.

Q. After the red division passed the rear of the enemy, did not you, in the Shrewsbury, wear and stand towards the enemy again, before any ship of your division?

A. I did.

Q. Do you remember your having declared, at the time you directed that to be done, that you intended to attack the rearmost ship as soon as you could get at her, or something to that purpose?

A. I do not recollect I ever did; I had no sooner wore, but I saw I should throw myself, and the ships towards me, into the greatest confusion; and I wore back instantly almost.

Q. As I make no doubt but Sir John's intentions were laudable, I should be glad if you would recollect what your intentions were, by wearing the first time?

A. As there was no signal out for line of battle, I certainly wore with an intention to pursue the French; but seeing it would throw my ship, and the other ships of the fleet into confusion, I wore back again momentarily.

Q. Do you remember, after the red division was out of the engagement, at any time taking notice of the Vice Admiral of the blue, whilst he remained engaged?

A. I do not remember any thing particular of the Formidable, but my remark was, that the blue division, and several other ships, were engaged with the French fleet till near forty minutes after one; they had then passed the French fleet, and the signal was then hauled down for engaging, which was repeated by the Vice Admirals of the red and blue squadrons.

Q. Did you take notice of the Formidable's laying her head towards the enemy again, after she came out of the action?

A. I did not, Sir, the reason of it was, at half past twelve o'clock, Vice Admiral Sir Robert Harland, made the signal to tack, we then tacked, stood after the French fleet, and my attention was chiefly taken up in conducting my ship.

Q. At

Q. At the time the last of our ships came out of the action, how was the Vice Admiral of the red situated, in respect to the rear of the enemy?

A. When the red squadron tacked, and stood to the northward, the sternmost of the French fleet were then a-head on our lee bow, when we were close to the wind.

Q. After your division had tacked, did not you make sail, Sir, and draw up with the rear of the enemy?

A. We were under sail, but what sail was up I cannot tell.

Q. Can you recollect whether some of you had not your main sails set?

A. No, I don't recollect.

Q. Did the red division tack some time before the center division wore?

A. They did, Sir, not that I can exactly mention the time the center division did wear, but they tacked before they wore.

Q. As you tacked before you wore, I presume your division was considerably nearer the enemy, than the center division?

A. We were nearer, but the distance I cannot ascertain.

Q. Can you form a judgment of the distance the Admiral of the center division was from the rear of the enemy, when they wore?

A. I realy cannot.

SEVENTEENTH DAY, TUESDAY, JANUARY 26th.

The Court being met at ten o'clock, the evidence of Sir John Ross was continued.

Prosecutor. Do you know what distance the red division stood beyond the enemy, before they tacked?

A. I cannot exactly tell, I have not minuted it down.

Q. Can you tell who first made the signal for battle, the Vice Admiral of the Red, or Commander in Chief?

A. I did not see the signal for battle, till I had passed the line of fire.

Q. Do you judge that a flag officer commanding a division, has a right to make any signal, contrary to those made by the Commander in Chief, to call in ships from chace, without the Commander in Chief first making the signal for it?

A. I should imagine not, Sir.

Q. You have said the red division was to windward

 of

of the rear of the enemy, after the red divifion had tacked; I afk whether, if the Admiral, when he was ftanding towards the enemy, had continued the fignal for battle out, whether the red divifion, from the fituation they were in, could not have bore down and attacked the enemy?

A. As they were to windward they could have edged down; but the point is, how proper it would have been in the fituation the fleet was in at that time.

Q. Was any part of the red divifion difmafted?

A. Not that I know of.

Q. Was any part of the fleet?

A. Not that I heard of.

Q. Was any part of the red divifion, any way difabled, to your knowledge, at that time?

A. The Shrewfbury was; as to what damages the other fhips received, I cannot anfwer.

Q. Do you mean the Shrewfbury was damaged fo that fhe was not fit to come into action immediately?

A. In half an hour fhe was fit for action.

Q. I underftood you gave an account of your wearing the fhip, with an intent to re-attack; I fhould be glad to know the particular damages of the Shrewfbury?

A. The main and fore fpring ftays, main tacks, top fail ftays, a great part of the running rigging, and moft of the fails fhot through in feveral places, one fhot through the main maft, one fhot through the rudder head, one fhot through the main piece of the rudder, and feveral others.

Q. From the very brifk fire that was kept up by the Englifh fhips that were engaged, have not you reafon to conclude, that the enemy fuffered in proportion to the Englifh fleet?

A. I fhould imagine fo; I could be no judge.

Court. Did they appear to you to be as much damaged in their fails and rigging as our fhips?

A. I thought not.

Profecutor. Did you obferve the enemy when they broke up their line of battle, and began to form a new line with their heads to the fouthward, towards the Britifh fleet?

A. I did obferve them, but I have not the particular time in my minutes; I beg pardon, I did obferve them about half paft three o'clock, with their heads to the fouthward.

Q. If the whole of the Britifh fleet had immediately wore, after paffing the rear of the enemy's line, inftead of

ftanding,

ſtanding to a diſtance, might not the engagement have been immediately renewed, and the French prevented from forming a new line with their heads to the ſouthward?

A. It depends upon the condition ſhips are in. It is matter of opinion.

Court. You ſaid yeſterday, that you did immediately wear as ſoon as you paſſed the French fleet, and that as ſoon as you had done it, you found ſeveral ſhips coming upon you, that would have entangled you; and therefore you judged it proper to wear back again, and ſtood the other way?

A. I did ſo; it was momentary; I had no ſooner wore but I brought back again.

Admiral Montague. As moſt of the queſtions that have been aſked here, are ſuppoſitions and opinions, I beg to know whether it is your opinion of the Britiſh fleet, when they came out of action, that if they had received little or no damage, the commander in chief, Admiral Keppel, would not have renewed the action again immediately?

A. Moſt certainly he would.

Proſecutor. The time you mention that the ſhips would have been put into confuſion, by his wearing in the Shrewſbury, does he mean to ſpeak of the ſhips of his own diviſion to be in that confuſion?

A. No, I mean if the Britiſh ſhips that were out of action had wore directly, they would have thrown thoſe of the Britiſh fleet that were coming up, into the greateſt confuſion.

Q. Did the ſhips in the van, by tacking before the ſternmoſt of them, cauſe any confuſion to the ſternmoſt; do not the leading ſhips weather thoſe that follow them?

A. Ships in the van tacking firſt, generally keep their wind; but in this caſe two or three things are to be conſidered as to the ſituation of the Engliſh and French fleets; Would you go to windward and fire through the Engliſh fleet? A ſhip in the van may always weather a ſhip aſtern.

Admiral Montague. Suppoſe the ſhips in the van had attempted to tack, and miſs'd ſtays, would it not have put thoſe aſtern of them into the greateſt confuſion?

A. Certainly would.

Q. I aſk it only as matter of opinion, as it ſeems much like paſſing the examination of a lieutenant.

Proſecutor. Did the red diviſion bear down into the Admiral's wake that afternoon, when the ſignal for a line of battle was flying, and the fleet on the ſtarboard tack, at any time in the afternoon?

A. At twenty minutes past three, the Admiral made a signal to wear; at half past three he made the signal to bear down into his wake; the French fleet some minutes before that, were rather ahead to the southwest, standing in a line of battle. The Admiral made the signal to form a line of battle ahead a cable's length asunder, which was obeyed.

Q. Did the red division first go down astern of the Admiral?

A. I do not understand your question. First go down?

Q. Go down first into the Admiral's wake, before you went ahead of them?

A. The Vice Admiral of the red made a signal to lead upon that tack, which I found afterwards was in consequence of orders from Admiral Keppel, to lead the fleet upon that tack.

Q. During the whole night of the 27th, were there any observations made on the French fleet, on board the Shrewsbury?

A. During the whole night we were under an easy sail, in a line of battle, a cable's length astern of Sir Robert Harland, the French fleet being to leeward.

Q. Did you observe them make any signals during the night?

A. I observed none myself, but was told about eleven there were some rockets, but I did not see them, though I was upon deck the whole time.

Q. Was it observed on board the Shrewsbury when they bore away in the night? A. No.

Q. Do you remember what time you lost sight of them in the night?

A. I do not, it was dark weather.

Q. How many of them was in sight the next morning?

A. At four o'clock we saw three sail of the French fleet, bearing S. E. and by E. five or six miles distant, they bore away and made all the sail they could.

Q. Were no more of the French fleet seen from on board the Shrewsbury?

A. At five o'clock one of the Lieutenants from the main topmast head, saw nine or ten sail, bearing S. E. and by E. six or seven leagues distant.

Q. Was any signal made to the Admiral by the Shrewsbury, or any other ship in your division, for seeing the French fleet?

A. The Shrewsbury made none, as I saw several pendants flying, the signal was made for several ships to chace, from the Admiral.

Q. Did

Q. Did any other ſhips of the red diviſion make their ſignal to the Admiral for ſeeing theſe nine or ten ſail?

A. I obſerved none, but part of the red diviſion had ſet their top-gallant ſails; I did not obſerve that any other ſhips did.

Admiral Montague. Did you ſee the Britiſh fleet run away, or have the appearance of a flight, or behave in ſuch a manner as to give the French Admiral a pretence to claim the Victory, or that the French Admiral purſued the Britiſh fleet, and offered it battle on the 27th of July?

A. Moſt aſſuredly at no period of that time did the Britiſh fleet run away, nor had the appearance of it.

Q. Then, Sir, did you ſee the honour of the Britiſh navy tarniſhed on the 27th or 28th of July?

A. I did not, in any reſpect.

Q. In the morning of the 28th, when you found the French fleet were gone away, did you not look upon it that they run away from the Britiſh fleet?

A. Certainly.

Admiral Keppel. Could the ſhips, in the cloſe order they were in, and coming out of action, have tacked clear of each other, till they had ſtood on and increaſed their diſtance?

A. It was abſolutely neceſſary to ſtand on.

Q. Was it by means of the Red diviſion having ſtood on that they got to windward?

A. Certainly.

Q. I ſhould be glad to aſk if I uſed every means as an officer, to get up with and bring the French fleet to battle, from the 24th to the 27th of July?

A. You did, by carrying a preſſed ſail both by day and night.

Q. If I had purſued the French in a line of battle, would it have been poſſible to have preſerved our nearneſs?

A. It could not.

Q. Was it not in the power of the French every day before the action, to have brought on an engagement with the Engliſh fleet?

A. Certainly, being always to windward.

Q. If I had formed my line of battle in the morning of the 27th, do you imagine I could have brought the French to battle that day?

A. No, becauſe if the Admiral had made a ſignal for a line of battle, and the weathermoſt ſhips had bore down to the wake of the leewardmoſt ſhips, we ſhould have been near five leagues to leeward of the center of the French fleet.

Q. At eleven o'clock, when the French were so near, and the change of wind gave advantage to the British fleet, must not the French Admiral have given up some of his rear ships, if he had not risqued his center battle to prevent it? A. Most certainly.

Q. Did it ever appear to you in the afternoon of the 27th, that I had given over intention of renewing the fight, if I could have formed a line in time to have done it.

A. Certainly at no time, and I think so, because the signal for a line of battle was out all night, it was on board the Shrewsbury.

Admiral Keppel. You are an officer of long experience in the service, and therefore I will venture to ask, and desire you to inform the court, of any instance, if you know any such, in which I negligently performed my duty on the 27th and 28th of July?

A. I know of none. In every respect the Admiral discharged his duty as far as I can judge, becoming a brave and gallant officer.

Ordered to withdraw.

CAPTAIN PEYTON, *of the Cumberland, sworn.*

Prosecutor. Do you recollect the time when you first saw the French fleet, on the morning of the 27th?

A. Some time before seven o'clock, as near as I can recollect.

Q. How were they then standing?

A. Upon their larboard tack, with their heads to the northward.

Q. Did you see them change their tacks?

A. About eight o'clock they wore, and formed their line on the other tack, leading largely.

Q. Did they wear successively in each other's wake, and so formed the line? A. They did.

Q. After they had all wore, did they appear to you to be in a line?

A. Yes, I think so, as far as I could judge of them at that distance.

Q. How long did they continue upon that tack?

A. I think till ten o'clock.

Q. What did they do then?

A. Then they laid their heads the other way; they returned to the larboard tack.

Q. Can you recollect whether they tacked or wore then, or was it at the time there was a thick squal, that you did not see them?

President. Did you lose sight of them at any time, betwixt

twixt their being upon the larboard and the ſtarboard tacks?

A. The ſquall was ſuch that they were not wholly come up, but ſome part of them ſoon diſcovered themſelves. I ſaw part of them at different times in the ſquall.

Q. You do not tell the court whether you ſaw them tack or wear.

A. I cannot charge my memory.

Proſecutor. When you ſaw them again upon the larboard tack, did they appear to you to have kept their wind cloſe, or to edge down to attack the Britiſh fleet?

A. They appeared to me to have kept their wind, and that their headmoſt ſhips crouded as much ſail as they could carry.

Q. When you ſaw them wear the firſt time were they to windward? A. Yes.

Q. Then by their being to windward, by their wearing and leading large afterwards, when they might have tacked and kept their wind, and afterwards changing their tack, and attacking the Britiſh fleet, do you conſider theſe motions as an indication of their intending to avoid coming to an engagement, or of their intention to do ſo?

A. About the time they wore I had my eye upon them, and I then thought that their intentions were different from what they had ſhewn for ſeveral days before, when we had been purſuing them. But when they came upon the larboard tack, and I ſaw they crouded ſail and kept their wind cloſe, I then thought they had an inclination to avoid action. And as I had it in my ideas ſeveral days before the 27th in the morning, that their fleet outſailed ours as a fleet and a body, I thought it a confirmation to me that they did not intend to come to action then.

Q. Did they continue to croud ſail, after the whole of them had laid their heads that way, or did they ſhorten ſail, and engage the fleet under their topſails only, or their topſails lowered on the cap?

A. They ſtood a very little while upon their larboard tack, before three or four of their headmoſt ſhips bore down: but there was one aſtern of them, and they began firing upon the Monarch, and from thence the action began.

Q. You ſay they edged down and fired upon the Monarch? A. Yes.

Q. Did you happen to obſerve whether, after they had continued to range along the Engliſh fleet, they crouded or ſhortened ſail.

A. After

A. After the firing began, it was very unexpected to me; by what I ſaw of their ſhips they were under different ſail; ſome brought to, to fire, others continued under that ſort of ſail which would naturally keep company with their line, but not with any appearance of crowding ſail after the firing began.

Q. Was the ſignal for engaging firſt made on board the Queen or the Victory do you know? A. I cannot ſay.

Q. Whilſt the Red diviſion was paſſing the enemy, was you ahead or aſtern of the Queen?

A. I was upon the Queen's weather quarter?

Q. Was you at any time obſtructed in your firing by other ſhips coming in your way, or you in the way of others, or any firing over them?

A. The Monarch was before the Cumberland's weather beam, but no obſtruction to her firing, the enemy paſſing us aſtern further than the Monarch, and we fired as they preſented themſelves to us, I don't know of any ſhips firing over the Cumberland.

Q. After the Red diviſion paſſed the rear of the enemy when the diviſion tacked, did not they look up to windward of the rear of the enemy?

A. Yes, but what I am ſpeaking of the Red diviſion is of the Cumberland, and the ſhips near her; we followed very cloſe, but that will not take up the whole diviſion.

Q. Do you know that the whole diviſion did not tack and ſtand the ſame way with the Admiral?

A. I do not know they did, I believe they did.

Q. Did you obſerve the Admiral and the center diviſion, after they paſſed the laſt of the enemy's rear?

A. I remember to have ſeen the Victory as we paſſed her, after we had got upon the larboard tack, we cheered the Victory as we paſſed her.

Q. Did you obſerve the Admiral and the center diviſion afterwards wear?

A. I do not recollect, but I have my ideas that they wore as well as the van did.

Q. After the center diviſion had wore, and had their heads the ſame way as the van diviſion; was the van diviſion then ahead and to windward of the center diviſion, or how ſituated?

A. The van diviſion for ſome time bore down, and the center diviſion did the ſame, to the beſt of my memory.

Q. During that time was the van diviſion ahead of the center diviſion, and to windward withal?

A. I can-

A. I cannot tell.

Q. After the van divifion had tacked or wore, did you make fail upon that tack, or fhorten fail, or draw up with the rear of the enemy, or how?

A. On our bearing up we neared the enemy, and paffed them at about two gun fhot, as near as I can judge, to windward of them. We then hauled our wind upon the ftarboard tack.

Q. At what diftance did the center divifion ftand beyond the rear of the enemy, before they tacked, at the time they ftood towards the enemy again?

A. I cannot judge of the diftance.

Q. At what diftance do you reckon the van divifion ftood, before they tacked or wore?

A. To the beft of my recollection firing ceafed about half paft twelve, and the Vice Admiral of the Red tacked about one o'clock.

Q. Do you remember the time of the fignal for battle being hauled down? A. No.

Q. From the fituation you have defcribed the van divifion to be in, within two gun fhot of the rear of the enemy, and the center divifion ftanding towards the enemy, if the fignal for battle had continued flying, and the body of the fleet had continued advancing towards the enemy, did any reafon appear to you at that time againft re-attacking the enemy?

Admiral Keppel. Captain Peyton has faid no fuch thing; he faid they were within two gun fhot of the French, who were upon the ftarboard tack. Now the queftion is put as if within two gun fhot, upon the larboard tack.

Profecutor. Captain Peyton did fay that they paffed them within two gun fhot on the ftarboard tack, does it not follow that they were within that diftance upon the larboard tack?

Admiral Keppel. No conclufion, that.

A. This is a matter of opinion, and opinion is fubject to error, and contrary to the latter part of the oath I have taken, to fpeak nothing but the truth.

Q. Did you take notice when the laft of the Britifh fleet came out of action? A. I cannot fay I did.

Q. Did you take notice of the Vice Admiral of the Blue after he came out of action?

A. I faw the Vice Admiral of the Blue to leeward of the Red divifion, and as it were prefented to the van of the French fleet, when drawing to their ftarboard tack.

Prefident. Sir John Rofs has fent a note, in which he begs leave to explain himfelf on an anfwer given to a queftion.

Sir

Sir JOHN ROSS, *called. It was in anſwer to a queſtion of Admiral Keppel's, nearly as follows:*

"Did I ſhew any appearance of having given over my intention of renewing the fight, if I could have formed a line to have done it." Upon recollection, I meant to ſay, that the Shrewſbury kept her ſtation in the line, all night; inſtead of ſaying "That the ſignal continued flying on board the Shrewſbury all night."

Admiral Montague. Were your colours hoiſted all night?

Q. Yes, they were certainly.

Capt. PEYTON *called in again.*

Q. Did you obſerve the French, during that afternoon, to continue to form into a line with their heads on the ſtarboard tack? A. Yes.

Q. Have you any reaſon to think, that the French fleet did not ſuffer in proportion to the Engliſh fleet during the engagement, conſidering the brisk fire our ſhips kept up?

A. They did not appear to me to have ſuffered ſo much in their maſts and yards, as our ſhips had done. One ſhip of theirs was more diſabled in their maſts and yards than any of ours.

Q. Did you obſerve any ſhip on either ſide diſmaſted?

A. No.

Q. Do you know of any ſhips in the red diviſion being diſabled at that time?

A. The Monarch, which had her fore-ſail yard carried away; I do not recollect any thing of any other ſhip very particular.

Q. Do you remember ſeeing the Admiral, when he laid his head to the ſouthward again?

A. It does not ſtrike me juſt now.

Q. Do you remember when you firſt ſaw, that he was laid with his head to the ſouthward again?

A. I muſt have ſeen her, as we were following on after the van diviſion to go ahead of him, but no particular time ſtruck me, it muſt have been the whole time I ſuppoſe.

Q. You have ſaid you obſerved the French begin to form a new line, with their heads to the ſouthward, was not that ſtanding towards the Britiſh fleet? A. Yes.

Q. Then did it appear to you by the enemy's ſtanding towards the Britiſh fleet, and forming a new line, that they ſhewed a diſpoſition to renew the engagement, or to avoid it? A. To renew it.

Q. The next queſtion, if Capt. Peyton conſiders it as a matter of opinion, I will not put it, I ſhall ſtate it. If the

the Admiral, with the ships that were with him, and the Vice Admiral of the red with his division, had advanced upon the enemy, at the time they were beginning to form their new line, and attacked them, would it not have prevented their forming a new line?

A. If you mean to ask, whether I would answer it as a matter of opinion, I beg to decline answering any matter of opinion.

Q. Did the red division bear down into the Admiral's wake, that afternoon?

A. They did bear down, there was a signal made to bear down, but I do not remember seeing them directly in the Admiral's wake; and to the best of my recollection, the van division bore down, and passed the Admiral, and took their station upon the starboard tack.

Q. Do you remember any notice being taken of the French fleet during the night?

A. Their lights were seen, and they fired some rockets about eleven o'clock.

Q. Did you perceive them to bear away in the night?

A. No.

Q. How many were in sight, in the morning, from the Cumberland? A. Three.

Q. Do you know of any signals being made by any ship, of a greater number being in sight?

A. By the Queen, and by the Monarch; there was the usual signal made for seeing a fleet from those ships.

Court. What was the signal made?

A. Top gallant sail flying, with the yard hoisted up.

Q. Do you remember whether there were signals made for seeing a fleet, or particular ships only, did you see them? A. Not from our ship.

Prosecutor. Did the British fleet chace those three ships you mentioned, or the fleet that was seen?

A. We stood towards them, some little time but I am not very clear in my recollection, how long.

Q. What weather was it that morning, do you recollect? A. Moderate weather.

Q. Do you recollect how the wind was?

A. To the northward of the W. I believe.

Q. With that wind, and moderate weather, did you consider Ushant as a lee shore, dangerous to approach, being summer time and short nights?

A. The question answers itself; there can be no danger in moderate weather, undoubtedly.

Admiral Montague. I do not ask as matter of opinion, because you have declared you would not answer it; therefore

therefore, did you fee the Britifh fleet run away, or have the appearance of a flight, or behave in fuch a manner as to give the French Admiral a pretence to claim the Victory, and that the French Admiral purfued it with his fleet, and offered it battle ?

A. There are many queftions in one.

Admiral Montague. I will afk you fingly: Did you fee the Britifh fleet run away? — A. No.

Profecutor. Thofe are not the words of the charge.

Admiral Montague. " So far as to publifh to the world that the Britifh fleet run away." The Profecutor has asked twenty and twenty times, " Whether the Victory did not carry preffed fail." I fhould be glad to have my queftions anfwered without interruption. 'Tis a proper queftion and the Court only have a right to correct me. It is the fame queftion I have asked before, and why it fhould be objected to I do not underftand.

Q. Did you fee the Britifh fleet have the appearance of a flight that day? A. No.

Q. Did you fee the French Admiral purfue it, and offer it battle?

A. The French fleet followed the fleet of England, and offered it battle, undoubtedly.

Q. Did you fee the honour of the Britifh flag tarnifhed on the 27th or 28th of July?

A. I believe that is matter of opinion.

Q. I afk whether you faw it?

A. No, by no means in the world.

Q. The French fleet, which you faw following and offering the Englifh fleet battle, did you fee it the next morning the 28th? were they not run away?

A. Yes, they were run away.

Court. When the French formed the line upon the ftarboard tack, if they had intended to renew the action, could they not have formed within piftol fhot, and renewed the action if they had pleafed?

A. I cannot judge how near they could have fetched the Englifh fleet. My words were, " offered us battle." They ranged themfelves to leeward of the Englifh fleet, at fuch a diftance as to admit of the Englifh fleet attacking them, whenever the Commander in Chief had thought proper.

Admiral Keppel. At the time you defcribe the French to have offered the Englifh fleet battle, I would afk if the Admiral had been able to form a line?

A. The line was not formed till late in the evening.

Q. Had not the fignal for a line been flying the whole afternoon,

afternoon, I mean both before and after their heads wore to the ſouthward, on the ſtarboard tack?

A. Yes, from two o'clock.

Q. And did it ever appear to you, that I had given over my intentions to have renewed the fight that afternoon, if I could have formed my line in time to have done it?

A. As to the Admirals intentions I could be no judge of them; but from the diſpoſition of the ſhips and their movements, they were endeavouring to form the line from the time the ſignal was made, as faſt as the diſabled ſhips would allow of it.

Q. I would aſk Captain Peyton, Whether I uſed every means as an officer, to get up with and bring the French to battle, from the 24th to the 27th of July?

A. If the Admiral means whether I ſaw him neglect any endeavours, I anſwer No; but as to the other part of the queſtion, it will not admit of my ſpeaking to facts I did not ſee.

Q. If I had purſued the French fleet in a line of battle, would it have been poſſible to have preſerved our nearneſs to them during the whole time?

A. I cannot judge.

Q. Was it not in the power of the French every one of the preceding days, to have brought on an action with the Engliſh?

A. At ſome parts of the time there was two much wind for fleets to wiſh to come to action, but after the 23d, as they were to windward, they might have taken their own time for it.

Q. In your deſcription of the ſituation the French fleet were in between eight and nine o'clock, it remains upon my thoughts, that you ſaid, that after that time they ran large, when on the larboard tack; I would aſk you whether, in the morning of the 27th, after having formed their line, (if they did form it) they did not keep their wind cloſe, and ſtand from the Britiſh fleet, carrying their uſual preſſed ſail?

A. In my former anſwer, I obſerved they wore in ſucceſſion, that they wore and hauled their wind large, about half after eight, and at ten they tacked.

Q. When the Engliſh fleet laid up for their rear, if the French had intended to come to action, would they not have ſhortened ſail, to enable the Engliſh fleet to have ranged up with them upon that tack, and not got upon a contrary tack?

A. I ſaid in a former part of my evidence, that the French

French fleet, when on the larboard tack, kept their wind, and at that time I had ideas of their not having an intention of coming to action.

Q. What number of ships of the red division were with the Admiral, when he tacked in the rear of the enemy, after having passed them?

A. I believe there were all, as I have no ideas of any ship being left behind; the Monarch was before, and she was the most disabled.

Q. Are you sure the Monarch was?

A. I am not sure, I speak to my belief.

Q. Was the Duke?

A. She was not in my eye; but I don't know why she should not.

Q. Do you recollect what time it was when you cheered the Admiral in passing?

A. I believe between one and two o'clock.

Q. Was the Admiral then upon the larboard or starboard tack?

A. Upon the starboard tack; we were then crossing each other pretty near.

Q. Can you recollect whether the Admiral had the signal up to wear, at that time?

A. I think he had not.

Q. Was the fleet upon the starboard tack, standing to the southward, at the time you stated the French within two gun-shot to leeward of you?

A. The English fleet, that is the van and center, were bearing down and drawing to a parallel on their starboard tack. The French were to leeward of the van, presenting themselves to each other. They were upon the larboard bow.

Q. Where was the Vice Admiral of the blue at this time, and his division?

A. I cannot tell the place where the Vice Admiral of the blue and his division were at this time; I saw them sometime during the afternoon.

Q. When the French formed their line of battle on the starboard tack, if they had set a good deal of sail, might they not have come up presently with the English rear. And do you recollect whether they did not come up to leeward under their topsails?

A. If they had made all the sail they could, undoubtedly. As to some, they came up under their top-sails, some had their foresails, and others their stay-sails and jibs; and so I suppose according to their different going they made different sail.

Q. With

Q. With the crippled ſhips that had been in action, is it ſafe to go down upon a lee ſhore on an enemy's coaſt, truſting to fine good weather when you get there?

A. What do you mean by a lee ſhore?

Q. You have ſtated the wind to the northward of the weſt. I mean a lee ſhore, when it blows upon the land that you may entangle yourſelf with, upon an enemy's coaſt, where the wind is fair to carry the enemy into port in ſafety.

A. In this inſtance, I don't know there was any lee ſhore, we were ſo far from the land.

Q. Can a crippled fleet go in with any land with ſafety, as a fleet that is not crippled?

A. Crippled ſhips cannot go in with any land; while ſhips that are not crippled may clear the land.

Q. How far on the 28th was you from Uſhant?

A. I cannot be a judge, as I have not my Journal nor log book with me.

Q. You do not know how far you was from the land of Uſhant? A. No.

Preſident. I ſuppoſe you had ſome ideas of it at that time?

A. I had an idea, that we were about forty leagues from Uſhant.

Q. Do you imagine at that time, on the 28th, when the French fleet were at ſuch a diſtance, that you could have come up with them, before they had got into Breſt?

A. I have mentioned in a former part of my evidence, that I thought from all circumſtances, the French fleet ſailed better than ours, therefore I imagined we could not come up with them, but as there were crippled ſhips beſides, more than there were in the other circumſtances, there was ſtill leſs likelihood of coming up with the other.

Q. But if you had come up with them, was there not danger on a lee ſhore with the crippled ſhips?

A. Undoubtedly, in bad weather.

Q. Can you recollect how long it appeared to you that the French fleet offered the Engliſh battle?

A. The greater part of the afternoon of the 27th.

Q. Did it appear to you at that time, that the whole of the Engliſh fleet was in a condition and ſituation to give them battle?

A. I have mentioned, the Engliſh fleet was not in a line the greater part of the afternoon.

Q. I aſk whether they were in a condition with regard to their being diſabled?

A. I did not ſee but the Engliſh fleet was in a condition to give them battle.

Q. Was the whole fleet in a condition to come into action?

A. There were six or seven ships laid repairing; of course they could not come into a line, and were not in a condition to come to action.

Q. During the course of your evidence you said, that some part of the time the weather was such, that it was improper for the French to come down and engage. The English then were to leeward. Had you commanded a squadron of British ships, and was to windward as the French was, and your enemy to leeward, should you have hesitated one moment in going down to engage them, as a British officer?

A. It seems matter of opinion; but if two fleets could have been brought together, it would have been my duty to be sure, as an officer, to have gone down and engaged them.

It being now near four o'clock, Captain Peyton was ordered to withdraw, and the Court immediately adjourned, until ten o'clock to-morrow morning.

EIGHTEENTH DAY, WEDNESDAY JANUARY 27th.

At ten o'clock this day, the members being assembled, and the Prisoner brought in, the Court proceeded, when

CAPTAIN SUTTON, *of the Proserpine, was called and sworn.*

Prosecutor. Was you stationed in the night of the 23d of July, to watch the motions of the French fleet?

A. I was.

Q. What orders did you receive for that purpose?

A. To keep between the French and the English fleets.

Admiral Keppel. I gave him the orders myself to go between me and the French fleet; but if the question is meant to imply any thing against me, I shall oppose it, because the 27th and 28th are the days on which I am accused of not doing my duty.

Prosecutor. It is relative to the charge itself.

Admiral Keppel. I admit the wind was fair for the French to get into Brest the 23d at night.

Prosecutor. Did you receive any orders in the afternoon of the 27th, to carry any message from the Admiral to any part of the fleet? A. I did.

Q. What time did you first receive the orders?

A. At two o'clock in the afternoon.

Q. What were the orders?

A. To

A. To desire Sir Robert Harland to keep the same position he was in, and to continue the same tack.

Q. What were the next orders?

A. To form astern of the Victory.

Q. What time was the next?

A. Both orders were given nearly at the same time.

Q. Which of these orders did you deliver to the Queen? A. The last.

Q. Had you any other orders or message from the Admiral that afternoon? A. No.

Q. At what time was it when you delivered your message to the Queen?

A. About three o'clock, I cannot be exact to time.

Q. Whereabout was the red division at that time, with respect to the rear of the enemy?

A. They were to windward, a few of them.

Q. What did that division do, in consequence of that message; did you observe them bear down?

A. They were bearing down when I came to the Vice Admiral Sir Robert Harland?

Q. Did they bear down, and form astern of the Admiral, agreeable to the directions you carried?

A. I think they did.

Q. Was that station in the line of battle the proper station of the Vice Admiral of the red, or the Vice Admiral of the blue?

A. The Vice Admiral of the blue.

Admiral Keppel. When you first came on board the Victory, did not I give you orders to go to Sir Robert Harland, with orders for him to lead upon the larboard tack? A. Yes.

Q. Was not the Victory then upon the larboard tack?

A. She was.

Q. Then sir, before you was able to get away in consequence of my orders, I thought it proper to wear to the southward; did I wear to the southward, and then give you the second order for Sir Robert Harland to form astern of me?

A. I went away with those orders, and the Victory wore immediately after.

Ordered to withdraw.

LORD MULGRAVE, *Captain of the Courageux, called and sworn.*

Prosecutor. What time did you first see the French fleet in the morning of the 27th of July?

A. I do not know.

Q. At the time you did take notice, can you remember which way they were ſtanding?

A. I do not, I cannot be clear in my recollection, my attention was moſtly taken up with my own ſhip, and obſerving the motions and watching the ſignals of the Admiral.

Q. Did you on any part of that morning before the action obſerve the French to tack or wear, and which tack were they upon?

A. The weather was hazy and the French ſhips at too great a diſtance. I cannot give account with that accuracy which I could wiſh to do, I did ſee them; but I cannot be ſo preciſe to the time as I ought, to have any weight as an evidence.

Q. Did they appear to you to be in a line?

A. They appeared to be in a line; but when ſhips are at a great diſtance, how far a line may be regular, or on what point, I cannot take upon me to ſay, whether they were in a regular line or not; they appeared to me to be in a line.

Q. With what part of the French fleet did you begin to engage?

A. I could be very accurate as to the time, but did not attend to the circumſtances of what part of the fleet; there were many ſhips ahead of the Admiral. I had enough to do to attend to my own ſhip, and watch the motions of the Admiral. I was fired at by ſeveral before I came near the Admiral; there were many ſhips ahead of the French Admiral.

Q. Did the French fleet edge down upon the Britiſh fleet, as they engaged?

A. It did appear ſo; I mean from the poſition of the ſhips I paſſed, mine being almoſt cloſe upon a wind, and our broadſides then to each other, I think they muſt have edged down.

Court. Did they edge down before the engagement began?

A. I was much more attentive to the motions of the Admiral, in whoſe diviſion I was, than to the motions of the enemy, becauſe it was from him that I was to take my conduct, and not from any obſervations I made upon the enemy, till I was in action.

Q. I believe the Courageux was in general more engaged in ſome part of the action, than any other of the Fleet; can you recollect whether the French engaged under more or leſs ſail, than the Britiſh fleet engaged under?

A. I hope

A. I hope the Court will forgive me if I ſubmit a wiſh to them that all queſtions that are put to me, may relate to the facts I am aſked. Every information that I can give the court I will; but I wiſh not to give an anſwer to the introductory part of the queſtion. The French fleet appeared to me to carry a great deal of ſail, ſome more than others, as muſt be the caſe in fleets that keep company together; ſome of them carried their topſails and foreſail, many of them had only their topſails, and ſome of thoſe were lowered as the largeſt ſhips ranged along them.

Q. Did your lordſhip obſerve whether any of them carried more than their topſails and foreſails during the action, and whether many of them had only their topſails, and ſome of them lowered as your lordſhip ranged along them.

A. I did not obſerve any of them without topſails lowered; I cannot ſpeak poſitively upon my recollection, whether they did carry more than topſails and foreſail, but I think I remembered ſome with their main-ſails; the impreſſion at that time was that they carried a great deal of ſail, and had a freſh way through the water. Some of them ſeemed attentive to their Admiral, and to carry ſuch ſail as to keep in a proper ſituation with him.

Q. Do you remember what ſail the French Admiral himſelf engaged under?

A. I did not at that time, I had not leiſure to make accurate obſervations.

Q. Can you ſay who made the firſt ſignal for engaging, the Vice Admiral of the red, or the Commander in chief?

A. I cannot. From the moment I ſaw the firing, my eyes turned to the Admiral's flag, and there they were fixed till he made his ſignal; my ſole attention out of the ſhip was directed to the Admiral.

Q. When the Victory paſſed the rearmoſt ſhips of the enemy's line, in what ſituation was you, in reſpect to her, at that time?

A. I do not know the preciſe time when the Admiral had paſſed the French fleet; I had paſſed before, and from that time I was endeavouring to put my ſhip in a condition to obey further orders. I was ahead of the Admiral certainly.

Q. Can you ſpeak to the time and the diſtance that the Admiral ſtood beyond the rear of the enemy, after he wore?

A. I have before ſaid I do not know the preciſe time when the Admiral paſſed the laſt ſhip of the enemy; I

 can

can tell the time I passed them, and the time that the Admiral wore, at least, that he made the signal to wear, if that will answer the question.

Q. Please to mention the time.

A. The watch that these minutes were taken by, when compared with mine, was a quarter of an hour slower than mine. By this watch it was a quarter of an hour after twelve, when we got past the enemy; it was eighteen minutes past eleven when the French began firing, and twenty minutes past eleven when the Admiral hoisted the red flag at the fore topmast head. The Admiral made the signal to wear at eighteen minutes past one; it appeared to me that he wore in a very short time, for I had not been able to get my ship in a situation to wear then.

Q. Do you remember what sail the Victory had set?

A. I remember before the firing began, when I passed the Victory.

Q. I mean after she had passed the enemy's rear?

A. I do not.

Q. Did you make any estimate of the distance the Victory was from the enemy after she wore?

A. I can describe the distance no other way than by the dates I have given. What time the Victory was in action I do not know. At forty minutes past twelve the Victory engaged, and at eighteen minutes past one the signal was made to wear; what part of the time betwixt forty minutes past twelve and eighteen minutes past one, the Victory was engaged, I do not know. I speak by the watch by which the minutes were taken.

Q. Did you take notice of the motions and situation of the red division?

A. At one the Queen, with the Cumberland, and some others of the red division, passed me, standing to the northward, on the other tack, (I was still on the starboard tack) with a good deal of sail, they having passed before; it was about one o'clock, or a quarter of an hour, at least, before the signal was made to wear. The Monarch, one of the red division, was at that time laying disabled, with her fore top sail yard down, just to leeward of us.

Q. Did you observe the red division after that time, when they shortened sail? A. I did not.

Q. Though you did not observe them at the time they shortened sail, did you take notice of them after?

A. I never observed them till they passed me, to take their station in the line in the evening.

Q. Did you observe when the signal for engaging was hauled down? A. I did, at forty-one minutes past one.

Was

Q. Was that after the Admiral had wore, and laid his head towards the enemy?

A. It was after the Admiral had wore, at eighteen minutes after one; he was upon the larboard tack when the signal was hauled down, at forty-one minutes past one.

Q. Was it observed by you when the French fleet broke up their line, and began to stand to the southward?

A. I observed from my situation part of the French fleet when they *were* standing to the southward, because it related to myself; but when they *began* to stand to the southward, or when they broke up their line, I know nothing about.

Q. At what time did you take notice of them with their heads to the southward?

A. The particular time was twenty-five minutes past two, when I hauled my wind, and set my sails upon the larboard tack, in obedience to the Admiral's signal to wear.

Q. Do you remember taking notice when the last of our ships came out of action? A. I did not.

Q. From the brisk fire kept up during the engagement on the part of our ships, does your Lordship believe that the French did not suffer in proportion with the English?

A. I desire not to answer any questions of opinion or conjecture.

Q. Did your Lordship see any of the ships of our fleet dismasted?

A. I saw the Foudroyant's mizen topmast gone, but no lower masts.

Q. Your Lordship has stated, that at twenty-one minutes past two the French ships were standing towards the British fleet, as the French ships were standing to the southward:---Can your Lordship mention the disabled ships they were pointing to?

A. I can; they were the Egmont, Ramillies, Robuste, and Sandwich. I think the Ramillies was to windward, because I had passed close to her, and hailed her.

Q. By your account, at this time the Admiral and the Vice Admiral were standing upon the larboard tack, towards the French?

A. The Admiral was; I did not mention the Vice Admiral of the Red, I did not attend to him; the Admiral was, but I said I took no further notice of the Vice Admiral of the Red till the evening; I do not mean to say it was not so, but I did not observe it.

Q. Whilst the French fleet, or part of them, were standing to the southward, and the British fleet to the northward, were they standing towards each other wide, or how?

 A. The

A. The Engliſh fleet was to windward of the French fleet, for I was working up to windward to get into my ſtation, and I juſt looked up for the headmoſt French ſhip. The French ſhips appeared to me to be ſtanding to the four diſabled; I am confident, becauſe five minutes after three I was uneaſy for theſe ſhips, and I obſerved then, if the ſignal for the line had not been out, I ſhould have thought it my duty to join them; I only ſpeak this to the Court as deſcriptive of the ſituation of that moment.

Q. From the ſituation you have deſcribed the two fleets in, did the Britiſh fleet wear and ſtand a contrary way, or did the French fleet wear and ſtand a contrary way, firſt?

A. I could wiſh to anſwer thoſe queſtions with reſpect to the different tacks they were upon, and not in any expreſſions that might involve opinion. The French ſhips that I mentioned I looked up for, were ſtanding upon the ſtarboard tack, the Admiral was at that time upon the larboard tack, and at ten minutes paſt three the Admiral made the ſignal to wear, to lay his head upon the ſtarboard tack.

Q. Did both fleets continue upon thoſe tacks the reſt of that afternoon?

A. The Admiral did, and the ſhips that wore with him, and the French alſo, as far as I ſaw; ſome particular ſhips getting into their ſtations did not, but the Admiral did, with the body of the fleet.

Q. Did you obſerve the French fleet to begin to form their line, at the time you have deſcribed that they were on your lee, when you was upon your larboard tack?

A. From the time the Admiral wore, my attention was ſo engaged to work my ſhip in ſuch a way as to get her into her ſtation, till I was in my ſtation a-head of the Admiral, that I made no further remarks.

Q. Did you take notice of the red diviſion coming down into the Admiral's wake that afternoon? A. I did not.

Q. After you did get into your ſtation, what obſervations did you make relative to the French fleet?

A. In the circumſtances I am going to mention I cannot pretend to fix time, becauſe it was at progreſſive motions; they only ſtruck me in the groſs. I tacked in my ſtation with the Admiral at three quarters after five; I think part of the French were forming a line to leeward; another greater part appeared to be nearly a-ſtern of the French Admiral's line, and formed one by one to leeward of that body. The Admiral's line was cloſe, at a cable's length aſunder. The French line appeared to be from three cables length to half a mile aſunder, and part of them

in

in the evening, after the van were got a-head of me, and the Admiral's division as far as I could see in a line a-head, formed. The second ship of the French line was rather abaft my beam.

Q. At the time you was upon the larboard tack, and you observed some of the French ships with their heads towards the disabled ships, did you observe any of the French ships fire upon one of our ships a-stern at any time that afternoon? A. I did not see any firing then.

Q. Did you observe what sail the Victory carried that afternoon, whilst she was standing to the southward?

A. I was only attentive to keep my own distance, and did not make any observations upon the sails.

Q. In the night of the 27th, was it observed on board your ship that any signals were made from the French fleet?

A. Not so accurately as to make a minute of it as signals, but we thought we saw some rockets between ten and eleven. I thought it was a signal.

Q. Was it observed on board the Courageux when the French fleet bore away? A. No.

Q. Was any signal made in the night by the Admiral for altering courses? A. I saw none.

Q. What part of the French fleet was in sight next morning?

A. I saw three strange ships, and I saw the signal made for a fleet by two of our ships, I think the Monarch and Queen.

Q. Did you judge those three ships to be French ships of war? A. I supposed so; I saw no colours.

Q. Did you judge them to be line of battle ships?

A. I formed no judgment about it.

Q. At what distance were they from the English fleet?

A. I do not know.

Q. Which way did they stand?

A. I don't remember; my ship was not in a condition to have her signal thrown out to chace, and I did not attend to it.

Q. Do you remember how the wind was that morning?

A. West, I believe.

Q. What kind of weather was it?

A. Moderate weather, and rather hazy; there was a swell.

Q. Can you speak to the latitude by reckoning, the 28th at noon?

A. I have extracts of the bearings and distances, 48° 16″ Ushant N. 79 E. dist. 74 miles.

Admiral Montague. To your knowledge and observation,

tion, did Admiral Keppel negligently perform the duty imposed on him on the 27th or 28th of July?

A. I have taken an oath to answer the truth to all questions that shall be asked me. I look upon opinion as liable to error. I have answered every fact as distinctly as I could, that came within my knowledge. I hope the Court will not press me to answer matters of opinion. I have always thought the opinion of individuals was sacred. I have declined giving my opinion on this to my most intimate friends. The Court are to form their opinion upon evidence; they take an oath not to divulge each other's opinion; and I hope the candour and justice of the Court will extend that protection to me, which the law has given to them, and that I shall not be called upon to give my opinion. The Court are to judge of facts, and I should think myself in a disagreeable situation, if I, as a witness, am called to answer upon oath to that which is matter of opinion, and after giving it to-day, may alter my opinion, and think it not a just one. To facts I speak, but to opinion I cannot.

Admiral Montague. I fancy your Lordship has misunderstood the question. I have not asked---I will not ask your opinion, nor the opinion of any other evidence. I do expect from every evidence that he will answer to such questions as he shall be asked; that upon oath he speaks the truth, the whole truth, and nothing but the truth. The question I ask is, From your own knowledge and observation, did Admiral Keppel negligently perform his duty on the 27th or 28th of July?

Lord Mulgrave. I perfectly understand the question, if I understand the language. It imports me much, when I am upon my oath, to go by my own understanding, and not by that of other people. The term of Negligence implies a crime, and I must be equal to the duty of the Admiral commanding in chief, before I can decide whether he did his duty properly upon either of those days. 'Tis the Court who are to decide, and not me. I have answered to facts, and if I am pressed more by the Court, 'tis not the Admiral that is accused, but me, because I am to form an opinion how that fleet was conducted, and not the Admiral. I think it not my duty, as a witness, to do that. If I am pressed by one member of the Court, I must desire the sense of the Court, and that they consider their own and my oath, and whether the opinion of an individual is necessary to influence the Court in a trial of such importance. If it is necessary, I hope the Court will withdraw, and that they will seriously and delibe-

rately

rately consider their own and my situation, before they call upon me to say whether Admiral Keppel is guilty of negligence or not; for a matter of fact which may be meritorious in one respect, in another may be criminal; and I am called upon to determine whether the conduct of the Admiral was meritorious or criminal. I have answered to every fact I observed, to every motion, to every signal of the fleet that I saw, and I am ready to give all the information in my power, as to facts; but to draw an inference from those facts, whether they imply negligence or not, does not become me; and I shall think myself an injured man, if I am obliged to answer questions imposed upon me by an individual. I hope the Court will consider my situation, and that I have said this much under a sense of the oath I have taken. It has happened to me during the course of the time I had the honour to serve under the honourable Admiral, to disapprove in my own mind of particular steps, and upon recollection found I was wrong. After that can the Court call upon me to give my opinion upon that, which I may perhaps hereafter conceive a different opinion of.

Admiral Montague. My lord, the language you have used this day, when it goes abroad, will appear strange without doors.

Lord Mulgrave. I must stop the Admiral before he proceeds any further. If I am to be corrected, I hope it will be by the Court, and not by an individual member.

Admiral Montague. My lord, I must tell you, that your language is a censure upon this Court, and of such a sort, that though I have been a seaman forty-six years, and a Captain and an Admiral upwards of thirty years, in which time I have attended many Court Martials, I never yet heard any thing equal to it; nor is there, I will be bold to say, a court in the kingdom where such disrespect would have been permitted.

Lord Mulgrave. I have treated the Court with no disrespect, but I conceive it to be the usage of the Service, if a witness is to be censured, that it be passed by the whole Court, and not by an individual. I confess I do not understand this new mode.

Admiral Montague. New mode! the whole trial is a new mode, unprecedented and strange to the last degree! But I must move the court to withdraw on this question. Such language and such treatment is not to be borne.

Admiral Arbuthnot. I confess I totally disapprove and must condemn the language. I think it exceedingly disrespectful. Every member has a right to ask questions,

but

but how far a witneſs is compellable to anſwer queſtions of opinion, the court muſt determine.

The Court withdrew, and after ſtaying out near an hour, the members reſumed their places, when the Preſident addreſſed Lord Mulgrave, as follows, " My Lord, the Court have come to a reſolution which the Judge Advocate will read to you."

Judge Advocate. " My Lord, I am directed to obſerve, " that in the courſe of the reaſoning you have uſed in " declining to anſwer a queſtion, which a member of the " Court has put, by the approbation of the Court; you " have made uſe of language unbecoming the dignity of " this Court; your treatment of them, is ſuch, as cannot " be paſſed over without cenſure.

" And it is their pleaſure, that I acquaint your Lordſhip, with their diſapprobation of your Lordſhip's behaviour.---It is agreed by the Court, that the queſtion " ſhall be put, but I am directed by the Court, to acquaint your Lordſhip, that as by the oath you have " taken, you look upon it, that you are not to anſwer " queſtions of opinion, you are at liberty to anſwer it or " not."

Lord Mulgrave. It is my duty to ſubmit to the determination of the Court. I had no intention to give offence. I ſtated my reaſons for refuſal.---It has appeared otherwiſe to the Court, and I am concerned for it. I can give no anſwer to that queſtion.

Here the Court interrupted his Lordſhip, by adjourning till to-morrow morning ten o'clock.

Nineteenth Day, THURSDAY, January 28th.

At ten o'clock this morning the Court being met, the priſoner was brought in, and audience admitted.

Proſecutor. I ſhall now call Lord Sandwich, to exhibit and prove ſuch letters as his Lordſhip may have received from Admiral Keppel, relating to the engagement. I would not have called for this mode of proof, if it had not been previouſly adopted by the Admiral. I would alſo call for the Admiral's private letters to his Lordſhip, relative to the engagement, if the Admiral has no objection.

Admiral Keppel. It is ſo far from my having any objection to what the Vice Admiral has propoſed, that there is not one act in my life, that I don't wiſh may come before the Court.

A motion was hereupon made for the Court to retire, to debate on the propriety of the Proſecutor's requeſt.---They retired, and

on

on their return, the Judge Advocate was about to read their resolution, when Sir Hugh Palliser addressed them in the following manner:

Prosecutor. To save my Lord Sandwich trouble, I would also beg leave to call for my own private letters. I have heard the prisoner say, that he means to call for them; I know not that they contain any thing to his prejudice, and I would not wish to call for them if disagreeable to himself.

Admiral Keppel. I object to it, since it belongs to me alone to make proof of the Prosecutor's letters; and if I call for them in the course of my evidence, I shall take care to give his Lordship timely notice.

The Earl of Sandwich then came forward, when Sir Hugh Palliser read again his request to the Court, respecting the production of his own private letters, and Admiral Keppel's objection to it. The resolution of the Court on the question was then read.

Resolution, "The Court has resolved that they cannot "take cognizance of letters, and admit them as proof, "which are of a private nature."

Lord Sandwich. I fancy that my presence then is not further required. I beg leave to say, that I do not think these letters are material evidence. I brought them with me; if it is the opinion of this Court that no private letters are to be admitted in evidence, I flatter myself the Court has no occasion of my presence, and I confess, I am pleased that they are not thought necessary, since there are two of them, that I should not have wished to have submitted to the Court, as they are chiefly reasonings with regard to the navy and officers.

Lord Sandwich ordered to withdraw.

LORD LONGFORD, *of the America, sworn.*

Prosecutor. Do you recollect the time when you first saw the French fleet, on the morning of the 27th, July?

A. I did not see the French fleet that morning, till signal was made for chace. I was not upon deck till day light, and so I do not know what time they were perceived.

Q. Do you recollect upon what tack they were when you first saw them?

A. They were upon the larboard tack, I think the same tack that we were.

Q. Do you remember when they changed their tack, whether they tacked or wore?

A. I cannot be certain, but I rather believe they wore; I saw some of them wear, but I do not know whether they all wore.

Q. Did

Q. Did they appear to your Lordship to be in a line?

A. They did at that time.

Q. Did you observe when they changed their tack again?

A. I did, I think so, it was a little before the firing began, I saw some of them upon one tack, and some upon the other.

Q. Did you observe that they wore that time, upon changing their tack? A. Some of them, I know wore.

Q. Did they appear to you, as they came upon the larboard tack to form the line again, upon that tack?

A. They did so.

Q. What part of the French line did your ship fall into, to begin the engagement with?

A. I believe we were fired at by the third ship of the van, and we returned our fire to the fifth, or sixth, the others were at too great a distance, I thought.

Q. At that time were any other of our ships so near the America, as to be of support to each other?

A. The Terrible was very near the America, a little upon her lee bow, and the Elizabeth, a little upon her lee quarter, we were near each other.

Q. Did you continue so during the engagement?

A. We did for a considerable time.

Q. Was not the America one of the Vice Admiral of the Blue's division? A. She was.

Q. Do you remember signal being made for six ships of that division to chace that morning? A. I do so.

President. Can you name them?

A. I cannot all. I know mine was one of them.

Q. If the ships of that division had been permitted to remain together, might not the whole division have been brought into action together, with their own flag, and engaged as their own flag did, if they had not been separated by the signal to chace?

President. 'Tis my duty to tell your Lordship, that whatever you look upon as matter of opinion, you may or may not answer, as you think proper.

Evidence. Very well, Sir. If the wind had continued as it was when that signal was made to chace, and the signal had not been made, I do not believe that any part of the Vice Admiral of the Blue's division, could have come into action at all.

Q. Under this circumstance that your Lordship mentioned, in that case would the centre division have been able to come into action at all, any more than the Vice Admiral of the Blue?

A. I do

A. I do not know. But the centre division must certainly have come into action sooner, because they were to windward of the Vice Admiral of the Blue.

Q. As you have answered questions that are somewhat matter of opinion; I would ask, whether if the signal had been made for the whole of that division to chace, instead of part, would it not have had the same consequence for the whole, as for that part, whatever that part was?

A. If they had been altogether, I believe it would, Sir.

Q. Can you remember how many ships the signal was made for? A. I cannot.

Q. How was the America situated with respect to the Victory, the latter part of the engagement?

A. Very soon after I had passed the sternmost of the French ships, I passed ahead of the Victory; she was then upon the larboard tack, standing towards the enemy. I mean when your ship was out of the action.

Q. Was the signal for battle flying then?

A. I don't recollect at that time?

Q. Was you ahead of the Vice Admiral of the Blue, when you came out of action? A. I was.

Q. At the time your Lordship was speaking of, when you passed ahead of the Victory, did you take notice of the Red division?

A. I did, a very short time before I passed the Victory, I passed under the lee quarter of the Queen, who was upon the larboard tack, standing towards the enemy.

Q. Did you take notice of the Vice Admiral of the Blue, when he came out of action?

A. I did not particularly, just at that time.

Q. Can you remember at what time you did happen to take notice of her?

A. I do not particularly.

Q. Did you observe the French fleet, when they began to lay their heads to the southward?

A. I believe I saw them soon after they began. I was upon the quarter deck, but did not see them at first.

Q. Was that before or after the Admiral had wore, and laid his head to the southward, that you took notice of them? A. I cannot recollect.

Q. You said you passed ahead of the Victory, and to leeward of the Queen, then by that description, the Red division were to windward of the Victory?

A. They were.

Court. Was it the whole division?

A. I do not know, but such as I saw, they stood after Sir Robert Harland at that time.

Q. Were

Q. Were they to windward of the rear of the enemy at that time?

A. I am not certain, I believe they might be to windward of the rear of the enemy at that time.

Q. Did you obferve when the Admiral wore, and laid his head to the fouthward? A. I did not.

Q. You faid you took notice of fome of the French fhips laying their heads to the fouthward. Which way was the Admiral then ftanding?

A. I anfwered that before. I do not recollect that I obferved which way the Admiral's head was, when I faw fome of the French fhips, with their heads to the fouthward?

Q. After that time did the French continue to ftand (the whole fleet) with their heads to the fouthward?

A. They appeared to me from that time to begin to form their line, they led out one fhip after another from the body of the fleet, as appeared to me very flowly.

Q. Did they continue to do fo all the afternoon?

A. The appeared to me to do fo all the afternoon.

Q. Did the Britifh fleet ftand to the fouthward all that afternoon?

A. They formed their line, with their heads to the fouthward, and continued to ftand upon that tack all the afternoon.

Q. From the very brisk fire kept up by our fhips that engaged, have you reafon to believe the French fleet muft have fuffered in proportion with the Britifh fleet, in fome fhape or other?

A. They did not feem to have fuffered fo much as fome of the Britifh fleet appeared to have fuffered in their fails and rigging, but I hope they fuffered more in their men.

Q. From the motions of the enemy during that afternoon, ftanding to the fouthward, and forming a new line of battle, did they fhow a difpofition to renew the engagement, or to avoid it?

A. If they had been inclined to have renewed the engagement, they might have fetched up within fhot of the Britifh fleet, there was nothing to prevent them. They fhewed a difpofition to fight if they were attacked, but I do not apprehend they intended to renew the engagement.

Q. Did you obferve that any of their fhips, as they advanced to the rear of the Britifh fleet, fired at one of our fhips that was left aftern? A. I did not fee.

Q. How many of the French fleet were in fight the next morning? A. Three fail.

Q. Did they appear to be line of battle fhips or frigates? A. I was

A. I was ſo far from them, that I could not diſcover whether they were line of battle ſhips, or frigates.

Q. Were they chaced? A. I do not know.

The Proſecutor obſerved he had no more queſtions to ask.

Admiral Keppel. Do you recollect when you made ſail in the morning by ſignal at five o'clock, what ſail the Vice Admiral of the Blue was under?

A. I do not know what ſail the Vice Admiral was under. I was under double reefed top-ſails, and fore-ſail.

Q. When ſignals were made for different ſhips of the Vice Admiral of the Blue's diviſion to chace, did the Vice Admiral ſet all his ſails to follow the chacing ſhips?

A. I did not obſerve.

Q. You have heard all the articles of the charge read, therefore, I muſt deſire you will ſtate to the Court, any inſtance, if you ſaw or know of any, in which I negligently performed my duty, or any part of it, on the 27th, or 28th of July?

A. I can ſtate no ſuch inſtance to the Court, for I know of none.

Lord Longford, ordered to withdraw.

ROBERT CHRISTIAN, *Maſter of the Ramillies, ſworn.*

Proſecutor. Have you brought your day's work of the 27th and 28th? A. I have.

Q. Give an account of the lat. bearing, and diſtance of Uſhant, on 28th July?

A. Lat. 48°. 20′. bearing N. E. ſix degrees E. diſtant 52 miles.

Preſident. How comes it that two leaves are torn out of your log book, betwixt the 26th and 27th of July?

A. They never were cut out, to my knowledge, if they were, it muſt be done by ſome of the young gentlemen of the ſhip; there is an addition put into the book.

Q. Did you end with the 26th?

A. The 27th began the new book.

Proſecutor. How was the wind the 28th in the morning? A. On the weſtward hank.

Q. What weather was it at that time?

A. Moderate weather.

Q. Do you conſider Uſhant as a dangerous lee ſhore, with the wind at weſt and moderate weather?

A. No.

Preſident. Would you have ventured upon that ſhore with crippled ſhips?

A. Not too nearly.

Q. Have you been uſed to cruize off Uſhant and Breſt?

A. In the late war I was.

Q. Do you apprehend any imminent danger in chacing ships in the middle of summer, even within Ushant, to Brest harbour? A. No.

Q. Can you inform the court how much the wind shifted in the morning, from six to ten o'clock?

A. I cannot, but it is down in the log book.

Q. Have not you a private log book?

A. Not with me, I have not.

Admiral Keppel. I beg nothing may be inserted from the log book where the leaves are cut out.

Prosecutor. The Formidable's was inserted.

Admiral Keppel. That was entered because it was under the accuser's inspection, for no other reason in the world. If the Court admits of it, they are the best judges, they will put down, in the morning of the 28th, wind at W. N. W.

Admiral Montague. When we come to debate, we shall be best able to judge whether to take any notice of those where the leaves are cut out, and how the wind was, and whether it shifted.

Admiral Keppel to the Prosecutor. I beg your pardon, Sir, the first time I ever did in my life, I am wrong.

Court. Will the Admiral ask the witness any questions?

Admiral Keppel. As I shall not condescend to measure my conduct as Commander of a fleet, by the opinion of the master of a ship, I shall put no question to the witness before you.

Ordered to withdraw.

RICHARD STORY, *Master of the Shrewsbury, called and sworn.*

Prosecutor. Do you remember the Shrewsbury wearing and standing towards the enemy, before any other ship?

A. Yes we did.

Q. Do you remember the occasion of it, and for what purpose it was declared to be at that time, and by whom? A. I really do not know.

Q. Do you remember about that time taking notice of the situation of the ships that remained engaged with the Vice Admiral of the blue?

A. None but the Formidable.

Q. What notice and observation did you make relative to her situation at that time, on board your ship?

A. Nothing more than seeing her engaged, I could not see her flag, nor the upper part of her top sail.

Q. What conversation passed amongst the officers and yourself relative to her situation? *Admiral*

Admiral Montague. As things of a private nature were not admitted by the court, respecting the Vice Admiral and Lord Sandwich, I think we cannot do it now. What the evidence sees and knows from his own knowledge, we must admit, but nothing else, no more than private letters of correspondence; with myself it will have no weight at all.

Q. Did you take notice of the Formidable after she came out of the action?

A. Not further than seeing her sails much shattered and shot.

Q. After the red division had tacked, did you observe under what sail the Victory was standing while she was standing upon the contrary tack?

A. I did not.

Q. How much did the wind shift on the 26th in the morning from six till ten o'clock?

A. I cannot say exactly.

Court. Did you know it was put down at that time?

A. No, not till the engagement was over, not till four o'clock in the afternoon.

Q. When it was inserted in the log book, was it not taken from the log board?

A. It was taken from the board.

Q. Do you remember from your own knowledge?

A. I do not suppose it shifted above two points and an half, or three points at most. On looking in his book he finds it shifted two points.

Prosecutor. There are two or three day's work in the log book crossed out, what was the reason of that?

A. There was not room in the page, that was ruled for the 27th, to insert every transaction; therefore I crossed it out, and it is in the following page as it stands. It is very fair, I wrote it myself.

Q. You said, by the log book it appeared that the ship was to windward two points; it is different in the log book?

A. I cannot say whether it may be marked till ten o'clock.

Q. Do you recollect whether the ships could have come to action that day, if the wind had not shifted?

A. We certainly could not.

Q. Do you remember seeing the French fleet, that morning, tack, or wear, once or twice before the action began? A. Yes I did.

Q. Did they wear twice?

A. They either wore or tacked.

Q. Cannot you ſay whether they wore or tacked?

A. The laſt time they wore, but the firſt time I am not certain.

Q. If the French fleet wore twice, would it not bring them nearer to the Britiſh fleet than they would have been if they had not ſo wore? A. Certainly.

Q. At the time they did wear, had not they run a good deal to leeward before they hauled their wind again on the contrary tack?

A. I cannot tell what diſtance they might run to leeward: It was very thick for ſome time, till it cleared away; when it did, I counted ſix ſail before the wind when I looked up.

Preſident. Do you recollect what obſervations you made in your log book at that time?

A. It is put down, I thought they were bearing away for Breſt.

Q. Then by their having gone before the wind, was not that the cauſe why the Britiſh fleet lay ſo well up with them when they tacked? A. Certainly.

Q. Do you remember how the wind was the morning of the engagement?

A. By the log book, it was W.

Q. What ſort of weather? A. Something hazy.

Q. As to wind?

A. The ſhips might have carried whole top ſails upon a wind.

Q. Do you conſider Uſhant as a dangerous lee ſhore in the middle of ſummer, moderate weather, and the wind at W.

A. Not dangerous in a ſingle ſhip, as for a fleet it is more dangerous certainly.

Q. Is Uſhant, with that wind, a dangerous lee ſhore at all: Is it a dangerous coaſt, with the wind at W. for any ſhip, or any number of ſhips?

A. It may be made a lee ſhore by leading too far to the ſouthward.

Q. I am ſtating my queſtion by ſuppoſing to be in the lat. of Uſhant, or nearly ſo?

A. Certainly it cannot be a lee ſhore, without a perſon makes it ſo himſelf by running on it.

Admiral Keppel. The Proſecutor has avoided aſking this gentleman for his day's work of the 28th; I ſhall be glad he would give his day's work, he may know it; I do not?

A. The 27th in the morning, at eight o'clock, Uſhant 84 E. diſtance nineteen leagues: I took it from the log book

book the following day myself, not after I made the land; I never do that.

Q. When we got upon the starboard tack, was not the Shrewsbury upon the weather bow of the Admiral's fleet?

A. About half an hour after we tacked, we were astern of the fleet.

Q. Did you look at the Admiral just before you came into action? A. I did not.

Q. Do you recollect, about four days before the English and French fleets came together, a very strong wind at N. W. that obliged the fleet to stand to the southward, and crippled many of them, and the Victory in particular?

A. I remember it blew very fresh some time before we saw the French fleet; and to the best of my remembrance, the Victory's main yard broke.

Mr. MATTISON, *Master of the Victory, sworn.*

Prosecutor. How came the interlinations in your log book?

A. I found the bearings omitted, at three o'clock in the afternoon (by log) the day of action.

Q. What did you take it from when you put it in?

A. From recollection and overhauling remarks, and I found it not as I put it on to the hour at three o'clock.

Q. Was it by desire of any body that you interlined them or made that alteration? A. No.

Q. The courses both ways, were they not? A. Yes.

Admiral Keppel. When did you insert it?

A. I don't know the day.

Q. Was it a great while ago?

A. It was some days before it was brought into court.

Q. Is this the original log that was kept for the log book, or your own, is there no publick log book for the use of the ship?

A. There was a rough log book which the mate used to keep, but he was negligent, and there were several days behind when I examined it, I found it not inserted, but this is the original book for the use of the ship.

Q. Was that log book taken from the board as the ship's log book?

A. Yes, from the log board and slate I kept for it.

Q. Was not there a rough log book kept for the use of the ship independent of this?

A. The other I am speaking of; that I had for the mate, to teach him how to take a log off; it was imperfect, and not copied from the board.

Q. Was this book taken off day by day?

 A. Yes,

A. Yes, by myself, from the log board.

Admiral Arbuthnot. Was the log book, said to be the rough log book, copied from this?

A. Yes, this is the genuine log book of the ship.

Q. *Prosecutor.* Look at your log book and give the court an account what alterations there were in the wind between six and ten o'clock in the morning of the 27th?

A. One point.

Q. Please to give the court your reckoning the 27th and 28th of July, of the latitude, bearing, and distance from Ushant.

A. On the 27th, lat. 48°. 31". N. bearing, Ushant S. 89 deg. E. distance 36 leagues. The 28th, lat. 48°. 10'. N. Ushant N. 75 deg. E. 27 leagues.

Q. Are these your correct reckonings, or back reckonings from the land?

A. They are the current reckonings of the ship, I made no alterations, they were worked each day.

Q. How was the wind and weather on the morning of the 28th?

A. The weather was squally. Wind, W. and by N.

Q. With that weather and that wind, was Ushant a dangerous lee shore in summer time?

A. With the wind and weather we had I should have thought it so, if we had been near a lee shore.

Q. Would you consider it so when you were in the latitude of it, or near it?

A. Ushant itself is a small spot, and a ship might clear it with the wind at W. N. W. in moderate weather.

Q. *Admiral Montague.* Should you chuse, if you was master of a flag ship, with a fleet of thirty sail of the line, all in good condition and not disabled, would you chuse in the afternoon of any day, though the weather was fine, to run any way on an enemy's shore nearer than five or six leagues; night coming on? A. No.

Q. Suppose you in the Victory going two knots, and a ship astern of you (tis a plain question) going three knots and four fathom, do you not think the ship astern will come up with the ship ahead that goes two knots?

A. I do, Sir.

Admiral Keppel. If the British fleet, after the action on the 27th, had been catched in with Ushant, as they were a week or eight or nine days before, with the wind at N. and by W. such a gale of wind as when the Victory broke her main yard, do you not think they would have been in a perilous situation?

A. With

A. With the wind as at that time, and blowing as hard as it did then at N. N. W. on that day they would have been in great danger.

Q. Do you remember whether the Vice Admiral of the Red, in the morning after he ſtood upon the other tack, was upon the weather bow?

A. I do not recollect ſeeing him upon the weather bow; when I ſaw him, which was juſt before the Victory wore, he was a point abaft the weather beam.

Q. Was the ſignal made for the whole fleet to tack together at ten o'clock on the 27th?

A. The ſignal was made to tack about that time.

Q. Do you remember upon ſome change of wind, whether it was a point or two that the Vice Admiral of the Red became upon the lee bow of the Victory, about 11 o'clock?

A. I recollect ſeeing him near two points upon a wind, or about two points.

Q. Do you remember my having diſtinctly looked to leeward, and obſerving the French fleet were in confuſion, and that one ſhip was almoſt aboard of another, did you obſerve they were in confuſion? A. I did.

Admiral Keppel. I ſhall take notice to the court that the alteration made in the Victory's log book, from recollection, is an inſertion of one of the principal facts which my accuſer makes the matter of his charge; ſo the alteration will not appear as a crime againſt Sir Hugh Palliſer.

Q. Did you fire into the Foudroyant during the engagement on the 27th? A. Not to my knowledge.

Q. Do you conſider Uſhant as a dangerous lee ſhore with the wind weſterly in moderate weather, and ſummer time within two leagues, and in the latitude of it nearly ſo? A. Yes, I do.

Adjourned till to-morrow, ten o'clock.

TWENTIETH DAY, FRIDAY, JANUARY, 29th.

The Court re-aſſembled at ten o'clock, when THOMAS READE, *Maſter of the Queen, was called and ſworn.*

Proſecutor. What was the ſituation of the Red diviſion with re-ſpect to the rear of the enemy in the afternoon of the 27th, when the Admiral made a ſignal to wear and ſtand to the ſouthward?

A. The Red ſquadron was about two miles as near as I can judge from the rear of the enemy.

Q. I am ſpeaking of three o'clock, when the fleet was to ſtand to the ſouthward; do you ſpeak of that, or a time earlier than that?

A. At the time the ſignal was made for wearing, we were rather nearer by two miles, than at firſt when we ſhortened ſail.

 Q. Upon

Q. Upon the larboard tack do you mean?

A. I mean when we wore from the larboard tack to the ſtarboard.

Q. Was you then to windward or to leeward, or in what poſition from them?

A. They were about a point upon the lee bow.

Q. Is this the original rough log book that was kept for the ſhip's uſe on board the Queen?

A. No, it is not; it is my own log book, kept daily and ſhewn every day.

Q. Where is the original proper ſhip's rough log book?

A. At Plymouth.

Preſident. Is it the log book that you kept every day during the time you was employed upon that ſervice?

A. It is, Sir.

Q. Can you ſwear to this more particularly than you can to the ſhip's book?

A. I can; I took it off every day at ten o'clock, myſelf, from the log board.

Q. Was the rough log book taken from this, or this from that?

A. The mate wrote that every day from the log board, and I wrote this every day from the log board.

Preſident. Have there been any alterations, corrections, or additions ſince, of any ſort whatſoever?

A. No, nothing reſpecting thoſe days.

Proſecutor. Did you never, at no time, copy the days work from the ſhip's log book into your book?

A. Not at ſea, harbour work frequently.

Q. Do you call by coming very near the rear of the enemy, the diſtance of two miles?

A. We were not within gun ſhot of them at that time.

Q. Then do you mean within leſs than two miles, by that? A. Yes.

Q. There is a reference inſerted in the log book, "*at this time the Victory hauled down the ſignal for engaging,*" that appears to be wrote with a different pen and different ink; was that reference wrote at the ſame time as the reſt of the day's work?

A. It was wrote in ſome part of the ſame day, not at the ſame time, and was omitted in taking off the log.

Q. What is the reaſon that there is no log marked from one o'clock till five in the afternoon, of the day of the engagement?

A. The reaſon was, the various courſes we ſteered were too complicated to admit of making any remarks. We were never without running faſt, or ſhortening ſail.

Q. Was

Q. Was it uſual for four or five hours to omit giving the ſhip ſome eſtimate of her rate and courſes, if you did not leave the log?

A. Yes, under thoſe particular circumſtances.

Admiral Montague. I aſk you by the oath you have taken, what you mean by the word various? do you mean at twelve o'clock, or till you took notice of the wind and weather again?

A. With reſpect to the variety of courſes, it is meant, ſhe was not under the ſame courſes from eleven till twelve o'clock.

Q. What time did the Queen come out of the engagement?

A. About half after twelve o'clock, as near as I could gueſs.

Q. Then the time ſpoken of, in which the log is not marked, is it not after that time, from one to five o'clock?

A. The log was not marked till we were a little ſettled, and in our ſtation.

Q. Are you ſure that there is nothing marked for thoſe hours, in the original rough ſhip's log book?

A. There is not, I have ſeen it.

Q. What is the reaſon why one of the leaves of that log book was cut out, the 24th, while the French fleet were in ſight?

A. Becauſe it was blotted I had it cut out, and made a fair book to ſhew to the Admiral every day.

Q. Inform the court how much the wind ſhifted from ſix o'clock till ten in the morning of the 27th.

A. About two points.

Q. Does it appear ſo by the log book? A. No.

Q. Was it one or two points by the log book?

A. One point.

Q. Do you remember taking particular notice of the French fleet in the morning of the 27th, and at what time?

A. I did not take particular notice of them till we tacked, at ten o'clock:

Q. Did you ſee them tack or wear before noon?

A. I did not take particular notice of their manœuvres, being buſily employed about our own ſhip.

Q. Have you brought your day's work? A. Yes.

Q. Give an account of the latitude, bearings, and diſtance of Uſhant, the 27th and 28th of July.

A. The 27th, lat. 48° 36″ N. Uſhant; S. 86 E. diſtance 28 leagues. On the 28th, 48° 8″. Uſhant N. 47 E. 26 leagues diſtance.

Q. In

Q. In the morning of the 28th, what part of the French fleet was seen from your ship?

A. Three sail, that I imagined to be part of the French fleet.

Q. Were no other ships seen that were supposed to be the French fleet? A. Not that I heard of.

Q. Was not the signal made on board the Queen for seeing a fleet? A. Not to my knowledge.

Q. How was the wind and weather on the morning of the 28th?

A. The wind was westerly, the weather moderate.

Q. Was the wind and weather such that you would advise not to chace a flying beaten enemy towards Ushant, from any apprehension of danger of Ushant's being a lee shore?

A. The ships might have chaced that were not disabled, without considering Ushant as a dangerous lee shore then.

Q. Was any part of the fleet then dismasted?

A. None were dismasted, many appeared very crippled.

Q. Was that appearance of being crippled in sails and rigging only, or how; did it appear they were crippled in their masts?

A. Many of them were preparing to fish their masts, several of their topmasts being uncapped.

Q. In what situation must a ship be, and with what weather, to make Ushant a dangerous lee shore?

A. When a ship is prevented from carrying sail, from a variety of accidents, or by blowing hard.

Ordered to withdraw.

The Master of the America, called and sworn.

Capt. Duncan. I must beg to object against examining any other log books. They were put on the table for our inspection, and not to find matter of accusation. We have been trying the master of the Queen for this hour past.

Admiral Keppel. I have no objection to the Vice Admiral's examining or looking into log books for accusation, or any thing else, that he can get at any one way.

Court. 'Tis not to the point, 'tis the masters we are trying, not the Admiral; 'tis delaying time.

Prosecutor. I presume I may be allowed to observe, that in the Victory's log book from the time of passing the enemy, till five o'clock, there is only one knot and five fathom marked upon it; the rest of the time is said to be laying to.

Court observed the words laying to did not seem to be evidence one way or other.

Admiral Keppel. I never saw that book, and I have nothing to do with what is marked at all.

Court. Is the log book here, the copy?

A. It is the book I wrote every day, without any alterations or erasement.

Q. What alteration of wind was there from six in the morning till ten, when the fleet tacked?

A. About 4 points S.W. to W. from nine to ten o'clock.

Admiral Montague. I must beg the master will give an answer to that question from his own knowledge. If he has a doubt, he may refer to his book if he wants it.

Q. Are the courses allowed in your reckoning according to that shift of wind, or according to what it is in the log book?

A. The courses are as they are in the log book, the shift of wind is not mentioned in the log book.

Q. How was the wind and weather in the morning of the 28th?

A. The wind was about west, as near as I can recollect, the weather moderate.

Q. Would you have advised not to have chaced a flying enemy at that time, for fear of making Ushant a lee shore, at that time of year too?

A. I should not have been afraid of making Ushant a lee shore, till I had been within three or four leagues of the land.

Q. Under what circumstances must the ship be to make Ushant a dangerous lee shore; what kind of weather must it be?

A. If a ship was between Ushant and the Seams, and blowing a gale of wind at W. or W. N. W. I should suppose her in great danger.

Q. Until she became between Ushant and the Seams, do you consider there was any great danger while she was without, supposing it moderate weather?

A. Not in the least dangerous, if she could carry sail.

President. Ask the same question of the Master for a fleet of thirty sail, and part crippled ships.

It was put.------Q. If a fleet of crippled ships, &c.

A. Not if they were three or four leagues without the lines of Ushant and the Seams.

Prosecutor. Be it one, or thirty, if they can carry sail, is it not all the same in moderate weather?

A. One ship could get off the land much faster than a fleet of ships could, even in moderate weather.

Admiral Keppel. I am not a Brother of the Trinity-house, and therefore I shall not ask this gentleman any more questions.

Ordered to withdraw.

Prosecutor.

The Master of the Foudroyant called and ſworn.

Proſecutor. Is this the original rough ſhip's log book, kept on board the Foudroyant?

A. Yes, it is the log book I received from the maſter I ſucceeded in the ſhip.

Q. Was there no other public log book kept for the uſe of the ſhip?

A. There was one for the uſe of the midſhipmen and mates.

Q. Was not part of this book copied from that book?

A. No, Sir.

Q. Then this is not the public ſhip's book that every body had acceſs to, or was the other for that uſe?

A. Only the Captain, and Lieutenants, had acceſs to this.

Q. Does the other log book and this, exactly agree?

A. I never looked at the other.

Q. Have you brought your day's work?

A. 'Tis in the log book.

Q. Mention the latitude, bearing, and diſtance on the 27th and 28th.

A. The 27th lat. 48° 38″, bearing Uſhant E. half S. diſt. 27 leagues; on the 28th, lat. 48° 17″, bearing Uſhant 11 deg. N. diſt. 21 leagues.

Q. Inform the Court, how much the wind ſhifted in the morning of the 27th, between ſix and ten o'clock?

A. I do not recollect it ſhifted at all in that time.

Preſident. Did it afterwards, at what time, how many points?

A. Betwixt ten and twelve it ſhifted two points.

Proſecutor. What kind of weather was it in the morning of the 28th?

A. Freſh gales and cloudy.

Q. As the wind and weather then was, would you as a maſter or pilot have objected to chace a beaten flying enemy, from any apprehenſion of Uſhant being a dangerous lee ſhore?

A. It muſt depend upon the circumſtances of the ſhip I was in.

Q. Suppoſe a ſhip that can carry ſail with that weather, and all her maſts ſtanding?

A. If they were all ſtanding as a man of war, I ſhould have no objection of chacing.

Q. In the ſituation the Foudroyant was in that day, would you have objected to chace? A. Yes.

Q. At that diſtance from the land, would you have thought yourſelf in danger? A. Not

A. Not at that diſtance.

Q. What ſail could ſhe have carried upon a wind?

A. Third reefed top ſails.

Q. Could you not have carried her top ſails three reefs, in ſuppoſing yourſelf within a few miles of Uſhant, with the wind at W. or W. N. W. the variation in your favour too, and in the latitude, or nearly in the latitude of Uſhant?

A. Yes, ſhe might have carried that, and not more.

Q. Would ſhe in theſe circumſtances have been in danger? A. Yes.

Ordered to withdraw.

JOHN FORBES, *Maſter of the Berwick, ſworn.*

Proſecutor. I ſhall aſk no queſtions about the log book, but obſerve there are a great many additions made to it on the 28th of July, wrote in a different hand, and with different ink. I dare ſay they are all facts, and you know your meaning by it. I only remark, there is that circumſtance attends it?

A. There is nothing in that book, but what I ſaw myſelf, and put down myſelf that day. It was done the ſame day.

Q. During the engagement of the 27th of July, did not ſome of our ſhips fire into the Berwick?

A. Not to my knowledge.

Q. Did you underſtand that it was ſo?

A. I heard ſo by report of the ſhip's company, but not to my own knowledge.

Q. By that report, was it not ſaid ſome men were killed by it? A. Not to my knowledge.

Q. Did you receive no ſhot on the larboard ſide?

A. Not as I ſaw.

Q. Was you told of any?

Admiral Keppel. That's not evidence I apprehend.

Ordered to withdraw.

Proſecutor. Mr. Preſident, as I apprehend the Court are pretty well tired of the chapter of log books and lee ſhores, I would not tire them any further, but beg leave to inform the Court, that the expreſſes that were ſent after Lieutenant Perry, who was ſuppoſed to have the minutes of the Formidable, have not procured any account of him; but by a letter from the Secretary, I am informed, expreſſes were ſent to meet him at the Nore, it being ſuppoſed the tender he commanded, was at the Nore, or on her paſſage thither; but if he ſhould come before the proceedings are cloſed, and the Court or the Admiral de-

ſire

fire any further explanation, I request Mr. Perry may be examined when he does come; I am also ready to produce any other information in my power, as to the Formidable's log book, which the Court or the Admiral requires. As to the log book of the Robuste, I think it not necessary to take up the time of the court with any further examination about it. Captain Hood acknowledges on the one hand, that the alterations and additions were made by his orders, and on the other, it has not appeared they were wholly contrary to truth; I shall drop the subject of log books, except the Court requires any thing from that particular person.

Admiral Keppel. I shall not trouble the Court with any further examination concerning the Formidable's log-book. With respect to the additions and alterations in the log-book of the Robuste, I shall take the freedom to offer some observations, as well as evidence, to shew the danger, mischief, and falsehood of such alterations.

Prosecutor. The letter that was read from Admiral Keppel to Mr. Stephens, mentioned another letter on the preceding day of the 24th of July; I beg that letter may be read.

The letter to Mr. Stephens was then read by the Judge Advocate, as follows:

"I dispatched the Peggy to you yesterday afternoon; "and about four o'clock the French fleet tacked, and "stood towards the English. As night was near, and "action to be avoided in the night, I brought the fleet "to, leaving it in the option of the French to engage in "the morning, but they were then discovered in the "N. W. quarter; they had been in the wind's eye all "that day, and had the choice in them to come to action.

"The French spread their frigates so greatly, that I "should be afraid single ships attempting to join my "fleet would be intercepted.

"P. S. We count of the French fleet, great and small, "forty sail."

Prosecutor. As the Admiral has signified his intention that he means to call for evidence to prove the falsehood of the additions and alterations in the Robuste's log-book, it is in justice due to the character of Capt. Hood, that I should intreat the Court will, in case of any such proceeding, give Capt. Hood an opportunity of justifying himself from such an attack.

Admiral Keppel. The Court will do what is just and right upon such an occasion.

Prosecutor. Mr. President, I have now finished my evidence,

dence, and have prepared a few words by way of addreſs to the Court, which I deſire that the Judge Advocate may read.

Admiral Keppel. Mr. Preſident, the evidence on the part of the accuſer being cloſed, I truſt it is not preſumption in me to declare, that I don't reſiſt the deſire of the proſecutor to addreſs the Court in a ſpeech, from any apprehenſions of danger; but as I have never heard nor known any ſuch attempts in Court Martials, and ſuch a precedent may be attended with bad conſequences in other caſes, I truſt that my caſe, which is ſufficiently new in many reſpects, will not be diſtinguiſhed by any ſuch innovation.

Proſecutor. Mr. Preſident, conſidering myſelf not ſuffered to addreſs the Court at the cloſe of my evidence for the Crown, I cannot aſſent to wave it, but muſt take the opinion of the Court.

Admiral Keppel. Mr. Preſident, I mean my accuſer has no right to make a ſpeech as to the merits of the cauſe, in this caſe.

The Court hereupon withdrew, and after ſtaying about half an hour, returned, when the Judge Advocate read the following reſolution:

" It not occurring to the recollection of any member
" of this Court, that it has ever been the uſage of Court
" Martials to receive any thing on the part of the accuſer
" after declaring that he had gone through all the wit-
" neſſes that he ſhould call, it is on this account agreed,
" that the paper now offered by the Vice Admiral cannot
" be admitted."

Proſecutor. As the Court was withdrawing, the Admiral inſiſted that the proſecutor had no right to addreſs the Court at all.

Admiral Keppel. I beg your pardon—

Proſecutor. 'Tis material to me to know whether I am to be at liberty to addreſs the Court with my obſervations, at the cloſe of the evidence on each ſide. I deſire the Court's opinion on that point.

Admiral Montogue. Admiral Keppel, do you propoſe immediately to go into your defence?

A. To-morrow morning I ſhall be ready for it.

The Proſecutor attempting to proceed, was ſtopped by Admiral Montague thus: I did underſtand, that when we withdrew to debate on what the Proſecutor deſired, that we had come to a determination, which determination has been read by the Judge Advocate. After that, it is cuſtomary that no more is ſaid upon the ſubject; but that the Priſoner is left at liberty to ſay what he has to ſay before

he

he calls his evidence. If the Court will then permit the Prosecutor to say any thing after, that is another matter, and must then be debated.

Ordered by the Court, That every thing on the side of the Prosecutor and Prisoner shall be expunged from the minutes, since the resolution.

Adjourned till to-morrow morning, ten o'clock.

TWENTY-FIRST DAY, SATURDAY, JANUARY 30th.

Soon after Ten o'clock, the Court being opened, and audience admitted, the Prisoner came forward, and, addressing himself to the President, made the following Defence.

ADMIRAL KEPPEL's DEFENCE.

SIR,

AFTER forty years spent in the service of my country, little did I think of being brought to a Court-martial, to answer to charges of misconduct, negligence in the performance of duty, and tarnishing the honour of the British Navy. These charges, sir, have been advanced by my accuser. Whether he has succeeded in proving them, or not, the Court will determine. Before he brought me to a trial, it would have been candid in him to have given vent to his thoughts, and not by a deceptious shew of kindness to lead me into the mistake of supposing a friend in the man who was my enemy in his heart, and was shortly to be my accuser. Yet, sir, after all my misconduct; after so much negligence in the performance of my duty, and after tarnishing so deeply the honour of the British navy, my accuser made no scruple to sail a second time with the man, who had been the betrayer of his country! Nay, during the time we were on shore, he corresponded with me on terms of friendship, and even in his letters he approved of what had been done, of the part which he now condemns, and of the very negligent misconduct, which has since been so offensive in his eyes!

Such behaviour, sir, on the part of my accuser, gave me little reason to apprehend an accusation from him; nor had I any reason to suppose that the state would criminate me. When I returned, his Majesty received me

with

with the greatest applause. Even the First Lord of the Admiralty gave his flattering testimony to the rectitude of my conduct, and seemed with vast sincerity to applaud my zeal for the service. Yet, in the moment of approbation, it seems as if a scheme was concerting against my life; for without any previous notice, five articles of a charge were exhibited against me by Sir Hugh Palliser, who, most unfortunately for his cause, lay himself under an imputation for disobedience of orders at the very time when he accused me of negligence! This, to be sure, was a very ingenious mode of getting the start of me. An accusation exhibited against a Commander in Chief might draw off the attention of the public from neglect of duty in an inferior officer. I could almost wish, in pity to my accuser, that appearances were not so strong against him. Before the trial commenced, I actually thought that my accuser might have some tolerable reasons for his conduct. But from the evidence, even as adduced to account for the behaviour of the Hon. Gentleman in the afternoon of the 27th of July, from that evidence, I say, sir, I find that I was mistaken. The trial has left my accuser without excuse, and he now cuts that sort of figure which, I trust in God, all accusers of innocence will ever exhibit.

I have observed, sir, that the opinions of officers of different ranks have been taken. I trust that the Court will indulge me with the same liberty, in the evidence for my defence. Some have refused to give their opinions. I thought it strange, as plain speaking, and a full declaration, are the best of evidences in a good cause.

I would wish, sir, the court to consider, that in all great naval, as well as military operations, unless the design be fully known, the several manœuvres may have a strange appearance. Masters have been called to give their opinions on the higher departments of command. Higher authorities should have been taken. Such authorities are not scarce, for I am happy to say, there never was a country served by naval officers of more bravery, skill, and gallantry, than England can boast at present. As to this court, I intreat you, gentlemen, who compose it, to recollect, that you sit here as a court of

 honour,

honour, as well as a court of juſtice, and I now ſtand before you, not merely to ſave my life, but for a purpoſe of infinitely greater moment——to clear my fame.

My accuſer, ſir, has been not a little miſtaken in his notions of the duty of a Commander in Chief, or he would never have accuſed me in the manner he has done. During action ſubordinate officers either are, or they ought to be, too attentive to their own duty to obſerve the manœuvres of others. In general engagements it is ſcarcely poſſible for the ſame objects to appear in the ſame point of view to the commanders in two different ſhips. The point of ſight may be different. Clouds of ſmoke may obſtruct the view. Hence may ariſe the difference in the opinions of officers as to this or that manœuvre, without any intentional partiality. Whether I have conceived objects in exact correſpondence with the truth; whether I have viewed them unſkilfully, (or, as my accuſer has been pleaſed to term it, *unofficer-like*) theſe are matters which remain to be determined. I can only ſay, that what Sir Hugh Palliſer has imputed to me as *negligence*, was the effect of *deliberation* and *choice*. I will add, that I was not confined in my powers when I ſailed; I had ample diſcretion to act as I thought proper for the defence of the kingdom. I manœuvred; I fought; I returned; I did my beſt. If my abilities were not equal to the taſk, I have this conſolation left, that I did not ſolicit, nor did I bargain for the Command. More than two years ago, in the month of November, 1776, I received a letter from the Firſt Lord of the marine department, wherein he obſerved, " That owing to the motions of foreign Courts, it might be neceſſary to prepare a fleet of obſervation." My reply to this letter was, " That I was ready to receive any command *from his Majeſty*, and begged to have the honour of an audience." This requeſt was complied with. I was cloſeted, and I told the King, that " I was willing to ſerve him as long as my health would permit." I heard no more until the month of March 1778, at which time I had two or three audiences, when I told his Majeſty, that " I had no acquaintance with his Miniſters, but I truſted to his protection and zeal for the public good."

good." I had no ſiniſter views; no paltry gratifications, I received nothing, I felt nothing but an earneſt deſire to ſerve my country. I even accepted the Chief command with reluctance. I was apprehenſive of not being ſupported at home. I foreſaw that the higher the command, the more liable I was to be ruined in my reputation. Even my misfortunes, if I had any, might be conſtrued into crimes. During forty years ſervice, I have not received any particular mark of favour from the Crown. I have only been honoured with the confidence of my Sovereign, in times of public danger. Neither my deficiencies, nor my miſconduct, were ever before brought forward to the public. And it is now ſomewhat ſtrange, that, ſo well acquainted as my accuſer muſt have been with my *deficient* abilities, it is ſtrange, I ſay, ſir, that he ſhould be the very perſon who brought me the meſſage to take the command upon me! Nay, further, ſir, he brought me that meſſage with great ſeeming pleaſure! There was, or there was not, reaſon at that time to doubt my ability. If there was reaſon, how could my accuſer wiſh me to accept a command, for which I was diſqualified? If there was not any reaſon to doubt my profeſſional abilities ſixteen months ago, I have given no reaſon why they ſhould be ſince called in queſtion. When I returned from the expedition, I did not complain of any thing. I endeavoured to ſtop all murmurings, I even truſted the *Firſt Lord of the Admiralty* in the ſame manner as I would have done my moſt intimate friend. This might be imprudent. It might be dangerous. But, ſir, I am by nature open and unguarded, and little did I think that traps would artfully be laid to endeavour to catch me on the authority of my own words.

It was in the month of March, 1778, that I was told a fleet lay ready for me to command. When I reached Portſmouth, I ſaw but ſix ſhips ready, and on viewing even thoſe with a ſeaman's eye, I was not by any means pleaſed with their condition. Before I quitted Portſmouth, four or five more were ready, and I will do the perſons in office the juſtice to ſay, that, *from that time*, they uſed the utmoſt diligence in getting the fleet ready

 for

for ſervice. On the 30th of June I ſailed with twenty ſhips of the line, and very fortunately I fell in with the Belle Poule and other French frigates, and the letters and papers found on board them were of material ſervice to the State. Captain Marſhall diſtinguiſhed himſelf with the greateſt honour. I confeſs that when I fell in with thoſe frigates, I was at a loſs how to act. On the one hand, I conceived the incident to be favourable to my country; and on the other, I was fearful that a war with France, and all its conſequences, might be laid to my charge. For any thing I can tell, this may yet be the caſe. It may be treaſured up to furniſh another matter for future accuſation. To this hour I have not received official approbation or cenſure for my conduct. With twenty ſhips of the line I ſailed. Thirty-two ſhips of the line lay in Breſt water, beſides an incredible number of frigates. Was I to ſeek an engagement with a ſuperior force? I never did, nor ſhall I ever fear to engage a force ſuperior to the one I then commanded, or that I may hereafter command. But I well know what men and ſhips can do, and if the fleet I commanded had been deſtroyed, we muſt have left the French maſters of the ſea. To refit a fleet requires time. From the ſituation of affairs, naval ſtores are not very ſoon ſupplied. Never did I experience ſo deep a melancholy, as when I found myſelf forced to turn my back on France! I quitted my ſtation, and courage was never put to ſo ſevere a trial.

I was permitted to ſail a ſecond time, without receiving official praiſe or blame for the part I had acted. Theſe were diſcouraging circumſtances. But they did not diſturb my temper. My principal object was to get ready for ſea with all poſſible haſte. I was ſurpriſed on my return to be threatened with the fate of Admiral Byng, and I was ſtill more ſurpriſed to be charged with *cowardice*.

With thirty ſhips of the line I ſailed early in July. The French Admiral ſailed from Breſt with thirty-two ſhips. I believe that when the fleets came within ſight of each other, the French were not a little ſurpriſed to ſee me ſo ſtrong. I deſire not to throw the ſlighteſt imputation

putation on the courage of the French admiral, I believe him to be a brave man, and one who had ſome particular reaſons for the line of conduct he purſued. I was determined, if poſſible, to bring the French to battle, as I had every reaſon to think that their having avoided an engagement when it was for four days in their power to attack me, was owing to their expecting ſome capital reinforcements. I therefore thought that the ſooner I could engage them the better; eſpecially as I knew that the principal fleets of our trade were daily expected in the Channel, and if the French fleet had been permitted to diſperſe without an action, our Eaſt and Weſt India fleets might have been intercepted, the convoys might have been cut off, and the ſtake of England might have been loſt. I beg leave to mention, that in the reign of King William, the gallant Admiral Ruſſel was *two months* in ſight of a French fleet, and he could not poſſibly bring them to action. My being in ſight of the French fleet *four days* before the engagement, will not therefore appear quite ſo extraordinary as it has been repreſented. Had it not been for the favourable change of the wind on the morning of the 27th of July, I could not have brought the French to action when I did.

I am exceedingly ſorry, Sir, that the Admiralty have refuſed me the liberty of producing my inſtructions. In all former Court-Martials, the inſtructions and orders have been ſent with the charge to the members of the Court. As it has been denied in this inſtance, I muſt and do ſubmit.

Although on the 27th of July *I fought and beat* my enemy, and compelled him to take ſhelter by returning into port, yet the efforts did by no means anſwer my wiſhes. I ruſhed on to re-attack the enemy. Why I did not accompliſh my deſign will be ſeen in the evidence I ſhall produce. I might, it is true, have chaced the *three* ſhips which were viſible on the morning of the 28th of July; but with very little proſpect of ſucceſs. I therefore choſe to return to Plymouth with my ſhattered fleet, to get ready for ſea again, not however forgetting to leave two ſhips of the line to cruize for the protection of our trading fleets, which, thank God! all arrived ſafe.

On my return, Sir, I moſt cautiouſly avoided to utter a ſyllable of complaint, becauſe it might have ſuſpended our naval operations, which at that time would have been highly dangerous. I could not think of attending to a Court-martial, when greater objects were in view.

With reſpect to the *ſecond edition* of the *Formidable's* log-book, it appears to have been fabricated rather for the purpoſe of exculpating *the Proſecutor*, than to criminate me. I ſhall therefore paſs it over, and permit the gentleman to make the moſt of ſuch an exculpation. I cannot, however, be ſo civil to the *alterations* and *additions* in the log-book of the Robuſte. Capt. Hood's conduct muſt have ſtruck the Court, as I believe it did every perſon, except the proſecutor, with aſtoniſhment.

A great ſtreſs, Sir, has been laid on my letter to the Admiralty. There is a paſſage in it where I ſeemed to approve the conduct of every officer in the fleet. The Court will obſerve, that I was not in my letter to inform all Europe that a *Vice Admiral* under my command had been guilty of neglect, whilſt there remained a poſſibility of excuſe for his conduct. As to Court-martials, one very bad conſequence will I am ſure reſult from this trial: it will terrify a Commander in Chief from accepting a commiſſion, if he ſhould be liable to be brought to a trial by every ſubordinate officer.

As I have touched on my letters, I will juſt obſerve, Sir, that the moſt diſagreeable task I ever experienced, was that of writing my letter on the 30th of July. However, if I writ ill, I am confident that I fought well, and the deſertion of the trade of France was evident from the number of rich captures which we made; a number far exceeding any thing ever known in ſo ſhort a period! his Majeſty noticed this in his ſpeech from the throne.

Mr. Preſident,

I now deſire that the Judge Advocate may be directed to read the charge, and I will anſwer the ſeveral accuſations.

The Charges were then read by the Judge Advocate, and the Admiral replied to them ſeparately, as follows:

The

The REPLIES *of* ADMIRAL KEPPEL, *to the* CHARGES *against him.*

The FIRST of the CHARGES, contained in the first Artice, is,

" That on the morning of the 27th of July, 1778, " having a fleet of thirty ships of the line under my " command, and being then in the presence of a French " fleet of the like number of ships of the line, I did not " make the necessary preparations for fight."

To this I answer, That I have never understood preparations for fight to have any other meaning in the language and understanding of seamen, than that each particular ship, under the direction and discipline of her own officers, *when in pursuit of an enemy*, be in every respect cleared and in readiness for action; the contrary of which no Admiral of a fleet, without a reasonable cause, will presume; *as from the morning of the 24th, when the French fleet had got to the windward, to the time of the action, the British fleet was in unremitting pursuit of them*, it is still more difficult to conceive that any thing more is meant by this charge than what is immediately after conveyed by the charge that follows it, viz. " That on " the same morning of the 27th I did not put my fleet " in line of battle, or into any order proper either for " receiving or attacking an enemy of such force."

By this second part of the charge I feel myself attacked in the exercise of that great and broad line of discretion, which every officer commanding either fleets or armies, is often obliged, both in duty and conscience, to exercise to the best of his judgment; and which, depending on circumstances and situations, infinitely various, cannot be reduced to any positive rule of discipline, or practice.—A discretion which I submit to the Court, I was peculiarly called upon by the strongest and best motives to exercise, which I therefore did exercise, and which, in my public letter to the Board of Admiralty, I openly avowed to have exercised. I admit, that on the morning of the 27th of July, I did not put my fleet into a line of battle, because I had it not in my choice to do so, consistently with the certainty,

tainty, or even the probability, of either giving or being given battle; and becauſe, if I had ſcrupulouſly adhered to that order, in which, if the election had been mine, I ſhould have choſen to have received or attacked a willing enemy, I ſhould have had no enemy either to receive or attack.

I ſhall, therefore, in anſwer to this charge, ſubmit to the Court my reaſons for determining to bring the enemy to battle at all events; and ſhall ſhew, that any other order than that in which my fleet was conducted from my firſt ſeeing them, to the moment of the action, was incompatible with ſuch determination.

In order to this I muſt call the attention of the Court to a retroſpective view of the motions of the two fleets from their firſt coming in ſight of each other.

On my firſt diſcovering the French fleet at one o'clock in the afternoon, of the 23d of July, I made the neceſſary ſignals for forming my fleet in the order of battle, which I effected towards the evening, and brought to by ſignal, and lay till the morning, when perceiving that the French fleet had gained the wind, during the night, and carried a preſſed ſail to preſerve it, I diſcontinued the ſignal for the line, and made the general ſignal to chace to windward, in hopes that they would join battle with me, rather than ſuffer two of their capital ſhips to be entirely ſeparated from them, and give me a chance of cutting off a third, which had carried away a topmaſt in the night, and which, but for a ſhift of wind, I muſt have taken. In this, however, I was diſappointed, for they ſuffered two of them to go off altogether, and continued to make every uſe of the advantage of the wind.

This aſſiduous endeavour of the French Admiral to avoid coming to action, which from his having the wind, was always in his option, led me to believe that he expected a reinforcement. This reflection would alone have been ſufficient to determine me to urge my purſuit, in as collected a body as the nature of ſuch a purſuit would admit of, without the delay of the line, and to ſeize the firſt opportunity of bringing on an engagement.

But

But I had other reaſons no leſs urgent.

If by obſtinately adhering to the line of battle, I had ſuffered, as I inevitably muſt, the French fleet to have ſeparated from me; and if, by ſuch ſeparation, the Engliſh convoys from the Eaſt and Weſt-Indies, then expected home, had been cut off, or the coaſt of England had been inſulted, what would have been my ſituation?—Sheltered under the form of diſcipline, I might perhaps have eſcaped puniſhment, but I could not have eſcaped cenſure. I ſhould neither have eſcaped the contempt of my fellow-citizens, nor the reproaches of my own conſcience.

Moved by theſe important conſiderations; ſupported by the examples of Admiral Ruſſell and other great commanders, who in ſimilar ſituations had ever made ſtrict orders give way to reaſonable enterprize; and particularly encouraged by the remembrance of having myſelf ſerved under *that truly great officer*, Lord HAWKE, when rejecting all rules and forms, he graſped at victory by an irregular attack, I determined not to loſe ſight of the French fleet by being out-ſailed from preſerving the line of battle, but to keep my fleet as well collected as I could, and near enough to aſſiſt and act with each other in caſe a change of wind or other favourable circumſtances ſhould enable me to force the French fleet to action.

Such were my *feelings* and *reflections* when the day broke on the morning of the 27th of July, at which time the fleet under my command was in the following poſition—Vice Admiral Sir Robert Harland was about four miles diſtant, on the Victory's weather quarter, with moſt of the ſhips of his own diviſion, and ſome of thoſe belonging to the centre. Vice Admiral Sir Hugh Palliſer at about three miles diſtant, a point before the lee-beam of the Victory, with his mainſail up, which obliged the ſhips of his diviſion to continue under an eaſy ſail.

The French fleet was as much to windward, and at as great a diſtance as it had been the preceding morning, ſtanding with a freſh Wind at S. W. cloſe hauled on the larboard tack, to all appearance avoiding me with the ſame induſtry it ever had done.

A

At this time, therefore, I had no greater inducement to form the line, than I had the morning of the former day; and I could not have formed it without greatly increasing my distance from the French fleet, contrary to that plan of operation which I have already submitted to the judgment of the Court.

The Vice Admiral of the Blue next charges, "That "although my fleet was already dispersed and in dis- "order, I, by making the signal for several ships in "his division to chace to windward, increased the dis- "order of that part of my fleet, and that the ships "were in consequence more scattered than they had been "the day before; and that whilst in this disorder I ad- "vanced to the enemy, and made the signal for battle."

In this part of the charge there is a studious design to mislead the understanding, and by leaving out times and intermediate events, to make the transactions of half a day appear but as one moment.——It is, indeed, impossible to read it, without being possessed with the idea, that at half past five in the morning, when I made the signal for six of the ships of the Vice Admiral of the Blue's division to chace to windward, I was in the immediate prospect of closing with an enemy, approaching me in a regular line, and all their motions plainly indicating a design to give battle—instead of which both the fleets were on the larboard tack, the enemy's fleet near three leagues, if not more, to windward, going off close by the wind with a pressed sail— My reason, therefore, for making that signal at half past five, was to collect as many ships to windward as I could, in order to strengthen the main body of the fleet, in case I should be able to get to action, and to fill up the interval between the Victory and the Vice Admiral, which was occasioned by his being far to leeward, and it is plain that the Vice Admiral must have himself understood the object of the signal, since it has appeared in the course of the evidence, that on its being made, the Formidable set her mainsail, and let the reefs out of her topsails; and indeed, the only reason why it was not originally made for the whole division, was, that they must have then chaced as a division, which would have

retarded

retarded the beſt going ſhips by an attendance on the Vice Admiral.

Things were in this ſituation, when, at half paſt nine, the French Admiral tacked, and wore his whole fleet, and ſtood to the ſouthward, on the ſtarboard tack, cloſe hauled; but the wind, immediately after they wore about coming more ſoutherly, I continued to ſtand on till a quarter paſt ten, at which time I tacked the Britiſh fleet together by ſignal. Soon after we wore about, on the ſtarboard tack, the wind came two points in our favour to the weſtward, which enabled us to lie up for a part of them; but in a dark ſquall that ſoon after came on, I loſt ſight of the enemy for above half an hour, and when it cleared away at eleven o'clock, I diſcovered the French fleet had changed their poſition, and were endeavouring to form the line on the larboard tack; which, finding they could not effect without coming within gun-ſhot of the van of the Britiſh fleet, they edged down and fired upon my headmoſt ſhips, as they approached them on the contrary tack, at a quarter after eleven, which was inſtantly returned, *and then, and not till then, I made the ſignal for battle. All this happened in about half an hour*, and muſt have been owing to the enemy's falling to leeward in performing their evolution during the ſquall, which we could not ſee, and by that means produced this ſudden and unexpected opportunity of engaging them, as they were near three leagues a-head of me when the ſquall came on.

If therefore by making the ſignal for the line of battle, when the van of my fleet was thus ſuddenly getting within reach of the enemy, and well connected with the centre, as my accuſer himſelf has admitted, I had called back the Vice Admiral of the Red, the French fleet might either have formed their line compleat, and have come down upon my fleet while in the confuſion of getting into order of battle, or (what I had ſtill greater reaſon to apprehend) might have gone off to windward out of my reach altogether, for even as it was, the enemy's van, inſtead of coming cloſe to action, kept their wind, and paſſed hardly within random ſhot.

My

My accuser next asserts, as an aggravation of his former charge,

" That the French fleet was in a regular line on that " tack which approached the British fleet, all their mo-" tions plainly indicating a design to give battle."

Both which facts have already been contradicted by the testimony of even his own witnesses. That the enemy's fleet was not in a regular line of battle, appeared by the French Admiral being out of his station far from the centre of his line, and next, or very near, to a ship carrying a Vice-Admiral's flag, and from some of their ships being a-breast of each other, and in *one*, as they passed the English fleet, with other apparent marks of irregularity. Indeed every motion of the French fleet, from about nine, when it went upon the starboard tack, till the moment of the action, and even during the action itself, I apprehend to be decisive against the alledged indication of designing battle; for if the French Admiral had really designed to come to action, I apprehend he never would have got his fleet on the contrary tack to that on which the British fleet was coming up to him, but would have shortened sail and waited for it, formed in the line on the same tack; and even when he did tack towards the British fleet, the alledged indication is again directly refuted, by the van of the French fleet hauling their wind again, instead of bearing down into action, and by their hoisting no colours, when they began to engage.

Notwithstanding these incontrovertible truths, my accuser imputes it to me that a general engagement was not brought on; but it is evident from the testimony of every witness he has called, that a general engagement was never in my choice; and that so far from its being prevented by my not having formed the line of battle, no engagement, either general or partial, could have been brought on if I had formed it; indeed it is a contradiction in terms to speak of a general engagement, where the fleet that has the wind tacks to pass the fleet to leeward on the contrary tack.

Such was the manner in which, after four days pursuit, I was at last enabled, by a favourable shift of wind to close with the fleet of France; and if I am justifiable

on

on principle in the exercise of that discretion which I have been submitting to your judgment, of bringing, at all events, an unwilling enemy to battle, I am certainly not called upon to descend to all the minutiæ of consequences resulting from such enterprize, even if such had ensued, as my accuser has asserted, but which his own witnesses have not only failed to establish, but absolutely refuted. It would be an insult on the understanding of the Court, were I to offer my arguments to shew that ships which engage without a line of battle, cannot so closely, uniformly, and mutually support each other, as when circumstances admit of a line being formed; because it is self-evident, and is the basis of all the discipline and practice of lines of battle. But in the present case, notwithstanding I had no choice in making any disposition for an attack, nor any possibility of getting to battle otherwise than I did, which would be alone sufficient to repel any charge of consequent irregularity or even confusion, yet it is not necessary for me to claim the protection of the circumstances under which I acted, because no irregularity or confusion either existed or has been proved; all the chacing ships, and the whole fleet, except a ship or two, got into battle, and into as close battle as the French fleet, which had the option by being to windward, chose to give them. The Vice-Admiral of the Blue himself, though in the rear, was out of action in a short time after the Victory; and so far from being left to engage singly and unsupported, was passed during the action by three ships of his own division, and was obliged to back his mizen topsail to keep out of the fire of one of the largest ships of the fleet, which must have continued near him all the rest of the time he was passing the French line, as I shall prove she was within three cables lengths of the Formidable when the firing ceased.

Answer *to the* SECOND ARTICLE.

THE moment the Victory had passed the enemy's rear, my first object was to look round to the position of the fleet which the smoke had till then obscured from observation, in order to determine how a general engage-

ment

ment might beſt be brought on after the fleets ſhould have paſſed each other.

I found that the Vice-Admiral of the Red, with part of his diviſion, had tacked, and was ſtanding toward the enemy with topgallant ſails ſet, the very thing I am charged with not having directed him to do; but all the reſt of the ſhips that had paſſed a-head of me were ſtill on the ſtarboard tack, ſome of them dropping to leeward, and ſeeming employed in repairing their damages. The Victory herſelf was in no condition to tack, and I could not immediately wear and ſtand back on the ſhips coming up aſtern of me out of action (had it been otherwiſe expedient) without throwing them into the utmoſt confuſion. Sir John Roſs, who very gallantly tried the experiment, having informed the Court of the momentary neceſſity he was under of wearing back again to prevent the conſequences I have mentioned, makes it unneceſſary to enlarge on the probable effects of ſuch a general manœuvre, with all the ſhips a-head. Indeed I only remark it as a ſtrongly relative circumſtance appearing by the evidence of a very able and experienced officer, and by no means as a juſtification for having ſtood away to a great diſtance beyond the enemy before I wore, becauſe the charge itſelf is groſsly falſe. In fact, the Victory had very little way while her head was to the ſouthward, and, although her damages were conſiderable, was the firſt ſhip of the centre diviſion that got round towards the enemy again, and ſome time before the reſt were able to follow her; ſince, even as it was, not above three or four were able to cloſe up with her on the larboard tack; ſo that had it been even practicable to have wore ſooner than I did, no good purpoſe could have been anſwered by it, ſince I muſt have only wore the ſooner back again to have collected the diſabled ſhips which would have been thereby left ſtill farther aſtern.

The Formidable was no otherwiſe left engaged with the enemy during this ſhort interval, than as being in the rear, which muſt always neceſſarily happen to ſhips in that ſituation, when fleets engage each other on contrary tacks; and no one witneſs has attempted to ſpeak

to

to the danger my accuser complains of, except his own Captain, who, on being called upon to fix the time when such danger was apprehended, stated it to be before the Formidable opened her fire, which renders the application of it as a consequence of the second charge, too absurd to demand a refutation.

ANSWER *to the* THIRD ARTICLE.

As soon as I had wore to stand towards the enemy, I hauled down the signal for battle, which I judged improper to be kept abroad till the ships could recover their stations; or, at least, get near enough to support each other in action. In order to call them together for that purpose, I immediately made the signal to form the line of battle a-head, and the Victory being at this time a-head of all the centre and Red division, I embraced that opportunity of unbending her main topsail, which was totally unserviceable, and in doing which the utmost expedition was used; the ships astern of me doing all they could in the mean time to get into their stations, so that no time was lost by this necessary operation.

The Formidable was a-head of the Victory, during this period; it was her station in the line on that tack. Yet at the very moment my accuser dares to charge me with not calling the ships together to renew the attack, he, himself, though his ship was in a *manageable condition*, as appeared by the evidence of his own Captain, and though he had wore, expecting, as he says, the battle to be renewed, quitted his station in the front of that line of battle, the signal for which was flying, passed to leeward of me, on the starboard tack, while I was advancing towards the enemy, and never came into the line during the rest of the day.

In this situation I judged it necessary that the Vice Admiral of the Red, who was to windward, and passing forward on my weather-bow, with six or seven ships of his division, should lead on the larboard tack, in order to give time to the ships which had come last out of action to repair their damages, and get collected together; and the signal appointed by the 31st article of the fighting

fighting inſtructions not being applicable, as the French fleet was ſo nearly a-head of us, that by keeping cloſe to the wind we could only have fetched them, I made the Proſerpine's ſignal, in order to have diſpatched Captain Sutton with a meſſage to Vice Admiral Sir Robert Harland, to lead the fleet to the larboard tack; but before he had left the Victory, with the orders he had received, the French fleet wore and ſtood to the ſouthward, forming their line on the ſtarboard tack, their ſhips advancing regularly out of a collected body, which they had got into from the operation of wearing, and not from any diſorder or confuſion which really exiſted. I could have derived no immediate advantage from it, not having a ſufficient force collected to prevent their forming, by an attempt to renew the attack. The Victory was at that time the neareſt ſhip to the enemy, with no more than three or four of the centre diviſion in any ſituation to have ſupported her, or each other in the action. The Vice Admiral of the Blue was on the ſtarboard tack, ſtanding away from his ſtation, *totally regardleſs of the ſignal that was flying to form the line*; and moſt of the other ſhips, except the Red diviſion, whoſe poſition I have already ſtated, were far a-ſtern, and five diſabled ſhips at a great diſtance on the lee quarter. Moſt of theſe facts are already eſtabliſhed by the accuſer's own evidence. I ſhall prove and confirm them all, by the teſtimony of that part of the fleet, whoſe ſituations will enable them to ſpeak with certainty.

I truſt they will convince the Court, that I had it not in my power to collect the fleet together to renew the fight at that time, and that, for their not being able to follow me, I conſequently could not advance with them: that I did not haul down the ſignal for battle, till it ceaſed to be capable of producing any good effect: that, during the whole time I ſtood towards the enemy, I endeavoured, by the moſt *forcible* of all ſignals, the ſignal for the line of battle, to call the ſhips together in order to renew the attack: that I did avail myſelf of the ſhips that were with the Vice Admiral of the Red, as far as circumſtances admitted; and that I therefore did do the utmoſt in my power to *take*, *ſink*, *burn* and *de-*

ſtroy,

ſtroy, the French fleet, which had attacked the Britiſh fleet.

ANSWER *to the* FOURTH ARTICLE.

THE French fleet having wore, and began to form their line on the ſtarboard tack, by the wind, which if they had kept would have brought them cloſe up with the centre diviſion, ſoon afterwards edged away, pointing towards four or five of the diſabled ſhips which were at a diſtance to leeward, and with evident intention to have ſeparated them from the reſt of the fleet; to prevent which, I made the ſignal to wear, and ſtood athwart their van in a diagonal courſe, to give protection to thoſe crippled ſhips, keeping the ſignal for the line flying to form and collect the fleet on the ſtarboard tack. As I had thus been obliged to alter my diſpoſition, before Captain Sutton left the Victory with my former meſſage, I diſpatched him with orders to Sir Robert Harland, Vice Admiral of the Red, to form with his diviſion at a diſtance a-ſtern of the Victory, to cover the rear, and to keep the enemy in check, till the Vice Admiral of the Blue ſhould come into his ſtation, with his diviſion, in obedience to the ſignal. Theſe orders the Vice Admiral of the Red inſtantly obeyed, and was formed in my wake before four o'clock; when, finding that while by the courſe I ſteered to protect the crippled ſhips, I was nearer the enemy, the Vice Admiral of the Blue ſtill continued to lie to windward, and by ſo doing kept his diviſion from joining me. I made the ſignal for ſhips to bear down into my wake, and that it might be better diſtinguiſhed (both being ſignals at the mizen peak) I hauled down the ſignal for the line for about ten minutes, and then hoiſted it again. This ſignal *he repeated*, though he had not repeated that for the line of battle; but by not bearing down himſelf, he led the ſhips of his diviſion to interpret his repeating it as requiring them to come into HIS WAKE INSTEAD OF MINE.

Having now accompliſhed the protection of the diſabled ſhips, and the French fleet continuing to form their line, ranging up to leeward, parallel to the center diviſion, my only object was to form mine, in order to bear down upon them to renew the battle; and therefore at a quarter before five o'clock, after having repeated

S the

the ſignal for ſhips to windward to bear down into my wake, with no better effect than before, I ſent the Milford with orders to the Vice Admiral of the Red to ſtretch a-head, and take his ſtation in the line, which he inſtantly obeyed; and the Vice Admiral of the blue being ſtill to windward, with his fore topſail unbent, and making no *viſible* effort to obey the ſignal, which had been flying the whole afternoon, I ſent out the Fox at five o'clock, with orders to him to bear down into my wake, and to tell him, *that I only waited for* HIM and HIS *diviſion to renew the battle.* While I was diſpatching theſe frigates, having before hauled down the ſignal to come into my wake, I put aboard the ſignal for all ſhips to come into their ſtations, always keeping the ſignal for the line flying. All this producing no effect on the Vice Admiral of the Blue, and *wearied* out with *fruitleſs expectation*, at ſeven o'clock I made the ſignal for each particular ſhip of the Vice Admiral of the Blue's diviſion to come into her ſtation; but before they had accompliſhed it, night put an end to all further operations.

It may be obſerved, that amongſt theſe ſignals, I did not make the Formidable's. If the Vice Admiral chuſes to conſider this as a *culpable neglect*, I can only ſay, *that it occurred to me to treat him with a delicacy due to his rank*, which had ſome time before induced me to ſend him the meſſage by Captain Windſor, the particulars of which he has already faithfully related to the Court.

I truſt I have little reaſon to apprehend that the Court will de inclined to conſider my conduct, as I have ſtated it, in anſwer to this fourth article of the charge, *as diſgraceful to the Britiſh flag.* After I had put upon the ſame tack with the enemy, to protect the diſabled part of my fleet, and to collect the reſt together, there would have been little to do to renew the battle, but bearing right down upon the enemy, if my accuſer had led his diviſion in odedience to the *repeated ſignals* and *orders* which I have ſtated. The Victory never went more than two knots, was under her double reefed top-ſails and fore-ſail much ſhattered, which kept the ſhips that were near her under their top-ſails, and ſuffered the French fleet, which might always have brought me to action, if they had been inclined

inclined to do it, to range up parallel with the centre, under very little ſail. It was to protect the five diſabled ſhips above mentioned, and to give the reſt time to form into ſome order, that I judged it might be more expedient to ſtand as I did under that eaſy ſail, than to bring to with my head to the ſouthward. The Court will judge whether it was poſſible for any officer in the ſervice, really to believe that theſe operations could give the appearance of a flight, or furniſh a rational pretence to the French Admiral to claim the Victory, or publiſh to the world that the Britiſh fleet had run away.

ANSWER *to the* FIFTH ARTICLE.

ON the morning of the 28th of July, the French fleet, (except three ſail which were ſeen upon the lee quarter) was only viſible from the maſt heads of ſome of the ſhips of the Britiſh fleet, and at a diſtance from me, which afforded not the ſmalleſt proſpect of coming up with them, more eſpecially as their ſhips, though certainly much damaged in their hulls, had not apparently ſuffered much in their maſts and ſails. Whereas the fleet under my command was generally and greatly ſhattered in their maſts, yards and rigging, and many of them unable to carry ſail. As to the three French ſhips, I made the ſignal at five o'clock in the morning for the Duke, Bienfaiſant, Prince George, and Elizabeth, to give them chace, judging them to be the propereſt ſhips for that purpoſe, but the two laſt were not able to carry ſufficient ſail to give even countenance to the purſuit, and looking round to the general condition of my fleet, I ſaw it was in vain to attempt either a general or a partial chace. Indeed my accuſer does not venture to alledge that there was any *probability*, or even *poſſibility*, of doing it with effect, which deſtroys the whole foundation of his charge.

Under theſe circumſtances, I could not miſtake my duty, and I was reſolved not to ſacrifice it in an empty ſhew and appearance, which is beneath the dignity of an officer, unconſcious of any failure or neglect. To have urged a fruitleſs purſuit with a fleet ſo greatly crippled in its maſts and ſails, after a diſtant and flying enemy, within reach of their own ports, and with a fresh wind blowing fair for their port, with a large swell, would have been not only wantonly exposing the British fleet under my command without end or object, but misleading and defeating its operations, by delaying the refitment necessary for carrying on the future service with vigour and effect.

My accuser asserts, by a general conclusion to the five articles exhibited against me, that from what he states as instances of misconduct and neglect in me, "a glorious opportunity was lost of doing a most essential service to the state," and that the honour of the British navy was tarnished.

The truth of the assertion, that AN OPPORTUNITY WAS LOST, I am not called upon either to combat or deny. It is sufficient for me, if I shall be successful in proving, that that opportunity was seized by ME, and followed up to the full extent of my power: if the court shall be of that opinion, I am satisfied; and it will then rest with the Vice Admiral of the Blue, to explain to what cause it is to be referred *that the* GLORIOUS OPPORTUNITY, he speaks of, *was lost, and to whom it is to be imputed,* (if the fact be true) *that the* HONOUR *of the* BRITISH NAVY *has been* TARNISHED.

Having now, Sir, finished my replies, I shall call witnesses to prove my innocence. I have heard it asserted as matter of right to alter a log-book. I will only say that there is a wide difference between correcting inaccuracies, and *malicious* alterations for the purpose of aiding malicious prosecutions.

As to my prosecutor, I have even his own letters, of as late date as the 5th of *October*, wherein he thus writes to me: "*I know that you would rather meet the French fleet* †." Yes, sir, that very French fleet which he after-

† The letter here referred to, was written by Sir Hugh Pallifer to the Admiral on the capture of some French vessels that fell in with the fleet. This letter is dated on board the Formidable at sea, Oct. 5th, 1778, and serves to shew, that at this time, which was upwards of two months after the action on the 27th of July, Sir Hugh Pallifer had not conceived any idea of his Admiral's MISCONDUCT or WANT of COURAGE. But of this the public will form their own judgment, by the Vice Admiral's own words at the conclusion of his letter, which are as follows: "THESE

wards accused me of running away from! I cannot produce these letters in evidence, but I will shew them to any gentleman out of Court who desires to see them. I will also shew to any gentleman a paper which my prosecutor requested me to sign but a very short time ago, and I refused to sign it *. In the news-papers my prosecutor denied receiving any message by the Fox frigate.

"THESE prizes coming in our way are not unacceptable, but "I know you would much rather meet the French fleet."

I am, with the greatest regard and respect,
Dear Sir, Your most obedient humble servant,
Hon. Admiral Keppel. HUGH PALLISER."

* So soon as the Gazette Account of the action off Ushant made its appearance, a general dissatisfaction took place, and it was in the mouth of every one, that *something must be wrong*. When part of the fleet arrived at Spithead, it was naturally asked, "How the Admiral could be so very complaisant, to suffer the French to form their line, and remain within gun-shot for a whole afternoon, and not re-attack them?" It was answered, "that the Admiral could not engage, because Sir Hugh Palliser would not obey the signal to form the line of battle, but kept at a distance till the opportunity was lost, although his signal had been out several hours, and the Admiral sent Captain Windsor to let Sir Hugh know, that he only waited for him to bear down, and then he should immediately re-attack the enemy." This report soon made its way into all the public prints. To get rid of so scandalous an imputation, he prepared an address to the public, in vindication of his character, which he inclosed in the following letter to Admiral Keppel, desiring him to sign and publish it as coming immediately from himself.

"I THINK myself so much intitled to have my conduct on the day we engaged the French fleet justified by you, Sir, as Commander in Chief, from those foul aspersions, that I confess I have been expecting your offer to do it; I have waited for your coming to town to ask it: being now informed of your arrival, I lose no time in desiring you will contradict those scandalous reports that have been propagated as aforementioned, by publishing in your own name the inclosed paper, which I have the honour to inclose herewith, or something to that effect, that may be more agreeable to you, and as may be agreed on, if you will permit me the honour to wait on you to-morrow morning.

"I must beg the favour of your speedy answer, that my honour and reputation may not be farther wounded by delays.

I am very respectfully, Sir,
Your very obedient, humble servant,
To the Hon. Admiral Keppel. HUGH PALLISER."

The Paper inclosed was literally as follows:

Having seen a paragraph in the General Advertiser of the 15th of last month highly reflecting on the conduct of Vice Admiral Sir Hugh Palliser,

Capt. Windſor ſwore to the delivery of ſuch a meſſage: He proved in evidence that he received the meſſage from me at *five o'clock*, and delivered it to the *Vice Admiral* at *half paſt five o'clock*: Captain Beazely endeavoured to refute his evidence. But I ſhall call witneſſes to prove the delivery of the meſſage. My conſcience is perfectly clear. I have no ſecret machinations, no dark contrivance to anſwer for. My heart does not reproach me. As to my enemies, I would not wiſh the greateſt enemy I have in the world to be afflicted with ſo heavy a puniſhment as—*my accuſer's conſcience.*

The Admiral having finiſhed his Defence, the Court, at the requeſt of the Judge Advocate, who deſired to have ſome time to adjuſt his papers, declined entering upon the examination of witneſſes in behalf of the Priſoner, 'till Monday morning ten o'clock, to which time they immediately adjourned.

TWENTY-SECOND DAY, MONDAY, FEBRUARY 1ſt.

The Court being opened at ten o'clock, and the members reſumed their places, Evidence was called in behalf of the Priſoner.

Sir ROBERT HARLAND *Vice Admiral of the Red, ſworn.*

Ad. Keppel. What day did you firſt ſee the French fleet?

A. On the 24th of July.

Q. Were they ſeen the next day?

A. They were ſeen next day from the Queen, at noon?

Palliſer, on the 27th of July laſt, when the fleet under my command engaged the French fleet; and the Vice Admiral having informed me that reports to the ſame purpoſe have been propagated by ſome officers of the Victory, I think it neceſſary in juſtice to Sir Hugh Palliſer to publiſh to the world, that his conduct on that day was in every reſpect proper, and becoming a good officer; and I further declare that when I made the ſignal in the evening for the ſhips to windward to bear down into my wake, and afterwards for particular ſhips of Sir Hugh's diviſion to do ſo, he repeated theſe ſignals properly, and that the calling his and Vice Admiral Sir Robert Harland's diviſion into my wake in the evening, was not for the purpoſe of renewing the battle at that time, but to be in readineſs for it in the morning; that in obedience to the ſaid ſignals ſuch of the ſhips of Sir Hugh Palliſer's diviſion as were in condition for it, did immediately bear down, as did the reſt ſo ſoon as they were able, ſo that Sir Hugh Palliſer and his whole diviſion were all in my wake accordingly the next morning [illegible] day light ready for engaging.

Q. Were

Q. Were they to windward, or leeward of the English fleet?

A. To windward of the English fleet?

Q. Was it in the power of the French to come to action, the 25th, and 26th?

A. The French had it in their power to come to action, either of those days.

Q. Did I pursue them with a pressed sail, till I brought them to action, conformable to the worst sailing ships?

A. You pursued them with a pressed sail, till you got up with them.

Q. If you had commanded an English fleet of the same number of ships as the French were with respect to the English, should you have hesitated one moment on bearing down to bring them to action, on account of the weather? A. Not a moment.

Q. If I had pursued in a line of battle, could I have preserved my nearness to the French fleet?

A. I think not.

Q. Did you see the French fleet on the morning of the 27th? A. Yes.

Q. On what tack?

A. On the larboard tack when day broke.

Q. On what tack was the English fleet at that time?

A. On the same tack.

Q. Did the French fleet, on the larboard tack, or when got upon the starboard tack, shew any more intention of coming to action, than on the preceding day?

A. If this question means when the French wore first upon the larboard tack till eight o'clock, and afterwards upon the starboard tack, till they changed again upon the larboard tack, they shewed no more disposition to engage, than on the preceding days.

Q. If at the time they got upon the starboard tack, I had formed my line of battle, would it not have deprived me of the power of getting to action that day?

A. If you had formed the line of battle, and continued in it, you could not have brought the French to action that day, unless the French had come to you.

Q. During the course of that time, while the French were upon the starboard tack, was there at any time a dark squall, that obscured them from your sight?

A. They were obscured frequently, it being hazy, and black clouds that morning.

Q. At what time did the firing begin, betwixt the British and French fleets?

A. Between eleven and twelve o'clock.

Q. Upon what tack? A. The larboard tack.

Q. Was not the centre and rear of the French fleet in a confused appearance, when the firing began, and you were passing them?

A. In passing them, the van of the French fleet were not well connected with the centre, nor the centre with the rear, as to distance or connection, and tho' there were six or eight ships that had got up nearly close together, and formed in a body out of the centre, there were two or three of those six or eight ships, which had the appearance of confusion.

Q. Did not the French begin firing at your ship at a very great distance?

A. The French when they began, with respect to the Queen, were at a great distance.

Q. I ask you as a flag officer, if I had ordered ships by signal of your division to chace to windward, and after that signal I became engaged in the ship where my flag was, by which I could not direct distant ships, if you should have thought yourself warranted to order those ships to you, if you had judged it for the general service of that moment to have done so?

A. I should have been happy in assisting you, and rendering any service to the fleet, while I had any command in it. The occasion as stated in the question would have been sufficient for me to have done it.

Q. After you had passed the rear of the French fleet, did you observe the Formidable before she was got out of the fire?

A. I do not recollect seeing the Formidable, before the fleet tacked in the morning. I was able but twice that day to make any observations upon her. The first was when she was coming out of the cannonade, the second was when I passed her to leeward, or left her upon my weather bow, in going down to form in your rear; these were the times I observed the Formidable, and no other.

Q. At the time you did observe the Formidable coming out of the firing of the rear of the French fleet, did there appear to you the smallest danger of the Vice Admiral of the Blue being cut off?

A. There did not appear to me to be the smallest intention of the French to do it.

Q. After you was out of the action and got upon the larboard tack, and leading upon the Victory's weather bow, the Victory upon the larboard tack also, how many of the ships of your division were connected with you?

A. At most seven.

Q. How

Q. How many points of the compaſs was your diviſion to windward of the French fleet?

A. I fancy they were upon my lee bow, and ahead withal, when I was upon that tack.

Q. If I had directed you to lead upon the enemy, did it appear to you, that I had force with me in a line, or connected, ſo as to have given you proper ſuccour in your re-attacking the French fleet, in the appearance they then made?

A. Moſt certainly, and moſt truly you had not.

Q. Did you obſerve the French fleet, whilſt upon the larboard tack, draw out of the body of their fleet, and begin forming their line upon the ſtarboard tack? A. I did.

Q. Did they appear to you diſordered, or were they in a cloſe body?

A. They were not in a regular line as to diſtance, and therefore not in a cloſe body.

Q. At that time had they a confuſed appearance, or only a natural appearance to the changing of poſition?

A. It did not appear to me to have any confuſion in it, but a well regulated appearance.

Q. Under the circumſtances and ſituation you have obſerved the Engliſh fleet to be in, was it in my power as an officer, to have prevented the French forming their line upon the ſtarboard tack?

A. It was no more in your power to have done that, than it was for you to have connected your ſhips to have done it with.

Q. What then would have been the conſequence, if I had ſent orders to you at that time to attack them?

A. I ſhould have obeyed, and the French would have deſerved to be hanged, if they had not taken me and the ſhips of my diviſion.

Q. At what time did I wear from the larboard tack to the ſtarboard tack, what hour of the day?

A. About two o'clock.

Q. Did I immediately after that, uſe my endeavours to get my line of battle? A. You certainly did.

Q. Did you receive any orders from me, from the Proſerpine, after the fleet wore to the ſouthward? A. I did.

Q. What were they?

A. To form with my diviſion aſtern of the Victory.

Q. If you had not received ſuch orders, did you ſee reaſon to have put yourſelf in the ſituation at your own riſque as an officer, for a moment?

A. Before I received theſe orders, I ſaw the neceſſity

there

there was of taking that post with my division without loss of time, and was doing it at my own risque.

Q. What was your inducement?

A. Seeing the Commander in Chief unsupported, within the power of the whole French force at his stern.

Q. If the Vice Admiral of the Blue, whilst you was with your division in the Victory's rear, had borne down with his division, to have taken his station, should you not have thought yourself justified, to have immediately made sail ahead, even before orders could have reached you?

A. I should have wished to have received those orders, if they could have come to me, but if it was plain that I could not receive them, the same reason that I have given for going into the rear of the fleet, would have carried me into the van of the fleet for the service, if I had seen the Vice Admiral of the Blue with his division standing for the rear.

Q. At what time did you receive orders from me in the afternoon, to go into your proper station?

A. At five o'clock.

Q. What was the situation and appearance of the French fleet at that time?

A. They had formed as far as I could see them, and were leading their line on to the southward.

Q. Was the signal for a line of battle in the afternoon, flying on board the Victory, from the time of my being on the starboard tack, to dark, except the short time it was hauled down, to shew plainer the signal for bearing down?

A. It was.

Q. Had the British fleet standing on to the southward, upon the same tack as the French were, and both forming their line, under the sail carried by the Victory, the appearance of a flight?

A. Oh, fie! no certainly.

Q. Were we then avoiding the French fleet, or exercising a proper manœuvre to form our line upon the same tack, and by that means when executed, to bring on a general and decisive engagement?

A. You were using every means to collect your force and form a line of battle, and after you had done so, I make no doubt you would have brought on a general and decisive action, if you could.

Q. Did I lose any favourable opportunity of re-attacking the French fleet in the afternoon, while there was day enough to have done it properly?

A. If

A. If I have not said it before, I say it now, that you never had the means of doing it.

Q. When you passed the Victory to go ahead into your station, did you pass to windward or to leeward of her ?

A. I passed the Victory to leeward.

Q. At what distance ? A. About a mile.

Q. Did you observe what sail the Victory was under during the afternoon ?

A. I must have observed it at the time.---As well as I can recollect, sometimes under her topsails, and sometimes under her topsails and foresail, her topsails might be reefed.

Q. Do you recollect what sail you carried on board the Queen during the night to preserve your station ?

A. Sometimes our topsails, and sometimes our topsails and foresail, topsails double reefed.

Q. Did you carry your distinguishing lights all night?

A. I always carry my distinguishing lights at night.

Q. Were the Victory's at her bowsprit-end, seen from the Queen all night ?

A. The Victory carried a very good light at her bowsprit-end, I saw it myself frequently that night.

Q. Do you recollect at what rate you went all night ?

A. To the best of my recollection, it was about two knots, and never above three knots.

Q. On the 28th in the morning, did it not appear that the French had run off in the night ?

A. The French made their escape in the night.

Q. On the morning of the 28th, was the French fleet seen from the Queen's mast head ?

A. They were steering to the south-east.

Q. Could it be discerned what sail they were making?

A. They were at too great a distance, sometimes they were seen, and sometimes they were not, we only catched sight of them twice, I think.

Q. If I had attempted pursuit of them with the wind and weather as it was, was there the least probability of getting up with them, before they reached the port of Brest, conditioned as the British fleet was after the action?

A. I think not.

Q. You have heard all the articles of the charge read; I must desire you will speak to the court, any instance, if you saw or know of any such, in which I negligently performed any part of my duty on the 27th, and 28th of July?

A. I know of none, and therefore I cannot speak it.

Sir Robert Harland, ordered to withdraw.

Mr.

Mr. Moore, *Secretary to the Admiral, called and ſworn.*

Q. Did I not appoint you to attend my perſon, and take minutes and obſervations for my uſe, on the 27th of July? A. You did, Sir.

Q. Do you recollect the relative poſition of the three diviſions of the Britiſh fleet with reſpect to each other, on the morning of the 27th?

A. At half an hour after five in the morning of the 27th, the Vice Admiral of the Red, with moſt of the ſhips of his diviſion, ſome of the ſhips of the centre diviſion alſo were from three to four miles to windward of the Victory, and a little before the beam to the quarter. The Vice Admiral of the Blue, with the ſhips of his diviſion, were from three to four miles to leeward of the Victory, from the beam to about the cheſtry, one or two of the ſhips might be before the cheſtry, the remainder of the ſhips of the centre diviſion were about the Victory. In ſpeaking of the rear diviſion, I muſt except the Ocean, ſhe was further aſtern, upon the quarter, and all the ſhips of that diviſion but her, I believe had their mainſails up.

Q. Do you recollect what ſail the Vice Admiral of the Blue had?

A. The Vice Admiral of the Blue's mainſail was up.

Q. What was the poſition of the French Admiral with reſpect to the Victory, in the center of the Britiſh fleet?

A. The French Admiral was rather before the beam of the Victory, nearly in the center of his own fleet, which was much the ſame in order of battle, as they were the preceding morning, they were about nine or ten miles to windward. The French fleet, in general, were under their topſails and foreſails.

Q. Did you ſee the ſignal, made by the Victory that morning, for ſhips of the Vice Admiral of the Blue's diviſion to chace to windward, and at what time?

A. May I make uſe of my minutes?

Q. Yes. When were they taken?

A. They were minutes I took in conſequence of the orders I received from the Admiral to attend his perſon, which I kept from firſt ſeeing of the French fleet till the morning of the 27th, and they were thus written at that day, and this is the book. At half after five, ſignals were made for the Shrewſbury, Robuſte, Egmont, America, Terrible, Elizabeth, Defiance, and Worceſter to chace to windward.

Q. What did appear to you to be the intention of that ſignal?

A. Moſt of the ſhips of the center diviſion were to windward of the Victory, but there was a large ſpace between

tween the Vice Admiral of the Blue's division, and the leewardmost ships of the center, and I apprehend it was meant to bring up the best sailing ships of the Vice Admiral of the Blue's division to support the center, in case the French would permit us to bring on an action.

Q. At the time the signal was made was there any greater indication of the French intending to fight than on the preceding days?

A. None, they were close hauled, carrying as much sail as their worst going ships could keep up with them, they were on the larboard tack.

Q. Did you observe the French fleet change their position any time in the morning of the 27th of July, betwixt the hours of eight and ten?

A. When I speak of the French fleet altering their position at any time, I mean to speak to the French Admiral, as my observation was particularly to him, and the extremes of his fleet were perpetually, some one or other of them, wearing or tacking to get into their stations. At half past nine the French Admiral tacked, most of his fleet were about before him, and continued carrying the same sail as they had on the larboard tack.

Q. At what hour did the British fleet tack after the fleet of France?

A. Soon after the French Admiral was about, the wind came a little to the southward, and the British fleet stood on till a quarter past ten, as we lay up better for them than we did before. The time I am speaking of is when we came to sail from the larboard to the starboard tack.

Q. Was there any alteration of the wind at that time, or soon after we had got upon the starboard tack?

A. The wind shifted near two points, which brought us to lay up for the sternmost of them; we soon after lost sight of the French fleet in a very thick squall.

Q. After this did you see the French fleet get on the larboard tack before the action began, and at what hour?

A. We lost sight of the French from twenty minutes after ten till eleven o'clock. When we then saw them at eleven o'clock, their fleet appeared in confusion, considerably so; a large body of them bearing S. S. E. they were then getting up their sails on the larboard tack.

Court. Do you mean bearing or steering?

A. They bore S. S. E. that large body which was particularly in confusion, the Admiral spoke to me about them, I went forward on the forecastle, thinking they were on board each other, they were in such confusion and

and so close, that the Admiral and most other people on the Victory's quarter deck, thought they were on board each other.

Q. What time did the firing begin between the two fleets?

A. At fifteen minutes after eleven, the wind was then W. S. W.?

Q. Was it the French ships that began firing, had they their colours hoisted at that time?

A. Neither the English nor the French ships had their colours hoisted at the time the firing began.

Q. At what time did I make the signal for battle?

A. At twenty minutes after eleven o'clock.

Q. Were the French fleet then in a regular line of battle, when the action was brought?

A. At a quarter past eleven when it commenced, the French van was very irregular, some more than a mile to windward than others of them, they all appeared to keep their wind as they approached us, they were at very unequal distances from each other, independent of their being to windward and to leeward. What was properly their center was pretty compactly formed, but they were not in a line. That which should have been their rear division, I could not make any observation upon, as they were far to windward of Monsieur d'Orvilliers, in the Bretagne and the ships about him, and must have passed us while we were engaged with what was properly their center.

Q. Were the greatest part of the ships of the British fleet when they came to battle, though not in a line, in a situation speedily to support each other?

A. They were.

Q. How soon after I made the signal for battle was it before the Victory was engaged with the French Admiral? A. About twenty-seven minutes.

Q. Did any, and how many of the French van fire at random a great way off from the Victory?

A. All the French van but three or four sail fired at the Victory, hardly any of their shot reached her.

Q. Did the Victory return the fire of any of those ships?

A. Not one.

Q. How many ships ahead of the French Admiral fired upon the Victory, in passing, to do execution?

A. Three sail fired upon us; but except two or three guns, there was no fire returned, which was ordered to be reserved for the French Admiral.

Q. When

Q. When the Victory began to fire upon the French Admiral on board the Bretagne, how did the French Admiral appear to be situated in regard to his fleet?

A. At a quarter before twelve, when we began to fire on the Bretagne, there was a three deck ship, with a white flag at her main top-mast head; close astern of the Bretagne, there were then three sail of private ships, a white and blue flag flying at her fore top-mast head, and two sail of private ships astern of her, and no other ships astern of the French.

Q. In passing the French Admiral, except the moment we were obliged to weather her head, not to run aboard the three decked ship with a white flag at her fore top-mast head, did not the Victory cling her wind not to lose one fathom of her position and nearness to them?

A. Till the Admiral mentioned that particular, I did not know the helm had ever been put up, I should have said that she was always to the wind as close as she could lay, the latter part of the action, I believe she would not lay close to the wind.

Q. What time did the Victory pass the rear of the French fleet? A. At one o'clock.

Q. What time did I make the signal to wear towards the French fleet?

A. The signal for wearing was made very soon afterwards, in ten minutes, as soon as you could see the smoke clear away, but the Victory could not be wore till a quarter before two.

Q. Can you remember what ship wore with the Victory, and when the signal for battle was hauled down?

A. Not a single ship wore with the Victory, the Prince George continued to stand on the starboard tack till we had passed her on the larboard tack, about a quarter of an hour afterwards, she, and one or two sail more, got round.

Q. Can you say what other ships were connected with, or near the Victory?

A. I cannot---the signal for battle was hauled down at a quarter before two o'clock, I have it not noted down but I know it was just at the time we wore, I will not be positive whether it was just before, or just after. I am sure, from a quarter before two till three o'clock, during which time we were on the larboard tack, standing after the French fleet, there was not a single ship formed with the Victory. We had passed all the ships that had fought astern of us. There was one ship with her mizen

mizen top-maſt gone, that was about abreaſt of our cheſtry at three o'clock, I took it to be Captain Jarvis, of the Foudroyant.

Q. At what hour was ſignal made for line of battle, after being upon the larboard tack?

A. At two o'clock.

Q. Did you obſerve any ſhips, while the Victory was upon the larboard tack, to fall into their ſtations, or cloſe with the Victory?

A. Whilſt we were on the larboard tack, there were no ſhips near on the ſame tack except the Prince George, Bienfaiſant, and Foudroyant; the Valiant could not join us, and none of thoſe ſhips were ever in their ſtation while we were on the larboard tack, from a quarter before two till three; they were all more than a mile from us except the Foudroyant.

Q. What was the poſition of the French fleet whilſt the Victory was ſtanding towards them?

A. The poſition of their fleet was, about three ſail of them, we ſaw to windward of the four ſail, a large body of their center right ahead of us, and their ſternmoſt ſhips not very open on the lee bow; at half an hour after two they were about three miles from us, they then began to get round and form on the ſtarboard tack, for ſome time they pointed their heads ſo as to weather the Victory, but a little before three o'clock they kept from the wind and pointed for four or five ſail of the Engliſh ſhips that were far to leeward, and appeared diſabled.

Q. Did you obſerve one of the French ſhips go off before the wind?

A. Yes; at half paſt two her main yard and mizen top-maſt being gone, ſhe went off, and was followed ſoon after by a frigate.

Q. What was the poſition of the red diviſion at this time, and how many ſhips wore of that diviſion when we wore on the larboard tack?

A. When I firſt ſaw the Vice Admiral of the Red with his diviſion, after the action, aſſiſting the van, they were on the Victory's lee bow, ſtanding towards us on the larboard tack; at five minutes after one, ſoon after the ſmoke cleared away, they continued to ſtand on the larboard tack, ſome of their ſhips paſſing us very cloſely. At a quarter before two o'clock, when we wore, the Vice Admiral of the Red, with about ſix or ſeven ſail, before we wore, were on the Victory's ſtarboard bow, or between that and the cheſtry; at half an hour after two, when the French were forming their line on the

ſtarboard

ſtarboard tack, and we ſtanding towards them on the larboard tack, the Vice Admiral of the Red, and the ſhips with him were a little before the beam of the Victory; at three o'clock they were hauled upon the lee bow of the Victory, about two miles and a half from us.

Q. At what time did the French draw out from their body, and begin forming their line upon the larboard tack, ſtanding to the ſouthward?

A. At half after two in the afternoon.

Q. Can you deſcribe the ſituation of the Britiſh fleet at that time?

A. The Vice Admiral of the Red, with ſix or ſeven ſhips were to windward, nearly abreaſt of the Victory. The Vice Admiral of the Blue was about paſſing us, continuing to ſtand on the ſtarboard tack; all the ſhips of his diviſion had paſſed us on the other tack, at that time there were four or five ſail far to leeward, abaft the beam a great way off the Victory. There was about four ſail of ſhips of the center diviſion, in a different poſition around us, at about a mile diſtant, which four ſail were all the ſhips excepting thoſe that were with the Vice Admiral of the Red, that were on the larboard tack.

Q. When was the ſignal made for the Britiſh fleet to wear to the ſouthward?

A. At ſeven minutes after three o'clock.

Q. Do you recollect the poſition of the Vice Admiral of the Blue and his diviſion at that time?

A. After we were about on the ſtarboard tack, ſtanding to the ſouthward, we paſſed the Formidable to leeward, from that time ſeveral of the ſhips of the Vice Admiral of the Blue's diviſion continued to join him; I cannot ſay the number of them at that time, but they continued to windward.

Q. Was the ſignal flying at that time to form a line of battle?

A. The ſignal to form the line of battle, was made at two o'clock, when we were on the larboard tack and was conſtantly flying all the afternoon.

Q. When was it hoiſted again?

A. It was hauled down at that time to let the fleet ſee the ſignal for the ſhips to windward to come down into the Admiral's wake, which was at that time hoiſted, in about twenty minutes after the ſhips having ſeen that ſignal, it was hauled down, and the ſignal for the line then hoiſted, and continued flying all night.

Q. Soon after the Victory was about on the ſtarboard tack, did ſhe lead from the wind to give protection to thoſe ſhips you before deſcribed diſabled to leeward?

 A. On

A. On the Victory's first coming about to sail on the starboard tack, seven minutes after three she was kept to the wind for about ten minutes to endeavour to collect some of the ships near us, but the Admiral gave that up, observing at the time he directed the Victory to be kept from the wind, *that the French had a design to affront him*, (these were his words) by an attack on those ships that were to leeward. The Victory was then kept away from the wind, steering S. S. E. The wind was rather abaft the beam a point or thereabouts. I am now speaking to about twenty or twenty-five minutes after three, for the wind afterwards came further to the westward.

Q. What time was the signal for ships to windward to come into the Admiral's wake made, during the course of the afternoon?

A. At the time I was last speaking, the signal for ships to come into the Admiral's wake had not been made, it was not made till forty minutes after three, and was hauled down ten minutes before four, when the signal for forming the line was again hoisted. At half past four the signal for the ships to come again into the Admiral's wake was again made, but the signal for the line of battle was kept constantly flying, it was not hauled down the second time.

Q. What was the position of the two Vice Admirals, and the ships that were with them at that time, and till five o'clock?

A. The Vice Admiral of the Red, with six or seven sail including himself, was forming astern of the Victory, in consequence of a message, which had been sent to him by Captain Sutton, in the Proserpine, there was no ship of the center division but the Foudroyant then astern of the Victory. The Vice Admiral of the Blue division, with seven or eight sail was to windward, betwixt the Victory's weather beam and her quarter, keeping their wind betwixt two and three miles from us. Captain Faulkner at that time gave me his glass, observing that we could count every gun and every port distinctly; the four sail were still to leeward upon our bow.

Q. What had been the conduct of the French fleet from three o'clock to that time, and how were they situated with regard to the English fleet?

A. The French fleet had continued forming their line, keeping a course parallel to that which was held by the Victory and the ships near her, they were at half after four the headmost ships, about three miles astern and to leeward of the Victory.

Q. At

Q. At that time what sail had the Victory set?

A. The Victory had her fore sail and fore and mizen top sails set, her main top sail was also set with two reefs in it, which was done when it was bent to the yard; the mizen top sail was unbent soon after we came on the larboard tack after the action, as it was unserviceable.

Q. Did you hear any message or orders sent by frigates in the afternoon of the 27th of July?

A. At five o'clock the Milford was hailed, and ordered to acquaint Sir Robert Harland, that it was the Admiral's orders he should make sail with the ships his division, then astern of the Victory, and form the van which was his proper station in the line of battle; the Fox was sent immediately after to Sir Hugh Palliser to tell him to bear down, as the Admiral only waited for him and his division to bring the enemy again to action.

Q. Do you recollect any other signal made at that time, or was there a general signal made for ships to get into their station?

A. Five minutes past five the signal was made for all shipsto get into their stations.

Q. What was that signal?

A. A Spanish flag at the main top mast head, in the Admiral's additional instructions.

Q. Were there no pendants out?

A. Not at the time the signal was made at the mast head; but the Prince George and Bienfaisant, whose stations were astern of the Victory when the signal for the line of battle was flying on the starboard tack, and who were on the larboard tack, but seeing the Vice Admiral of the red, forming his division astern of the Victory, and fallen into the line in the manner they would have done had there been a signal set up for forming the line of battle reverse, it was to communicate to them, that the Admiral had sent orders to Sir Robert Harland to form ahead, that he then directed these two ships pendants to be thrown out.

Q. Did they not obey it as quick as possibly could be expected?

A. They obeyed it immediately.

Q. Then before they got astern into their stations, and after the Vice Admiral of the red had gone from the rear, how many ships were there formed astern in the line with the Victory?

A. The Foudroyant only.

Q. Did the Vice Admiral of the blue lead down the ships of his division in obedience to the general signal I

had

had made, or by orders fent by the Fox, in the afternoon of the 27th of July? A. No.

Q. What was the pofition of the Vice Admiral of the blue, from five till feven o'clock?

A. He kept nearly the fame bearings as us, but kept his wind betwixt the beam and the quarter.

Q. Were there any particular fhip's fignals made that afternoon, for them to come into their ftations?

A. At feven o'clock, the particular fignal belonging to every fhip of the Vice Admiral of the blue's divifion, excepting the Formidable, was made; thefe fignals were for fhips to come into their ftations; the fignal was kept conftantly flying.

Q. What fail was the Victory under the remainder of the afternoon, after the time you fpeak of?

A. Double reefed top fails and fore fails, going about two knots and an half.

Q. Did fhe make a lefs fail than before dark?

A. At eight o'clock, we clofe reefed our topfails.

Q. What was the relative pofition of the two fleets when night fet in?

A. The Vice Admiral of the red was formed ahead of the Victory; the fhips belonging to the center divifion had all, except one or two, joined us; the Foudroyant, Prince George, and Bienfaifant, were formed in a line aftern of us. A confiderable way aftern of them, but not in the line, there was another fhip endeavouring to get up; I took her for the Vengeance. The Vice Admiral of the blue, and the fhips of his divifion, were to windward about three miles, ftanding on, excepting three or four fail, who had begun to obey the fignal for coming down into their ftations in the line.

Q. Did the Vice Admiral of the blue repeat that fignal? A. Not that I faw.

Prefident. What fail were the French fleet under at that time; and how were they fituated with refpect to the Britifh fleet?

A. The French fleet were fteering a parallel courfe with the Victory, we were very near the wind at that time, we had hauled our wind an hour before them. The third fhip of the French van was abreaft of our quarter; about a mile and a half to leeward of us, the French line was formed with fourteen fail ahead of the French Admiral, and the fame number aftern of him; their beft going fhips were under their top fails; only their heavy failing fhips wore under fore fails and top fails, and fome of them with their main fails fet.

Q. Was

Q. Was the ſignal for forming the line, and for ſhips to come into their ſtations, flying till dark?

A. They were flying after dark.

Q. Did you ſee the Formidable repeat the ſignal for a line of battle any time in the afternoon, or the Spaniſh flag at the main top maſt head, for ſhips to come into their ſtation?

A. We paſſed the Formidable twice, from about half an hour after two till half after three; ſhe had at that time no ſignal flying of any ſort. At the time the ſignal was made for ſhips to come into the Admiral's wake, a little before four, the Formidable repeated that ſignal; but I never ſaw her repeat any other in the courſe of that afternoon.

Q. Where was the Formidable when you firſt ſaw her in the evening of the 27th of July?

A. Three miles, or thereabouts, to windward of the Victory, ſtanding upon a wind before the quarter, betwixt the quarter and abaft the beam, about a point and an half or two points.

Q. In the morning of the 28th of July, how many of the French fleet were in ſight?

A. Three ſail, one much larger than the other two.

Q. What diſtance were they from the Victory?

A. Three miles the neareſt.

Q. Were any ſhip's ſignals made to chace?

A. The Bienfaiſant, Duke, Prince George, and Elizabeth's ſignals were made to chace; but the Elizabeth informed you, ſhe could not carry ſail on her maſt. It was viſible the Prince George could not make ſail as a ſhip in chace ſhould.

Proſecutor. Do you take upon you to ſwear poſitively that the Formidable did not repeat the ſignal for the line of battle, when ſhe was abreaſt of the Victory?

A. I believe ſhe did not.

Q. Nor while aſtern, till dark?

A. I did not ſee it, as I obſerved before.

Ordered to withdraw.

Mr. ROGERS, *Secretary to the Admiral, called and ſworn.*

Admiral Keppel. Did I not deſire you to take notes on the 27th and 28th of July?

A. You did ſo on the 27th.

Q. Have you always done ſo the time you was in ſervice with me during the laſt war?

A. I attended the Admiral, in that ſituation, during the whole of his ſervice in the laſt war, and 'tis the greateſt pride I have.

Q. At what hour did they begin their fire on the 27th of July?

A. At twenty minutes before eleven.

Q. What time did I make the signal to engage?

A. At forty minutes past eleven.

Q. What hour was it the Victory made her fire upon the French?

A. At one quarter before twelve.

Q. At what French ship did the Victory first fire?

A. At a three decked ship, with a flag at main top mast head, some guns were fired before, but the whole of the fire was directed to be reserved for the Admiral.

Q. Did I pass in action near any other three decked ship of the enemy?

A. Yes there was another which followed the first, and approached much nearer the Victory.

Q. How near was she?

A. Very close indeed, so as to appear as if she was coming on board us.

Q. What part of the French fleet were those two Admirals situated in?

A. Very near the rear.

Q. At what time did the Victory pass the rear of the French fleet and cease firing?

A. At one o'clock.

Q. At what time did I make the signal for the fleet to wear?

A. At forty-five minutes past one.

Q. At what time was the signal for battle hauled down?

A. Very near the same time.

Q. Do you know what number of ships did wear with the Victory, when she wore to get on the larboard tack?

A. I cannot say.

Q. What time was signal for line of battle ahead made after being on the larboard tack?

A. At two o'clock.

Q. At what time was the signal made to wear to the southward again?

A. At ten minutes past three.

Q. Did you observe the French fleet at this time, and were they forming their line upon the starboard tack?

A. They were drawing out from a body and forming their line.

Q. Had they been standing towards the Victory before she wore, and how were they steering?

A. I cannot be exact as to the first, but when I obſerved them, they were layIng up for the Victory's ſtern, after the Victory had got about on the ſtarboard tack.

Q. Before the Victory wore on the ſtarboard tack, had either the center diviſion, or the Vice Admiral of the blue's diviſion got connected in their ſtation in the line with the Victory?

A. There were no ſhips that could be ſaid to be connected with the Victory; the Vice Admiral of the red and part of his diviſion were to windward.

Q. After wearing to the ſouthward, did you obſerve any part of the Britiſh fleet much to leeward, repairing?

A. Yes, I particularly took notice of four.

Q. Did the van of the enemy ſeem to point towards them?

A. They did ſo, they kept away for that purpoſe apparently.

Q. Did you obſerve the Victory edge away two or three points to get near thoſe ſhips and ſecure their junction?

A. I do recollect very perfectly that ſhe did.

Q. Was the ſignal for the line of battle flying from the time the Victory wore to the ſouthward, till dark; or was it ever hauled down to ſhew the ſignal plainer for the ſhips to bear down into my wake?

A. I don't know it from my own knowledge: I ſhall ſay, the ſignal for the line of battle was kept flying from two o'clock till dark. I underſtood that it had been hauled down ſome ſhort time, to ſhew the blue flag that had been hoiſted for ſome other purpoſe, but I did not ſee it hauled down myſelf.

Q. Did you ever obſerve the ſignal for a line of battle ahead, to have been repeated on board the Formidable, during the afternoon?

A. I never ſaw the flag flying on board the Formidable for the line of battle the whole afternoon.

Q. What time did I ſend the Milford to Sir Robert Harland in the afternoon, after being on the ſtarboard tack?

A. At three quarters paſt four by my watch?

Q. At what time did I ſend the Fox to Vice Admiral Sir Hugh Palliſer?

A. I cannot be exact as to the minute, but it was immediately after hailing the Milford, which I have conſidered as five o'clock, or rather before it.

Q. What orders did I ſend by the Fox?

A. To deſire Sir Hugh Palliſer to bear down into his ſtation in the line, that you only waited for him to renew the action.

Q. Did you obſerve the Fox ſpeak to, or range near the Formidable ?

A. I ſaw the Fox cloſe under the Formidable's lee quarter.

Q. At what time muſt that be ?

A. I ſuppoſe about half an hour after ſhe left the Victory.

Q. Did the Vice Admiral of the Blue, bear down in conſequence of the meſſage ſent by the Fox ?

A. I did not ſee any motion made on board the Formidable, to comply with theſe orders, tho' I looked for it.

Q. At this time, how far upon the weather quarter did ſhe appear to be ?

A. I wiſh not to be preciſe as to diſtance, but ſhe was far upon the lee quarter.

Q. Were there any ſignals made at ſeven o'clock ?

A. There were ſeveral pendants thrown out for ſhips to come into their ſtations.

Q. How was the Vice Admiral of the Blue then ſituated ?

A. I cannot ſay I obſerved any alterations from what I had obſerved before.

Q. Did you ſee any, or how many of the ſhips bear down, of the Vice Admiral of the Blue's diviſion ?

A. There were ſome bore down, but I cannot mention them.

Q. Was the French fleet ſeen on the morning of the 28th, from the Victory ?

A. At opening of day I ſaw only three ſhips, one of them I think, I kept my eye upon moſt part of the night.

Q. Did I ſend ſhips to chace them ?

A. There were ſignals made for ſhips to chace.

Q. Do you know what ſhips ?

A. The Prince George, Elizabeth, Bienfaiſant, and I believe the Duke, but will not be poſitive as to the Duke.

Q. Was it obſerved after the ſignal was made to chace, that ſome of them were crippled ?

A. I obſerved particularly the Prince George could carry no ſail on the fore top maſt.

Q. Have you any recollection of the perplexity and trouble both to myſelf and your copying, in penning my letter relative to the attack on the 27th of July, to the Admiralty, ſo as to convey no cenſure upon the conduct of the Vice Admiral of the Blue ?

A. I recollect you had great difficulty in forming the rough draft of your letter, to relate facts, without cenſuring the man, whom you then thought your friend, and of whoſe courage, I know you thought well.

Admiral

Admiral Montague. If the signal for a line of battle had been flying on board the Formidable, was you in such a situation in the Victory as to see it, or did any other ship betwixt you and the Formidable intercept your view?

A. If it had been flying on board the Formidable, as I looked for it with eagerness and great attention from many different parts of the ship, I think I must have seen it.

Q. From the time the signal was thrown out for ships to windward to come down into the Admiral's wake, to the time of its being hauled down, did you hear the Admiral express his displeasure at the ships not bearing down agreeable to the signal for that purpose, and that if he could form the line, he would again renew the action?

A. The Admiral expressed great anxiety and uneasiness at the ships not bearing down in consequence of the signal, and it was my idea, and I believe the sense of every body on board the Victory, that he only waited for those ships, to renew the action with the French fleet.

Prosecutor. The time you speak of giving orders to the Fox, does the hour and minute stand in your minutes?

A. The time of delivering the message was very near to that of the Milford, which is marked three quarters past four, the hailing the Fox succeeded so immediately, that I have made no distinction, but I can say it did not exceed five o'clock.

Q. Is the time of speaking with any other ship regularly entered, except that of speaking to the Fox?

A. The Milford and Fox are both entered particularly.

Q. You described the Formidable to be astern from the Victory's quarter, might not the signal at the mizen peak be out, and you not see it; are you positive you saw the mizen peak open and clear of her sails?

A. I looked at the Formidable at different times, and I did not see the signal for the line flying on board her. I looked at the mizen peak, and knew that to be the place to look for the signal.

Mr. Rogers ordered to withdraw. After which the Court adjourned till to-morrow morning ten o'clock.

TWENTY-THIRD DAY, TUESDAY, FEBRUARY 2d.

At ten o'clock this morning the Court being met, the prisoner was brought in, and audience admitted.

ADMIRAL CAMPBELL, *called in, and sworn.*

Ad. Keppel. What day was the French fleet first discovered? A. On the 23d of July.

Q. Do

formed the line of battle, instead of closing with the French fleet in the manner I did?

A. Increased our distance from them, as much as ever it had been from the first time of seeing them.

Q. Would that have been the way to have brought them to action? A. No.

Q. What time did I tack, and continue upon that tack, till my passing the rear of the French fleet?

A. The whole of the English fleet tacked by signal at ten o'clock, or a little before, and the wind very soon after veering about two points, we hoisted our staysail and main top gallant sail, and wore, in order to near the French with the greater expedition. We had lost sight of them in a squall, but when it cleared away, in about three quarters of an hour, we saw they had altered their position, and were on the contrary tack, the larboard tack, and were at no great distance from Sir Robert Harland's division, who was then in the van of the fleet; whereupon the Admiral ordered the signal to be made for them to engage, and observed to me, in the gangway, that several ships of the French fleet seemed to be in confusion, and believed they were running aboard each other. We passed on with all the sail we had then abroad, attended by all the ships of our own division, pretty well connected, till we came abreast of the French Admiral.

Q. In drawing near to the French ships, and in passing them, did they appear to you to be in any regularity?

A. The van of the French fleet appeared to be in a pretty regular line, except in point of distance, they were not at regular distances from each other; the rest of the French fleet was in an irregular line.

Q. I am charged with having stood at too great a distance beyond the enemy, before I wore to stand to them again, please to inform the Court, whether it was practicable or expedient for me to wear sooner than I did?

A. No, it was not.

Q. When I did wear, wore there any ships about me, able to wear with me.

A. No, none of them wore immediately, that I saw.

Q. Had you any reason to believe from any thing that you saw, or was acquainted with, that the Vice Admiral of the Blue was exposed to be cut off? A. No.

Q. When was the signal for battle hauled down?

A. The signal was made for hauling it down, immediately as those ships ceased firing which were then out of engaging distance.

Q. I am charged with shortening sail when I advanced towards the enemy, I desire to know whether I had ships

enough

enough with me to admit of my advancing faster than I did?

A. The whole time that the Admiral remained upon the larboard tack, standing towards the enemy, he had not above one or two ships stationed a-head of him, that were got into their proper stations; the Vice Admiral of the Blue was ahead of the Victory, after we wore towards the enemy, but instead of remaining there, and repeating the signal for the line to call the ships of his division into their station, he passed on the starboard tack, astern of the Victory, in direct disobedience to the signal then flying.

Q. Where was the Vice Admiral of the red at this time, and what number of ships of his division were with him?

A. He was upon the weather bow of the Victory, but I do not know the number of ships he had with him; I did not count them.

Q. Where was the French fleet at this time after we were on the larboard tack?

A. They were right ahead, as near as I can recollect; rather to windward, I think.

Q. As the two fleets were then situated was the signal appointed by the 31st article of the fighting instructions, applicable to the purpose of directing the Vice Admiral of the red to lead on the larboard tack, for the rest of the fleet to form?

A. Certainly not; because the signal directed by the 31st article has a precise and determinate signification affixed to it, and can be applicable to nothing else.

Q. While I was on the larboard tack did you see the French fleet in disorder?

A. No, I did not see them in any other disorder than what must appear from their changing from one tack to the other, which they did, a little while before we wore.

Q. Had I, at any time while I stood on the larboard tack, a sufficient force collected to renew the fight?

A. I have said the whole time we were upon the larboard tack you had not one ship stationed a-head of you got into their station, and I believe, not more than four, at most, of these stationed astern.

Q. Was the signal for the line flying all the time I was upon the larboard tack, to collect them?

A. Yes, the signal was hoisted very soon after we got upon the larboard tack, and was not hauled down from the time it was hoisted.

Q. Then, under these circumstances, did I not do the utmost in my power to take, sink, burn, and destroy the French fleet. A. I think you did.

Q. I

Q. I am charged with having wore at this time, and making ſail directly from the enemy, and leading the Britiſh fleet from them; I deſire you would explain all you know of that tranſaction?

A. On ſeeing the French wear and ſtand towards the Engliſh fleet, the Admiral ordered Captain Sutton to go to Vice Admiral Sir Robert Harland, and direct him to form the line, as there were none of the ſhips ahead of us in their proper ſtations; but before Captain Sutton got away from the Victory, the French edged away, and ſeemed to point to four of our ſhips to leeward, on the lee quarter, whereupon the Admiral made the ſignal for wearing; we wore, and got down to ſuccour theſe ſhips, the ſignal for the line being ſtill flying, and after we were about, keeping much away, I remarked to the Admiral, that we ſhould join ſome of the ſhips faſter, if we did not keep ſo much to the wind; whereupon he ſaid, Don't you ſee thoſe ſhips pointing directly to leeward? I muſt not receive an affront there; and ſo ordered the ſhip to be carried away to the ſuccour of the diſabled ſhips.

Court. Were there any ſhips near you at that time?

A. Yes, there were ſeveral of our own diviſion near us at that time, and others followed us down; they had been collecting the whole time that we were upon the larboard tack.

Q. Was the ſignal for the line ſtill kept flying?

A. I have ſaid ſo.

Q. What ſail did I carry at this time?

A. To the beſt of my recollection, double reefed top-ſails and fore-ſails; indeed the main top-ſail was not bent when we wore. We had, while on the larboard tack, bent our main top-ſail, which was much wounded with ſhot, ſeeing we could do ſo without any loſs of time, before the ſhips could be collected, and we were juſt beginning to haul it out to bend it, when we wore to go down to the ſuccour of theſe ſhips, and it was bent with as much expedition as any main top-ſail I ever ſaw.

Q. Do you recollect my ordering the Milford to Sir Robert Harland, to direct him to leave the rear, and form a-head, and at what time?

A. I had forgot to mention, that on our wearing to go to the ſuccour of the diſabled ſhips, Captain Sutton was ordered to go and direct Sir Robert Harland to form in our rear; and I remember Sir William Burnaby was ordered, at five o'clock, to go and direct Sir Robert Harland to reſume his ſtation in the van.

Q. Do

Q. Do you recollect at the same time my ordering the Fox to go to the Vice Admiral of the Blue?

A. I do.

Q. What orders were sent by the Fox?

A. Captain Windsor was directed to go to the Vice Admiral of the Blue, and acquaint him, that the Admiral wanted him to come down with the ships of his division, with all expedition, as the Admiral only waited till that was performed, to renew the action.

Q. Did you add any thing to that message, as he was going off?

A. I did add a little to the message, but I believe Capt. Windsor did not hear it; the people on board his ship were making a great noise at that time, and he was increasing his distance from us; he was then steering from us.

Q. Do you recollect what the words were?

A. I directed him to tell the Vice Admiral that we had long waited for him.

Q. Do you recollect my calling myself, from my gallery, at the time the message was delivering?

A. Yes, I heard the Admiral's voice, but I cannot be precise what he said. I had repeated the message myself to Captain Windsor; I attempted it from the quarter deck; I then went into the gallery, because I thought I should be better heard, and then I thought I heard the Admiral's voice from the stern gallery.

Q. Where was the Vice Admiral of the Blue, at this time?

A. Wide upon our weather quarter, at a considerable distance.

Q. After being upon the starboard tack, did I not the whole afternoon express my uneasiness, as well as surprise, at the Vice Admiral's remaining to windward, without making any effort to come down with his division, in obedience to the signal.

Q. You frequently did; and I remember very well, upon one of the occasions, I expressed my apprehensions of the Vice Admiral's being wounded, as, I said, I was sure the Formidable could not behave so, if he was in health.

Q. Was not my constant conversation with you that afternoon, that I only waited for Sir Hugh Palliser's coming down, to re-attack? A. It was.

Q. Did I ever seem to have given up the design of re-attacking, till evening was coming on? A. No.

Q. Do you recollect what degree of sail I made in the evening, to regulate the fleet going by night?

A. Yes

A. Yes: At eight o'clock we took the third reef in the top-sails, and handed the mizen top-sail, that it might not obstruct the sight of the top light from the ships stationed astern; and we went with our two top-sails reefed, and fore-sail all night. The French fleet reefed immediately after we did.

Q. May I beg the indulgence of the Court, to have the Robuste's log-book read to that time, with the alterations?

Ordered to be read.

N. B. The time and alteration alluded to is, at eight o'clock, "the Admiral making much sail."

Admiral Keppel. I must observe, that the alteration speaks for itself; and after Admiral Campbell's examination upon this matter, there requires no comment upon it.---(*To Admiral Campbell*) You have heard the five articles read, wherein I am charged with not pursuing the enemy on the 28th of July; please to inform the Court all you know concerning it.

A. In the morning of the 28th, the French fleet were not in sight, that I know of; but there were three ships at a considerable distance from each other, and a little to leeward of our rear-most ships; but before we could well make out what they were, they had bore away, and were at a great distance, crowding sail to leeward, the first confirmation I had of their being French ships. The signal was instantly made for ships to chace; the Bienfaisant was the nearest ship, the Prince George, Elizabeth, and, I think, the Duke's signal was made, because we knew she had not suffered in the engagement; at the same time we bore away in the Victory, and made the signal for the fleet to spread N. and S. as well as I recollect; but the Prince George and Elizabeth neither of them made sail like chacing ships, and soon after the Elizabeth hailed us, and told us that she could not carry sail. The Admiral in a short time called in the chacing ships, as the French ships had got a great start of ours before the signal could be made for them to chace, and we soon after brought to on the larboard tack, and made the signal for ships to set up their rigging, and refit.

Q. If I had pursued to the eastward with the fleet, in the condition it was in after the action, the wind and weather such as it then was, do you think there was any sort of probability of getting up with the French fleet, before they would have reached the port of Brest?

A. I am clearly of opinion, that if we had pursued with the fleet in the state it was, they could not have been kept together, nor carried their chacing sails; the disabled

ships

ſhips muſt have fallen aſtern. One thing I would beg leave to remark, that by diſabled ſhips, I mean diſabled in their maſts and rigging, which prevented their carrying chacing ſail. I do not know that they were otherwiſe diſabled.

Q. While I was upon the ſtarboard tack in the afternoon of the 27th, under the degree of ſail you have deſcribed, and the ſignal being out for a line of battle, had it the leaſt appearance of a flight?

A. Certainly not.

Q. Did you ever obſerve the ſignal for a line of battle repeated on board the Formidable, any time in the day, or in the evening of the 27th of July?

A. No; I think it would have been very improper to have repeated it, except it had been obeyed by the Formidable; it would have been very unofficer-like to have repeated it.

Q. Admiral Campbell, you have heard all the articles of the charge read, therefore I deſire you to ſtate to the Court any inſtance, if you ſaw or know of any ſuch, in which I negligently performed my duty on the 27th or 28th of July.

A. I never ſaw any then, or at any other time ſince I ſerved under the Admiral. I never ſerved under any officer that was more diligent in the execution of every part of his duty, as far as came within my obſervation.

Q. I would aſk whether I did not give inſtructions, upon my ſailing again with the fleet, to direct an inverted line, when I ſhould ſee occaſion for it, by way of providing for the calling ſhips into their ſtation, and changing the order of their line, when I thought it was for the public advantage?

A. Yes, you did.

Q. Do you recollect my giving thoſe additional orders in the fighting inſtructions at ſea, in theſe words:---"In "the line of battle, the flag of the Admiral commanding "in Chief, is always to be conſidered as the principal point "of direction for the whole fleet, in forming and pre- "ſerving their line?"

A. Yes.

Preſident. Do you know at what time the Vice Admiral of the Blue got into his ſtation in the line, the 27th at night?

A. The Vice Admiral of the Blue did not get into his ſtation, while it was light enough to ſee him do ſo.

Q. Did you obſerve him carry his diſtinguiſhing lights moſt of the night?

 A. I did

A. I did not see any thing of the Vice Admiral of the Blue, from the time the day shut, till the next morning.

Q. What distance was he in the line in the morning of the 28th, when you did see him, from the centre division?

A. I did not take notice of him; the three French ships to leeward engrossed my attention.

Prosecutor. You have mentioned, that when the Admiral was standing with his head towards the French, the Formidable was the only ship a-head of him; I ask, if the Formidable was not laying with her head after the enemy, within gun shot, till the signal for battle was hauled down, and the fleet had shortened sail, the Admiral at that time at a great distance?

A. I never saw the Formidable upon the larboard tack, after passing the French line; nor did I ever hear she had been upon the larboard tack, till the Vice Admiral of the Blue told me so himself, at Admiral Keppel's house, in London.

Q. When was the first time you saw her, which enabled you to say she was a-head of the Victory, when you was standing that way?

A. A little before the two ships met, the Victory upon the larboard tack, with her head towards the enemy, and the Formidable upon the starboard tack, approaching near the Victory. I then saw the Formidable, and continued to look at her, till she passed the Victory to leeward.

Q. From the Victory, with her head towards the enemy, as you have described, was it possible to see a signal out on board the Formidable, till she came so near as to open her.

A. The Victory was not the ship the Vice Admiral of the Blue should have looked to for the signal; there was a gun fired for a signal when it was made, and that naturally should have led the Vice Admiral of the Blue to look to the repeating frigate, where the signal was made.

Q. Was not the Captain of the repeating frigate on board the Victory at the time when the Formidable came close to her?

A. I do not recollect. I remember he was on board the Victory at the time we wore to go down to succour the three ships, but that was at least a quarter of an hour before the Formidable had passed; I really do not know whether he was on board at the time the Formidable and Victory passed each other.

Q. Whilst he was on board, was not the frigate near the Victory to be in readiness to take up the Captain's boat, and steering as the Victory did?

A. I be-

A. I believe ſhe was; I do not know; I cannot ſpeak poſitively to it; I did not take much notice of it.

Q. But then that being the caſe, was not the ſignal on board the frigate equally imperceptible to the Formidable as it was on board the Victory?

A. The ſignal had been repeated by the frigate long before Captain Marſhall came on board the Victory; but indeed that queſtion I cannot anſwer, the people on board the Formidable ſhould anſwer that queſtion.

Q. Inform the Court whether or not the ſignal for wearing, a blue pendant at the enſign ſtaff, was flying on board the Victory before the Formidable came the length of her?

A. I cannot ſay it was not, but I do not believe it was; theſe are things that ſlip one's memory, and 'tis impoſſible to anſwer them at ſuch a diſtant period.

Q. Do you recollect then, when the Captain of the repeating frigate left the Victory, whether it was at the time ſhe was actually wearing?

A. No, really, I do not preciſely recollect when he left the Victory; I only remember that he was on board, from a circumſtance that he was on the quarter deck, and helped to haul out the main topſail.

Q. You have ſaid before, that was the time of wearing?

A. Yes.

Q. As you cannot preciſely ſay that the ſignal for wearing was out before the Formidable came the length of the Victory, or a-breaſt of her, have you not been precipitate, in charging the Vice Admiral before this Court, of acting in direct diſobedience to the ſignal?

A. No, I do not think ſo; the ſignal for a line had been made full three quarters of an hour before the ſignal for wearing; and even if the ſignal for wearing was out before the Formidable paſſed the Victory, he ſtill was diſobedient to the ſignal, becauſe he ſhould not have wore till the Victory wore.

Q. Do you mean to ſay, Although it was impoſſible for him to have ſeen the ſignal for the line, till that time when he ſaw the ſignal for wearing out?

A. I do not mean to reproach any man with diſobeying ſignals he never ſaw; but it was the Formidable's duty to have ſeen that ſignal, and think they might have ſeen it if they had looked properly for it.

Admiral Montague. I humbly preſume this is not the trial of Admiral Keppel. The queſtion had been better let alone.

Evidence. If it does not trouble the Court, I ſhall anſwer any queſtions he may put.

Proſecutor. Was it poſſible to ſee ſuch a ſignal on board of the ſhip directly and on?

A. When there were two ſhips with the ſame ſignals flying, and both at conſiderable diſtances, and to windward, I think no ſhip can be ſituated ſo as not to ſee it on board one or the other.

Q. You ſay you do not know where the repeating frigate was at that time; where was ſhe when the ſignal was firſt made?

A. I do not know when the Formidable paſſed her, but I ſaw her conſiderably to windward with the ſignal for the line flying; I believe if the Formidable did not ſee it, ſhe muſt be the only ſhip in the fleet that did not ſee it.

Q. You ſaid the Formidable paſſed to leeward of the Victory, when the Victory was with her head to the northward towards the French fleet; did you ſee her then in a proper poſition, ſo as to have ſeen the ſignal for the line, if it had been flying on board her?

A. To be ſure; I ſaw her the whole time ſhe paſſed, and the ſignal for the line was not flying on board her.

Q. Did you not ſee it very ſoon after that, hoiſted on board the Formidable?

A. No, I did not ſee it at any part of the day hoiſted on board the Formidable; I had occaſion to look frequently at her, with and without the glaſs; I ſaw her hoiſt the blue flag at the mizen peak, a ſignal for ſhips to bear down, but I never ſaw her with the ſignal for the line the whole day: I ſaid ſo before.

Q. Did not the Victory wear very near under the Formidable's ſtern, and run to leeward of her?

A. I have before ſaid the Formidable paſſed the Victory to leeward, and at no great ſpace of time after we wore, and by edging away to cover thoſe ſhips to leeward, we approached to leeward of the Formidable; I did not take notice how far we were aſtern of the Formidable when we croſſed her wind.

Q. At the time that blue flag was hoiſted on board the Victory, which you ſaw the Formidable repeat, was it not within leſs than half an hour after making the ſignal for wearing?

A. No, to the beſt of my remembrance it was not within an hour after we had wore.

Q. But ſuppoſing it was only half an hour, at what diſtance could the Formidable then be from the Victory?

A. I really cannot anſwer queſtions of ſuppoſition, that muſt

must depend upon the sail that the two ships carried, and the different courses they steered.

Q. I would ask whether the Formidable, or some of the Vice Admiral of the Blue's division, were not the last ships that came out of action? A. Certainly they were.

Q. Can you inform the Court of the reason why the Admiral thought proper to order the Vice Admiral of the Red division, to take the station of the Vice Admiral of the Blue, at that time, being just after they came out of action?

A. Because not only the Vice Admiral of the Blue's division, but also the centre division, and those ships stationed astern of the Admiral, had passed on, and had not then wore when the Admiral himself wore, and therefore they could not take that station; he thought proper to have some ships there; but the order was not delivered nor performed?

Q. What time does the question mean?

A. Both times, the time the Admiral intended to take their stations ahead and astern. Because neither the ships of the centre division, nor those of the Vice Admiral of the Blue, were then in a position immediately to take it; but when the Admiral ordered the Vice Admiral of the Red to resume his own station ahead, the greatest part of the ships belonging to both divisions were then in a condition to resume their stations, according as it appeared to the Admiral on board the Victory.

Q. As you mentioned the orders sent by the Fox to the Formidable, I ask whether in the minutes kept on board the Victory, the hour and minute is entered of the delivery of that order?

A. Yes, I have always understood that it was in both, and I have one of the minutes ready myself, they were minuted in both of them, and one of them I have got.

Q. Part of the message is said to be, that the Admiral was waiting for me; Was the Admiral waiting, or was he not, had not he continued sail as he did before the time?

A. Yes, we had the same sail out, after we set our maintopsails, we had the same sail till eight at night.

Q. Did the Victory ever lay to that afternoon?

A. No, we went with the same sail.

Q. Was it not known on board the Victory before twelve o'clock at night, that the French had bore away?

A. No, it was not known till day light, and was matter of surprise to every body on board.

Q. Were there any frigates stationed between the two fleets that night, to give notice of the motions of the

 French

French to the Admiral, as had been done on former nights?

A. No, nor do I know any good purpose frigates could have anſwered; for had the Admiral known of their bearing away in the night, I do not know of any ſtep he could have taken to prevent it. His ſignals had been ſo ill obeyed by the Vice Admiral of the Blue that day, that he durſt not make a ſignal in the night to have purſued an enemy, at the riſque of having found a great part of his fleet laying to windward in the morning.

Q. In the morning when ſignal was made for ſhips to chace the three French ſhips; you mentioned the Duke as one, was not ſhe a very heavy ſailing ſhip indeed?

A. When I mentioned her ſignal being made, I gave a reaſon for it. We were pretty well aſſured the Duke had not ſuffered, and that was the reaſon I ſuppoſe why her ſignal was made.

The Proſecutor declining to aſk any further queſtions, Admiral Campbell was ordered to withdraw.

CAPT. MARSHALL, *called, and croſs examined.*

Admiral Keppel. Did you ſee the ſignal for a line of battle hoiſted on board the Victory after the action, whilſt on the larboard tack?

A. In my evidence I have ſaid, to the beſt of my memory, I did ſo, and it appears ſo by the minutes that I repeated it.

Q. Did you keep it abroad ſo repeated, all the time I ſtood on the larboard tack?

A. I think ſo.

Q. Did you ſee the Formidable whilſt I was ſtanding on the larboard tack? A. Yes.

Q. How was the Arethuſa ſituated with reſpect to her?

A. On the Formidable's weather quarter.

Q. Was the ſignal for the line of battle then flying on board the Arethuſa? A. I think ſo.

Preſident. Did you keep the ſignal out as long as the Admiral did?

A. I certainly did.

Proſecutor. Capt. Marſhall ſaid, he had not his papers about him, as he did not expect to be called; I aſk him by whom and when he had notice to attend?

Admiral Keppel. I ſent him word I ſhould call him concerning a ſignal in diſpute; I ſent for him to prove a matter of fact.

Capt. Marſhall. I received notice that the Admiral would want me, juſt now, as Admiral Campbell went out.

Admiral

Admiral Keppel. I would wiſh to know, whether the Proſecutor admits, or denies, or will put me to the trouble to prove, whether the paper, ſigned Hugh Palliſer, in the morning poſt of the 4th of November, is his.—*The accuſer ſaid, he admits it.*

CAPT. FAULKNER, *of the Victory, called, and ſworn.*

Admiral Keppel. What would have been the conſequence, if I had formed a line of battle, inſtead of cloſing with the French fleet as I did, in the morning of the 27th of July?

A. That they never would have been brought to battle.

Q. What part of the French fleet did the Victory begin action with?

A. The Victory fired ſome ſhot into the ſhip that led the French Admiral; we began cloſe action with the Bretagne; orders were given that we ſhould reſerve our fire for the French Admiral.

Q. Was your ſhips company in good order, obedient, and obſervant that day?

A. In every reſpect they were.

Q. Was the centre of the French fleet, as we came up to them, in appearance to you in any regular order?

A. No, they were not in regular order, they were in ſailing order, that ſort of order that is neareſt a line, but not what an officer would call a line of battle.

Q. Was there more French Admirals than one together.

A. There was only one ſhip betwixt the Admiral and the Bretagne, both thoſe Admirals were in three deck ſhips.

Q. Did they keep their wind, and avoid nearing the Victory, as ſhe paſſed?

A. They hauled their wind as cloſe as ſhips could poſſibly do.

Q. Did they paſs out of gun-ſhot, and how much out of gun-ſhot?

A. The fourth or fifth ſhip ahead of the Bretagne began her fire on the Victory, the firſt of theſe ſhips, that is the fourth or fifth, led the Bretagne, her ſhot ſcarce touched the Victory, the ſhips that were ahead of theſe four or five were ſtill further off.

Q. I am charged when I got out of action, with having ſtood at a great diſtance beyond the enemy before I wore, and ſtood towards them again; you will inform the court whether it was poſſible for me to wear ſooner, and when I did wear, whether any of the ſhips of my own diviſion were able to wear with me?

A. The Victory was wore ſoon after ſhe came out of battle, as ſoon as poſſible; I believe ſooner than many of the ſhips could have ſeen the ſignal. I do not recollect ſeeing any of the Admiral's own diviſion bearing down at that time.

Preſident, Give the defects of your ſhip?

A. The Victory had a large ſhot through the centre of the main maſt, about eight feet above the quarter deck; another ſhot in the main maſt, in the wake of the main yard; the mizen maſt was ſhot through, with a large ſhot in the centre about eight feet above the poop deck; the bowſprit was ſhot through before the ſtep; the main yard ſhot in the wake of the ſlings; the mizen yard ſhot in the lower arm, ſo as to make it neceſſary to cut it off immediately after battle, about ten or eleven feet; the jib boom was ſhot about three feet without the cap; the main topſail yard arm was ſhot upon the ſtarboard quarter; two of our lower deck mid-ſhip ports were much ſhot; the ſtanding and running rigging, the ſtarboard foretack ſheet and bowling, ſhot away; the foretop maſt ſtay, one of the gammons of the bowſprit, ſix fore ſhrouds, and four geer blocks, one at the yard and one at the maſt head, the foretopſail ſheet; the mizen top maſt ſtay, the main preventer ſtay, two foretopſail back ſtays, and five ſhrouds, five main top maſt ſhrouds, the main truſſel, four mizen ſhrouds, two mizen top maſt back ſtays, ſeveral braces, bowlings, &c. were either ſhot away, or cut to pieces. Our topſails were ſhot much, particularly the main topſail, which was ſhot to pieces; the running rigging was much damaged.

Q. Had you reaſon to believe, from any thing you ſaw, that the Vice Admiral of the Blue was expoſed to be cut off? A. No.

Q. Do you recollect when the ſignal for battle was hauled down?

A. I gave the orders for that ſignal being hauled down, having received them from Admiral Campbell, while the Victory was upon the ſtarboard tack. It was not reported to me that it was hauled down, nor did I look to ſee, nor do I preſume to give any information to the Court, when it was hauled down.

Court. What time did you receive the orders to haul it down?

A. About half paſt one, or ſomething later.

Q. Then I ſuppoſe your orders were obeyed?

A. Certainly, but I was much employed in preparing to wear again, which took off my attention from looking at that buſineſs.

Admiral

Admiral Keppel. Was signal made immediately for a line, after the Victory got upon the larboard tack?

A. Directly.

Q. Was it kept flying till she wore to the starboard tack again? A. It was.

Q. Were any ships got into their stations, in the line of battle, before we did wear to the starboard tack again, conformable to that signal?

A. The ships that should have led the Victory, were not ahead of her. Some of those that were astern were probably near their stations to follow him.

Q. I am charged with shortening sail after I wore to stand towards the enemy again, instead of advancing towards them. Had I ships enough with me to admit of my advancing faster than I did? A. No.

Q. Do you remember the main top sail being unbent?

A. Perfectly well.

Q. Did not that cause the ship to close up faster, and was the main top sail fit for service?

A. The main top sail was not fit for service, and it being unbent, the ships we left astern of us certainly had it more in their power to follow us.

Q. Was the main top sail being unbent, any public detriment to the business of that morning?

A. It was not, it certainly gave the ships an opportunity to get up ahead of us, if they had it in their power.

Q. Could any ships get ahead of us, even with their main topsails unbent, of our own division or the Vice Admiral of the blue's division, before we wore to the southward again?

A. I have already stated, that none got ahead of the Victory, and I should therefore presume, they had it not in their power; for, as the signal for the line of battle was out, every man would get into his post as fast as possible.

Q. Did your people replace that main top sail soon, that was unbent, in a seaman-like manner, in point of expedition?

A. The main top-sail was replaced in little more than half an hour.

Q. After the main top sail was replaced, did not you, and all the officers, notwithstanding the defects and damages you have stated to the Court, think the Victory was fit for action again?

A. By the time the main top sail was replaced, the rigging was repaired in such a manner as is done after action,

tion, the powder in the different magazines replaced, and ſhe was then as fit for action as ſhe could be.

Q. Did you ſee the French fleet wear, and begin to form on the ſtarboard tack? A. I did.

Q. Had I, at that time, ſufficient force collected with me, to have ſtood on to interrupt their forming?

A. I am ſure you had not.

Q. What time did I wear to the ſouthward?

A. A little paſt three o'clock.

Q. Did I keep the ſignal for a line of battle flying, after being upon the ſtarboard tack, to collect and form the ſhips?

A. Yes, Sir, the ſignal was not hauled down.

Q. What ſail did I carry upon the ſtarboard tack?

A. After the main topſail was unbent, double reefed topſails, fore ſail, mizen, and mizen ſtay ſail.

Q. Do you recollect Sir Robert Harland coming into the rear with his diviſion, whilſt upon the ſtarboard tack? A. I do.

Q. Do you recollect my ordering him to leave the rear, and form ahead, and at what time, and by what ſhip?

A. About five o'clock, a ſignal was made for the Milford and Fox to come within hail; the Milford came upon the lee quarter, and I hailed him by order of the Admiral, and directed him to go to Sir Robert Harland, and tell him it was the Admiral's directions that he ſhould make ſail, and form ahead, and carry a preſſed ſail in that ſervice.

Q. Do you recollect my ordering the Fox at the ſame time, to go to the Vice Admiral of the blue?

A. I recollect the Fox's coming on the ſtarboard quarter of the Victory, and ſhe was hailed by ſomebody in the ſtern gallery, the meſſage I did not hear given, but I ſaw the Fox immediately make ſail to windward on the larboard tack, keeping her wind cloſe, and carrying a preſſed ſail.

Q. Was that at the time you hailed the Milford?

A. No.

Q. How long might it be after?

A. It appears to me, upon recollection, to be from five to ſeven minutes; the ſignals were thrown out at the ſame time; the poſition of the Milford brought her up firſt.

Q. Do you recollect you heard what ſervice ſhe was ſent upon?

A. It

A. It was the language of the quarter deck, that ſhe was ſent to the Vice Admiral of the blue.

Q. Did you hear that meſſage delivered?

A. I did not hear it delivered.

Q. Where was the Vice Admiral of the blue at that time, Sir?

A. From two to three points abaft the Victory's weather beam; I ſhould ſuppoſe two miles up to windward.

It being four o'clock, the Court adjourned, till ten o'clock tomorrow morning.

TWENTY-FOURTH DAY, WEDNESDAY, FEBRUARY 3d.

At ten o'clock this day, the members being aſſembled, and the Priſoner brought in, the evidence of Capt. Faulkner was continued.

Admiral Keppel. Did you obſerve the Formidable's fore top ſail unbent in the afternoon? A. I did.

Q. How long was it ſo? A. Near four hours.

Q. Did you obſerve any other damages in that ſhip?

A. The Formidable had all her maſts and yards in their places, none ſhot away, when I ſaw her.

Q. Did you ever underſtand, I had given up my deſign of re-attacking the enemy that afternoon?

A. Quite otherwiſe in my opinion, you did not give it up, you did mean to re-attack.

Q. Did you obſerve any effort on board the Formidable, to obey the ſignal, after the Fox went to her?

A. I never did obſerve any effort made to obey the ſignal by the Formidable, either before the Fox went to her or afterwards.

Q. Did you, during the afternoon, at any time ſee the ſignal for the line of battle repeated on board the Formidable?

A. I did not; I ſaw it repeated on board the Arethuſa, who was then on the Fox's lee bow, near her.

Q. At the time you obſerved the Formidable in the afternoon, was ſhe ſo well up, as to enable you to diſcern any of her lee ports diſtinctly from one another?

A. I looked at the Formidable ſeveral times, in the courſe of the afternoon, with my glaſs, and could have counted her guns, if I had been aſked to have done it, at any time.

Q. In the evening of the 27th, what ſail did I eſtabliſh for the night?

A. Two treble reefed topſails, fore and main topſails, foreſail,

foresail, mizen and mizen stay sail, and mizen topsail, handed at the usual time, before the day closed.

Q. Were the distinguishing lights kept burning all night

A. I gave orders that every socket in each light should have a candle in it; it had been the custom to burn three, but that night there were four burning in each light. We carried an exceeding good light at the bowsprit end; I caused it to be looked at several times.

Q. Was there any encrease of sail during the night?

A. None; no alteration.

Q. Did you observe the French fleet bear away and go off in the night?

A. I did not; between ten and eleven o'clock it was reported to me that a rocket had been thrown into the air, upon which I came out of Admiral Campbell's cabbin, and their lights appeared in the same position they did before; I was on the Victory's quarter deck four or five times during the middle watch, and still saw lights in different places to leeward.

Q. In the morning of the 28th, what part of the French fleet were seen?

A. I never saw or heard of more than three sail under our lee, the northernmost of which I took to be a large line of battle ship, the southernmost a large frigate, and a smaller frigate between, nearly at equal distances from each other.

Q. Did I send any ships to chace them?

A. The signal was made for the Prince George, Bienfaisant, and Elizabeth, to chace to the N. E. they bore then from us rather to the northward.

Q. Was it not soon after discovered that the Prince George and Elizabeth were two much damaged to chace?

A. The Prince George and Elizabeth hailed the Victory, and accounted to the Admiral the reason of their not carrying more sail; I think the Prince George complained of her foremast, and the Elizabeth of her topmast?

Q. If I had chaced with the fleet, was there any probability of coming up with the French fleet before they reached the port of Brest, wind and weather as it was, and the ships crippled as they were?

A. Not the smallest; if there had, I am sure the Admiral would have pursued.

Q. When the French fleet brought to with their heads to the northward, how many ships made the signal for setting up rigging?

A. I was

A. I did not particularly count them, but I should ſuppoſe, from ten to fifteen, at leaſt.

Q. You have heard all the articles of the charge, therefore ſtate to the Court any inſtance, if you ſaw or know of any ſuch, in which I negligently performed my duty, or any part of it, on the 27th and 28th of July.

A. I cannot ſtate to this Court any inſtance wherein the Admiral did not conduct himſelf like a great and able ſea officer.

Q. Did not I ſend you with my public diſpatches to London? A. You did ſo.

Q. Do you recollect whether I entruſted you with any other meſſage to the Earl of Sandwich, than my public letter?

A. You did, ſir, and this is it: 'Give my compliments 'to Lord Sandwich, and tell him, I have more to ſay to 'him than I think it proper to put in my public letter; 'and if it is his Lordſhip's pleaſure to ask me any queſ- 'tions, I am ready to wait upon him."---This meſſage I 'repeated twice to Lord Sandwich.

The Proſecutor not chooſing to croſs examine Capt. Faulkner, he was ordered to withdraw.

CAPTAIN GEORGE STOREY, *late Second Lieutenant of the Victory, ſworn.*

Admiral Keppel. Had you the morning watch of the 27th of July? A. I had, Sir.

Q. Do you recollect the ſignal being made for ſeveral ſhips of the Vice Admiral of the Blue's diviſion to chace to windward? A. I do.

Q. Do you recollect at that time how the Vice Admiral of the Blue bore from the Victory?

A. About a point, or a point and a half before the lee-beam.

Q. How far?

A. About four miles.

Q. What ſail was the Formidable under at that time?

A. To the beſt of my recollection, fore-ſail, treble-reefed top-ſails, mizen ſtay-ſail, and mizen.

Q. What ſail had the Victory ſet at the ſame time?

A. Fore-ſail, treble-reefed top-ſails, mizen, and mizen ſtay-ſail.

Q. What watch had you in the evening of the 28th?

A. The firſt watch.

Q. What ſail was the Victory under during your watch?

A. Fore-ſail, treble-reefed fore and main top-ſail; it

was

was the ſame during the greateſt part of the watch, till the mizen maſt was ſecured, when the mizen ſheet was hauled aft, and ſhe ſcarcely ſteered before for want of aft ſails. I judged that to be about ſeven bells.

Q. Was there any other alteration in the ſails during the watch? A. None.

Q. Did your top and other diſtinguiſhing lights burn well?

A. They did, the lanterns being frequently wiped for that purpoſe.

Q. Did you ſee any rockets thrown from the French fleet into the air? A. I did.

Q. At what time? A. Nearly eleven, rather before.

Q. Did you not ſee ſeveral lights to leeward after that?

A. I did ſee ſome flaſhes, which I took for ſquibs alſo.

Ordered to withdraw.

LIEUTENANT CALDER, *of the Victory, called and ſworn.*

Admiral Keppel. Do you recollect the Fox being ſent with a meſſage to the Vice Admiral of the Blue, in the afternoon of the 27th? A. I do.

Q. Can you ſay at what time of the day it was?

A. From the heighth of the ſun, I ſuppoſe it to be between four and five; I did not obſerve, I had not my watch about me.

Q. At two o'clock were not your people at quarters, under the beſt order, obedience, and alertneſs that was poſſible? A. They were ſo.

Ordered to withdraw.

The Honourable G. C. BERKELEY, *late Firſt Lieutenant of the Victory, called and ſworn.*

Admiral Keppel. Do you remember what time of the day the Fox was ſent to the Formidable, on the 27th of July?

A. I came upon deck, and aſked the Quarter-Maſter what o'clock it was; he anſwered me that it was after one bell, or almoſt five o'clock. I was then ſhewed the Fox, ſtanding to windward towards the Formidable, with a meſſage, as I was told, from the Admiral.

Q. What watch had you the night of the 27th?

A. The middle watch.

Q. Did you ſee the lights of the French fleet during your watch?

A. The officer that I relieved ſhewed me the French lights, as he ſaid, about three points abaft the beam; I

kept

kept my eye on them the whole watch; when day-light broke, I plainly perceived two ships where the lights had appeared, and a third a good way astern of them.

Q. What sail was the Victory under during your watch?

A. Treble reefed fore and main top-sail, fore-sail, and mizen; I believe the mizen stay-sail, but am not sure. Her mizen top-sail was taken in, in order to shew the lights in the main-top. She carried her helm a-lee almost the whole watch.

Q. Were the distinguishing lights kept burning, and well, that night?

A. More so than they had been any other night before; I myself went aft, to see that the stern lights were kept in proper order.

Q. Where was you quartered?

A. Upon the middle deck, forward.

Q. Were the men in good order, alert, and obedient, in every matter they were employed about that day?

A. They were particularly so, more so than ever I saw people in any ship I ever sailed in.

Ordered to withdraw.

SIR JACOB WEAK, *Second Lieutenant of the Victory, sworn.*

Admiral Keppel. Do you remember my sending the Fox to the Vice Admiral of the Blue, on the 27th, and at what time was it?

A. I perfectly recollect standing by the Admiral on the starboard side of the quarter deck, when he ordered a frigate to be sent to Sir Hugh Palliser, with orders, that he only waited for him and his division coming down, to renew the action.

Q. Do you recollect the hour the frigate was sent?

A. I cannot speak positively to ten minutes; but it was within ten minutes of five o'clock.

Q. Where was you quartered then?

A. On the fore part of the deck, near the whale.

Q. Were the people under your command orderly, alert, and temperate, and did not they give you great satisfaction? A. Perfectly so.

Ordered to withdraw.

Sir JOHN LINDSAY, *of the Prince George, called and sworn.*

Admiral Keppel. From my first seeing the French fleet, to the time they were brought to action, did they shew any intent of coming to action; or did they avoid it?

A. In the close of the evening on the 23d, they got a-

bout

bout twelve ships formed, and they then stood towards the British fleet, passed to leeward, and next morning we saw them to windward, forming their line. The Admiral made signal for a general chace; if they had had any intention of giving us battle, they would not have suffered us to separate two capital ships from them; and the whole of the time afterwards they carried a pressed sail, to endeavour to avoid us, till the afternoon of the 27th.

Q. Did not I do my utmost as an officer, to endeavour to bring them to action during those days?

A. The Admiral carried as much sail, as to keep the fleet together in a connected body, would admit of. Had he continued in a line of battle, they would in a very short time have got out of sight, by their superiority over us in sailing.

Q. Had you commanded a British fleet, in the situation the French fleet was in with respect to the English, wind and weather as it was, would you have hesitated a moment to lead it down to battle, on account of the wind and weather during any part of the time?

A. I think an officer that had hesitated a moment, would have been unworthy of any command in the British fleet.

Q. Do you remember signal being made early in the morning of the 27th of July, for several ships of the blue division to chace to windward.

A. At this distance of time I cannot recollect with certainty, whether I saw the signal or not, but I remember such signal having been made.

Q. Was there at that time any greater indication of the French fleet designing to come to action, than before on the preceding days? A. None.

Q. Do you recollect the position of the Vice Admiral of the blue, and his division, at the time the signal was made?

A. I cannot say the exact position of the Vice Admiral of the blue's division at that time, but recollect in the morning they were at a considerable distance to leeward.

Q. What, in your judgment, was the object of that signal, or do you think it was a proper one under the circumstances in which it was made?

A. It appeared to me to be with an intention to bring up the leeward ships to close with the center division, and if it had not been made, I apprehend a great part of that division would not have come into action at all.

Q. In your opinion, what would have been the consequence, if I had formed a line of battle in the morning, instead

instead of bringing up the leeward ſhips by ſignal to chace?

A. As the French fleet were continually avoiding us, it might have enabled them to have eſcaped entirely; and I am fully ſatisfied we ſhould not have exchanged ſhot with them that day.

Q. Did you ſee the French fleet getting upon the larboard tack, juſt before the action began?

A. There was a ſqual which intercepted them from our ſight, a ſhort time before the action; when it cleared up I ſaw them in the manœuvre of wearing from one tack to the other.

Q. Was not our getting within reach of the enemy, very ſudden and unexpected from the ſhift of wind?

A. After we got upon the ſtarboard tack, the wind changed two points, which enabled us to lay up for them, as it appeared to me they had tacked their whole fleet together, their rear diviſion was obliged to bear down to get into the wake of their van, to form their line of battle. It was ſo unexpected that I had but juſt got my long boat cut away from the ſide of the ſhip, before the enemy began to fire upon me.

Q. What would have been the conſequence, if I had formed the line of battle at this time?

A. It would have thrown the fleet into ſuch confuſion, that if the enemy had bore down to the attack, it might have been attended with very fatal conſequences.

Q. As I am charged with having advanced on the enemy, and made the ſignal for battle without forming the line, pleaſe to inform the court whether you think I was juſtifiable in doing ſo, under the circumſtances you have ſtated.

A. There was no alternative; you were obliged either to advance and attack the enemy without forming the line of battle, or not have attacked at all. To me it was a very animating ſight; it appeared bold, daring, and becoming the character of a Britiſh officer, who felt his ſuperiority over an enemy he was accuſtomed to beat; and the ſucceſs juſtified the meaſure; it threw the enemy into ſuch confuſion, that I found two French Admirals cloſe together, which could not have been their ſtation in the line of battle, and I fired upon three ſhips abreaſt of each other.

Q. Did I make the ſignal for the line of battle as ſoon as I had wore, after paſſing the rear of the French fleet?

A. As ſoon as the Victory got upon the larboard tack, the ſignal for the line of battle was hoiſted.

Q. I am charged with having ſtood to a great diſtance beyond the enemy's rear, before I wore and ſtood towards them; I muſt beg to know of you, as being the firſt ſhip that wore after me, whether the fact be true?

A. The Admiral wore before any other ſhip was ready to follow, my rigging was ſo much cut, that I was obliged to paſs and wear under his ſtern; it appeared to me to be done with great expedition.

Q. Was the ſignal for battle the moſt proper ſignal I could make, to collect the fleet together?

A. I know of no ſignal ſo proper.

Q. I am charged with having ſhortened ſail, inſtead of advancing towards the enemy; I beg to know if I had a ſufficient force collected, to permit me to advance faſter than I did?

A. I do not remember above three or four ſhips that were cloſe to the Victory; the Vice Admiral of the Red was advancing; but it does not appear to me it was with an adequate force to attack the enemy.

Q. Had I at any time while I ſtood on the larboard tack, a ſufficient force collected to renew the fight?

A. There was not.

Q. Did you ſee the French fleet wear, and begin to form their line on the ſtarboard tack? A. I did.

Q. Had I a ſufficient force collected at this time, to have prevented their forming?

A. If the Red diviſion had advanced, with the ſhips of the Admiral, they muſt have ſuffered a great deal before the others could have come up with the enemy: and therefore it would have been highly improper to have attempted it.

Q. I am charged with having at this time wore, and made ſail directly from the enemy; I deſire you would explain this manœuvre to the court.

A. On the French firſt drawing out their line of battle, they ſtood for the center diviſion; but the Vice Admiral of the Red placing himſelf between the Admiral and the enemy, obliged them to relinquiſh their intention of attacking the fleet; they then bore away, and pointed for ſome of our diſabled ſhips that lay to leeward; a ſhort time after the Admiral made a ſignal for wearing, and bore down under an eaſy ſail to ſupport thoſe ſhips.

Q. Did I make every neceſſary ſignal to form the line and collect the fleet, on the ſtarboard tack?

A. every ſignal I think that could be, was made on the occaſion.

Q. What

Q. What sail did I carry?

A. Topsails, the foresail I am not certain that I saw; the Prince George was only under her topsails.

Q. Was not the sail I carried necessary for the protection of the disabled ships; or could the sail I carried possibly have prevented the Vice Admiral of the Blue from coming into the line?

A. If the Victory had carried less sail, it would have been difficult for the other ships to have kept under command, and preserved their stations in the line of battle; and it does not appear to me that it could prevent any ship from getting into her station.

Court. You said you had your topsails, were they reefed?

A. Yes, double reefed, and the fore top-sail not hoisted.

Q. Did not the easy sail I carried, permit the French fleet to range up under their topsails?

A. It did.

Q. Had this manœuvre, as you have stated it, the least appearance of a flight? A. Not the least.

Q. Could not the French fleet have attacked the British fleet at any time they thought proper?

A. It was in their power to do so all the afternoon.

Q. Did you see the Vice Admiral of the Red leave the rear, to form ahead? A. I did.

Q. At what distance was the Vice Admiral of the Blue from his station at this time, and how did he bear from you?

A. At that time I was not in my station, having placed myself ahead of the Victory, expecting an inverted line would have been formed, on the Vice Admiral of the Red's going ahead; my signal, as well as the Bienfaisant's, were made to resume our proper stations. After I got astern of the Admiral, I observed the Vice Admiral of the Blue, with his division, about two miles to windward, one point abaft upon our weather beam.

Q. What course must the Vice Admiral of the Blue have steered, to come into his station?

A. I should suppose nearly before the wind.

Q. Did any thing appear to you to prevent his bearing down?

A. He had then his fore top-sail unbent, but it appeared to me he was capable of making more sail.

Q. Did he ever make any visible effort to come into the line? A. I saw none.

Q. How long did you observe his fore top-sail to be unbent?

A. It was unbent, I apprehend, about half an hour after three or four o'clock, and continued ſo till the ſun ſet.

Q. Did you ever ſee the repeating ſignal for a line of battle?

A. I never ſaw it on board of the Formidable.

Q. Can you aſſign any reaſon why the French Fleet were not re-attacked that afternoon?

A. I ſuppoſe if the Vice Admiral of the Blue had led down his diviſion into the line of battle, they would have been re-attacked.

Q. You think then I ſhould have renewed the battle that afternoon, if the Vice Admiral of the Blue had led his diviſion down? A. I certainly do.

Q. You have read the fifth article of the charge, in which I am charged with not purſuing the French fleet in the morning of the 28th; I beg you would inform the court of all you know of that matter.

A. The ſignal for the Prince George, Elizabeth, Bienfaiſant, and Duke were made to chace the three ſhips that lay in ſight; the Prince George was ſo much ſhattered in her maſts, that ſhe was not able to make ſail, therefore the ſignals were made to call them in, the whole fleet appearing ſo much crippled, that the chace could not have been continued with any proſpect of ſucceſs.

Q. The fleet being ſo crippled in the action of the 28th, was there any probability of getting up with the French fleet before they had reached the port of Breſt, the wind and weather as it was?

A. There was not the leaſt probability of it. It might have been attended with great danger to have carried a fleet on a lee ſhore, in the ſtate they were.

Q. Your ſituation being very near me, which you preſerved the whole time I was in purſuit of the enemy, and on the day of action, which gave you an opportunity of ſeeing objects nearly in the ſame point of view with myſelf, I beg you will ſtate to the court any inſtance, if you know of any ſuch, in which I negligently performed my duty on the 27th and 28th of July?

A. I can ſtate no ſuch inſtance, becauſe the Admiral fulfilled his duty in every particular. I have had the honour of ſerving under his command in the laſt war, and had ſuch ſtrong proofs of his bravery, ability, and knowledge in his profeſſion, as pointed him out to me, as one of the greateſt ſea officers this country has ever produced. And the whole of his conduct during his late command,

command, was ſuch as further convinced me my former opinion was juſt.

Proſecutor. Sir John Lindſay has mentioned the ſhips having chaced on the morning of the 27th, I would aſk then, if thoſe ſhips had been permitted to ſtay with their Admiral, could they not have gone into action with their Admiral as he did, and if they had done ſo, whether they would not have rendered more ſervice, and ſupported themſelves and their Admiral?

A. Several of the ſhips whoſe ſignals were made, were to leeward of the Vice Admiral, therefore if the ſignal had not been made, they could not have had the advantage of the change of wind, and therefore I apprehend could not have come into action at all.

Q. Can you name any one ſhip that was to leeward, except the Ocean?

A. I cannot tell the name of any ſhip, but they were all aſtern of the Vice Admiral when the ſignal was made, and conſequently could not have received the advantage of the wind, when the ſignal was made.

Q. At the diſtance you was at, can you judge better of the ſituation of the ſhips one from the other, than the Captains of that diviſion themſelves?

A. I certainly cannot.

Q. Do you know the Ocean was the ſternmoſt ſhip, and to leeward of the whole?

A. I cannot recollect at this diſtance of time.

Q. Do you know whether the Ocean fetched in the action with the French Admiral? A. I do.

Q. If the ſternmoſt and leewardmoſt of the ſhips which were not chacing ſhips, did fetch into action with the French Admiral, could not the whole have done the ſame, if they had not chaced, as the Formidable likewiſe did?

A. If the leewardmoſt of the ſhips did fetch into action in the manner it was ſtated, I ſuppoſe they could.

Q. You ſeem to have taken a good deal of notice of the motions of the French after the action; I would aſk if you remember taking notice of the Formidable, immediately after the firing ceaſed?

A. I did not ſee the Formidable till ſhe was paſſing to leeward of the Victory.

Q. You took notice of the firſt of the ſhips that began to draw out of the body of the French fleet, did you obſerve thoſe ſhips firſt haul their wind, and ſteer for two of our ſhips that were laying at a ſhort diſtance aſtern of the remains of the French line?

A. I do not recollect.

Q. Do you know whether the Formidable wore close to the rear of the French line? A. I do not.

Q. If the Admiral had wore himself within gun-shot of the sternmost of the enemy's line, whether you in the Prince George, and all the rest of the ships, could not have done the same?

A. My rigging was so much cut, that I could not wear at the time the Admiral did, and as the other ships did not follow, I suppose they were in the same situation.

Q. Do you not suppose that a ship is capable of wearing with all her masts standing, and sails set, though some of the running rigging may be cut, and damaged, in moderate weather?

A. Without there are braces and bowlings, I do not see how a ship can wear and get upon the wind upon the other tack.

President. Would it have been prudent to have wore, when ships were firing and still engaging?

A. It would have thrown his ship into great confusion; and I should have thought it highly inexpedient, as it must have thrown the ships astern into confusion, besides running a risque of getting foul of each other?

Prosecutor. If those ships that were behind continued to stay in action upon his having done so, would there have been any risque in it?

A. There would have been no risque in it if they had first wore, and got upon the same tack with the enemy, otherwise I think there would have been a great deal.

Q. With regard to the risque, is not the sea wide enough for ten or twelve ships to go clear of one another?

A. I must answer, that in all the manœuvres of a fleet, when they have their sails and rigging in good condition, when they get into confusion, there is a great risque of falling aboard, and it requires the utmost attention of an officer to prevent these accidents happening; and it cannot be supposed that a ship after coming out of action can be worked with that ease, as on other occasions.

Admiral Montague. If they had wore, must not every one of these ships have been raked by the enemy in so doing?

A. They certainly would.

Q. If you had been coming down the French line, and had seen the rearmost of the enemy re-attacked by a ship that passed before you, would not you have run the risque of that short time of wearing, in order to have got upon the same tack, to have continued the engagement?

A. I do not suppose that such a case can exist, for no officer

officer would wear and attack a ſhip ahead of me, while I was ſtanding and looking on, on the other tack; but if I found a ſhip in that ſituation, I certainly would endeavour to wear and attack at any riſque.

Q. If the ſhip that had received moſt damage in her rigging and ſails, or at leaſt as much as any other ſhip, was immediately able to wear when ſhe came out of action, why might not the reſt have done ſo?

A. That muſt depend greatly upon the nature of the damages ſhe had received; if the braces and bowlings are entire, the ſhip may be wore, but I do not ſee how a ſhip can get upon the wind, upon the other tack, without them.

Q. But if a ſhip that had all her braces, except one or two, cut, was enabled by ſingle ropes, or by making uſe of other expedients, to wear, might not any one elſe have done ſo too?

A. I think what one man can do another may.

Q. Were not the laſt ſhips that came out of the action, the Vice Admiral of the blue, and ſome of his diviſion?

A. I believe they were.

Q. Do you know that they ſuffered more than any other equal number of ſhips of the fleet; more in men killed, and damages to the rigging and ſails?

A. I can only ſpeak to my own obſervation; it did not appear to me to be more than other ſhips of the fleet, and I believe the Prince George ſuffered more, or as much as any one of the fleet.

Q. Had the Prince George all her fore ſhrouds, and fore topmaſt ſhrouds, and ſtays, and ſpring ſtays, except one that was to leeward, ſhot away?

A. They were not.

Q. Could the lateſt ſhips that came out of action, and received the moſt damage, be expected to be in a condition to take their ſtations in a cloſe line, ſo ſoon as the other ſhips that had been longer out of action, and leſs engaged?

A. If they were more damaged they certainly could not.

Q. If they were equally, and had come much later out of action? A. They could not.

Q. What do you ſuppoſe might be the Admiral's reaſon, for ordering the Vice Admiral of the red to take the ſtation of the Vice Admiral of the blue; do you ſuppoſe it was becauſe the blue diviſion was juſt come out of action?

A. The reaſon appeared to me, that the red diviſion

had not suffered so much, therefore the Admiral placed those ships betwixt him and the enemy, as no ships were there.

Q. Whilst the red division were laying, by orders, in the station of the Vice Admiral of the blue's division, could any of the ships of that division go into their proper stations, such of them as were able, while that division remained there? A. They could not.

Q. You have noticed the Formidable's laying to windward with her topsail unbent, and that she was a point off the Prince George's beam. Did Sir John set her by compass? A. I did not.

Q. Did Sir John know the reason at that time, that her fore topsail had not been set? A. I do not.

Q. Upon the question relative to chacing, Sir John mentioned the whole fleet being crippled; did the whole fleet appear so to you?

A. I only took a cursory view of them, the greatest part of them appeared so to me.

Q. You was asked, if you thought the Admiral did not intend to renew the engagement that afternoon; do you think that the Admiral intended to renew it so late as seven or eight o'clock in the evening, at the risque of a night engagement, and with the ships that last came out of the engagement, that had been most damaged, in preference to other ships that had been less damaged, and longer out of the engagement?

A. I certainly thought the Admiral intended to renew the engagement, when I got astern into my station in the afternoon. I can give no opinion in regard to seven or eight o'clock, I should not have apprehended that.

Sir John Lindsay ordered to withdraw.

Capt. WINDSOR, *cross examined.*

Admiral Keppel. When you received orders from me to go to the Formidable, was not the Fox obliged to get upon the contrary tack, and could she fetch the Formidable?

A. She was obliged to go upon the contrary tack, and could not fetch the Formidable.

Q. Did you carry a great deal of sail?

A. My courses, and top gallant sails, and main topmast stay sail were set.

Q. You mentioned the Formidable's having cheered the Fox; I shall beg to know if the Formidable returned any cheer, after you returned her cheer?

A. To the best of my recollection, she did.

Court.

Court. When you was upon the larboard tack, going towards the Formidable, did you keep your wind close?

A. The Fox was close hauled.

Q. Do you know what part of the Formidable that cheer was returned from, the last that was given you?

A. As near as I remember, from the forecastle.

Prosecutor. You have never said from what part of the ship the first cheer was given?

A. From the main and mizen shrouds.

Lieut. BERTIE, *of the Fox*, *sworn*.

Admiral Keppel. Do you recollect the Fox being called to the Victory, in the afternoon of the 27th? A. I do.

Q. Do you recollect the message given to Capt. Windsor for the Vice Admiral? A. I do.

Q. What was the purport of it?

A. The Admiral desired Capt. Windsor to go to Sir Hugh Palliser, to let him know, it was his orders, that he came down into the Victory's wake, with his division, and that he waited for them to renew the action.

Q. What hour of the day was this?

A. I did not minute the time, but I think it was between five and six o'clock.

Q. Do you know whether the message was delivered to the Vice Admiral?

A. Capt. Windsor delivered it twice, punctually; not contented with that, he ordered me to repeat it, which I did, twice more; the answer each time was, from the stern gallery, "Sir, I understand you perfectly."

Q. Was the message delivered, to the exact purport of the direction I gave?

A. Word for word, to the best of my recollection.

Q. In standing from the Victory, was you able to fetch the Formidable?

A. No, the Fox was too far upon the weather quarter, we were obliged to tack.

Q. Had you much sail set?

A. A pressed sail, our top gallant sails were out, and I remember we stood by the halliards and lee sheets.

Q. How fast do you think you went, Sir?

A. I do not exactly recollect, but she had very fresh way through the water: I suppose from six to eight knots.

Q. How long might you be going from the Victory to the Formidable?

A. About half an hour.

President.

President. I think you said you heard a voice from the gallery; who did you at that time apprehend it to be.

A. I fancy it was Sir Hugh Pallifer. I am not certain.

Q. Did you observe any manœuvre on board the Formidable after you had received that answer?

A. She manned ship and cheered us.

Q. Did she make any alterations in her sails?

A. I do not recollect.

Q. Was she under sail, or laid to at that time?

A. I think her foretopsail was set, I know there were hands in each top, and upon the topsail yard.

Q. You have mentioned the hour between five and six o'clock. Do you mean when the message was received, or when it was delivered?

A. When it was received.

Ordered to withdraw.

MR. GEO. WM. COURTNEY, *Midshipman of the Fox, called, and sworn.*

Admiral Keppel. Had not you the charge of a prize to bring her into port, taken by the Fox? A. Yes.

Q. Was you on board the Fox when the English and French fleets came to action? A. I was.

Q. Do you remember the Fox being hailed by the Victory, on the 27th in the afternoon? A. I do.

Q. Do you remember at what time it was?

A. Between five and six o'clock.

Q. Do you recollect what orders were given, or message sent to the Vice Admiral?

A. You desired Captain Windsor to go under Sir Hugh Palliser's stern, and inform him, that you only waited for him, and the ships of his squadron, to bear down into your wake, to renew the engagement.

Q. Was that the direction that was delivered to Sir Hugh Palliser? A. Yes.

Q. Do you know if there was any answer given to it?

A. There was; but I do not recollect the words.

Ordered to withdraw.

The HON. FRED. MAITLAND, *Captain of the Elizabeth, called, and sworn.*

President. I am directed by the Court to inform you, that upon your examination, and cross examination, you may answer upon your opinion, and give your answers or not, as you please.

Admiral

Admiral Keppel. On what day was the French fleet first seen?

A. We saw them on board of the Elizabeth the 23d, between eleven and twelve o'clock.

Q. Were they seen the next day, and what was their position, with regard to the English fleet?

A. I think that the Arethusa made the signal for them about six o'clock, and we did not see them till about that time, it was very hazy weather.

Q. Was it in their power to have come down to the English fleet and engaged them?

A. There is no doubt of that, for they were right to windward.

Q. Did I use every means as an officer, from that time to the 27th, to get up with, and bring them to action?

A. To the best of my judgment you did.

Q. Can you remember I made signal to form the line of battle, on the 24th in the afternoon? A. I do.

Q. Had I pursued the French in that order, would it have been possible to have preserved our nearness?

A. No, we continued as near our stations as we could for forming the line.

Q. Did you judge from the motions of the French, on the 24th, 25th, and 26th, that they intended to come to action with the English, or avoid it?

A. To avoid it; they did every thing in their power to avoid coming to action.

Q. If you had commanded a British fleet of the force of the French, in the situation the French were with respect to the English on those days, wind and weather as it then was, should you have hesitated one moment to have gone down and brought them to action, on account of such wind and weather?

A. No, nor any other officer in the fleet, I believe.

Q. What part of the French fleet did you begin action with?

A. About the fifth or sixth ship from the van.

Q. How near was you to the Vice Admiral of the Blue?

A. We began firing about a quarter after twelve; we backed our mizen topsail, and began firing within two or three cables length of the Formidable.

Q. Were there any other ships near you at this time?

A. There were two or three ships astern of us; the Worcester, I know was one, but I cannot say what the others were. Q. At what distance?

A. I was so engaged, I cannot say the exact distance; I looked

I looked forward towards the enemy; Lord Longford paſſed us juſt before we began action.

Q. Do you look upon it the ſhips in the rear were near enough to afford you ſuccour?

A. We found no inconveniency from want of ſuccour; I do not chuſe to ſpeak as to the exact nearneſs, I am certain they were not far aſtern.

Q. Did you paſs the rear of the French before, or after the Vice Admiral of the Blue?

A. At a quarter paſt one we were very cloſe to the Formidable, and a midſhipman upon the poop called out, that there was a ſhip coming on board, on the weather bow; I put the helm to bring the ſhip to the wind, and found when the ſmoke cleared away, I was ſhot up under the Formidable's lee. The Formidable was then engaged with the two laſt ſhips in the French fleet; as I could not fire at them without firing through the Formidable, I was obliged to ſhoot on, and paſs the rear of the French fleet before the Vice Admiral of the Blue.

Q. Did it appear to you at this time when you paſſed the rear of the enemy, being forced away by that ſhip, or at any time before, that the Vice Admiral of the Blue was in danger of being cut off by the enemy?

A. No, I never thought any ſuch thing.

Q. Did you ſee four or five ſhips to leeward of the body of the Engliſh fleet, that the French fleet led up to in the afternoon, whilſt the Engliſh were got upon the ſtarboard tack, ſeeming to be repairing their damages?

A. I ſaw them very plain, while the Britiſh fleet was on the ſtarboard tack in the afternoon, with the ſignal for the line of battle flying, and the French forming on the ſame tack, with the ſame ſail as the Victory was under?

Q. Had it the appearance of a flight?

A. No, very far from it; I had a very different idea of it, and I will give my reaſons why: When the Admiral was ſtanding to the N. W. and firſt made the ſignal for the line of battle, in the afternoon at two o'clock, I was laying with my head towards the enemy, to leeward of the fleet; I had wore and ſtood to the ſouthward, with an intention to weather our line that I might get into my ſtation, as they ſtill ſtood on; juſt as I was putting about to go on the ſame tack as the Admiral was, he made the ſignal to wear, and he wore. Our helm was then a lee, I let the ſhip come round upon her heel without hauling the ſails; I then ſaid to my firſt Lieutenant, tho' the ſignal was out for the line, that as the red diviſion was all aſtern, and the French ſeemed to endeavour to cut off five of our diſabled

ſhips

ships that were to leeward, I thought it my duty to stay where I was, and to lay down to cut off the French van, which we did. About an hour after they bore away, the van of the French was within random shot of us, we were then pretty near our own disabled ships, and two of them made sail, the Courageux and Sandwich. I saw the red division come forward to windward of the Admiral; I tacked, and went under the lee of our line till I passed the Vigilant, and then hauled to in the line. I imagine this will satisfy the Court that we were not running away.

Q. Did you see the French fleet go off in the night?

A. No.

Q. What French ships were seen in the morning of the 28th? A. Three in the morning early.

Q. Was your signal made to chace them? A. Yes.

Q. Do you remember hailing the Victory after the signal was made, telling me of the crippled state of the Elizabeth's fore top mast?

A. I told you both my main and fore top mast were crippled, we had a very large shot that took away near half the diameter of the topmast, and it was sprung from that shot.

Q. If I had chaced towards Ushant, with the ships crippled as they were, was there in your opinion any possibility of getting up with them, before they reached the port of Brest?

A. No. I do not think there was any probability, which is evident from the former part of the chace we had.

Q. You have heard all the articles of the charge read, therefore I desire you will state any instance to the Court, if you know of such, in which I negligently performed my duty, on the 27th and 28th of July?

A. I saw none; I think you did every thing that a gallant and experienced officer could do upon the occasion.

Ordered to withdraw. After which the Court adjourned till ten o'clock to-morrow morning.

TWENTY-FIFTH DAY, THURSDAY, FEB. 4th.

The Court being assembled at ten o'clock this morning, the Prisoner brought in, and audience admitted,

CAPT. LEFOREY, *of the Ocean, was called, and sworn.*

Admiral Keppel. What time did the Victory cross you upon the larboard tack, standing towards the enemy?

A. I be-

A. I believe about half an hour after the Ocean came out of action.

Q. Can you inform the court how many ships were with the Victory, formed ahead and astern of her, as you passed her on the starboard tack?

A. I am certain there were none ahead of her, nor do I recollect there were any astern of her on the same tack.

Q. How soon after you passed her, was your ship in a condition to wear on the larboard tack?

A. I wore to the larboard tack about half after two.

Q. Did you hail the Worcester after you came out of action   A. Yes, I did.

Q. Was you then to the southward or northward of the Victory?

A. I was then to the southward of the Victory. I hailed the Worcester while I was wearing, telling them to get out of the way; they gave me for answer, they should be clear enough.

Q. How far was you from the Victory?

A. I don't well recollect how far I was from the Victory, but I was a mile and a half or two miles from the Formidable; I could not be so far from the Victory, because I met her upon the starboard tack, as I returned upon the larboard tack to take my station.

Q. What tack was the Worcester upon when you hailed her?   A. Upon the starboard tack.

Q. Did you observe the signal for the line of battle flying on board the Victory the whole afternoon?

A. I saw the signal for the line of battle flying on board the Victory, and do not recollect seeing it hauled down.

Q. How soon had you got the Ocean in repair to renew the action?

A. The Ocean was ready when I wore to the larboard tack at half past two.

Q. Was your ship then in a condition to obey the signal for a line of battle?   A. Yes.

Q. What prevented your obeying it?

A. I did not think myself at liberty to go down into the line before the Vice Admiral of the division I belonged to; I waited for him.

Q. What hour was it that the signal was made on board the Victory for your ships to bear down?

A. About seven.

Q. How near was you to the Vice Admiral at that time, and how was you situated with regard to the Formidable?

A. I was

A. I was aftern of the Vice Admiral of the Blue, and upon his lee quarter. I cannot afcertain the diftance, but I was not far from him.

Q. When you bore down in obedience to the fignal that called you, how far from the wind did you lead before you got into your ftation?

A. I bore down into that part of the line, which I thought would give room for the rear of the Admiral's divifion, and the van of the Vice Admiral's divifion to lead betwixt me and the Admiral. I do not recollect how many points I went from the wind, I muft have bore down a pretty large courfe; when I placed myfelf in the line, the Vice Admiral was nearly upon my weather bow.

Q. Can you recollect what fail the Victory was under in the afternoon? A. I do not know.

Q. How many knots did the Ocean go upon a wind?

A. From two knots to two and a half; and after ten, from two to three knots. I was obliged to haul my main tack on board, as about ten o'clock we had fallen down fo much upon the French line.

Q. What fail had you fet till ten o'clock?

A. Fore top-fails and forefail; the fore top-maft being much wounded with a double headed fhot, above the cap, I do not recollect whether I had ftay-fails or not.

Q. How many reefs had you in the topfails?

A. I think they were clofe reefed, the fore topfail I know was, for I reefed it at the beginning of the action, on account of the maft being wounded.

Q. After the Admiral ftood to the fouthward upon the ftarboard tack, in the afternoon, the French fleet being aftern, had it, to you, the appearance of a flight?

A. Not in the leaft.

Q. Did the Vice Admiral of the blue, in the afternoon, repeat any fignal that was made from the Victory?

A. I faw the blue flag at the mizen peak; I do not recollect any other fignal; though I do not infer from thence, that any other fignal was not made, I do not recollect whether they were or not.

Q. Do you recollect whether you faw the blue flag at the mizen peak, before or after your particular fignal was made for battle? A. Before.

Q. Did the Vice Admiral, when he made that fignal, fhew any appearance of bearing down himfelf?

A. I did not fee any.

Q. Did you confider his repetition of this fignal for you to keep in his wake, or bear down to the Victory?

A. I be-

A. I believe I have anſwered that in reply to a former queſtion.

Q. Did you obſerve any ſignal or movement of the Victory, in the afternoon of the 27th of July, that conveyed to you any idea that the Admiral did not intend to renew the action that afternoon? A. I did not.

Q. If the Vice Admiral of the Blue had led down his diviſion at five or ſix o'clock, was there not day light ſufficient to renew the action, and did there appear to you any reaſon that could prevent it?

A. I think if the line of battle had been formed by ſix o'clock, there was day light enough to renew the action; and I do not recollect any other impediment to it.

Q. In the ſituation the Engliſh and French fleets were after the action, when the enemy began to form their line of battle, could the French have brought the Engliſh to battle if they had been diſpoſed ſo to do?

A. I am convinced it was in the power of the French fleet to have attacked us, becauſe after I had placed my ſhip in the line, I ſent for the officers commanding the guns on the different decks, to ſhew them three of the French line laying up for the Ocean, in order that they might be prepared to receive them when they came up.

Q. Was the French fleet ſeen in the morning of the 28th, or had they gone off in the night?

A. I ſaw but three ſail in the morning, one of them nearer to me than the other two.

Q. Of what force did theſe ſhips appear to be?

A. The neareſt I obſerved was a line of battle ſhip, the other two were carrying ſail at a diſtance, and I did not form any judgment of them.

Q. If I had chaced towards Uſhant on the morning of the 28th, in the ſtate the fleet were in, their maſts, yards, and rigging diſabled, the wind and weather as it then was, was there the ſmalleſt probability of coming up with the French fleet, before they reached the port of Breſt?

A. Not the leaſt probability whatever.

Q. What were your bearings, and diſtance from Uſhant at noon, on the 28th?

A. Uſhant E. N. E. ½ E. 23 leagues by reckoning.

Q. Did you ſound?

A. I don't recollect whether we ſounded that day or not, but on the 23d it was eighty-four fathom, foul ſand and broken ſhoals.

Q. You have heard all the articles of the charge, therefore I deſire you would inform the court of any inſtance,

if

if you know or ſaw any ſuch, in which I negligently performed my duty either on the 27th or 28th of July?

A. I know of none. I was convinced at that time as far as my judgment extended, that Admiral Keppel left no means untried to bring the French to action, and continued them afterwards; and I have remained in thoſe ſentiments ever ſince.

Proſecutor. You have deſcribed the Ocean to have been upon the Formidable's weather quarter, when the ſignal was made for chace; you have alſo ſaid the Ocean was upon the lee quarter of the Formidable; what do you mean by fetching up, when you was upon the weather quarter?

A. I did ſay ſo; and I afterwards ſaid, that when the Formidable came into action, the Ocean fetched under her lee bow; I ſaid likewiſe that upon tacking to the ſtarboard tack, the Vice Admiral had weathered me out of gun-ſhot, conſequently when I tacked, I was upon the Formidable's lee quarter, the ſhift of wind enabled me to fetch under her lee bow, my ſtation was upon her quarter, I could not fetch it, but I fetched under her lee bow, and came to action as I deſcribed.

Court. How wide was you upon the Formidable's weather quarter, and how far aſtern, when the ſignal was made for thoſe ſhips to chace to windward?

A. I cannot exactly aſcertain the preciſe diſtance, but I imagine the Vice Admiral of the blue's diviſion might be about three points upon my lee bow, and I think I was full four miles aſtern.

Proſecutor. Four miles aſtern! then were you cloſe to the Victory?

A. I was not cloſe to the Victory, I was to the leeward of her wake, and aſtern of her.

Q. Where was your ſtation upon the larboard tack?

A. On the Vice Admiral's lee quarter.

Q. In the line, where?

A. Does the Admiral mean the line ahead, or the line abreaſt?

Q. The line ahead?

A. Ahead of the Vice Admiral and next to him.

Q. You ſaid, if I recollect right, that you once intended to edge down, in order to get into your ſtation with reſpect to the Vice Admiral of the blue, which was upon the weather quarter, and in the line, the next ſhip ahead of you; if you had continued to do ſo, inſtead of being four miles aſtern, would you not have been in a better ſituation, with reſpect to your own Admiral, for fetching

 up

up further towards the enemy's van after tacking, than by ſtaying where you was?

A. I muſt beg the Vice Admiral to put that queſtion in another way, or elſe to eſtabliſh the fact. He is pleaſed to infer that I ſtaid where I was, which I imagine implies that I was not getting into my ſtation. I do not admit of the fact. I ſaid I hauled my wind upon the ſignal being made for ſhips to chace; as I concluded the intention of that was, to bring the Vice Admiral's diviſion, which was too far to leeward, into the body of the fleet; on which I hauled my wind, but carried all the ſail I could to get into my ſtation. I ſprung my main topmaſt the Sunday morning, which was the occaſion of my being thrown to leeward. I had worked with all the ſail I could carry all night, and in the morning found myſelf where I was. I do not admit my ſtaying there at any rate.

Q. You ſaid you was upon the Formidable's lee bow, when you came into action; what ſhip was next ahead of you? A. The Egmont.

Q. Did you continue to follow the Egmont during the engagement?

A. The diſtance betwixt the Formidable and the Egmont was ſo ſhort, that it was with difficulty I could keep betwixt them to engage, without firing upon them, and I was once very near on board the Egmont.

Q. Did you proceed to keep that diſtance near the Egmont the time you was engaged?

A. I think I have anſwered that in a preceding anſwer, but I will anſwer it more fully in any part the Vice Admiral wiſhes. From the firſt to the laſt I had difficulty even in keeping clear of the Egmont; but I was nearer to the Egmont the whole time of action, than to the Vice Admiral, which was about an hour and an half.

Q. Did you at no time get up to the Victory during the action, or do you remember the circumſtance of being near the Thunderer when ſhe fired into the Egmont?

A. The action had begun before I got into it, and the ſmoke was ſo thick, and the firing ſo inceſſant, that I do not recollect to have ſeen any ſhip ahead, during the time I was engaged, but the Egmont.

Q. Do you remember the circumſtance of the Formidable's backing her mizen topſail before the action began, you being to leeward, to let you ſhoot ahead, that you might fire clear of her?

A. Upon coming up, I found the Formidable with her mizen topſail aback, but I do not know when ſhe backed it.

Q. After

Q. After you got ahead of her, did you observe that she continued it aback, to let the ships astern close with her?

A. I observed when I got ahead, that the Formidable did continue her mizen topsail aback, but I will not ascribe it to the motives that possibly the Vice Admiral may ascribe it to. The smoke was so thick that I could see but two or three ships astern of the Vice Admiral I attributed it to an act of gallantry, to give the French as much of his fire as he could, as they passed along. I mention this because it was my ideas at the time, and I believe I mentioned it to my officers.

Q. Was not the Ocean consequently increasing her distance from the Formidable, if she did not back her mizen topsail?

A. The Ocean's mizen topsail was backed more than once during that time, and her topsails lowered down during the action, on account of her shooting too near the Egmont.

Court. You have said when you came out of action, you believed yourself to be about three cable's length from the Formidable; did you believe at any one time, of the action, you was at a greater distance from her?

A. I was not in general so far; and in that distance it must be included, what I was to leeward; I was not that distance in a straight line.

Prosecutor. The signal being made for seven ships of my division, to chace, as it is now come out; how many ships of my division remained, whose signals were not made to chace?

Admiral Keppel. I must beg leave to refer to Mr. Leforey's evidence to confirm that.

Admiral Montague. This seems not a Court Martial, but a point between two lawyers, whether it shall or shall not be so.

Court withdrew and resolved, "That it is admitted, the Prosecutor has no right, upon the cross examination of witnesses, to enter into new matter, but must confine himself to such facts as have fallen from the witness on his first examination by the Prisoner. And therefore that the question now standing upon the minutes, is not a proper one."

Prosecutor. Can you give any account how the Formidable was situated at that time?

Court observed, That they could not see it had any tendency to prove the charge, by enquiring where the Ocean or Formidable was; what the Court wanted to know

 was

was, whether the Admiral had done his duty, neglected it, or run away. Keep to the point, the charge.

Prosecutor. The whole transaction must be mentioned, in order for the Court to form a judgment.

Court. This evidence is not called to support the charge, he is called in defence of the prisoner. There ought not to be fresh matter sought for to support the charge.

Q. What did the Formidable after she came out of action?

A. I cannot tell. From the time I came out of action to the time I wore, which was about four o'clock, I was so engaged in repairing the damages of my ship, that I did not attend to the Formidable at all.

Q. Then you cannot say whether she wore and laid her head again to the enemy?

A. No, I did not see her, I went on.

Q. Did the Ocean proceed on upon that tack, till she passed the Victory on the contrary tack?

A. I have already answered that in reply to a question put by the Admiral; the Ocean proceeded on upon the starboard tack, till she passed the Victory upon the larboard tack.

Q. When did the Ocean see the signal for the line, on board the Victory?

A. When we passed upon different tacks.

Q. Where was the Ocean's proper station, when that signal was made on the larboard tack?

A. A-head of the Foudroyant, whose station was a-head of the Victory.

Q. Were not the ships of the Vice Admiral of the blue division, the last that came out of the engagement?

A. They were.

Q. Did they all proceed to pass the Victory whilst they were upon the starboard tack?

A. I do not recollect; the Worcester was the only ship of that division that I have any knowledge of after I came out of action.

Q. You don't know that the Formidable wore, and laid her head towards the enemy again; do you that she was the last ship that got the length of the Admiral, and that at the moment when the signal was made?

A. I have said that I saw nothing of the motions of the Formidable, from the time I came out of action till the time I joined her on the starboard tack.

Q. If on passing the rear of the enemy you had found the Admiral and the other ships tacking or advancing to the enemy's rear, could you not in the Ocean have wore

and

and laid your ſhip on the other tack alſo, or was the condition of your ſhip ſuch, that you could not have done it?

A. I do not underſtand the queſtion; the Vice Admiral ſays, "If in paſſing the rear I had found the Admiral on the other tack." I could not find him on the other tack when he was not out of action.---- Mr. Preſident, it appears to me, that this queſtion is like trying me.

Proſecutor. By no means.

Evidence. I have no objection to anſwering any thing. I will anſwer that queſtion.---- I wore the Ocean as ſoon as I thought her in condition to wear; after reeffing my fore topſail to ſave my fore topmaſt which was wounded with a double headed ſhot. I believe it might be about an hour before I wore; but I was rather delayed in coming upon the other tack, by putting my ſhip in a condition to tack inſtead of wearing, in order to recover my ſtation, being too far to leeward before.

Admiral Arbuthnot. There is a very great diſtinction betwixt putting a ſhip in a condition to wear, and being in a condition inſtantly to go into a line of battle. Was your ſhip at the inſtant you wore, in a condition to go into a line of battle, and keep your line?

A. I do not recollect any impediment to the Ocean's going into action immediately after her wearing.

Proſecutor. When you came out of action, was you ſo much diſabled, if you had been along ſide of any ſhip that you might have engaged with upon the ſame tack, as not to have maintained the engagement, but have been obliged to quit her?

A. I do not think the Ocean received ſo much damage the time of the engagement, as two frigates would in half an hour, if they had been along ſide of each other; and I cannot ſay we were well warmed, in regard to the damage ſuſtained in her hull and among the men; I don't mean the running rigging.

Q. Could you have immediately re-engaged, if you had met another ſhip, to have run along ſide of her?

A. Yes, independent of manœuvering the ſhip in regard to ſails and rigging.

Admiral Montague. Then we are to underſtand that the ſails and rigging were in ſuch a condition that you could not immediately renew it? A. We could not.

Admiral Arbuthnot. I aſk you, as an experienced gallant officer; if I had the honour of being intruſted with the command of a ſquadron, and you had a pendant under me; if, when we came to action, you had diſcovered in me any

 omiſſion

omiſſion, which mankind are liable to, in the heat of action, ſhould you not have thought it your duty, for the honour of the colours, (ſetting my honour out of the queſtion) to have informed me what your opinion was, and how you could have remedied it, either by yourſelf or officers?

A. Moſt certainly, if my information could have tended to remedy any omiſſion or miſtake.

Q. Is it not equally proper for a ſuperior, to obſerve to an inferior, when he ſees any error, as it is for an inferior to go to his ſuperior with his obſervations?

A. I think the obligation is reciprocal.

Q. You have mentioned that in the evening, when you went down into your ſtation in the line, you obſerved three of the enemy's ſhips laying up with the Ocean; were theſe ſhips, the leading ſhips of the enemy's line, or were they then forming?

A. I think they were not forming, neither were they the leading ſhips of the French line; I think the line was further formed before I got down.

Q. What hour was it when you made the obſervation of three of the enemy's ſhips laying up for the Ocean?

A. It was betwixt ſeven and eight, I believe.

Q. Was our fleet then upon a wind?

A. I think they were, or nearly ſo.

Q. In the ſituation theſe ſhips were, looking up for the Ocean, does not that mark them to have been very much aſtern, near your wake, or were they far to leeward?

A. The ſhips that did look up for the Ocean were not far to leeward, but the diſtance of time is ſo great, that I do not recollect how our fleet was going at that time, whether before the wind, or whether two or three points from it, for that makes a wide difference in regard to the queſtion.

Q. You have ſaid that you was doubtful whether theſe three ſhips were the leading ſhips or not; can you recollect where the leading ſhips were, in reſpect to their bearings from the Ocean, at that time?

A. I don't recollect, they paſſed us very faſt, playing with us, as it were, ſome with their mizen topſails aback, and ſome ſhifting their main topſails at times.

Q. The time you are ſpeaking of, is about ſeven or eight o'clock, is it not, after you got down?

A. It was after I was in the line, while the enemy were forming their line.

Q. How far was you from the neareſt of the three French ſhips you diſcovered on the 28th in the morning?

A. They

A. They were about three miles from the Ocean, abaft our lee beam.

Q. Was the Formidable ahead or astern of the Ocean, between the Admiral and your ship, or how otherwise?

A. The Formidable was then ahead of the Ocean, bearing down athwart her.

Capt. LEFOREY *ordered to withdraw.*

Capt. BRADBY, *of the Plato Fire-ship, called and sworn.*

Admiral Keppel. Was not you Captain of a fire-ship on the 27th; Did you see the French and English fleets engage on the 27th of July? A. Yes.

Q. Did you pass to leeward out of gun-shot?

A. Yes.

Q. Do you recollect what time you passed the French fleet in the fire ship you commanded on the 27th of July?

A. About twenty minutes past one.

Q. Did you observe the Vice Admiral of the blue at that time. A. Yes.

Q. Where was he in respect to the bearings from your ship?

A. I was a little before his lee beam.

Q. At what distance? A. About random shot.

Q. Did you observe the Vice Admiral of the blue in danger of being cut off by the French? A. I did not.

Q. At the time you passed the rear of the French, had the Vice Admiral ceased firing? A. No, Sir.

Q. How soon after that?

A. He was engaging the last ship.

Q. At this time did you observe which way the Victory was standing? A. On the larboard tack.

Q. Did you observe whether she had the signal out for battle, or was it hauled down?

A. I did not observe the signal for battle on board the Victory, I saw it on board the Queen.

Q. At the time the Vice Admiral of the blue came out of the action, what ships of his division did you observe astern or ahead of him, and how near?

A. The Worcester was immediately astern; there were two ships ahead, but I do not recollect what they were; the Worcester appeared to be close.

Q. When you first saw the Victory upon the larboard tack, how far was she from you?

A. About a mile.

Ordered to withdraw.

A. Certainly to near the enemy, becauſe at four o'clock, when the carpenter reported to me he had ſtopped the leaks, I ordered the maſter to put the ſhip about; indeed ſhe miſſed ſtays, and I immediately ordered her to be wore, and the mizen to be hauled up. We wore within random ſhot of the van of the French fleet, hauled the wind, and joined the Admiral.

Q. Did you obſerve the Victory at this time, with any ſignals flying?

A. At four I obſerved the ſignal for the fleet to bear down into the Admiral's wake; at a quarter before five, I obſerved the ſignal for the line of battle ahead, a cable's length aſunder; at half paſt five, for three particular ſhips being out of their ſtations; at a quarter before ſix, for ſeveral of the Vice Admiral of the Blue's ſquadron to make more ſail.

Q. Did you obſerve, in paſſing the Victory, what ſail ſhe had ſet in the afternoon?

A. I endeavoured to head the Victory to get into my ſtation; had a little heat with the maſter when we drew near, and I told him to keep to windward, for we wore ſo near I was afraid of being aboard each other. I paſſed the Victory to leeward, ſo cloſe as to receive orders from Admiral Campbell perſonally, to wear immediately; ſhe then ſeemed to have her foreſail and reefed topſails.

Q. Did thoſe ſignals and motions of the Victory convey any idea to you, that the Admiral did not intend to renew the action on the 27th of July?

A. By no means! No.

Q. Had theſe manœuvres, as you have ſtated them, the leaſt appearance of a flight from the enemy?

A. No; I have anſwered that when he was bearing down to them, as I paſſed him.

Q. Did you ſee any partof the French fleet on the morning of the 28th? A. I ſaw three ſail.

Q. Did you make any obſervation what ſize they were?

A. One was nearer than the other two, I took her for a capital ſhip, and the others frigates.

Q. How far diſtant were they from you?

A. Four or five miles.

Q. Was the Sandwich in condition to chace, if the general ſignal had been made to chace?

A. Not in a condition to chace.

Q. Did you obſerve any particular ſhips ſignals made to chace on board the Victory?

A. I did not, for as they ran away, I had done with my minutes.

Q. Then

Q. Then do you think we should have come up with them if we had chaced, before they reached the port of Brest? A. No.

Q. You have heard all the Articles of the charge read, therefore I desire you will state to the court any instance, if you saw or know of any such, in which I negligently performed my duty on the 27th or 28th of July?

A. I cannot state any, for I saw none.

Ordered to withdraw.

Hon. Capt. Walsingham, *of the Thunderer, called and sworn.*

Admiral Keppel. From the 24th, after seeing the French fleet, till the moment they were brought to action, did they shew any intention of coming to action, or to avoid it?

A. They never shewed any such intention, they always avoided it.

Q. Did I do my utmost to bring them to action, from the 24th to the day we brought them to battle?

A. It was impossible you could do more.

Q. Had you commanded a British fleet, in the same situation the French fleet were in with respect to the English fleet, on the 24th, 25th, 26th and 27th of July, wind and weather as it then was, would you have hesitated one moment to have gone down and brought them to action, notwithstanding such wind and weather?

A. Not a moment.

Q. What would have been the consequence if I had formed a line of battle on the 27th, instead of pursuing as I did?

A. You never could have brought them to action.

Q. What part of the French fleet did you begin action with?

A. I believe about eleven or twelve sail from the rear.

Q. Did it appear to you to have been the intention of the French fleet to have gone off to windward, if they could have passed the English fleet far enough to windward?

A. I have not the least doubt but they would have gone off, if they could.

Q. I am charged with advancing towards the enemy, without forming and making signal for the line; you will inform the court whether, in your opinion, I was justifiable in attacking the French without forming the line?

A. You

A. You certainly was, for you had no other chance of bringing them to action.

Q. I am charged with having ſtood at a great diſtance from the enemy after I had paſſed them, before I wore and ſtood to them again; I deſire to know whether you obſerved the Victory did ſo?

A. I think you wore very ſoon; I had ſome difficulty in following you.

Q. Did I make the ſignal for the line of battle as ſoon as I had wore? A. You did.

Q. Was that the propereſt ſignal I could make to collect my ſhips? A. Without all manner of doubt.

Q. I am charged with ſhortening ſail, I deſire to know if I had a ſufficient force collected, to have allowed of my advancing faſter than I did? A. No.

Q. Had I at any time while I ſtood on the larboard tack, a ſufficient force to renew the fight? A. No.

Q. Did you ſee the French fleet wear, and begin to form their line on the ſtarboard tack? A. I did.

Q. Did I make every neceſſary ſignal to form the line, and collect the fleet on the ſtarboard tack?

A. Every ſignal you could poſſibly make.

Q. What ſail did I carry?

A. Reefed topſails and foreſail.

Q. Did you obſerve any ſhips diſabled to leeward?

A. I did.

Q. Did you obſerve me lead down to the wind for their protection?

A. I obſerved to my officers, that I thought you bore down for that purpoſe.

Q. Was not the ſail I carried neceſſary for the protection of the diſabled ſhips, and could ſuch ſail as I did carry poſſibly have prevented the Vice Admiral of the Blue from coming down?

A. As far as it appeared to me it could not.

Q. Did not the ſail I carried permit the French to range up with me under their topſails?

A. It did for ſome time, and very often their mizen topſails aback.

Q. What ſail had you ſet in the Thunderer, to keep in your ſtation?

A. Topſails in general, ſometimes mizen top-ſail aback, one reef in my topſail.

Q. Was not what you had for a main top-ſail, a mizen topſail? A. It was.

Q. By this degree of ſail, although the French were aſtern and to leeward of the Victory, had it the leaſt appearance of a flight? A. No,

A. No, Sir; I hear the queſtion with indignation, and reprobate the idea.

Q. Did you ſee the Vice Admiral of the Red leave the rear to form ahead? A. I did.

Q. Was there not day light at that time ſufficient to have attacked the French fleet, and do you not believe I ſhould have done it, if the Vice Admiral of the Blue had immediately bore away, and taken his ſtation in the rear of the fleet; the period of time I mean is, when the Red diviſion left the ſtern?

A. There certainly was time enough, and as a ſtrong proof that I ſuppoſed it was your intention to renew the fight that night, my hands were never from their quarters.

Q. Can you aſſign any reaſon why I did not attack the French fleet whilſt there was day light enough for action?

A. There was one that appeared to me, and that was, that you was not ſupported by the Vice Admiral of the Blue.

Q. Did the Vice Admiral of the Blue ever make any viſible effort to come into the line?

A. Not that I ſaw.

Q. How long did you obſerve the Formidable's fore top-ſail unbent? I believe four or five hours.

Q. Did you obſerve any other defect in that ſhip?

A. None.

Q. Did you ſee any ſignal from that ſhip that ſhe was in diſtreſs on the 27th in the afternoon, as the inſtructions direct? A. No.

Q. Did you obſerve any ſhips to be called by the Vice Admiral of the Blue, for the purpoſe of chaining his flag, by which I ſhould have known his diſtreſs, as the 25th article allows to do? A. No.

Q. Did you ever ſee the Vice Admiral of the Blue repeat the ſignal for the line of battle, during the afternoon? A. No.

Q. What ſail did you carry during the night of the 27th, to keep in your ſtation?

A. Top-ſails, main ſtay-ſail, and ſometimes when I ſhot ahead, my mizen ſtay-ſail aback.

Q. Did you ſee the French fleet in the morning?

A. No.

Q. Did you ſee any French ſhips?

A. I ſaw three ſail to leeward, and I ſaw your ſignal thrown out to chace them.

Q. If I had made a general ſignal that day to chace to leeward, in the ſtate the fleet were in after the action of the

the 27th, with the wind and weather as it then was; was there the least probability of coming up with the French fleet, before they reached the port of Brest?

A. I should think not, because the French ships in general were not much damaged in their masts and rigging, and the three ships that we saw the next morning, set their top-gallant studding sails.

Q. You have heard all the articles of the charge, therefore I desire you will state to the court any instance, if you saw any such, in which I negligently performed my duty on the 27th or 28th of July.

A. I know of none; I have been always taught to look to you as an officer of ability, courage, and good conduct; I never had the honour to serve under you before, but prejudiced as I was in my good opinion of you, your conduct exceeded my most sanguine expectations.

Admiral Keppel. Please to explain the Thunderer's firing into the Egmont.

A. The misfortune of the Thunderer's firing into the Egmont happened, and was occasioned by the Egmont's shooting upon her starboard quarter, while I was in the heat of action; upon the smoke clearing away, the first notice I had of her was seeing her jib beam abreast of my main shrouds, I immediately sent orders to cease firing. The time it happened was during the action, and after I saw her upon my quarter there was not one gun fired. At the same time I must take notice, there was not the least confusion in the Thunderer's ships company.

Court adjourned, till to-morrow morning, ten o'clock.

TWENTY-SIXTH DAY, FRIDAY, FEBRUARY 5th.

At ten o'clock this day, the members being assembled, the Evidence of the Hon. Captain Walsingham was continued.

Prosecuter. Was the ship you first began to engage with, ahead or astern of the French Admiral?

A. Upon my word I cannot say what ship I fired at first; I believe the Bretagne; many ships fired at me whose shot fell short, and I received the fire of two or three ships that went through my sails, before I fired at all; I did not fire till I thought myself within point blank shot.

Q. During the time you was engaged, was you ahead or astern of the Victory the whole time, or part of it.

A. I was

A. I was aſtern of the Sandwich, who was aſtern of the Prince George, the ſhip next the Victory; and there I remained the whole action.

Q. Was you in the evening while the fleet was forming, ahead of the Victory?

A. Upon the ſtarboard tack, I was ahead of the Victory.

Q. At what time did the red diviſion quit the ſtation of the Vice Admiral of the Blue?

A. To the beſt of my knowledge before five o'clock.

Q. After you was out of action did you obſerve the Vice Admiral of the Blue, and the ſhips of his diviſion?

A. As ſoon as I was out of action I paid particular attention to the Formidable, and upon my word it was a ſatisfactory manner in which I ſaw her engaged, much to the honour of her officers and ſhip's company; I particularly expreſſed it I believe to the Vice Admiral himſelf.

Ordered to withdraw.

CAPTAIN CLEMENTS, *of the Vengeance, called and ſworn.*

Admiral Keppel. Did the enemy, from the firſt moment you ſaw them, to the day I brought them to action, ſhew any deſign of coming to battle? A. No.

Q. Did I do my utmoſt endeavours as an officer, to bring them to action, during thoſe days?

A. Yes, I think you did.

Q. Had you commanded a Britiſh fleet, in the ſituation the French fleet were in with reſpect to the Engliſh, during the 24th, 25th, 26th and 27th of July, wind and weather as it then was, would you have heſitated one moment to have gone down immediately, and brought them to action? A. No.

Q. I am charged with having advanced towards the enemy, and made the ſignal for battle without forming my line; what in your judgment would have been the conſequence, if I had formed my line, without making in the morning the ſignal to chace?

A. I do not think that they would have been brought to action, and the conſequence of that would have been, loſing ſight of them.

Q. I am charged with not having advanced to attack the enemy, and to have paſſed on the larboard tack; had I at any time a ſufficient force collected, to prevent their forming their line upon the ſtarboard tack? A. No.

Q. Was

Q. Was not the signal for the line kept flying all that time to collect them?

A. I was so busily employed in my own ship, that I saw no signal for a line on the larboard tack.

Q. I am charged with having wore again, and made sail directly from the enemy; was not my wearing at that time, and standing to the southward, a necessary manœuvre for the protection of the disabled ships, and collecting my ships to renew the battle?

A. It was, and well executed by the Victory.

Q. Had it then the appearance of a flight?

A. No, the reverse, it was nearing the enemy.

Q. Did you see the French fleet in the morning of the 28th. A. No.

Q. If I had chaced towards Ushant in the state the fleet was in, from the action of the 27th, with the wind and weather as it was; was there the least probability of coming up with the enemy? A. No.

Q. You have heard all the articles of the charge read; therefore, I desire you will state to the court any instance, if you know of any such, in which I negligently performed any part of my duty on either of those days?

A. I have long had the honour to know Admiral Keppel, I ever had the highest esteem for him as a man of honour and most gallant officer. I do not conceive that it was possible for more to be done by the Admiral, than was done during the time the French fleet were in sight.

CAPTAIN MACBRIDE, *of the Bienfaisant, called and sworn.*

Admiral Keppel. What day was the French fleet first seen?

A. Between one and two o'clock on the 23d, I made the signal for seeing them at N. E.

Q. Did you see them next morning?

A. The weather did not open before seven in the morning, when I saw them in the N. W. and made signal for so doing.

Q. Did not you come on board the Victory in a small boat, and report to me the observations you had made?

A. I did.

Q. What were those observations?

A. As I observed before, the weather was exceedingly close when I discovered them. I saw a few sail considerably to leeward of the rest, one with the foretopmast gone, the other with a main topsail close reefed down upon the cap, by which I conceived she was much crippled, and the weather was then so close, that I imagined the Ad-

miral

miral might not see them, which was the reason of my going down to him?

Q. Was the body of the French fleet to windward of those ships?

A. They were from N. W. to W. and by N. the three sail I spoke of bore about N. and by W. and were at least three leagues to leeward of the body of the fleet; there were two other sail still further to leeward than those, and bore N. N. E.

Q. What orders did you receive from me in consequence of the report you made?

A. The Admiral observed that those two ships must be cut off, or the enemy must come down to support them, and by that means perhaps be brought to action, and therefore I had your orders to hail Capt. Maitland of the Elizabeth, who was about a mile on his starboard bow, and to acquaint him it was the Admiral's orders that we should chace and attack those two ships, and notwithstanding he should make the signal for the line of battle, we were to proceed, unless he made the signal for the cruizers in that quarter to return.

Q. Was the weather at that time such as to prevent the ships from fighting their lower deck guns, under the degree of sail your ship could fight under?

A. Any ship could have fought her lower deck guns, when I could go in a six-oar cutter, and row as fast as those ships sailed.

Q. Did not the signal I made for carrying the fleet to the northward, cause a separation of two of their capital ships from their fleet? A. It did.

Q. If the French fleet had intended battle, was not the prevention of such separation a great temptation to bring it on? A. Most assuredly.

Q. Did the enemy at any time, from the 24th to the 27th at noon, shew any inclination of coming to battle?

A. They never did.

Q. Did I do my utmost endeavours as an officer to bring them to action during those days?

A. You did, by carrying as much sail as the slow sailing ships would admit of so as to keep up with you.

Q. Had you been senior officer of a squadron of ships, and had been in sight of a fleet as the French were, and in the same situation as they were in with respect to the English, on the 24th, 25th, and 26th of July, would you have hesitated to lead it down to battle, on account of the wind and weather during those days?

 A. If

A. If I had, I ſhould never deſerve to have ſet my foot in this country again.

Q. After the Victory had paſſed the French fleet in action, and had wore and was ſtanding to the enemy again, did it appear to you at that time, or at any time while the Victory was upon the larboard tack, that I had ſufficient force to attack them immediately on wearing, or to interrupt their forming their line again, upon the ſtarboard tack? A. You had not.

Q. Did you ſee the ſignal for the line, whilſt on the larboard tack, flying on board the Victory?

A. I did: In a few minutes after the ſignal for battle was hauled down, the ſignal for the line was made.

Q. Did you ſee the Formidable paſs the Victory on the ſtarboard tack, while I was advancing on the larboard tack, after the ſignal for the line was flying?

A. I did.

Q. Had ſhe paſſed the Victory aſtern of her, before I made the ſignal to wear to the ſouthward?

A. She had.

Q. Did you ſee the ſignal for the line of battle on board the Victory, when ſhe was afterwards on the ſtarboard tack? A. I did.

Q. Had the fleet, ſtanding to the ſouthward with ſuch ſail ſet, with the ſignal for battle flying, the leaſt appearance of a flight?

A. It had not; it ſtruck me as a manœuvre of a judicious officer, and the only one in his power, at that time, to collect a fleet which was in great diſorder from the damages they had received, and to cover five ſhips to leeward of the enemy, who were advancing towards them, and I imputed it to that, that the French were prevented from advancing at a very critical time upon the Engliſh fleet.

Q. Could not the French have attacked the Britiſh fleet while they were ſtanding to the ſouthward, if they had choſe to have done it?

A. If good fortune had placed us in their ſituation, and they in ours, if we had not demoliſhed them, we ought to have been ſent to the Juſtitia ballaſt lighter.

Q. Did you obſerve the ſignals that were made on board the Victory in the afternoon, and repeated by the repeating frigate? A. I did.

Q. Did the ſignals or motions of the Victory, at any time, convey to you an idea that the Admiral did not intend to renew the fight in the afternoon?

A. Not in the leaſt degree.

Q. Can

Q. Can you assign any reason why they were not re-attacked in the afternoon?

A. I apprehend you waited for the Vice Admiral of the Blue to come down, agreeable to the signal then flying.

Q. Did the Vice Admiral of the Blue bear down?

A. He did not.

Q. If the Vice Admiral of the Blue had bore down as late as six o'clock, do you not think there was still day-light enough to have fallen upon the enemy, attacked them, and obliged them to have surrendered or run away before night?

A. We certainly should have known whether they meant to stand their ground, or run away. There was still two hours, or two hours and a half of good day-light, after six o'clock, at that time of the year.

Q. At what distance was the Vice Admiral of the Blue from his station, at five o'clock, and how did he bear from you?

A. Between two and three miles, I believe, upon my weather beam.

Q. Did any thing appear to you to prevent his bearing down?

A. His fore top-sail only was unbent; any other reasons I can be no judge of.

Q. How long was it unbent?

A. Upwards of four hours.

Q. Did he ever make any visible effort to come into the line?

A. None that I could observe.

Q. At the close of the evening, how far was the van of the French fleet drawn up with the English fleet?

A. The French van was abreast of me, two miles to leeward.

Q. What sail did you carry during the night of the 27th, to keep in your station?

A. Close reefed top-sails, sometimes the main top-sail a-back, and sometimes the mizen top-sail. We had but just steerage way to come into our station in the line of battle.

Q. Did you observe any motions of the French in the night of the 27th?

A. It was very dark, there was not the least appearance of a signal light till between ten and eleven o'clock, when a rocket was thrown up in the centre, and repeated from van to rear, after which every half hour, and sometimes oftener, a light was shewed, and a flash like that of a musket repeated and continued till day-break.

 Q. Did

Q. Did you see the French fleet, or any part of them, on the 28th in the morning?

A. Three sail early in the morning.

Q. What did you take them to be?

A. The ship a-breast of me was a line of battle ship, the centre one was a frigate, but what the other was I know not.

Q. How far was she from you?

A. About four miles.

Q. Was there any ship between you and these ships?

A. None.

Q. Was any signal made to chace them?

A. Yes, mine among others, and I did chace that ship till I was called in, so that if any other had been between me and her, I must have seen her.

Q. If I had continued the chace, would it have been of any effect?

A. I cannot say what would have been the consequence.

Q. Did you gain upon the ship you chaced?

A. It was so short a time we chaced, I cannot tell; but as no other ship could back us, I must have been left with three, and that was the reason, I supposed, the Admiral called me in.

Q. If I had followed you in the state the fleet was in, after the action of the 27th, and the wind and weather as it was, was there the least probability of coming up with the French fleet, before they reached the port of Brest?

A. I do not think that if our fleet had not been damaged, they could have come up with a fleet that had so great a start a-head, in the space we had to chace them. I was only twenty-one leagues from Ushant, and half our ships were a twelvemonth foul, and some two years. I believe the French ships were clean.

Q. You have heard all the articles of the charge read, therefore I desire you to state to the Court any instance, if you know of any, in which I negligently performed any part of my duty on the 27th or 28th of July?

A. I know of none; and I think Admiral Keppel realized every good opinion as an officer this country formed of him, on those days.

Prosecutor. Have you not frequently passed from ship to ship in such cutters, when it was not possible for ships to open their lower deck ports.

A. Perhaps I might; but that was not one of these days.

Q. Had it not blown very strong that night, when one of the French ships carried away her fore topmast?

A. It

A. It had blowed ſtrong, but I don't apprehend that's a proof of its carrying her foretopmaſt away?

Q. In what part of the line did you engage?

A. I engaged between the Valiant and Foudroyant.

Q. Was that a-head of the Victory? A. Yes.

Q. Whether, in that ſituation, the Duke, or any other ſhip fired into her?

A. No, the Duke did not fire into me, but the French did. I was ſummoned here by the Vice Admiral, as well as Admiral Keppel; if he had any queſtions to aſk reſpecting the priſoner, he might have done it: as the priſoner is now upon his defence the Vice Admiral has no right to aſk me any queſtions.

Admiral Keppel. I have ſaid before, I have no objection to the accuſer's picking up any thing he can, any where.

Q. When the Admiral was ſtanding upon the larboard tack, towards the enemy, did any of thoſe ſhips that were ſtationed in the line ahead of you get into their ſtation before the Admiral wore again.

A. They did not; becauſe I ought to have been ahead of him myſelf; but as the Vice Admiral of the Blue was ſtanding upon the ſtarboard tack, leaving the Victory, I thought the line was going to be inverted, which kept me aſtern of the Victory, as well as the Prince George.

Ordered to withdraw.

The Hon. LEVISON GOWER, *of the Valiant, called and ſworn.*

Admiral Keppel. Did you ſee the French fleet on the morning of the 24th of July? A. Yes.

Q. Were they to windward or leeward?

A. At firſt they were nearly ahead, but the wind came to the northward, and we wide off, and they came upon our weather bow; that is to ſay, the body of them; for they were two broad upon the lee bow, and another a little upon the lee beam.

Q. Did I order a general chace? A. Yes.

Q. Was the weather ſuch, that the Valiant carried her whole topſails upon a wind?

A. When I firſt made ſail, I had a reef in my topſails, ſoon after I let that reef out, and then I had topgallant ſtay ſails ſet, with all the reefs out, and topgallant ſails upon them, and had ſo till the ſignal was made to call me in?

Q. Did I make the ſignal for the line of battle in the afternoon of the 24th.

A. Yes, between ſix and ſeven o'clock.

Q. Did I purſue the French fleet from this time to the hour I brought them to action?

A. Yes, they went off as faſt as they poſſibly could, and we uſed every endeavour to get up with them.

Q. Had you commanded a Britiſh fleet, and in the ſituation the French fleet were, in reſpect to the Engliſh, wind and weather as it then was, would you have heſitated to lead them down to battle on eithet of thoſe days?

A. I certainly ſhould not have heſitated.

Q. Was there on the 27th in the morning any greater indication of the French fleet coming to action, than on the preceding days? A. No.

Q. What in your opinion would have been the conſequence, if I had formed a line of battle early in the morning of the 27th, inſtead of bringing up the leewardmoſt ſhips, by ſignal, to chace?

A. They would have got clear off without being brought to action.

Q. As I am charged with having ſtood a great diſtance beyond the enemy before I wore, and ſtood to them again, I deſire to know of you if that fact is true?

A. 'Tis not true, for you wore in ten minutes after the firing ceaſed from the Victory.

Q. Did I make the ſignal for the line of battle as ſoon as I had wore?

A. Immediately after having paſſed me, the ſignal for the line of battle was up at a cable's length aſunder.

Q. Was that the moſt proper ſignal I could make to collect the fleet together?

A. I think ſo.

Q. I am charged with ſhortening ſail, inſtead of advancing to the enemy; I deſire to know if I had ſufficient force collected, that admitted my advancing ſooner than I did?

A. The Valiant was not in a condition to make ſail for near an hour after I came out of the fire, and there were ſeveral ſhips aſtern of the Valiant, that is, aſtern of you a great way.

Q. Did you ſee the French wear and begin to form their line on the ſtarboard tack?

A. Juſt as I made ſail upon the larboard tack, to ſtand after the Victory, I was told they were wearing; I then ſaw two or three had got round upon the ſtarboard tack, and others ſeemed to be wearing before the wind upon the larboard tack; they all came up upon the ſtarboard tack together.

Q. Had

Q. Had I a sufficient force collected at this time, to prevent their forming their line?

A. No, you had not.

Q. I am charged with having wore at this time, and making sail directly from the enemy; was it so, or not?

A. The enemy soon edged away towards four or five of our disabled ships that were to the southward; and soon after I wore; you kept away for these disabled ships, to prevent their being cut off, I suppose, and steered about parallel with the French fleet in general, sometimes a little more up, and sometimes a little more away. I soon got down into my station ahead of the Admiral, and when I was ahead of him, he went right down for the disabled ships.

Q. Did I make every necessary signal to form the line, and collect the fleet on the starboard tack?

A. Yes, I think so; the signal for the line of battle was made, and the signal for ships to get into their stations.

Q. Do you remember what sail the Victory carried?

A. Double reefed topsails and foresail.

Q. Did not that permit the headmost of the French fleet to range up with me, under their topsails?

A. In general they had thier topsails set with staysails, they once set their foresails for a little while.

Q. What sail did the Valiant carry when ahead of the Victory upon the starboard tack?

A. Double reefed topsails, the fore tack on board; sometimes the fore sheet hauled aft, and sometimes the mizen topsail aback.

Q. Had this manœuvre, and the manœuvres of the English Admiral, as you have stated them, the appearance of a flight?

A. Not in the smallest degree.

Q. Could not the French have attacked the English fleet, if they had thought proper, during the afternoon?

A. Certainly.

Q What distance was the Vice Admiral of the blue from his station at five o'clock?

A. Broad upon the weather quarter, between two and an half and three points,

Q. Did any thing appear to you, to prevent his bearing down?

A. The Formidable's fore topsail was unbent; but I saw no masts or yards gone.

Q. How long was it unbent?

A. I never saw it bent, it might have been betwixt

 eight

eight and nine o'clock, but after I gave over all thoughts of action, I did not trouble my head about him.

Q. Can you recollect whether he made any signal to inform the Admiral that he was disabled?

A. Not that I saw.

Q. Did you ever see him repeat the signal for the line of battle in the afternoon of the 27th?

A. I never saw any signal on board that afternoon, but the blue flag at the mizen peak; there were pendants in the evening flying.

Q. Can you assign any reason why the French fleet were not re-attacked?

A. 'Till about four o'clock very few ships were with the Victory, and from that time till night, the rear division did not come down into their station, with an exception to two or three, till pretty late.

Q. Do you think I should have renewed the battle that afternoon, if the Vice Admiral of the blue had led his division down?

A. From your very spirited behaviour before that, I have not a doubt of it.

Q. What sail did you carry to keep in your station during the night?

A. Reefed topsails, and foretopmast stay sails; sometimes mizen topsails a-back.

Q. Did you see the French fleet on the morning of the 28th? A. Only three sail.

Q. If I had chaced towards Ushant in the condition the fleet were, from the action of the 27th, wind and weather as it then was, was there the smallest probability of my coming up with the French fleet before they got into Brest? A. I think not.

Q. Your station being near me during the pursuit of the enemy, and on the day of action, which gave you an opportunity of observing my conduct, and seeing objects in the same point of view with myself; I desire you would state to the court any instance, if you know of any such, in which I negligently performed my duty, or any part of it, on either of those days?

A. I do not know of any such instance; I then thought, and I now think, that your whole conduct was spirited, able, and brave.

Prosecutor. You have stated when the Admiral wore and stood towards the enemy, that he had not a force collected sufficient to advance with during the time the enemy were forming their line; I wish to know the reason why

why the Admiral's own division, and such other ships as had joined him, could not support him?

A. At that time there were five sail to the southward of me, one of which was a three decked ship, I believe the Sandwich; the Elizabeth I passed, and she was standing upon the starboard tack, and there was another ship abaft my lee beam, standing with her head to the southward, and two of the Red Division, one with her fore topsail yard gone, and another disabled, I do not know what was the matter, it was the Berwick, and my own ship, between two and three miles from the Admiral at that time. Our fore top-sail yard was gone, and the crotchet yard, our mainsail was shot all to shivers, the foot of the foresail cut in two, the mizen yard gone, and almost every brace, bowling and stay in the ship cut to pieces. I mention this as a reason for my being there.

Q. By your account there were two of the Red division among them, besides those I mentioned?

A. These two ships belonging to the Red division was to windward, but separated from the others a long way.

Q. Was the rest of the Red division, as far as appeared to you, in a condition of immediately re-attacking the French, if it had been thought proper to have done so.

A. I was not near enough to see their condition; they were a long way upon my weather bow; the Admiral was upon my lee bow, and they were to windward of him a good deal.

Q. Was not the Red division far the least damaged of any of the three divisions, first out of action, and consequently the soonest fit to renew the action?

A. They were soonest out of action; how much they had of it I cannot tell.

Q. In answer to a former question you have said, that the Admiral had not a sufficient force with him to re-attack; do you attribute that to the ships not being able to close with him?

A. I do. I judge from my own situation, I could not.

Q. From your account of the position of our ships and their situation, are we to understand that the British fleet were so much beaten, that they were not capable of renewing the attack as soon as the French wore?

A. About four o'clock a great many ships were got into their stations, I suppose they were cut in the manner as my ship was. They joined as soon as they put to rights, and after that I do not know of any reason we might not have renewed it, except what I mentioned before, Sir, that your division did not come down. I don't pretend to ſay why they did not come down; but they did not come down.

Q. At the time you ſpeak of, about four o'clock, was not the Red diviſion formed in the ſtation of the Vice Admiral of the Blue?

A. Yes, but they ſoon after went ahead.

Q. Was not the Vice-Admiral of the Blue, and part of his ſhips, the laſt that came out of action?

A. Certainly.

Q. Can you ſuppoſe any other reaſon for the Admiral's ordering down the Red diviſion into the ſtation of the Blue; but becauſe they were juſt come out of action, and by appearance to him, they were not capable of taking their proper ſtation at that time?

A. I do not exactly know when the Vice Admiral of the Red got there; I only ſaw him there at four o'clock, at which time you muſt have been a great while out of action.

Q. You have mentioned obſerving three of the French ſhips drawing out of their body; did you obſerve them firſt ſhape their courſe directly towards the Formidable, who was laying with her head towards the enemy, and within gun ſhot of their rear?

A. Not having occaſion to look for the Formidable, I did not ſee her at that time. I was in the Admiral's diviſion, and therefore had no buſineſs to look after her; I do not exactly know when they drew out, but it was not more than a quarter of an hour after I was told of it, that I ſaw them bear away, ſteering two or three points from the wind.

Q. Did you obſerve them range up, under the lee of one of our ſhips that was left a great way aſtern, and fire upon her, and afterwards point towards the cripplied ſhips you mentioned?

A. I never ſaw them fire after they paſſed upon a different tack.

Q. Were not theſe the ſhips that afterwards became the leading ſhips of the enemy's new-formed line of battle?

A. I think they were; but theſe were intervals that I never looked at them.

Q. If theſe ſhips had been attacked, would not that have prevented them forming a new line.

A. Theſe ſhips could not have been attacked, without attacking the whole of the French fleet.

Q. Do you attribute the ſhips being left ſo far aſtern as the Vengeance and Formidable, were then three miles, to to the Victory's out sailing them, or that they were not able to carry sail to keep up with him?

A. I did not say the Formidable was astern, I said broad upon the weather quarter, that is rather abaft my beam two or three points.

Q. Did you set her by compass?

A. No; I saw her as I walked the quarter deck, therefore she must be broad upon the weather quarter.

Q. What time did the Red division quit the rear?

A. To the best of my recollection between four and five o'clock, it was a little after I got into my station.

Q. You say you did not see the signal for the line of battle on board the Formidable, but that you saw a blue flag at the mizen peak; can you recollect, so as to speak with precision, whether that blue flag was not hoisted under the signal for the line of battle?

A. I am very sure it was not when I saw it; did not look at the Formidable from first to last; but when I saw that blue flag, there was no other over it.

Ordered to withdraw.

CAPT. JERVOIS, *of the Foudroyant, called, and sworn.*

Admiral Keppel. From my first seeing the French fleet, to my coming to action, did they shew any intention of coming to action; or did they always avoid it?

A. On the 23d of July, in the afternoon, when we first discovered them, I thought they shewed a disposition to come to action; but on the 24th in the morning, as soon as they discovered the force of the English fleet, I am convinced they never did design to give battle?

Q. Did I do my utmost endeavour, as an officer, to bring them to action, from the morning of the 24th, till they were brought to action?

A. You used your most unremitting endeavours.

Q. Had you commanded a British fleet in the situation the French was with respect to that under my command, wind and weather as it then was, would you have hesitated one moment to have gone down and attacked them?

A. Any officer that would have hesitated a moment, would have been unworthy of commanding the English fleet.

Q. Do you remember the signal being made early on the 27th for several ships of the Vice Admiral of the Blue's division, to chace to windward? A. I do.

Q. Was there at that time any greater indication of the French fleet coming to action, than on the preceding days?

A. There was not,

Q. What

Q. What was the position of the Vice Admiral of the Blue, and his division, at this time?

A. To the best of my recollection he was in the Formidable, upon the lee bow of the Foudroyant, about three miles distant.

Q. What in your judgment was the object of that signal; and do you think it a proper one, under such other circumstances in which it was made, required?

A. I made reflections upon the signal at the time, that it was made to combine the division of the Vice Admiral of the Blue with the centre.

Q. What would have been the consequence, in your opinion, if I had made the signal for forming the line in the morning, instead of the signal to chace?

A. I am clearly of opinion that you would not have brought them to action that day.

Q. Did you see the French fleet upon the larboard tack, just before the action began? A. Yes, I did.

Q. Was not our getting within reach of the enemy very sudden and unexpected, from the shift of wind?

A. That was the principal event which produced it.

Q. What would have been the consequence if I had formed a line at this time?

A. You would have given time to the enemy to have got into some form, when they were in disorder, and subjected your fleet to have been attacked before they could have got into order, or given the French an opportunity of escaping out of gun-shot, if they had been disposed so to do.

Q. As I am charged with having advanced towards the enemy, and made signal for battle without forming the line, I desire you would inform the Court, if in your opinion, I was justifiable in doing so under the circumstances you have described?

A. To the best of my judgment and ability you certainly was.

Q. I am charged with standing a great way from the enemy, before I stood towards them again; I desire to know if the fact be true? A. 'Tis not true.

Q. Did I make the signal for the line of battle as soon as I had wore? A. You did.

Q. Was that the properest signal I could make to collect the fleet?

A. It was the properest signal, and the signal that required the most prompt obedience to.

Q. I am charged with having shortened sail, instead of advancing towards the enemy; I desire you will inform the

the Court whether I had sufficient force collected to admit my advancing faster than I did?

A. To the best of my recollection when I approached you on the larboard tack, about three o'clock, you had not above two or three ships near you of your division, and the rest were at a considerable distance astern.

Q. While I stood upon the larboard tack, had I at any time a sufficient force to renew the action?

A. You had not.

Q. Did you see the Formidable at any time on the larboard tack, after the action? A. I did not.

Q. Did you see the French fleet wear, and begin to form their line on the starboard tack? A. I did.

Q. Had I at this time a sufficient force to have prevented their forming?

A. You had not the means in any sort.

Q. I am charged at this time with having wore, and led the British fleet directly from the enemy; I desire you will explain this matter to the court.

A. It appeared to me at this time, that you had two great objects in view, in wearing the British fleet, and standing as you did; the first and principal was to cover the four or five disabled ships in the S. S. E. and the other, to give opportunity to the Vice Admiral of the Blue, and his division, to form in their station astern of the Admiral.

Q. Did I make every necessary signal to form the line, and collect the fleet on the starboard tack?

A. I do not know a signal that you could have made, that was not made to produce that effect.

Q. What sail did I carry during the afternoon?

A. To the best of my recollection you carried double reefed topsails, and foresail, the former much shot, as well as the foresail.

Q. Was not the sail I carried necessary for protection of the disabled ships; and could the sail I carried possibly prevent the Vice Admiral of the Blue from coming into the line?

A. The sail you carried appeared to me well proportioned to effect both these purposes.

Q. Did it not permit the French fleet to range up with me under their topsails? A. It did.

Q. Had this evolution, or my subsequent conduct, as you have stated it, the least appearance of a flight?

A. Very much otherwise.

Q. Could not the French fleet have attacked the British fleet at any time they thought proper, during that afternoon? A. They

A. They could, and at the ſame time, with great advantage.

Q. Where was your ſtation, in the line of battle a-head, on the ſtarboard tack?

A. The next ſhip aſtern of the Victory.

Q. When did you get into it, and did you preſerve it?

A. I got into it as you wore, at or about three o'clock, and I never got out of it till four o'clock next morning.

Q. Did you think I intended to renew the battle; if I could have formed the line?

A. I did, and as a proof, I turned my people up, thinking it adviſeable to ſay a few animating words to them.

Q. What prevented my forming the line?

A. The Vice Admiral of the Blue not leading his diviſion down into his ſtation.

Q. Was he in a ſituation to have led his diviſion down into the line? A. He appeared ſo to me.

Q. Did any thing appear to you to prevent his bearing down:

A. There was nothing viſible to me, but his fore topſail unbent.

Q. How long did you obſerve it unbent?

A. It appeared to me to be near four hours unbent. I cannot ſpeak poſitively.

Preſident. Could he have got into his ſtation under his main topſail and foreſail?

A. I believe he could.

Q. How many points might he keep away?

A. Four at leaſt, he appeared to me to be always in the wind's eye in his ſtation.

Q. Did the Vice Admiral of the Blue ever make any ſignal, to inform the Admiral that he was diſabled?

A. I never ſaw any ſuch ſignal.

Q. Did you ever ſee him repeat the ſignal for a line of battle? A. I did not.

Q. What ſail did you carry in the night, to keep your ſtation?

A. Double reefed topſails pretty much ſhot, ſo as to make it dangerous to hoiſt them tight, and I don't recollect any other ſail but a ſtayſail bent for a mizen.

Q. Was your mizen maſt damaged?

A. The mizen maſt head had been ſhot away juſt under the cap; the mizen yard had been ſhot away, that is divided.

Q. Have you got the bearings and diſtance of Uſhant on the 28th at noon?

A. On

A. On the 28th Ushant bore N. 79 degrees, E. 29 leagues by log that day.

Q. Your station being near me during the pursuit of the enemy, and after the action, gave you an opportunity of observing my conduct, and seeing objects nearly in the same point of view; I desire you will acquaint the Court of any instance, if you saw or know of such, in which I negligently performed my duty on the 27th or 28th of July.

A. With great respect to you, and great deference to the Court, I hope I shall be indulged with having that question put by the Court.

It was then put by the Court.

A. I think myself bound, by the oath I have taken, to answer that question. I believe it consonant to the general practice of all sea Court-martials. I cannot boast a long acquaintance with Admiral Keppel, I never served under him before; but am happy in this opportunity to declare to this Court, and to all the world, that during the whole time the English fleet were in sight of the French fleet, he displayed the greatest naval skill and ability, and the boldest enterprize on the 27th of July, which, with the promptitude and obedience of Vice Admiral Sir Robert Harland, will be subjects of my admiration and imitation as long as I live.

Court. Please to relate the chief defects of your ship, after coming out of action?

A. The mainmast had one shot very near through the head of it, and was wounded in several other places; many shot in the foremast, bowsprit, and fore topmast; the mizen mast was totally disabled, which was of very ill consequence to the Foudroyant; every rope of the running rigging was, I believe, cut; the shrouds in a great measure disabled; there was no brace nor bowling left in the ship; halliards, fore stays, and spring stays much shot and damaged; our sails in general much shattered.

It being four o'clock, the Court adjourned till ten o'clock to-morrow morning.

TWENTY-SEVENTH DAY, SATURDAY, FEBRUARY 6th.

At ten o'clock this morning the Court being met, according to adjournment, the evidence of Capt. JARVOIS *was continued.*

Admiral Keppel. Did you see the French fleet on the 28th of July?

A. I did not see the French fleet; I saw three sail, and afterwards the man at the mast-head said he could just discern eight sail, pointing to the S. E.

Q. Did you see any signal made to chace the three French ships?

A. To the best of my recollection I saw signal made for three sail to chace to N. E.

Q. Was your ship in a condition to chace? A No.

Q. If I had chaced towards Ushant, with the fleet in the condition it was, was there the least probability of coming up with the fleet of France, before they reached the port of Brest?

A. There certainly was not the smallest probability.

Prosecutor. I think you said, that in the morning of the 27th the French shewed no more inclination to come to battle than on the preceding day; why then was it necessary to take seven of the Vice Admiral's division from him that day, more than on any other.

A. I have stated in my answer to that question, that the Vice Admiral and his division were full three miles to leeward of the Foudroyant, which would give them three miles from the Victory; they were under a very easy sail, the Foudroyant with her mainsail up, still going further to leeward, though in my opinion it was necessary for them to get to windward. I would add, that in my judgment at the time, the Vice Admiral accepted the meaning of the signal, for he made considerably more sail soon after the signal, than he had made before.

Q. If my memory don't deceive me, Capt. Jarvois said yesterday, that I was upon the Foudroyant's lee bow, three miles distant; now you convey an idea of my being wholly to leeward full three miles?

A. I did not mean to quibble about an idea; when I said upon the lee bow, I did not say upon what point of the lee bow. It is a very common expression, when a ship is to leeward, to say she is upon the lee bow; but to the best of my judgment, I was very near the beam of the Victory, abaft the beam. I did not mean to take any advantage of you, Sir, or to say any thing in favour of the Admiral, that was not true; this I say, that the Formidable was much further to leeward, than her station in the order of sailing prescribed; that is positively my meaning.

Q. If these ships had been permitted to remain with their proper Admiral, might not they have gone into action with him, as he did, in the same place where the Commander in Chief began the action?

A. I can give no reason why they could not; but I am not a competent judge of that part of the fleet. I must beg leave to state to the Court the cause which brought the

the fleet into action, and which did not exist when those ships were directed to chace. To make it as short as possible, I would wish to fix it as the fact really was: by a material shift of wind in our favour, the action was brought on, which shift of wind did not happen till four or five hours after those ships began chacing.

Q. Will you take the trouble to look at your own ship's log-book, which is upon the table, and inform the Court how much the wind shifted between six and ten o'clock that morning.

A. It shifted one point at eight o'clock, and between eight and twelve four points.

Q. Which way?

A. In our favour. It stands S. W. at eight o'clock, and at twelve W. S. W. but I do not suppose a very great stress will be laid to a shift of wind while we were in action, a great deal was due to an evolution which was performed successfully, and much beyond my expectation, which was tacking the fleet together.

Q. Can your memory stand to wind and courses?

A. I only speak to the ships looking up, I govern myself by the ship; I cannot speak to any point, nor will I. I don't speak to points of wind or compass, nor do I refresh my memory by log-books, for I have looked at none, nor do I pay any regard to it, though I would not have a log book altered by any means. When officers look to their Commander in chief, they don't note down every shift of wind. I have no minutes, I bring nothing but the charge, I have no other thing to guide me.

Prosecutor. Look at your log book.

Admiral Montague. Captain Jervois has said he does not want his log book, and why it should be crammed down his throat I cannot think!

A. I will not be bound by any thing that the prosecutor repeats out of that book, or that is read by his orders, which I am very ready to obey in every thing that is proper.

Prosecutor. You call the shift four points?

A. I did, but it is a mistake; I took this for W. N. W: I beg your pardon.

Admiral Montague. Shut the log-book up, and let us hear no more of the log-book for God's sake, let us come to matter of fact, from your own knowledge.

Prosecutor. Did you ever know or hear of a commander of the third post, having his ships drafted from him, and he left unsupported by his own fleet to go into action.

 A. Before

A. Before I anſwer that queſtion, I muſt beg leave to obſerve to the Court, that I don't know that ſuch a fact exiſted on the 27th of July; I certainly never heard of ſuch a thing; but I would have it underſtood that I do not admit the fact to be ſo.

Q. I would ask Capt. Jervois, whether the French fleet's manœuvre of wearing, did not contribute to bring them to leeward, and enable the Britiſh fleet to lay up better with them than if they had not wore.

A. I beg you will fix the period of wearing.

Proſecutor. If they wore at any time before coming to action?

A. I ſaw them between eight and ten o'clock in the operation of wearing, and by that wearing they did fall to leeward, that muſt certainly have brought them further to leeward than they were before, there is no doubt of that.

Court. Could you fetch the van of their fleet, when you came into action?

A. No, Sir, not in the ſhip I commanded; a very conſiderable part of their fleet paſſed to windward. There were various other circumſtances that intervened between our wearing and coming to action.

Proſecutor. You ſaid there was another manœuvre of the French fleet?

A. That manœuvre was much obſcured by thick weather; I am not certain, but I think it was an attempt to perform the ſame evolution that they had obſerved ſucceſsfully performed by our fleet, to paſs us to windward, and avoid action; and I obſerved that many of their ſhips ſtayed, and others miſſed ſtays, and to that I attribute the confuſion that afterwards appeared in their fleet.

Judge Advocate. Muſt this be entered in the minutes?

Admiral Montague. Put it down, it will ſwell the volume, and make it ſell the better.

Q. In a diſtant view of a fleet that was changing their poſition from one tack to another, does it not naturally give an appearance of confuſion, though they may be performing ther evolutions ſucceſſively in each other's wake?

A. It certainly does; but the diſorder in part of the centre and rear continued from that time, till the centre and rear paſſed me during the whole time I was in action with them. I don't ſpeak of the confuſion, but of the diſorder, for they were in no line.

Q. Can you ſay, while the French were upon the ſtarboard tack, after having wore, as you have deſcribed, whether they did not lead large?

A. I

A. I cannot ſpeak otherwiſe to that fact, than by deſcribing them; in the act of wearing they were leading large, but I do not recollect they were leading large, after the whole had wore.

Q. You ſaid, if the fleet had formed in a line of battle, an action could not have been brought on that day; I would aſk whether, if the Admiral had made the ſignal as appointed by the eleventh article of his additional fighting inſtructions, for the ſhips neareſt to the enemy to form into a line, without regard to the general form delivered, and the reſt as they came up to form in a line, in like manner, and other ſhips following to form likewiſe, in that caſe would not our ſhips have engaged with more advantage than in the promiſcuous manner they did?

Preſident. Captain Jervois has ſaid before, that they would not have engaged at all.

Court. Read the eleventh article of Admiral Keppel's fighting inſtructions.

The eleventh article was read, as follows:

"If at any time while the whole fleet is in chace, I would have a certain number of ſhips neareſt the enemy form in a line, I will hoiſt a red flag with a white croſs; when I would have five ſhips draw out in a line, I will fire one gun; when ſeven a-head, two guns; then theſe ſhips are to form the line, without any regard to diſtance or ſeniority. The headmoſt are to lead, and the rearmoſt to follow."

Preſident. I think you ſaid, that no other manœuvre than what the Admiral made uſe of, could have brought on the action that day?

A. I admit that I ſaid ſo.

Proſecutor. If the rear diviſion of the Vice Admiral of the Blue had remained together, and engaged in like manner in a connected body with their own Admiral, as the other diviſions of the fleet did, would they not have ſupported each other, done more execution, and ſuffered leſs than by engaging ſingly and ſeparate?

Preſident. I do not underſtand they were together.

Evidence. They never were together. I do not know that any part of the queſtion did really exiſt.

Q. Were not the ſhips that chaced by ſignal ſeparated at a diſtance from their Admiral, and at diſtances from each other, different to what they were before?

A. I did not know it exiſted at the time the Vice Admiral came into action; but I am not a competent judge of that part of the fleet, for I was very attentive to my own buſineſs.

Q. After the action was over, and the Admiral laid his head to the northward again, what was the situation of the red division at that time, before the Admiral wore the second time?

A. I shall beg leave to answer the first part of the question. In the Foudroyant I weathered a great part of the Vice Admiral of the Red's division; I was very covetous of the wind; disabled as I was, that advantage alone could carry me into action: When I approached him upon his larboard tack, I observed the Vice Admiral of the Blue upon my weather beam, but I cannot say to the point; they were to windward of me.

Q. Were they a-head withal?

A. I cannot recollect; they were of me, but not of the Victory, I believe; the distance of time is great, and I cannot recollect. There are some things that struck me forcibly, which I remember, but others that my memory does not go to. I little expected to have been called upon this occasion, or I might have remembered them better.

Q. You said, whilst the Admiral was standing towards the enemy upon the larboard tack, he never had a force collected proper to advance with; that none of the ships took their stations in the line of battle; that the Admiral made the properest signal for collecting the ships, which was the signal for the line. I would ask, if while the Admiral was upon that tack, he ever made a signal for ships to windward to bear down, or for any particular ships to make more sail, or the signal for observing any particular ships out of their stations?

A. There is one part of the answer, I believe, does not come exactly out in my evidence yesterday; that is, none of the ships did take their stations in the line. I am sure I did not, nor was it in my power. I did not see those signals made that the Vice Admiral alludes to, while we were upon the larboard tack. If they had been made, very few ships could have obeyed them, from the situation they were in. I could not.

Q. Whilst we were upon the larboard tack, I mean?

A. The signal for the line is established by my former evidence.

Q. You said you saw the French wear and stand to the southward; I would ask if you can give any reason why it was necessary to require an exact line of battle for our advancing and attacking the enemy at that time, more than it was requisite in the morning?

A. The Admiral is charged with not collecting his ships together, and not keeping so near the enemy as to renew

renew the battle ſo ſoon as it was proper. In reply I ſay, the Admiral made the ſignal for the line of battle, which in my judgment was the propereſt ſignal for calling the ſhips together, for the purpoſe of renewing the action, and leading them down to the enemy, at that time, diſabled as we were.

Proſecutor. That is not an anſwer to my queſtion.

Evidence. 'Tis the anſwer I chuſe to give.

Q. Am I to underſtand of your account in general, that the condition of the fleet was ſuch, that it was not proper to face the enemy, and renew the attack, when they ſtood towards us, before they formed their new line?

A. The fact is, that we did face the enemy, Sir.

Q. But whilſt they were facing us, did not we wear and ſtand the other way?

A. We wore certainly. I have deſcribed the object of that yeſterday.

Q. Did you ever know or hear of an Engliſh fleet turning their ſtern to an enemy of equal or inferior force, that enemy ſtanding towards them immediately after engaging with them?

A. I deny the fact in all its extent and meaning.

Q. You ſaid that whilſt the Engliſh fleet was ſtanding to the ſouthward, the French fleet could have fetched and attacked them; in that caſe, was not our ſterns towards them?

A. I anſwered that queſtion yeſterday, and explained the whole manœuvre to the Admiral; I ſhall not explain it any further, unleſs the Court requires it.

Q. In an anſwer you made yeſterday, you mentioned the fleet edging down to four or five crippled ſhips; were thoſe ſhips of my diviſion?

A. I did not at that time know what ſhips they were.

Q. Do you now know whether they were of my diviſion or not?

A. I ſaw two of them join the center diviſion; what the other ſhips were I do not know.

Q. I think you ſaid yeſterday, that the ſail the Admiral carried during the afternoon, would not prevent the Vice Admiral of the blue from keeping up with him, and getting into his ſtation; I would aſk you, whether from your own knowledge, the diſtance you have deſcribed the Formidable to be at, three miles from the Victory, was occaſioned by any neglect on board the Formidable to keep up with her.

A. I have not ſtated any ſuch thing as you deſcribe in

either the firſt or laſt part of your queſtion; there was no diſtance ſpecified in the afternoon.

Q. Did you know the particular condition of the Formidable at that time?

A. I never pretended to any ſuch knowledge.

Q. When did the red diviſion quit the ſtation of the Vice Admiral of the blue?

A. The red diviſion was never in it in the afternoon.

Q. Were not they nearly ſo?

A. No, by no manner of means.

Q. Whereabout was you during the afternoon, ahead or aſtern of the Admiral?

A. Aſtern of the Victory, in my ſtation, which I never quitted a moment.

Q. Did not the red diviſion form aſtern of the Admiral?

A. I believe you underſtand it by order of the Admiral; I know nothing of any order; part of the red diviſion did, at a conſiderable diſtance from me.

Q. What time did they quit that ſtation?

A. To the beſt of my recollection, about five o'clock.

Q. Was not the Vice Admiral of the Blue, and the ſhips of his diviſion, the laſt that came out of action?

A. They certainly were; they muſt have been, from their ſituation.

Q. Did not you underſtand they ſuffered more than any other of the diviſions?

A. It did not appear to me, at that time, that they ſuffered more than the centre diviſion; the Formidable appeared to have ſuffered much, but I believe my own ſhip ſuffered as much, or more than any other ſhip in the fleet, in every ſenſe, except in killed and wounded.

Q. Was not the red diviſion the firſt part of the fleet that came out of action, and conſequently had been the longeſt out of it?

A. Yes, I believe they were.

Q. I would aſk Captain Jervois, if the ſailing and fighting inſtructions he received were ſigned by the commander in chief, or by the flag officers of the different diviſions?

A. I never was of any diviſion, but that of the commander in chief.

Court. This is new matter, and not proper on a croſs examination.

Proſecutor. You ſaid you did not ſee the ſignal for the line repeated on board the Formidable; I would aſk, whether the ſignal flying on board the commander in chief, was not a ſufficient warrant for every ſhip to take their ſtations, when they were able to do ſo?

Evidence,

Evidence. I muſt beg the interpoſition of the Court, for this queſtion leads me to reflect upon the character of the Captains of the blue diviſion, of whom I have the higheſt opinion.

Court. You may anſwer it or not.

Evidence. I do not ſee any other application that it will bear.

Proſecutor. There was no ſuch application meant by the queſtion; I only meant to ask, whether they could have taken their ſtations, while they were occupied by other ſhips? A. I have already denied that fact.

Q. You have been asked if you ſaw the Vice Admiral of the blue make any ſignal of diſtreſs; I would ask what ſignal of diſtreſs was applicable at that time?

A. Though I am not accountable for anſwering the queſtions I have been already asked, I will repeat, that I did not know the particular ſituation of the Formidable, and I never pretended to any ſuch knowledge.

Q. Was the weather ſuch that a boat could live at that time?

A. The beſt proof of it is, that a boat was floating between the French fleet and ours without any body to guide her; at that time it certainly was ſuch that any boat could live.

Q. You ſaid you kept cloſe to the Victory all the afternoon?

A. After three o'clock, when the Admiral wore.

Q. Then your courſes and rates of going muſt be the ſame? A. Undoubtedly.

Q. Was you fired into by the Duke or any other Britiſh ſhip, during the engagement that day?

A. I never knew the Duke fired a ſhot that day, nor for ſeveral days afterwards; nor do I think any Engliſh ſhip fired into the Foudroyant, but the French did; I never heard that a ſhot approached the larboard ſide of the Foudroyant.

Q. Had you any men killed?

A. Five killed, and one died of his wounds, and about eighteen more wounded.

Q. Had you any men blown up by an exploſion of gunpowder?

A. I did not know of any exploſion during the action, but afterwards the Lieutenant who commanded one deck reported to me, that a man had been killed in the act of putting a cartridge into a gun, and I believe two men and a boy were ſent to the hoſpital, but they recovered, and are now in the ſhip.

President. I think you said yesterday, you thought yourself bound by the oath you had taken, to answer to every part of the charge; I would therefore ask whether to your knowledge, as the fourth article states it, Admiral Keppel did any one act, between the 23d and 29th of July, disgraceful to the British flag?

A. I have already answered that question very fully, in a reply I made yesterday; but am still ready to say, I do not know of any one instance in his conduct disgraceful to the British flag.

Q. Do you know of any opportunity Admiral Keppel lost, of doing a most essential service to the state; and by losing that opportunity, tarnishing the honour of the British navy? A. I know of no such instance.

Capt. JERVOIS *ordered to withdraw.*

Capt. KINGSMILL, *of the Vigilant, called and sworn.*

Admiral Keppel. I am charged with advancing towards the enemy without making the signal for forming the line; what in your judgment would have been the consequence, if I had formed it instead of closing with them as I did?

A. That the French fleet could not have been brought to action that day.

Q. I am charged with not having advanced towards the Enemy to renew the action on the larboard tack; had I at any time a sufficient force collected together to renew it, or to prevent the enemy from forming their line on the starboard tack? A. No.

Q. Was not the signal for the line kept flying all that time? A. It was.

Q. I am charged with having wore again, and made sail directly from the enemy; was not my wearing again at that time to stand to the southward, a necessary manœuvre for the protection of the disabled ships, and for collecting the ships to renew the battle?

A. I think it was very proper, both for the protection of the disabled ships, and to collect the ships together in order to renew the action.

Q. Had it the least appearance of a flight?

A. No, certainly not.

Q. Do you recollect what sail I carried in the afternoon, and during the night of the 27th?

A. I do not recollect what sail the Victory had; we were under, in our station ahead of her, double reefed topsails, and very often our mizen topsail was aback.

Q. Did you see the French fleet in the morning of the 28th?

A. I saw

A. I saw three sail of the French fleet in the morning, going before the wind large, with all their studding sails set.

Q. Did you see the signal out for any ships to chace them?

A. There were some pendants out, but I do not recollect for what ships; I remember one of the Lieutenants told me, ours was out, but on my looking, found it was not.

Q. If I had chaced with the fleet towards Ushant, in the condition it was in after the action of the 27th, with the wind and weather as it then was; was there the least probability of coming up with the French fleet before they reached the port of Brest?

A. I do not think there was the smallest chance.

Q. You have heard all the articles of the charge read, therefore I desire you will state to the Court, any instance, if there be any such, in which I negligently performed any part of my duty on the 27th, or 28th of July?

A. I can state to the Court no instance of negligence, nor do I know of any; but that you discharged your duty with the ability of a great and gallant officer.

Prosecutor. Do you remember stopping your fire, on board the Vigilant, because of firing into one of your own ships? A. No, I do not.

Ordered to withdraw.

Sir CHARLES DOUGLAS, *of the Stirling Castle, called and sworn.*

Admiral Keppel. Did the French fleet shew any intention of coming to action, from the time they were discovered to the 27th, when they were brought to battle?

A. By no means; to the best of my knowledge, they ever did endeavour to avoid it.

Q. Did I do my utmost endeavour, as an officer, to bring them to action during those days?

A. To the best of my knowledge you did, with unremitting assiduity.

Q. Had you commanded a British fleet, and in the situation the French fleet were in with respect to the fleet under my command, wind and weather as it then was, would you have hesitated one moment, to have gone down and attacked them?

A. To the best of my remembrance, and to the best of my judgment, if I had the honour of commanding a British fleet under such circumstances, I could not have desired a better opportunity than what daily offered, to have given

given battle to an enemy turning up towards me, and endeavouring, as the British fleet actually did, to bring on an action.

Q. As I am charged with advancing towards the enemy on the 27th of July; and made the signal for battle, without forming the line; what in your judgment would have been the consequence if I had formed it, instead of closing with them as I did?

A. Judging of their future conduct by the past, had the Admiral formed his fleet in a line of battle, on the 27th in the morning, I do not think we could have brought them to action at all; and even without forming the line, had it not been for a shift of wind, I do not think we should have fetched near enough within cannon shot of any part of their fleet.

Q. How many ships had the Vice Admiral of the red with him advancing towards the enemy, on the larboard tack, after the action?

A. I really do not possitively recollect.

Q. Was your ship one of them?

A. I was one of the number that followed Sir Robert Harland towards the rear of the fleet, in the Stirling Castle, which I had then the honour to command.

Q. I am charged with having hauled down the signal for battle, by which the red division was prevented from renewing the fight upon the larboard tack; I desire you would acquaint the Court, what in your judgment would have been the consequence, if by keeping abroad that signal, or making any other, I had ordered the Vice Admiral of the red to advance with the ships at that time to the attack?

A. To the best of my judgment, such a measure would have been very disadvantageous to the red division, for such a part only of the fleet, was not of sufficient force to have attacked the whole of the French fleet, and moreover they were not close up together.

Q. Did you see the French fleet wear and begin to form their line on the starboard tack?

A. I do recollect to have seen a part of the French fleet, I cannot say the whole, making sail ahead on the starboard tack, and some of them formed themselves into a line of battle ahead, but I cannot say exactly at what time; there were more, but I cannot fix how many of them were formed at the time I allude to.

Q. I am charged with having wore to stand to the southward at this time, and leading the British fleet directly from the enemy; did my wearing at this time appear

to

to you to be a neceſſary manœuvre, or had i. the appearance of a flight?

A. Your wearing to the ſouthward appeared to me to be a moſt neceſſary meaſure, nor had it ſurely by any means the appearance of a flight, nor did it ever in the ſmalleſt degree make an impreſſion upon me to that effect?

Q. What ſail was you under during the night of the 27th?

A. During the night of the 27th, in general double reefed topſails and mizen ſtay ſail, ſometimes the fore tack was abroad, the foreſail very often hauled up, much to the fatigue of my ſhip's company; my ſhip was foul, and I could not uſe the common expedient of backing my mizen topſail, for fear of driving down to leeward, and putting the fleet into confuſion. I don't recollect how often the foreſail was hauled down, but it was very often; my main top maſt having been ſhot thro' above and below the cap, and the bowſprit two turns into the near gammon; I did not dare to let a reef out to follow my Admiral, ſo faſt as I otherwiſe ſhould have done. I thought it better to compromiſe with the weather to preſerve my maſt with double reefed topſails, than run the riſque of having my maſt carried away. I now allude retroſpectively to my having followed Sir Robert Harland. Sometimes we hauled aft the main top maſt ſtay ſail ſheet, and once or twice hoiſted the fore top maſt ſtay ſail; now I hope I have been ſufficiently minute.

Q. From the very bad ſailing of your ſhip, did it not occaſion your falling ſo far aſtern of the Red diviſion, as to mix with the centre diviſion? A. Not that I remember.

Q. Did you, during the night of the 27th, and at what time of the night, call your men to quarters, upon a ſhip's ranging up nearly with you, which you thought was a ſhip of the enemy.

A. At or about the firſt dawning of the day, having my leader the Berwick in my eye, coveting to keep myſelf to windward, and being then actually upon her weather quarter, that I might have it in my power to aſſume my exact place with more preciſion in the line of battle, as day light ſhould advance, I obſerved a ſhip ranging up upon my weather quarter. When firſt I ſaw her, I think about three points upon the weather quarter, not knowing who it might be, I thought it prudent to order my ſhip, company to their quarters, and reſume our preparation for battle, which had been for ſome time diſcontinued.

Q. What ſhip was it?

A. As that ſhip approached towards our beam, I could plainly

plainly discern a flag at her fore top mast head, the colour thereof I could not yet ascertain with certainty; passing further along, and no act of hostility having passed betwixt us, I presumed it to be the Formidable, although she had neither top nor poop light, nor ensign flying, nor no light at her bowsprit end. About this time I bore up a little, as the day opened, and I could do it with safety, to get more precisely into my station in the line of battle. The ship in question still passing along, until she came further forward, and then I observed her having her ensign flying. Seeing a ship approach us in the morning as this did, I confess I was not without some apprehension that the enemy had, by stretching away on the larboard tack, doubled upon our rear in order to regain the windward gage; and at or about the same time, seeing other ships in the same quarter of the compass, my suspicions grew stronger in that respect, insomuch that I ruminated and entertained a thought of making the signal for seeing strange ships in the N. W. quarter. I had proceeded so far in my own mind, as to be pondering whether to make the day or night signal, which nearly fixes the time of my being under that apprehension.

Q. Did you see the lights of the Admiral of your own division at that time?

A. I do not recollect that circumstance.

Q. When day came, was you then sure it was the Vice Admiral of the Blue that you had seen before?

A. To the best of my knowledge and remembrance it could be no other.

Q. On the 28th if I had chaced towards Ushant, in the condition the fleet were in after the action of the 28th, in their masts and yards, was there the least probability of coming up with the French fleet before they had reached the port of Brest?

A. Had the French fleet observed their former line of conduct, there could not be the least probability of your coming up with them before they reached the port of Brest. By their line of conduct I mean constantly avoiding an engagement.

Q. You have heard all the articles of the charge, therefore I desire you will state to the Court any instance, if you saw or know of any such, in which I negligently performed my duty, or any part of it, either on the 27th or 28th of July?

A. I did not observe any thing done or left undone by Admiral

Admiral Keppel, on the 27th or 28th of July, bearing the appearance of his negligently performing his duty.

Sir Charles ordered to withdraw.

CAPT. COSBY *of the Centaur, called and ſworn.*

Admiral Keppel. I am charged with advancing towards the enemy, and making ſignal for battle on the 27th of July, without forming the line; what in your judgment would have been the conſequence if I had formed it, inſtead of cloſing with them, as I did?

A. We ſhould have increaſed our diſtance from the enemy, and could not have brought them to action that day.

Q. How many ſhips had the Vice Admiral of the Red advancing with him on the larboard tack, after the action?

A. I believe ſix or ſeven, I am not certain which.

Q. Was yours among thoſe ſhips?

A. The Centaur, which I commanded, was one of them.

Q. I am charged with having hauled down the ſignal for battle; by which the red diviſion was prevented from renewing the fight on the larboard tack; I deſire you will inform the Court what would have been the conſequence, if by keeping abroad that ſignal, or making any other, I had ordered the Vice Admiral of the Red to advance at that time with the ſhips he had with him, to the attack?

A. If the red diviſion had been ordered to attack, I am ſure the Admiral of the red diviſion would have done it; but it would have been a dangerous experiment, for from the apparent ſituation of the fleet in general, he could not have been ſupported.

Q. Did you ſee the French fleet wear, and begin to form their line on the ſtarboard tack? A. I did.

Q. I am charged with having wore at this time, and ſtood to the ſouthward, leading the Britiſh fleet directly from the enemy; did my wearing appear to you to be a neceſſary manœuvre, or the appearance of a flight?

A. As to a neceſſary manœuvre, the Commander in Chief is the beſt judge; but as to a flight without wings, the idea could never ſtrike me, from the apparent ſituation of the fleet.

Q. You have heard all the articles of the charge read, therefore I deſire you will ſtate to the Court any inſtance, if you know of any ſuch, in which I negligently performed my duty, or any part of it, on the 27th and 28th of July?

A. If I am allowed, from the experience of thirty years ſervice, to aſſume an opinion upon a commander in chief, and

and more particularly upon so great an officer as Admiral Keppel, I am of opinion, and I do firmly believe, he did do his utmost for his Majesty's service. 'Tis the first time I ever had the honour of being under his command, and 'tis one of the most unfortunate events in my servitude, that I have not been under it before.

Ordered to withdraw.

CAPT. NOTT, *of the Exeter, called, and sworn.*

Admiral Keppel. I am charged with advancing towards the enemy, and having made a signal for battle on the 27th of July, without forming the line; what in your judgment would have been the consequence; if I had formed it, instead of closing with them as I did?

A. That we should not have got into action that day.

Q. How many ships had the Vice Admiral of the Red advancing with him on the larboard tack?

A. I cannot say how many, six or seven I believe.

Q. Was your ship one of them? A. Yes.

Q. I am charged with hauling down the signal for battle, by which the red division was prevented from renewing the fight on the larboard tack; I desire you will inform the Court, what would have been the consequence, if by keeping abroad that signal, or making any other, I had ordered the Vice Admiral of the Red to advance at that time, with the ships he had with him, to the attack?

A. The destruction of the red division.

Q. Did you see the French fleet wear, and begin to form a new line?

A. I did not see them wear, I saw them after they had wore?

Q. I am charged with having wore and stood to the southward at this time, and leading the British fleet directly from the enemy; did my wearing appear to you to be a necessary manoeuvre, or had it the appearance of a flight?

A. It appeared very necessary. I have been thirty years in the service, and I never saw an Englishman turn his back on the French?

Q. You have heard all the articles of the charge read, I desire you will state to the Court any instance, if you saw or know of such, in which I negligently performed my duty, either on the 27th or 28th of July?

A. I had the honour of serving under you before, and it was the greatest pride of my heart, when I was commissioned to serve under you again. I know you to be a gallant officer, and one of the first naval commanders in the world.

world. Your conduct during the whole time that you saw the French fleet, convinced me that my judgment was right respecting your abilities.

Ordered to withdraw.

The HON. KEITH STEWART, *Captain of the Berwick, called, and sworn.*

Admiral Keppel. I am charged with advancing towards the enemy, and making the signal for battle without forming the line; what in your judgment would have been the consequence if I had formed it instead of closing with them as I did?

A. I do not apprehend they would have been brought into action that day, if the line of battle had been formed.

Q. How many ships had the Vice Admiral of the Red advancing with him on the larboard tack?

A. I do not know, the Berwick was not there.

Q. Did you see the French form their line on the starboard tack? A. I cannot say I did.

Q. I am charged with having wore and stood to the southward at this time, and leading the British fleet directly from the enemy; did my wearing appear to you to be a necessary manœuvre, or had it the appearance of a flight?

A. To the best of my judgment it was a necessary manœuvre, I never conceived it as a flight; on the contrary, I expected to have been in action before five o'clock in the afternoon.

Q. Did I make every necessary signal in order to collect and form the fleet on the starboard tack, to renew the battle? A. Yes.

Q. Did you see the French fleet on the morning of the 28th? A. No.

Q. If I had chaced towards Ushant in the state the fleet were in from the action of the 27th, wind and weather as it then was, was there any probability of coming up with the French fleet before they reached the port of Brest?

A. I think certainly not.

Q. You have heard all the articles of the charge, and therefore I desire you will inform the court any instance, if you saw or know of any such, in which I negligently performed my duty, either on the 27th or 28th of July?

A. I know of none.

Ordered to withdraw.

It being near four o'clock, the Court adjourned to ten o'clock to morrow morning.

TWENTY-

Twenty-ninth Day, MONDAY, February 8th.

The Court being re-assumed, and the Prisoner brought in, the Honourable Lieutenant Lumley, *of the Robuste, was called and sworn.*

Admiral Keppel. Is the log book you have in your hand, an exact copy from the original Robuste's log book?

A. Yes, Sir; with two or three additions of my own, which I have put in between parentheses.

Q. At what time were the additions made?

A. At the time I wrote the log.

Q. Then Mr. Lumley's log book will ascertain the alterations that have been made in the log book of the Robuste, and I beg they may be compared.

Mr. Lumley's notes were then read, as follows:

"Fresh breezes, and still in chace of the French fleet to windward, under two reefed topsails. A signal for the Defiance, Worcester and Elizabeth, to make more sail. At six o'clock squally, reefed topsails. At seven, a signal for particular ships to tack. At five o'clock, let the reef out of the main topsails; a swell from the westward. A signal for the Vice Admiral of the Blue squadron to make chace to windward. Out second reefed main, and second and third reefed topsail. At ten o'clock tacked by signal, the body of the French fleet S. and by W. five or six miles. At half past ten our headmost ships were engaged with the French; we passed to the windward of them, and had the signal to engage. Bore down to the enemy, and passed to leeward of them within musket shot, and begun the action with the headmost of them. Moderate and cloudy, still in action within musket shot. A little before two o'clock, the signal for battle was hauled down, and a signal made to wear. Soon after the signal was made for a line of battle ahead, a cable's length asunder, at which time having passed all the enemy's ships, and exchanged broadsides with twenty five of them, we found our mainmast, foremast, and bowsprit much wounded, our main topmast yard, and fore topgallant mast shot away, and three feet water in our hold, from a shot in the hull betwixt wind and water. At three, tacked, kept all the pumps going, got down the broken main topsail yard and sail and the fore topsail yard and sail, close reefed the topsail, and knotted and spliced the rigging shot away."

The

The first difference in comparing them was, that the original log book had the words "*still in chace of the French fleet,*" which were not in the altered edition of it. In the original it stood, "*A signal for the Vice Admiral of the Blue squadron to give chace to windward.*" In the altered log it was, "*A signal for us and several other ships of the Vice Admiral of the Blue's squadron to chace to windward.*" The words at twelve, "*the weather more moderate,*" were wanting. The following (which the Admiral conceived to affect his life) was very material. In the original log it stood, that "*At six in the afternoon the Robuste tacked and bore down, and resumed her station in the line.*" But in the altered edition it stood thus; "*Between six and seven o'clock, observed a signal on board the Victory for ships to bear down, which was repeated by the Formidable, and in the evening we resumed our station in the line, as well as a disabled ship could do,* THE ADMIRAL MAKING MUCH SAIL."

Admiral Keppel. What time did you first come on deck, in the morning of the 28th? A. At three o'clock.

Q. Was it your watch upon deck?

A. No; Mr. Pitt sent down to me at three o'clock, that he would be obliged to me to relieve the last hour of his watch, as he was very sleepy.

Q. Where was the Robuste when day-light came?

A. On the Vice Admiral of the Red's weather quarter, within hail of him.

Q. What sail had the Robuste when you came upon deck?

A. Close reefed topsails, foresail, and lower staysails.

Q. Did you shorten sail or continue it?

A. Soon after I came upon deck the first Lieutenant came up, and finding out that it was a red flag at the fore topmast head of the ship to leeward, we hauled the mainsail up, backed the mizen top-sail, and hauled the staysails down.

Q. Was the Vice Admiral of the Red ahead of the center division at that time? A. Yes, he was.

Prosecutor. Was you present when those corrections took place in the log book of the Robuste?

A. No, I was once present when I saw some leaves taken out of the log book, which made me believe there was an alteration to take place.

Admiral Montague. Present with whom?

A. The master and some of the officers. I don't know exactly who was in the ward-room. The captain was not present.

 Prosecutor.

Prosecutor. Can you speak of the time when it was, with any degree of precision?

A. It was about the sixth of December last.

Court. Where was your ship then?

A. I am not certain whether she was come into the harbour, or not.

Q. Do you know what became of that leaf or leaves that you saw misplaced? A. No, I do not.

Q. Have you seen any thing of them since that time?

A. No.

Q. You said you relieved the deck at three o'clock; was the mainsail set then? A. Yes.

Q. Did the officer whom you relieved, tell you the occasion of his setting the mainsail?

A. Yes, he said that after consulting the captain he was obliged to do it, to keep sufficiently ahead of the Vice Admiral of the Blue.

Q. Did he shew you the Admiral's lights, or any lights that he took to be the Admiral's?

A. No; the ship which he pointed out as the Formidable, had no lights on board, I saw none.

Q. That ship was astern of you, was she not?

A. Yes.

Q. What I ask you is, with respect to the Admiral's lights?

A. I did not take notice of the Commander in chief at all.

Q. Did you distinguish the lights, before you knew the flag at the fore topmast head to be red?

A. He had lights, but I did not take notice how many.

Q. I understood you did not know where the Commander in chief was, from the time of your coming upon deck till day light? A. No, I did not.

Admiral Montague. When it was day-light, where did you see the Vice Admiral of the Blue, in the Formidable?

A. I did not see her at all on the quarter deck; the First Lieutenant went abaft on the poop to look for her.

Ordered to withdraw.

ROBERT ARNOLD, *Master of the Robuste, sworn.*

Admiral Keppel. When were the alterations made in the Robuste's log book?

A. The 12th of December, the last alterations were made.

Q. Do

Q. Do you recollect what time of the day the last alterations were made?

A. Betwixt eleven in the morning and two in the afternoon.

Q. By whose orders? A. By Captain Hood's.

Q. Do you know if Sir Hugh Palliser was at Portsmouth at that time? A. I do not.

Q. Do you know where the Robuste was in the morning of the 28th, at day-light?

A. Yes; she was upon the starboard quarter of the Queen, at the distance of about two cables length.

Prosecutor. When Captain Hood ordered the alterations to be made in the Robuste's log book, did not he desire that they might be such as would swear to the truth of, in case they should be called for, or to that purpose?

At the time Capn Hood had these alterations made, I received it as his orders; and never made any scruple to do it. I remember upon returning from the cabin, Captain Hood did say, he only wished it might be as correct as possible; turning to me and the Lieutenant, and said, I suppose you can attest them. These, I think were his words.

Q. What Lieutenant was that?

A. The first Lieutenant.

Court. Do you know whether the Admiral carried much sail, the Commander in Chief at that time?

A. I was not upon deck in the night myself.

Prosecutor. When Captain Hood had mentioned to you and the First Lieutenant, whether you could attest these corrections, what answer did you make either of you, or both?

A. I answered yes; meaning those parts that fell under my observation.

Ordered to withdraw.

Admiral Keppel then addressed himself to the Court, as follows:

Capt. Hood, in justification of his conduct, says, that he revised his log-book for his own protection, not knowing but he might be brought to this bar as a prisoner, instead of an evidence; but I appeal to the sense of the Court, whether the alterations are such as can support either the belief or existence of such a measure, how could the signal for chacing, in the morning of the 27th, if made for several ships of the Vice of the Blue's squadron, instead of the whole Blue's squadron, on which my accuser founds his first charge, possibly affect the character of Capt. Hood? how much less, whether the three French ships were seen or not, near or at a distance, on the morning of the 28th: he could not possibly be affected by

 the

their escape, nor could any guilt arise in him from their chaced or not.

But that which remains behind, tends directly to affect my life, and to destroy that which ought to be still dearer to every British seaman, MY HONOUR. I must beg leave to take notice of it, more particularly as it cannot tend in the smallest degree to have exculpated him; had he, as he says, been brought to your bar as a prisoner, had the Robuste fallen astern, indeed, there might have been some advantage in asserting, that the Admiral made much sail; but instead of the Robuste's struggling to keep in her station, from the Victory's making *much sail*, it has come out in proof, that in the space of a short night she run miles ahead of the Victory. It is therefore evident that this alteration was made to support the charge of my accuser. I declare 'tis a subject of pain to me, that a man, with whom I lived in familiarity and friendship, and of whose bravery and merit as an officer, I am well convinced, should be led into such a snare, and seduced by any party or persuasion to have deviated so far from that honourable line of conduct, which every British seaman ought to preserve. And I hope it will be believed, after this, that I have not investigated this point for the sake of myself, so much as for the security of the service.

As to the officers who commanded in the blue division, I honour them all as brave men, and it was to my astonishment that I heard a question put yesterday by my accuser, that struck directly at their honour; but I was well pleased to see it so nobly repelled by the officer to whom it was put.

The prosecutor begged that he might be permitted to offer something in justification of Capt. Hood, to which Admiral Montague replied, "If Captain Hood had done a bad thing he must acquit himself in the Morning Post, or some other paper."

Sir JOHN HAMILTON, *of the* Hector, *sworn.*

Admiral Keppel. As I am charged with having advanced to the enemy, and made the signal for battle without forming the line, what in your opinion would have been the consequence, if I had formed it, instead of closing with them, as I did. A. You never could have come to action.

Q. How many ships had the Vice Admiral of the Red advancing with him on the larboard tack?

A. Not more than five.

Q. Was your ship one of those five? A. It was.

Q. I

Q. I am charged with having hauled down the signal for battle, by which the Red division was prevented from renewing the fight on the larboard tack; I desire you will inform the Court, what in your judgment would have been the consequence, if by keeping abroad that signal, or making any other, I had ordered the Vice Admiral of the Red to advance at that time, with the ships he had with him, to the attack.

A. The Vice Admiral of the Red, at that time, was in a critical situation, advancing towards the enemy's ships, and had no ships near enough to support him, but the Hector; and if the signal had not been hauled down, they would have been exposed to be cut off.

Q. I am charged with having wore and stood to the southward at this time, and leading the British fleet directly from the enemy; did my wearing appear to you to be a necessary manœuvre, or had it the appearance of a flight?

A. A necessary manœuvre, and no appearance of a flight.

Q. If I had chaced towards Ushant on the morning of the 28th, in the condition the fleet was in after the action, wind and weather considered, was there the least probability of my coming up with the French fleet before they had reached the port of Brest?

A. Not the least probability.

Q. You have heard all the articles of the charge, and therefore I desire you will state to the Court any instance, if you saw or know of any such, in which I negligently performed my duty, either on the 27th or 28th of July.

A. I know of none.

Prosecutor. You have mentioned there was only five sail of the Vice Admiral of the Red with him; at what period do you speak of?

A. At the time the signal for the action was hauled down.

Q. How many ships were with him at the time when you wore to the southward, to go down to the Admiral?

A. I cannot say what ships were with him then, most of the division, I believe.

Q. Do you remember how many of the division went with the Vice Admiral of the Red, when they formed astern of the Victory?

A. About six sail.

Q. Can you give any account where the rest of the division were at that time?

A. Some of the ships were to leeward, and others refitting after the action.

Q. Do

Q. Do you remember when they were to windward in the manner you have described, seeing the Formidable lay with her head the same way as the Red division were then? A. I do not.

Q. While the Victory was upon the larboard tack, standing towards the enemy again, did you observe where the rest of the ships of that division were, whether they were about him, or separated from him, or how?

A. I was too much taken up with attention to my own duty, to observe.

Q. Whilst the Admiral was with his head to the enemy, upon the larboard tack, did you observe any signal being made for ships to windward to bear down?

A. I did, the signal for ships to bear down was made at four o'clock.

Q. I am speaking whilst the Admiral's head was towards the enemy?

Admiral Keppel. I admit there was none.

Q. Was there at that time any particular ship's signal made to make more sail, or for ships to get into their stations.

Admiral Keppel. There was no signal made whilst the Victory was upon the larboard tack, but the signal for the line of battle; no other.

SIR JOHN HAMILTON *ordered to withdraw.*

CAPT. PRESCOTT, *of the Queen, sworn.*

Admiral Keppel. I am charged with advancing towards the enemy and making the signal for battle, without forming the line; what in your judgment would have been the consequence, if I had formed it, instead of closing with them, as I did?

A. That you could not have brought them to action.

Q. How many ships had the Vice Admiral of the Red advancing with him on the larboard tack? A. Seven.

Q. I am charged with hauling down the signal for battle, by which the Red division was prevented from renewing the fight on the larboard tack; I desire you will inform the court what, in your judgment, would have been the consequence, if by keeping abroad that signal, or making any other, I had ordered the Vice Admiral of the Red to advance at that time, with the ships he had with him, to the attack?

A. I am very certain that the Vice Admiral of the Red would have punctually and cheerfully obeyed, if the signal had been made; but the consequence must have

b.en

been fatal, the French must, with common professional knowledge, without bravery, have destroyed every ship of that division, before you could have given them support.

Q. Did you see the French fleet wear, and begin to form on the starboard tack?

A. I saw many of their ships before the wind; I afterwards saw them in a line.

Q. I am charged with having stood to the southward at this time, and leading the British fleet directly from the enemy; did my wearing appear to you to be a necessary manœuvre, or had it the appearance of a flight?

A. It appeared to me to be a most necessary manœuvre, nor did it ever strike me with the idea of a flight.

Q. Did I make every necessary signal to collect and form the fleet on the starboard tack, to renew the action?

A. You did.

Q. Did you see any signal on board the Victory, that conveyed to you an idea that the Admiral did not intend to renew the action that day, if he could have formed the line?

A. Not at all; I never thought but he meant to renew it, if he could have formed his line.

Q. Did the Queen carry distinguishing lights in the night of the 27th, and did you see the Victory's light at the bowsprit end?

A. The Queen did carry her distinguishing lights. I did not see the lights at the Victory's bowsprit end myself, though I was informed by the officers that they had seen them.

President. Did you see any on board the Formidable that night? A. I did not.

Admiral Keppel. Did you see the French fleet on the morning of the 28th? A. I did not.

Q. Did you see three sail? A. I did.

Q. What distance were they?

A. Two were very near hull'd down, the other was half hulled down.

Q. If I had chaced towards Ushant in the morning of the 28th, in the condition the fleet was in after the action of the 27th, was there the least probability of my coming up with the French fleet before they reached the port of Brest, wind and weather as it then was?

A. I think not.

Q. How far was you from Ushant the 28th of July?

A. Twenty-six leagues.

Q. You

Q. You have heard all the articles of the charge read: I defire you will ftate to the Court any inftance, if you faw or know of any fuch, in which I negligently performed my duty, either on the 27th or 28th of July?

A. I cannot point out to the Court any inftance wherein you negligently performed your duty, on the 27th or 28th of July. I received an early part of my naval education under your care. I have always looked up to you with a degree of filial refpect. Your character ftands too high to ftoop to my judgment; but thus called upon, I declare, and am happy to make the declaration upon oath, that your conduct on that day added luftre to your name, and holds you up a worthy example to every officer in the navy.

Profecutor. You have faid, that if the Vice Admiral of the Red had advanced, and re-attacked with his divifion, it would have been attended with fatal confequences: I would ask you, if the whole Britifh fleet had advanced and re-attacked, what fatal confequences were there to be apprehended?

A. I do not apprehend that the whole fleet were in a ftate to advance and renew the attack.

Q. Was not the French fleet advancing towards the Britifh fleet?

A. Not that I obferved.

Q. I mean after the time you mentioned, of feeing fome of them before the wind, and afterwards in the line?

A. At the time they were in a line, they were to leeward of us, and I apprehend the Admiral then meant to renew the attack; but *you* was fo far to leeward, that I do not apprehend we had it in our power to renew the action.

Ordered to withdraw.

Mr. WACE, *Builder's Affiftant at Plymouth Yard, fworn.*

Admiral Keppel. I call him to ftate the condition of the fleet, as they were when they came into Plymouth.

Mr. Wace accordingly delivered in an account, on oath, of the damages the fleet received, as they were when they came into Plymouth, which was laid upon the table, and Mr. Wace ordered to withdraw.

The Admiral then defired the letters in the poffeffion of the Court, No. 62, 67, and 83, might be read, to prove there was no material circumftance he would keep from the public. They were read accordingly. They were the Admiral's letters to Mr. Stephens, Secretary to the Admiralty, which contained the principal circumftances that occurred during all the time the two fleets were in fight of of each other. Two letters from the Secretary were alſo read, expreſſing his Majeſty's approbation of his conduct, and the congratulations of the Admiralty on his victory over the French fleet. The Admiral received thanks for having ſo prudently provided for the ſecurity of our Weſt India fleets, in the appointment of Capt. Leviſon Gower, with orders to teſtify to the Captain their approbation of his conduct.

Admiral Keppel. The Court will ſee by theſe letters, that I have not concealed any part of my conduct from the public, nor put a falſe gloſs upon it.

The Admiral then addreſſed himſelf to the Preſident thus:

"Mr. Preſident, I have now cloſed my evidence, and "ſhall make no obſervations upon it. I ſubmit the whole "to the wiſdom and juſtice of this Court."

The Proſecutor then addreſſed himſelf to the Court, that as there were no other witneſſes to examine, it was his intention to make ſome obſervations, not only on his own evidence, but alſo on the defence and evidence of the Admiral, eſpecially as the Admiral, in defending himſelf, had criminated him. And as the trial had run to ſuch a length, and ſuch a maſs of evidence, he could not be immediately prepared, therefore hoped the Court would indulge him till Wedneſday for that purpoſe.

Admiral Keppel. I am in the judgment of the Court, with reſpect to the accuſers right to reply; even in the caſe of Admiral Byng, where the proſecution was carried on by the Solicitor in the name of the Crown, no ſuch attempt was made; and I am at a loſs to conceive, on what Sir Hugh Palliſer grounds ſo unprecedented an attempt.

On this the Court retired, and reſolved to the following purport:

"That having on a former occaſion reſolved, after the "Proſecutor had concluded his evidence, that they could "not receive a paper preſented to them by him; and it "being declared, that the evidence on both parts is con"cluded, it is therefore reſolved, that nothing further, "by way of addreſs from any quarter, can be received."

Agreed to adjourn till to-morrow morning, ten o'clock.

THIRTIETH DAY, TUESDAY FEBRUARY 9th.

The Court met according to Adjournment, at ten o'clock this morning, and Adjourned till ten o'clock to-morrow morning.

THIRTY-

THIRTY-FIRST DAY, WEDNESDAY FEBRUARY 10th

The Court met according to Adjournment, at ten o'clock this morning, and adjourned till ten o'clock to-morrow morning.

THIRTY-SECOND DAY, THURSDAY FEBRUARY 11th.

The Court being met according to Adjournment, the doors were thrown open, and audience admitted, when the Judge Advocate was directed to read the Sentence on Admiral Keppel, as follows:

At a Court-Martial assembled on board his Majesty's ship Britannia, the 7th of January 1779, and held by adjournment at the house of the Governor of his Majesty's Garrison at Portsmouth every day afterwards (Sundays excepted) till the 11th of February inclusive,

PRESENT,

Sir *Thomas Pye*, Knt. Admiral of the White, President.
John Montague, Esq. Vice Admiral of the Red.
Marriott Arbuthnot, Esq. Rear Admiral of the White,
Robert Roddam, Esq. Rear Admiral of the White,

Capt. *Mark Milbank.*
Fra. Sam. Drake.
Taylor Penny.
John Moutray.

Capt. *William Bennett.*
Adam Duncan.
Philip Botteler,
James Cranston.

THIS Court, pursuant to an order of the Lords Commissioners of the Admiralty, dated the 31st of December, 1778, and directed to Sir Thomas Pye, proceeded to enquire into a charge exhibited by Vice Admiral Sir Hugh Palliser, against the Hon. Augustus Keppel, for *Misconduct* and *Neglect of Duty* on the 27th and 8th of July last, in sundry instances as mentioned in a Paper that accompanied the said order, and to try him for the same—and the Court having heard the evidence and the prisoner's defence, and maturely and seriously considered the whole, are of opinion that the charge is MALICIOUS and ILL-FOUNDED, it having ap-

 peared

peared that the Admiral, so far from having by misconduct and neglect of duty on the days therein alluded to, lost an opportunity of rendering essential service to the state, and thereby tarnished the honour of the British Navy, behaved as became a JUDICIOUS, BRAVE, and EXPERIENCED OFFICER.

The Court do therefore UNANIMOUSLY and HONOURABLY ACQUIT the said ADMIRAL AUGUSTUS KEPPEL of the several Articles contained in the charge against him, and he is FULLY and HONOURABLY ACQUITTED accordingly.

SIR THOMAS PYE, President.
JOHN MONTAGUE.
MARRIOT ARBUTHNOT.
ROBERT RODHAM.
MARK MILBANK.
FRA. SAM. DRAKE.
TAYLOR, PENNY.
JOHN MOUTRAY.
WILLIAM. BENNET.
ADAM DUNCAN.
PHILIP BOUTTELER.
JAMES CRANSTON.

GEORGE JACKSON,
Judge Advocate.

Sir Thomas Pye, on delivering to Admiral Keppel his sword, addressed him in the following words :

" *Admiral Keppel,*

" It is no small pleasure for me to receive the com-" mands of the Court I have the honour to preside at, " that in delivering you your sword, I am to congra-" tulate you on its being restored to you with *so much* " *honour*, hoping, ere long, you will be called forth by " your Sovereign, to draw it once more in the defence " of your country."

www.ingramcontent.com/pod-product-compliance
Lightning Source LLC
Chambersburg PA
CBHW030902270326
41929CB00008B/535

* 9 7 8 3 3 3 7 3 2 0 4 2 3 *